ΘΕΟΦΡΑΣΤΟΥ ΧΑΡΑΚΤΗΡΕϹ

MACMILLAN AND CO., LIMITED
LONDON · BOMBAY · CALCUTTA
MELBOURNE

THE MACMILLAN COMPANY
NEW YORK   BOSTON · CHICAGO
ATLANTA · SAN FRANCISCO

THE MACMILLAN CO. OF CANADA, LTD
TORONTO

ΘΕΟΦΡΑΣΤΟΥ ΧΑΡΑΚΤΗΡΕC

THE
CHARACTERS OF THEOPHRASTUS

AN ENGLISH TRANSLATION
FROM A REVISED TEXT
WITH INTRODUCTION AND NOTES

BY

R. C. JEBB, M.A.

FELLOW AND ASSISTANT-TUTOR OF TRINITY COLLEGE, CAMBRIDGE,
AND PUBLIC ORATOR OF THE UNIVERSITY,

1870;

A NEW EDITION

EDITED BY

J. E. SANDYS, Litt.D.

FELLOW OF ST JOHN'S COLLEGE, AND PUBLIC ORATOR

MACMILLAN AND CO., LIMITED
ST. MARTIN'S STREET, LONDON
1909

All rights reserved

24/7/09

A.284286
First Edition Crown 8vo 1870
Second Edition 8vo 1909

PREFACE TO THE FIRST EDITION.

AT a time when the desire to see ancient life more vividly on every side from which it can illustrate our own is perhaps the strongest with which the classics are widely read, it seems possible that the Characters of Theophrastus may have some general interest. To Englishmen who do not read Greek they are probably best known through the French translation of La Bruyère. In an edition of the Characters published in 1852 the Rev. J. G. Sheppard mentions an English translation by Mr F. Howell (1824)[1], and another by Mr H. Galley, of which he does not give the date[2]. But he does not speak of either with approbation, and I have not been able to learn that there is any other[3].

The first object of my book is to make these lively pictures of old Greek manners better known to English readers. But

[1] ('Francis Howell' was really the pseudonym of Isaac Taylor (1787—1865), the artist, author, and inventor. See *The Family Pen*, I 64, II 414, by his son, the Rev. Isaac Taylor. Mr Jebb's attention was first drawn to this fact by a letter received in 1870 from the Rev John Gwynn, D.D., Dublin. It may be added that 'Francis Howell's' translation was published (in 1824) by Josiah Taylor, and that, in A J. Valpy's reprint of the same (in 1831—6), 'Howell's' name is omitted, while the initial T is added at the end of the Preface Owing to Isaac Taylor s translation having been first published under the pseudonym of Francis Howell, the Cornell translators of 1902 have been accidentally led to draw a distinction between two works which are in fact identical.)

[2] (The date is 1725; the author was the Rev Henry Gally, of Corpus Christi College, Cambridge, whom Sheppard erroneously calls Galley.)

[3] (The *Characters* had already been translated by Eustace Budgell (London, 1714), who had 'read over' the notes of Casaubon and Duport in Needham's 'very neat' edition (1712), and who also mentions, in his Preface, an earlier English translation, doubtless that of J Healey (1616), since reprinted, with Earle's *Microcosmographie*, in the 'Temple Classics,' 1899.)

some critical labour has been given to it, and I venture to hope that in certain points of view it may have interest for scholars.

A translator of the Characters is forced to become also an editor. The text is corrupt, and has long been a field for the ingenuity of critics. It is thickly studded with passages on which hardly two commentators agree, and there is no edition with which I am acquainted in which the editor has not adopted several of his own conjectures. A student of the book who is capable of forming a judgment upon its difficulties is thus driven to make a text for himself. Where doctors differ so often and so utterly, it is absolutely necessary that he should be 'nullius addictus iurare in verba.' He must, in the disputed passages, first inquire what the MSS have, and whether sense can be made of it. If he concludes that it is nonsense, he has the conjectures of previous critics to choose from. If no one of these appears satisfactory, or if he has thought of something which seems to him more probable than any of them, he is justified in adopting his own emendation. A critic ordinarily competent to weigh the opinions of other critics has in every case a right to give so much of weight to his own. In the case of the Characters this right is especially clear. Each chapter consists of a string of short sentences not necessarily connected in meaning. When, therefore, in any one of these the genuine reading has been lost, no sure clue for its recovery can be looked for from the context; for it is possible that the sentence, as written by the author, had no connexion with the sentences which precede and follow it. Every such passage must be treated as a separate riddle, and the limits within which the answer may lie are wide. Open competition in conjecture affords the best hope of the true answer being found. A paper by Dr O. Ribbeck in the *Rheinisches Museum* for January, 1870, entitled 'Critical Remarks on the Characters of Theophrastus,' illustrates the freedom with which German scholars are disposed to apply this principle.

In forming the text from which this translation has been made I have used the editions of (1) F. Ast, Leipzig, 1816: (2) J. G Sheppard, London, 1852 · (3) H. E. Foss, Leipzig, 1858: (4) E. Petersen, Leipzig, 1859. (5) J. L. Ussing, Hanover, 1868. The editions of Foss and Petersen give in full the readings of the three principal MSS,—viz of Par A and B, from Herr Fr Dübner's collation, and of the Vatican MS from Mr Badham's; also the readings of several other MSS where they are important. The essential apparatus criticus is thus provided The commentaries of Ast, Foss and Ussing give the conjectures of various other editors and commentators, and make the constant use of the older editions (as of Needham's) practically unnecessary for the purposes of textual criticism. A Critical Appendix at the end of the book contains the results of my work on the text as regards all important points. In a great number of cases it will be found that I have adhered more closely than previous editors to the MSS as reported by Foss and Petersen In a few cases, where neither the MSS nor the critics solved a difficulty to my satisfaction, I have adopted conjectures of my own. The chief of these are:—

In Ch. VIII (XXVII) 14, συναυλήσοντας for συναύξοντας.

In Ch. XIV (IV) 18, λευρόν for λυπρόν.

In Ch. XVI (VI) 22, οὐδὲ καπήλων for οὐδ' ἅμα πολλῶν.

In Ch. XXI (XVIII) 8, Κορινθιακῶς for κρινοκόρακα.

In Ch XXVIII (XVI) 30, ἑστιώμενον for ἐστεμμένων.

In Ch XXIX (XXVI) 1, ἰσχύος, οὐ κέρδους for ἰσχυροῦ κέρδους.

The grounds upon which these emendations rest are stated in the Appendix.

If the moderate use of conjecture is a privilege which few, perhaps, will challenge, the translator who presumes to expurgate must expect protests. In assuming the unpopular and much-suspected office of expurgator, I was sensible that I was imperilling the pretensions of this little book to a severely high tone of scholarship, and risking the censure of that large majority who prefer the integrity to the purity of a text. There are, however, in the Characters about a dozen passages or phrases which I was unwilling to translate, and which I have omitted both in the English and in the Greek. The curious can discover them by comparing this edition with any other in the chapters περὶ ἀγροικίας, ἀπονοίας, βδελυρίας, περιεργίας, ἀναισθησίας, δυσχερείας, ἀηδίας, ὀψιμαθίας. At least three objections may evidently be made to such omissions. First, that a translator so fastidious would have done better to have left the Characters alone altogether. To this it may be replied that the coarseness in the delineations of Theophrastus is but a small element, accidental, not essential, and can in every case be separated from the portrait without injuring it as a whole. Secondly, it may be asked—'Where is the line to be drawn? Why is this struck out and that left in?' Here I have nothing to say but that I have used my best discretion. Thirdly, an objector may contend that, granting the advisability of omitting certain passages in the English translation, there was no sufficient reason for omitting them in the Greek text. It is enough to answer that, in this book, the Greek text is printed only as an adjunct to the translation; and that, therefore, passages omitted in the translation could not, with due regard to symmetry, be left in the text. So to leave them, it may be added would have been nearly equivalent to printing them in capital letters.

The order in which the MSS arrange the Characters has been changed, in this Translation, for an order less embarrassing to the reader. The reasons for this change are stated in the Introduction, pp. 19—21.

The illustrative notes have been made to consist, as much

as possible, of short translated extracts from Greek or Roman writers. The choice of these extracts cost some time and trouble; but, while making them, I often thought of a passage in that delightful book, the *Oxford Spectator*—the account of the Oxford Commemoration given by an historian writing in 4000 A.D.:—'On the last day of the Commemoration festival it appears that there was a procession to Nuneham, a pleasant spot some miles down the river: "the whole University goes to Nuneham," says the writer of a private letter.' Anyone who attempts to write notes on the details of ancient life is pretty sure to make some statements of this kind. He can only take precautions to keep the number down as much as possible.

R. C. JEBB

TRINITY COLLEGE, CAMBRIDGE,
April 4, 1870.

PREFACE TO THE SECOND EDITION.

THE first edition of the present work was published in 1870 as a small octavo volume of 328 pages under the title of *The Characters of Theophrastus, an English Translation from a revised Text, with Introduction and Notes*, by R. C. Jebb, M.A., Fellow and Assistant-Tutor of Trinity College, Cambridge, and Public Orator of the University. The permanent interest of the original, and the immediate aim of the translation, are set forth as follows in a letter written by the translator a year after the publication of the work, and printed for the first time thirty-six years later:—

'I sent off *Theophrastus* three days ago. You will be amused, I think, by the Eresian, if you have not expected too much of him. His real interest is this / Other writers, whose name is legion, prove to us that the great, the organic, lines of human nature are the same to-day, yesterday, and for ever. Theophrastus is one of the few who survive to remind us that the lighter traits also of character are permanent and universal. The bore of the Fourth Century B.C. is essentially the bore of the Nineteenth Century A.D / Do not be frightened by the occasional appearance of Greek type in the notes at the end. The notes consist, mainly, of translated extracts from old authors. They are specially meant to be intelligible to English readers. They aim at illustrating the Life of Ancient Hellas (as far as may be) in contemporary language."[1]

The essential permanence of the old Athenian types of character is similarly noticed in the *Impressions of Theophrastus Such*, published by George Eliot in 1879, six years

[1] *Life and Letters of Sir Richard Claverhouse Jebb, O.M., Litt.D*, by his wife Caroline Jebb (University Press, Cambridge, 1907), p. 102.

PREFACE TO THE SECOND EDITION

after the authoress had renewed her first acquaintance with the translator —

'I gather ..from the undeniable testimony of Theophrastus that there were bores, ill-bred persons, and detractors even in Athens, of species remarkably corresponding to the English, and not yet made endurable by being classic.'[1]

The edition of 1870, warmly welcomed on its first appearance, has long been out of print,—a fact quoted by the Cornell translators of 1902 as a plea for their own translation,—a translation, which (like that of 1870) was 'intended not for the narrow circle of classical philologists, but for the larger body of cultivated persons who have an interest in the past.' Even editors of the text in Holland, Italy, and Germany, have failed to find a copy of the former edition, or have only had an indirect knowledge of its contents. The work was, however, well known to the English authors of the illustrated school-edition of 1904, no less than to the German contributors to the edition published in 1897 by the *Philologische Gesellschaft* of Leipzig. Jebb's latest legacy to classical literature, the elaborate edition of *Bacchylides*, published in 1905, was the ultimate result of Dr Kenyon's publication of the *editio princeps* in 1897. Similarly, the Leipzig edition of Theophrastus, which appeared in the very same year, led to his returning with renewed interest to the study of the *Characters*. I have before me a complete abstract of the 45 pages on the Recension of the Text contributed to that edition by Otto Immisch. This abstract was written on 25 quarto pages in the Library of the House of Commons, and was concluded on April 14, 1904,—a day on which the House was engaged in debates on army estimates and underground railways.

The discussion of the date of the *Characters*, contributed to the Leipzig edition by Conrad Cichorius, is carefully analysed

[1] c. II.

in the margin of Sir Richard Jebb's copy of that work, which I owe to the kindness of Lady Jebb. There can be little doubt that, had Sir Richard lived for even a few years longer, he would have prepared a new edition of his Theophrastus. This had been repeatedly urged by his friends during his life-time, and, after his death, three years ago, it was definitely suggested by one of them, Professor Tyrrell. By the desire of Lady Jebb and Messrs Macmillan the preparation of the new edition was accordingly undertaken by the present editor, who has now to state the points in which it differs from its predecessor.

In the *Introduction*, a few references to the later literature of the subject have been added, and the considerations urged by Cichorius, and analysed (as above noticed) by the translator, have been accepted as a sufficient reason for holding that the historical allusions in the *Characters* point to the year 319 as the date of their composition, and not to the year 316, as suggested in the previous edition.

Among the very few changes in the *Greek text* is the alteration of Πολυσπέρχων in XX 13 into Πολυπέρχων, which is now known to be the reading of the best Paris MS as well as of the Munich Epitome, besides being the only form recognised in Attic inscriptions of the age of Theophrastus. In V 20, the text has been brought into harmony with the translation by abandoning the transposition printed in the Teubner text by Foss, and accidentally followed by the printers of the first edition. In XVIII 10, the word πλεῖον, which had been removed, under the mistaken impression that it was omitted by both of the Paris MSS, has now been reinstated, and the translation of the sentence has accordingly been brought into agreement with the translator's own quotation of it in the note on XXVII 7:—
'If Zeus would (be gracious enough to) send *more* rain, the crops would be better.' In the former edition the earlier Attic form κναφέως appeared in XXIII 14, and the later Attic form

γναφεῖς in XXIV 26; in the present, the later form in γν, which is supported by inscriptions of the fourth century, has been adopted in both passages. There are other points, in which the text is uncertain, but further alterations would have involved corresponding changes in the translation, and it has been thought best that the latter should remain, so far as possible, intact.

In the *Translation*, the punctuation has been carefully revised, and a few necessary corrections have been introduced. Thus, in VII 7, 'when he pays a mina, he will cause the slave to *pay it with a new coin*,' has been altered into '*pay the sum in new coin*,' the mina being a sum of money and not a single coin. In VIII 6, 'the festival of a hero' has been altered into 'the festivals of heroes,' with a view to a closer correspondence with the plural ἡρῷα In XXVIII 25, 'convolvulus' has been altered into 'smilax,' as the description of the plant in one of the botanical treatises of Theophrastus shows that it corresponds to the *smilax aspera*, and not to the convolvulus. Lastly, certain clauses, accidentally omitted in XVIII 9 and XXIII 8, have now been duly inserted.

To facilitate reference, the number and the title of each chapter has been printed at the head of the page, the lines of the text and the translation have been numbered in the margin; and every note, whether explanatory or critical, is now preceded by the number of the line to which it refers.

For the convenience of the reader, the *Explanatory Notes* have been transferred from the end of the text to the foot of the page In these Notes only two items have been omitted :— (1), in XV 13, where the inference from a disputed passage in Plato's *Apology*, 26 E, that a drachma was charged for the best places in the theatre, had already been tacitly given up in Jebb's article on THEATRUM in the *Dictionary of Antiquities*; and (2), in XXVI 22 f, where the summary of Boeckh's views on ancient money-standards (on p 258, ed 1870), has been withdrawn, as the text refers only to measures of capacity and not to money-standards, while Boeckh's opinions on the latter are superseded by those which have resulted from the discussions raised by the tenth chapter of Aristotle's *Constitution of Athens*. On this point, and on many others, supplementary notes have been added Not a few of these have been suggested by texts discovered since the publication of the first edition. The above-mentioned treatise of Aristotle has thus been quoted, as well as the *Mimes* of Herondas, while a few further illustrations have been gleaned from the fragments of Menander, the pupil of Theophrastus[1] There are also repeated references to the recent literature of the subject, including the papers by Canon E. L Hicks, and by Professors Ribbeck and Gomperz, and the commentary of the Leipzig editors, while several illustrations have been derived from the province of classical archaeology A marginal memorandum (the only one of its kind) shows that the original editor intended to revise his note on the *Odeum* (XVIII 13). this note has accordingly been recast. It has also been necessary to revise the note on the Panathenaic procession (XXIX 5).

In the text 'square brackets,' [ ], are uniformly used in this edition to denote words that ought to be omitted, and 'angular brackets,' < >, to distinguish words that have been inserted The additions due to the present editor are, in the case of the Explanatory Notes, placed in parentheses distinguished from the ordinary parentheses by the use of blacker type; in the Critical Appendix (as in the notes to the Preface), ordinary parentheses have been found sufficient for the purpose

In the *Critical Appendix* the account of the MSS has been revised. It is now known that the MS, which the editor (following the precedent set by Petersen) described as the

[1] Pamphila, ap. Diog. Laert. v 36

'Palatino-Vatican' (P Vat.), is not identical with any one of the four Vatican MSS of the *Characters*, which were formerly in the Library of the Palatinate Accordingly, throughout the critical notes, the MS in question is simply called the 'Vatican MS' (V). The Bibliography has also been revised and supplemented by the addition of more than three pages on the literature of the subject between 1869 and the present time. These pages also contain references to works, in which many suggestions have been made for the correction of the text; but, of these suggestions, only those that appear to have a high degree of probability have been quoted in the critical notes.

In the course of some correspondence with Professor von Wilamowitz-Moellendorff, who had included several of the *Characters* in his well-known 'Greek Reader,' I had the good fortune to learn that his colleague, Professor Diels, whose *Theophrastea* of 1883 is one of the landmarks in the recent study of the text, was engaged in preparing a critical edition for the Clarendon Press. Professor Diels and myself were thus happily enabled to arrange for communicating our proof-sheets to one another. The result was that the Berlin Professor was put in possession of Jebb's opinions on the text, which had previously been inaccessible to him, while I had the advantage of obtaining accurate information as to the disputed readings in the two Paris MSS and the Vatican MS, all three of which had been completely photographed with a view to the Oxford edition I have also had the satisfaction of being enabled to record the excellent emendations now proposed by Professor Diels, to whom my best thanks are due for the promptitude with which he has kindly supplied me with all the information I could possibly desire.

The *Greek Index to the Text* is on a considerably larger scale than the corresponding index to the notes in the former edition. As a simple *Index Verborum*, arranged in the order of the alphabet, it will enable the reader to find any important word or phrase with, perhaps, greater facility than is possible in the case of any elaborately classified and subdivided index, such as those which accompany the editions of 1897 and 1904. The *English Index to the Notes* includes practically all the items in the corresponding index to the first edition, and many more besides. It is hoped that the enlargement of both the Indexes will furnish scholars and students with a ready means of referring to any passage they desire to trace in the text or notes, and that the new edition of this work will find many friends in the generation that has grown up since the date of its first appearance eight and thirty years ago.

J. E. SANDYS.

MERTON HOUSE, CAMBRIDGE,
  December, 1908

ADDENDUM

On page 58, line 3, after περαιτέρω insert ὡς (omitted in the text of the first edition, but inserted in the *Critical Appendix*).

INTRODUCTION.

I.

PROBABLE ORIGIN OF THE BOOK.

THE book of Characters which tradition ascribes to Theophrastus, the pupil of Aristotle, contains thirty sketches from Athenian society in the age of Alexander the Great. If they do not go far into human nature, they touch things upon its surface with a good deal of humour and acuteness. As illustrations of manners, again, they have this merit, that they treat of commonplace people and of everyday life. But it is not as pictures of men or of manners that they seem most interesting.

Besides the language which a literature can preserve, every civilised people has another which necessarily dies with it, the language of society. The general sense of a word survives in books, and it is sometimes possible by a comparison of passages to discriminate shades of meaning; but it is seldom or never possible to be sure that we have seized the precise notions which the word conveyed long ago to the men in whose mouths it was a part of living speech. A thousand associations which we cannot guess at, reaching back into the infancy of the people, becoming more complex with its growth, intertwining themselves with every part of its civil and social being, were blent together in every word through which this life found utterance, and dyed each with tints which are lost for ever when the glow from which they were caught is extinct. The words of a dead language are like panes of stained glass seen on a bleak morning. The genius of the design which they make up can be felt; and, if the separate colours seem hard in the grey light, it is possible to imagine them deepened; but no imagination can see them as they looked when the evening sunshine was streaming through the window. When the life of a nation is over, the forms of the language which it once warmed remain, and sympathy can still quicken them, perhaps, with a tinge of the old spirit; but the very soul which gave its meaning to the shape can never be lit up again.

This loss is at once severest and least remediable in the case of those terms which every society invents or adapts to express familiar ethical facts from points of view peculiar to itself, but which either do not come into books, or are not fully explained there. Even in a living language such terms are seldom so well understood by a foreigner that he can be sure of using them in exactly the right cases. For instance, the ironical application of 'shocking' occasionally met with in French novels is not always what we should consider happy; and few Englishmen would dare to say that they knew precisely what is meant by certain French and German terms of the same kind. This is one of the obvious reasons against interlarding one's mother-speech with words borrowed to express ideas pithily; the words so borrowed are usually just those which a foreigner is most likely to use wrongly. They are saturated more deeply than any others with the mind of the people to whom they are peculiar. For the same reason, when it is possible to arrive at a tolerably clear notion of what they mean, no helps are so valuable towards understanding the ways in which a foreign people feels and thinks.

Now in the Characters of Theophrastus we have thirty such words explained and fully illustrated. The precise idea, for example, which an Athenian attached to 'Meanness' is put beyond a doubt by a list of the things which the Mean man will do. To make clearness doubly clear, qualities nearly akin to each other are in some cases described. Thus the province of Meanness has its border still better defined by juxtaposition to Avarice and to Penuriousness. We have, in fact, in this book, a fragment of the social language of Athens interpreted by a very full and explicit commentary. The value of such a fragment to the study of Greek history and literature is surely not slight. A series of men, vividly seen, with all the tricks of speech and manner which marked them in Athenian society, passes before us; and for once we know that we are viewing them from an absolutely Athenian standpoint, and can name every one of them as an Athenian would have named him. It would be a dull imagination which were not helped by this to understand better the drama played on a larger stage, and to feel the language which the actors spoke as if it were one of which the shades could still be caught from the tones and gestures of living men.

It is well known that the text of the Characters is corrupt, though there is scarcely a place where the general meaning cannot be seen, and that one manuscript, now in the Vatican library, is the sole authority for two of the chapters, as well as for certain additions to thirteen others. A short account of the manuscripts and of the principal editions will be found in another place[1]. Here it will be enough to say that there have been three epochs in the modern history of the book; the appearance of Casaubon's edition in 1598; the discovery of the two long-missing chapters in 1786; and the publication, in 1834—6, of three essays by Herr H. E. Foss, by which the disputed authenticity of these chapters and of the other additions in the Vatican MS may be said to have been established.

The origin of a book so singular in style and with a history so peculiar has been the subject of various theories. It is proposed briefly to review the principal of these; to consider the chief arguments for and against them; and to separate, as far as possible, what is certain or probable from what remains mere matter of conjecture.

Two questions occur. Were the Characters written by Theophrastus? And, if so, did they originally form an independent work, or have they been extracted from some other book or books?

Burney[2] believed that the Characters were composed by a writer who lived under the Roman Empire, and who derived them from the pictures of old Greek life in the dramatists of the Middle or New Comedy. The second part of this theory scarcely requires to be disproved. No incident, no trait of style in the book warrants the supposition that a writer whose aim was to describe manners turned from living men to portraits of the dead. It is only necessary to read the 'Letters' in which Alciphro, a rhetorician of the Empire, attempted to revive the Athens of Menander, in order to feel the difference between a clever cento and a sketch from life[3]. There remains the more general proposition,—that the Characters, if not a patchwork, are yet the production of an age later than that of Theophrastus. This opinion no longer finds many supporters, but it is due to some names whose authority it has had to state the grounds on which it appears improbable.

Authorship of the Characters —Burney's view.

---

[1] Critical Appendix.

[2] The authority for Burney's opinion is a note by Dobree on Ar. *Plut.* 1021 (in his *Porsoni notae in Aristophanem*, Cambridge, 1820):—'Docte et acute suspicabatur desideratissimus Burneius, tempore imperatorum Romanorum ex comoediis esse consarcinatos (Characteras).'

[3] Alciphro probably lived in the latter part of the second century A.D. His imaginary Letters, in three books, are intended to illustrate the Athenian manners of an earlier time. One of them purports to be written by Menander, who was contemporary with Theophrastus. It is probable that the ludicrous adventures of parasites and rustics which they describe were taken in part from pieces of the Middle and New Comedy. If this be so, we have here sketches actually constructed as Burney supposed the Characters to have been—'ex comoediis consarcinati'. The artificial and elaborate drollery of the Letters is in striking contrast with the simple humour of the Characters.

INTRODUCTION

Date of the Characters.— External evidence.

The earliest writer who ascribes the Characters to Theophrastus is Diogenes Laertius, early in the third century. Supposing him to have been deceived, further evidence to their higher antiquity can be found only in themselves. The internal evidence which they supply is of two kinds, general and particular.

Internal evidence—that of the language.

The general evidence is, in the first place, that of the language. As far as the state of the text allows us to judge, the book contains scarcely a word or a construction which would not be admissible in what is usually called 'classical' Greek prose[1]. Changes in the language and in literary style proceeded rapidly from the beginning of the third century B.C., and even those later writers who, like Lucian, especially studied Atticism, use words and constructions which, as far as we can judge, an old Attic writer would not have used. As regards the ordinary style of the later prose-writers, there is no possibility of mistaking it for the 'classical': not only is the language different, but the old straightforward way of writing has given place to a general taste for antithesis and for what was thought melodious arrangement. The plain, short sentences of the Characters, the series of infinitives strung together on the οἷος at the head of each chapter, like papers of all sizes on a file, do not resemble such work as the disciples of the rhetorical schools loved to produce. The only case which has been alleged of a post-classical usage is δεισιδαιμονία in the sense of 'superstition.' The word, it is said, did not 'acquire' a bad sense till after the time of Theophrastus. As we have endeavoured to show in a note on c. xxviii, it is inaccurate to speak of the word 'acquiring' a sense which potentially it must always have had. And that, as early as the time of Theophrastus, it was actually used in this as well as in its better sense, is sufficiently shown by the fact that Menander wrote a comedy with the title Δεισιδαίμων.

Evidence of the manners

Another kind of general evidence may probably be derived from the nature of the social manners which the Characters describe. Here, indeed, we are on ground far less sure than that of language. But it is certain that we may recognise in these sketches that frank homeliness which marked old Athenian life, and which faded there, as elsewhere, when men began to take their tone from the new capital of the world. This homeliness is seen in frequent allusions to the details of a small household, to petty loans between

---

[1] If καίπερ ἔχεις occurs in the character of the Flatterer, it should be remembered that the same construction is found in Plato's *Symposium*.

neighbours, to minute economies in dress and the like[1]. The simple life thus opened, and the candour which opens it, remind us rather of Aristophanes than of any writer whose taste in manners and in literature had been formed under imperial Rome[2].

Evidence of particular passages. The particular evidence consists in passages which allude to Alexander the Great and to his immediate successors as to persons with whom the speakers were contemporary.

In c. XXIII (VI of this edition) the Boastful man brags of having served with Alexander; and afterwards states that Antipater has conferred upon him the privilege of exporting timber from Macedonia free of duty. This appears to refer to the three years (322—319 B.C.) during which Antipater, first as regent of the province of Macedonia, afterwards as supreme regent of the whole Macedonian empire, was master of Athens, and in particular to the first half of 319 B.C.[3] In c. VIII (XX in this edition) the Newsmonger,—or, as he is styled, the Newsmaker,—pretends that he has just had news of a battle between Cassander and Polyperchon. These leaders were at war in the years 319—309 B.C.; and the particular time referred to is probably the latter half of the year 319[4].

Now a writer who wished to illustrate character by sketches of representative men might of course, if he pleased, throw them back into history. By so doing, however, he would not only give himself much needless trouble, but would lose nearly all the freshness and effect. An English character-writer of the present day, who wished to convey a distinct idea of how a braggart speaks and acts, would scarcely place him in the reign of Elizabeth, and make him boast of his adventures with Raleigh, or affect to have received private advices from the Low Countries. Or, if he chose to proceed in this way, he would at least take care that the allusions should be such as ordinary readers could easily recognise. On Burney's hypothesis, however, the author of the Characters neglected even this precaution. The allusion which he has placed in the mouth of his Newsmonger is to an obscure episode in the complicated quarrels of Alexander's successors. To an Athenian who

---

[1] See esp. cc. 14, 15, 23.
[2] The tone of social life in the small republics of ancient Greece is described, with the inspiration of a true feeling for Aristophanes, by Mr G. O Trevelyan, in the paper 'A Holiday among some Old Friends,' reprinted from the *Cornhill Magazine* in the same volume with 'Ladies in Parliament' (pp. 141—196, ed. 1869).
[3] See note on VI 14. (In the former edition the date adopted was 316; but the discussion by Conrad Cichorius, in the Leipzig edition of 1897, has made it clear that the true date is 319)
[4] See note on XX 15.

lived just then the episode happened to be important, and in his mind
it would fill a large space: but it is scarcely one which a literary man,
writing long afterwards, would have brought into a popular sketch.
The probability that the composer of the Characters was contemporary
with the events of which they speak may be illustrated from the case
of a similar book in our own literature. Let us suppose that, several
centuries after the English language was dead, a critic with no external
testimony before him, and who could not trust himself to decide surely
between the literary styles and social manners of different periods, wished
certain from internal evidence when Hall's 'Characterismes of
and Vices' were written. He would be struck, in the first
by a passage in the sketch of the Busie-Bodie. 'What euerie
ventures in *Guiana* voyage and what they gained he knows to a
haire Whether *Holland* will haue peace hee knowes, and on what
conditions; and with what successe is familiar to him ere it bee
concluded.' Another passage to which he might look for help is in the
sketch of the Vaine-glorious man. 'His talke is...what exploits he did
at *Cales* or *Nieuport.*' If he then consulted histories, he would find
that voyages to Guiana were most in fashion in England during the
latter part of Raleigh's life, who made his first expedition thither in
1595, and his second in 1618. A truce for twelve years between the
States-General and Spain was signed on the 9th April, 1609. Calais
was taken by the Spaniards April 17th, 1596[1], and remained in their
hands until Henry IV regained it by a treaty with Philip signed at
Vervins, May 2nd, 1598. In the interval he more than once asked
Elizabeth to help him in a siege for the recovery of the town[2]. The
battle of Nieuport, in which the army of the States-General, led by
Maurice of Nassau, with the English allies under Sir Francis Vere,
defeated the Spaniards under Albert of Austria, was fought July 2nd,
1600[3]. Here, then, are four distinct allusions to events comprised in a
period of about twelve years. It would be a reasonable inference that
these were events of the writer's own time; and that the 'Characterismes'
were written either soon before or soon after the end of the war between
Spain and Holland. If the inquirer could assume that the sketch of
the Busie-bodie, who discusses the prospects of peace, was written while
peace was really future, then he would have ascertained that part of the
book at least was composed not later than the spring of 1609. If he
hesitated to assume this, he would merely pronounce it probable that

---

[1] Motley, *United Netherlands*, III 346, 470.
[2] *Ib.* III 347, 432.
[3] *Ib* IV 27—47

the book was written in or about the years 1600—1610. We know that, in fact, it was published in 1608.

On evidence of the like kind, confirmed by the general evidence first noticed, it is probable that the Characters were written in or about the years 322—300 B.C. If the inference which would have been safe in respect to Hall's 'Busie-Bodie' is safe in respect to the Greek sketch of the 'Newsmaker,' then that chapter, at least, was written late in the year 319 B C.; but this is uncertain and unimportant.

The life of Theophrastus, though its precise limits are doubtful, falls in the period 373—284 B.C.[1] The Characters are expressly ascribed to him by Diogenes in the century, and were known as his to the later grammarians, Eu.. Suidas, and Tzetzes. A story preserved by Athenaeus further that the tradition of antiquity represented him as having a genius for lively description[2]. On the whole, then, there seems to be no good reason for doubting that the Characters are his genuine productions[3].

<small>Date of Theophrastus.</small>

But did they originally form a separate book? Or have they been extracted from some other work or works of Theophrastus? This question, unlike the former, cannot be answered with any confidence: we can only balance the probabilities.

<small>Original form of the Characters.</small>

The principal champion in recent times of the belief that the Characters represent an independent work has been F. Ast, the author of the *Lexicon Platonicum*. When his edition was published at Leipzig in 1816, the theory of extracts was already current in Germany. In his Prolegomena he re-asserts the older view by an appeal to the evidence of style. There are, he says, three styles in which character may be described. First the philosophical, having for its aim to teach. Secondly the rhetorical, having for its aim to move. Thirdly, what he calls the 'mimicum genus,' the farcical; having for its aim simply to amuse. The proper subjects for this style

<small>The opinion that they formed an independent work.</small>

<small>Ast's argument.</small>

---

[1] According to Apollodorus *ap.* Diog. v 58 he died in Ol. 123 (288—284 B.C.). According to Diogenes (v 40), he died at 85 years of age. This places his birth in 373—369 B.C; and makes him 11—15 years younger than Aristotle.

[2] Athen. I p. 21 A.

[3] Dobree thus refers to the opinion of Porson:—'Putabat scilicet, nisi me vehementer fallit memoria, falso tribui Theophrasto Characteras, antiquos tamen esse concedens' (Pors. Notae in Ar., *Plut.* 1021). Had Porson left on record his reasons for this opinion, they would have been of great interest. As it is, we have only a dictum vaguely reported.

are qualities neither virtuous nor vicious[1], but morally indifferent; its excellences are truth, tact, brevity; its results should be 'witty pictures—idylls—of human character, drawn from nature itself, with no purpose but to please'[2]. These conditions are, he thinks, fulfilled by the Characters of Theophrastus. They are essentially in this humorous style; they cannot, therefore, have been culled from a philosophical or rhetorical work. As we shall endeavour to show by and by, there is an element of truth in this view. But, in the precise form which Ast gives to it, it appears slightly fantastic. Granting that the laws which he lays down for the 'farcical' style are just, it cannot be said that the Characters of Theophrastus strictly obey them. Truth, tact, conciseness, are doubtless among the merits of these sketches. But the qualities described are not such as the author, at least, thought 'morally indifferent.' Many of them are identical with 'vices' treated by Aristotle and Eudemus; all of them, as being extremes, are vices in the meaning of the Peripatetic school to which Theophrastus belonged. Ast's rule that such descriptions should *simply* amuse is a test not easy to apply; but he saves us this trouble by avowing that three chapters—the Oligarch, the Patron of Rascals, and the Superstitious Man—do not satisfy it; and regards them, on this and other grounds, as spurious. The same objection might surely be urged with equal force against some others,—notably against the chapters on Irony and on Evilspeaking.

But, when we have rejected Ast's theory of the style in which the Characters are composed, we have still to consider the value of his general result. The theory that these sketches formed part or the whole of a special work starts with an advantage; the burden of proof rests with those who deny it. Nor, indeed, can it be disproved. But a number of circumstances, which severally are not of great weight, combine to render it improbable. In the first place, not only do the manuscripts vary much in the number of chapters which they contain, but they represent three distinct revisions or editions; in one of which the same chapters are longer, and in another shorter, than in the third. If the Characters once formed a definite whole, the volume has had a fate which could not easily be paralleled, for, whereas its original unity ought to have secured something like a uniform tradition, it has been handed down, not merely with various texts, but in a number of

---

[1] *Proleg* p 13 'res vel materia ..neque praestans et ad virtutem insignis neque turpis et foeda erit, sed eiusmodi quae propter suam ipsa naturam iocum et risum admittat; igitur ex earum rerum numero erunt quas indifferentes dicimus'

[2] *Proleg.* p. 26 'mimos, h. e. lepidas humanorum morum imagines (quasi εἰδύλλια) ex ipsa natura expressas, quibus mera delectatio sit proposita.'

different shapes and sizes. Next, if we consider that portion of the contents, and that arrangement of them, upon which the manuscripts agree, we shall discover a want of symmetry and a confusion hardly reconcileable with the supposition that the book was put forth in this form by its author. Some qualities are treated, for no evident reason, with much greater fulness than the rest. Three chapters are given to the Love of Money, considered in finer gradations than are recognised in any other case; Talkativeness, again, and the qualities allied to Shamelessness, are especially favoured; while such complex ideas as Pride and Cowardice are dismissed in one chapter each. The order of the chapters is also capricious. Qualities so much alike that juxtaposition is necessary for distinction, are placed apart; nor is contrast, any more than resemblance, a principle of the arrangement. Yet upon this arrangement the manuscripts agree. Unless such an order had ancient authority, it could scarcely have maintained itself against reason and convenience in all the manuscripts; on the other hand it is scarcely conceivable that it can represent the author's final design. An explanation of the fact will be suggested presently; we are now concerned only with the fact itself. Three things, then, seem against the view that the Characters, as now extant, originally formed a single work; the multiform tradition; the unsymmetrical plan; the confused arrangement. If it is contended that the Characters, though not the whole, may be a fragment of such a work, the first and third of these difficulties have still to be met; for the second is substituted that of explaining how it happened that part of a volume presumably small should have been preserved in a number of copies which testifies to its popularity, while the other part has been so completely lost that no trace remains of it.

The opinion that the Characters are extracts from some other work or works is less open to obvious objections, and is that to which recent scholars have generally inclined. It has been held in different forms, which have gradually become more and more precise. Schneider, in the preface to his edition published in 1799, was content to surmise that these extracts were made 'at various times and by various persons' from 'some larger ethical work' of Theophrastus. This is certainly to put the theory in its least probable shape. The gradual formation of the book would account, indeed, for the confused order of its chapters; but how can it be supposed that such a collection was made gradually 'by various men and at various times'? If, when the first of these had selected two or three sketches, he held his hand, what

Theory that the Characters are extracts

Schneider's view.

singular good fortune transmitted to the next labourer this small beginning of a book, and so passed the slowly growing volume through these mysterious inheritors of a purpose? It is surely simpler to suppose that a task of such very moderate compass was completed by the person who conceived it. But upon what book or books did this person draw? Schneider says merely on 'a larger ethical work'; but some later writers have spoken more definitely.

Works from which the Characters may have been taken. Theophrastus is known to have been the author of two large works on moral philosophy; one of these was called ἠθικά[1], and was perhaps a collection of special treatises; the other was entitled περὶ ἠθῶν, and was probably analogous in plan to the Nicomachean Ethics of Aristotle, but more comprehensive. It is now[2] a favourite opinion that the Characters were derived from the latter of these works[3], or perhaps from both[4]. The claims of the περὶ ἠθῶν have been urged in an elaborate and able essay by Dr E. Petersen (1859). We will attempt to give an outline of his argument, and to consider its value.

---

[1] Plutarch in his *Life of Pericles*, c. 38, quotes an anecdote as given by Theophrastus ἐν τοῖς ἠθικοῖς. The other work, περὶ ἠθῶν, is mentioned by a scholiast on the *Nicomachean Ethics*, IV 2, p. 1121 A, in Cramer's *Anecdota Parisina*, I p. 194, who says that the avarice of Simonides of Ceos, on which Aristotle touches, was noticed also by Theophrastus ἐν τοῖς περὶ ἠθῶν. Athenaeus says too (XV p. 673 E), that Adrantus (or as it is now generally read, Adrastus) wrote 'five books on the questions of history and language (τὰ καθ' ἱστορίαν καὶ λέξιν ζητούμενα) in the περὶ ἠθῶν of Theophrastus, and one book on those in the *Nicomachean Ethics* of Aristotle.' That the περὶ ἠθῶν and the ἠθικά were distinct works, and that each consisted of several books, appears from the statement of the grammarian Eustratius (on the *Eth. Nicom.* V 2, p. 1129 B) that a certain verse there quoted was ascribed by Theophrastus, in the first book of the περὶ ἠθῶν, to Theognis; but, in the first book of the ἠθικά, to Phocylides. Zeller agrees with Petersen in supposing the περὶ ἠθῶν to have been a work of the same kind as the *Nicomachean Ethics*, but 'more comprehensive.' Usener, in his *Analecta Theophrastea* (1858), an examination of the catalogue of the works of Theophrastus in Diog. V 42—50, supposes that the ἠθικά was a collection of essays like those περὶ εὐδαιμονίας, περὶ εὐτυχίας, περὶ κολακείας mentioned by Diogenes,—put together by the grammarian Andronicus, who is said by Porphyry (*Vit. Plot.* 24) to have rearranged the writings of Theophrastus (*Anal. Theophr.* p. 22). Besides these special treatises, and the Characters, Diogenes mentions only ἠθικῶν σχολῶν α', which, Zeller thinks, may have been identical with part of the περὶ ἠθῶν or of the ἠθικά.

[2] 1870.

[3] Speaking of the epitomes from the writings of Theophrastus mentioned by Diogenes, Usener says: 'eodem pertinent etiam ἠθικοὶ χαρακτῆρες, in rhetorum usum, quae est Hermanni Sauppii coniectura ueri simillima, ex Theophrasti libris περὶ ἠθῶν excerpti' (p. 18).

[4] 'Aus einem dieser Werke, *oder auch aus beiden*, scheinen...die Schilderungen von Fehlern entlehnt zu sein, welche in unsern "Charakteren" zusammengestellt sind' (Zeller *Philos. der Gr.* II 2, p. 684 note). (E. T. of ed. 3, *Aristotle and the earlier Peripatetics*, II 400; cp. 355, 407.)

ORIGIN OF THE BOOK

After touching upon some notices of the lost work περὶ ἠθῶν, which suggest that it went over nearly the same ground as the Nicomachean Ethics, Petersen expresses the belief that yet clearer traces of this work are to be found in an extant author. Stobaeus in his 'Eclogues' sketches the ethical system 'of Aristotle and the other Peripatetics,' and in one place quotes Theophrastus by name in support of a particular statement. Petersen endeavours to show that the whole of this exposition was probably derived from the περὶ ἠθῶν of Theophrastus; that, therefore, the περὶ ἠθῶν treated of (at least) all those qualities which are cited in illustration by Stobaeus; and that, since twelve of these correspond with qualities described in the Characters, it is so far possible that the Characters may have been derived from the περὶ ἠθῶν. The first position is defended at length. To make it probable that Stobaeus was indebted to a work which not only is not extant, but of which the nature can only be conjectured, is certainly no easy task; and, on the other hand, we would not willingly undertake to show that it was improbable. It will suffice to quote a criticism upon this part of Petersen's theory by the historian of Greek philosophy, Dr E. Zeller[1]. 'Since the latest source used by Stobaeus is at all events a much later one (than Theophrastus),— as one sees from the frequent introduction of Stoic terminology and the elaborate apologetic references to Stoic doctrines, and as is also probable from Cic. *de Fin.* v;—since, too, a partial agreement with Theophrastus warrants no conclusion as to the remaining contents of the extract;— we cannot use it (with the exception of one passage in which Theophrastus is named, p. 300) as evidence for the doctrine of this teacher.'

It appears to us, however, that Petersen might resign his special theory regarding the passage in Stobaeus without damage to his main position, viz. that the Characters were derived from the περὶ ἠθῶν. Everyone would allow that if, as is likely on other grounds, the περὶ ἠθῶν was a work similar to the Nicomachean Ethics, it probably treated of many qualities identical with those described in the Characters. The real difficulties are of a kind out of which Stobaeus could not help us.

The first may be stated thus. Admitting that many, or that most, of the characters may have been extracted from a formal treatise on morals, are there not some for which such a source is inconceivable? Consider, for instance, the sketches of the Newsmaker, of the Late-learner, of the Oligarch, of the Patron of Rascals. Each of these must,

---

[1] Zeller *Philos. der Gr.* II 2, p. 684 (*Peripatetics*, II 401 *note*). *note* (E T, *Aristotle and the earlier*

on Petersen's assumption, have been treated in the lost philosophical work; and, if this work was on the plan of Aristotle's Ethics, each must have been considered in relation to an opposite and to an intermediate quality. Petersen labours hard to reconstruct these συζυγίαι or trios; but it is not surprising that personages such as those just named are somewhat refractory under the process. The Newsmaker, with all that is distinctive in his genius unrecognised, subsides into a place under the notion of Loquacity, though doubts are expressed whether he would not have been an equally loyal dependent of Boastfulness. The names of the vicious character to which he is opposite, and of the virtuous one in regard to which he is extreme, are not specified. The Late-learner is dealt with yet more summarily. He is merely pronounced to be a variety of the Idly-laborious, and, when it has been briefly suggested that Industry is the virtue from which he has strayed, he is left with his more special relations unexplained. The Oligarch is declared—with a partiality somewhat oligarchical—to be the opposite of the Reckless man (ἀπονενοημένος); the intermediate character being the Popular (δημοτικός). The Patron of Rascals is still more strangely situated, he is given for his vis-à-vis the Arrogant Man, and the character between them is styled φιλόδημος, the Friend of the People.

Whether such groups can have had place in a work on moral science, is a question which everyone must judge for himself. It would not, perhaps, be easy, with the given materials, to form an arrangement which should not be liable to criticism in at least the same degree as Petersen's. The Newsmaker, the Late-learner, and the rest, could never be accurately fitted into any of those round or square holes which are prepared for abstractions. They are not ideal men, in each of whom a quality is personified; they are real, and therefore complex. Moreover they have been regarded, not from the philosopher's, but from the artist's point of view; they have not been analysed, but drawn as they strike the eye, in such wise that the laws of anatomy are of less moment than the rules of perspective. Now, as Petersen himself has conclusively shown elsewhere, the genuineness of all thirty Characters rests upon the same evidence. No hypothesis of their origin can be accepted which will not apply to every one of them. If, then, the derivation from a formal work on morals appears unlikely for some chapters, it must be pronounced unlikely for all.

The second difficulty involved in the view which we are discussing

Second objection —Style of the Characters generally. arises from the style of the Characters generally. Would descriptions of this kind have been admitted into a philosophical work? Petersen has met this objection fairly, though not, as it appears to us, victoriously Theophrastus merely wished, he says, to embody each fault, with the utmost truth and clearness, in a person who should be typical of a class. If the resulting portraits 'move laughter rather than indignation,' this is due partly to the nature of the subject, partly to that of the author. Most of the qualities described are such as hurt the possessor more than anyone else, and Theophrastus seems to have had a very keen sense of the ridiculous To these remarks we readily assent; but they do not appear to meet the case. The difficulty is, not that the descriptions are amusing, but that they are written as if their principal aim was to amuse. No one would object to philosophical truths receiving humorous illustration. But when a delineation of character has been so worked up that every sentence is a point or a witticism, its fitness to illustrate general truths is spoilt by the interest of its details. A writer whose first object was to show by examples how certain principles work, would do ill if he set before the imagination a mass of particulars so humorous that the thought of principles must at least be undermost.

Petersen contends, however, that passages similar in style to the Characters are actually found in Aristotle's Ethics. We will now turn to these, and inquire how far the resemblance goes.

The first passage in which he discovers an approach to the manner of Theophrastus is the discussion upon Courage (*Eth.*

Analogy of passages in the Nicom. Ethics to the Characters examined.

N. IV 5—9). We translate the remarks which he cites.— (1) 'The rash are headlong, and, though ready enough before dangers, yet in dangers fall away; but the courageous are in action keen, and, before it, quiet'. *Eth. N.* IV 7. (2) 'Regular troops turn cowards when the peril becomes pressing and they are inferior in numbers· or equipment. They are the first to run away': IV 8. (3) 'Such' (i e occasions of sudden death) 'are especially the chances of war; not but that the courageous man is fearless also at sea'· IV 6. And (4) from the comparison of Intemperance with Cowardice, IV 12: 'Such things distract the mind with pain, so that men throw away their arms and otherwise incur disgrace.'

Aristotle refers here to particular occasions on which cowardice is displayed, and even to particular acts which the coward does. But these are referred to in general terms, and in direct connexion with the general laws which they exemplify. Turn now to the chapter on Cowardice in the Characters of Theophrastus. It consists of two little stories, each elaborated to the highest point, and set off with a profusion of lively details. The first runs thus:—'The Coward is one who, on a voyage, will protest that the promontories are privateers; and, if a high sea gets up, will ask if there is anyone on board who has not been initiated. He will put up his head and ask the steersman 'if he is halfway yet'; remarking to the person sitting next him that 'a dream makes him feel uneasy'; and he will take off his tunic and give it to a slave; or he will beg them to set him ashore.'

Is it easy to suppose this embodied in a work similar to the Nicomachean Ethics?

But more stress is laid by Petersen on two other cases,—the delineations of the Magnificent and of the Magnanimous Man. From the former he makes this extract:—'There are cases of expenditure which we call honourable; for instance, the presentation to the gods of offerings, temple-furniture, sacrifices; all things, in like manner, which concern the divine nature generally, or which are subjects of honourable rivalry in regard to the common weal; as when men deem in any case that they are bound to put a chorus on the stage, to equip a trireme, or perhaps to feast the town, in splendid style. ..In private life [the occasions for magnificence] are those which occur but once,— a marriage, for instance, or anything of that kind,—and those which excite the interest of the whole community, or of its most respected members; preparations, again, for the reception or for the departure of guests; and the making or the recompensing of gifts. It also belongs to the Magnificent Man to furnish his house suitably to his wealth.' (*Eth.* IV 2)

With the particulars of this statement Petersen compares some special points in the three chapters of Theophrastus on Penuriousness, Meanness, and Avarice. But a safer mode of proceeding is surely to compare the general style of the passage in Aristotle with the general style of any one of these. Take, for example, the first few sentences of the chapter on Meanness:—'The Mean Man is one who, having gained the prize in a tragic contest, will dedicate a wooden scroll to Dionysus, having had it inscribed with his own name. When subscriptions are being raised in the ecclesia, he will rise without saying a word, and walk out of the assembly. When he is celebrating his daughter's marriage, he will sell the flesh of the animal sacrificed, save what is due to the altar; and will hire the attendants at the marriage festival on condition that they find their own board. When he is trierarch, he will spread the steersman's rugs under him upon the deck, and put his own away.' Here, as in the former case, the difference between the two kinds of writing is well seen. Aristotle, bent on illustrating principles, touches on facts by the way. Theophrastus, studying to produce a picture, combines groups of facts within a framework which is itself scarcely observed.

It remains to consider the passage upon which Petersen chiefly relies,—the famous description of the Magnanimous Man, which he pronounces 'most like of all, both in matter and in manner,' to the Characters. *Eth. N.* IV 3 '—'Now the Magnanimous Man despises others justly...It is of his nature to confer benefits, but he is ashamed to receive them. He seems, also, to remember whom he has benefited, but not those from whom he has received benefits. Again, it is characteristic of him to ask no favours, or to ask them reluctantly, but to do a service readily; to show himself haughty to men of rank or fortune, but kindly to those of middle station...He will not court objects of common ambition, or go where others are foremost.. He will be inactive and dilatory save where there is question of great honour or of a great work; he will engage in few things, but these shall be great and famous. He must needs be frank, too, in his hatreds and in his likings: for disguise belongs to fear....He will speak and act openly.. He will be ironical to the many...not prone to admire. .not apt to bear a grudge...no gossip. Nor, again, is he lavish of praise; and for the same reason he speaks no evil; not even of his enemies, unless it be to show his scorn...Again he is apt to possess beautiful and unfruitful things rather than those which yield fruit and profit; for this better becomes an independent man. Slow movement, also, deep tones, deliberate speech, seem to become the man of a great soul...Such, then, is the Magnanimous Man.'

Is it true that 'this description is removed only by the smallest interval from those of Theophrastus', and that 'the differences are in things which must, if the nature of his genius is considered, have given rise to his style of description'?

In the first place it should be noticed that the above extract, which we have given as Petersen gives it, does not accurately represent the general tenor of the passage. To every special characteristic of the Magnanimous Man Aristotle subjoins, as usual, a statement of the principle on which it depends. Thus to the remark that 'it is his character to confer benefits, but he is ashamed to receive them,' is added, 'for the one becomes a superior, the other an inferior'; and so, throughout, each action has its theory appended to it. The complexion of the entire passage is therefore very different from that of the epitome. It is not simply a series of picturesque instances. These instances are ranged upon a groundwork of connected reasonings;

and it is never for a moment obscure that the artistic purpose is secondary to the philosophical. If in the next place we consider the terms in which the particular actions of the Magnanimous Man are described, the difference between Aristotle and Theophrastus will again be clear. These terms are always general. The Magnanimous Man 'shows himself haughty to men of rank or fortune.' When Theophrastus is describing Arrogance, he is not content with saying that the Arrogant Man is haughty to all the world. 'The Arrogant Man,' he tells us, 'is one who will say to a person who is in a hurry that he will see him after dinner when he is taking his walk.' Aristotle says that the Magnanimous Man 'will not court objects of common ambition.' Theophrastus would have told us that such a person scorns to walk through the Market-place in his spurs, or to speak of the privilege which Antipater has conferred upon him of exporting timber free of duty.

To conclude: The theory that the Characters are extracts from a philosophical work appears to us improbable for two reasons. First, because of the subjects of certain chapters. Secondly, because of the style of all; and the latter objection cannot be overcome by a comparison of passages in the Nicomachean Ethics.

In the course of an attempt to examine several views of this question, it has been impossible to do full justice to the learning and ability with which Dr Petersen has urged his own. It is an opinion which has struck deep root in Germany, which many of her foremost scholars in recent times have asserted or allowed, and which will probably remain the general faith about the Characters of Theophrastus[1]. We have endeavoured to give fairly the substance of the chief arguments for it, and to explain why they do not satisfy us. If, then, the theory of an independent book and the theory of extracts are both to be rejected, what hypothesis remains? We will suggest in as few words as possible that solution of the question which appears to us least improbable.

Theophrastus wrote from time to time, for his own amusement and that of his friends, short sketches of characters common in everyday life, allowing free scope in these to his gift for lively satire. These playful pieces were handed about in his intimate

Another hypothesis

---

[1] (The opinion that the Characters are *extracts* from a philosophical work has, however, been opposed by Diels and Gomperz, *Sitzungsberichte* of Vienna Academy, 1888, CX no. 10, pp. 10, 19. Both of them regard the Characters as a collection of materials bearing the same relation to the *Ethics* of Theophrastus, as the *Politeiai* to the *Politics* of Aristotle; but both admit the existence of interpolations. In 1898 Gomperz described the 'excerpt-theory' as having no defenders.)

circle, but were never formed into a regular book; either because sketches so desultory did not readily lend themselves to a plan and an arrangement, and their author did not care to force them; or because he thought pieces so slight unworthy of his reputation and of his position as Aristotle's successor. At his death these several pieces, already famous among a few, passed into a wider currency than had been permitted to them during his life. Copies were multiplied; but some contained more pieces, some fewer; in some a particular piece was given at greater extent than in others. For there was no authentic volume to which appeal could be made; the sketches had been circulated privately, and not necessarily all together; no public edition had furnished a standard text, or stamped the collection as a definite whole. Thus may be explained the circumstance which has already been noticed as adverse to Ast's theory of an independent book, and which Zeller notices as favourable to the theory of extracts,—the looseness of the manuscript tradition. Thus, too, the absence of symmetry in the contents, for either Theophrastus, writing as fancy prompted, may have dwelt most largely upon certain characters in which the materials for description were peculiarly full and rich; or part of what he wrote about others may have been left out in the copies from which ours have come. Lastly, the order in which the chapters are arranged, which can hardly have been due to the author's design, but which yet has ancient authority, is intelligible if it represents the order into which the sketches chanced to have fallen in one or more of the collections made soon after the death of Theophrastus, and which, as being known to date nearly from his time, was respected by the Alexandrian grammarians. With these advantages the view just suggested combines the chief recommendation of that which supposes the Characters to represent an independent book published by Theophrastus. It justifies the grotesque subjects of some chapters, and the pointedly humorous style of all, on the plain ground that these sketches were written for their own sake, and were never episodes of a graver work[1].

---

[1] It may be mentioned, merely as an illustration, not of course as an argument from analogy, that the history here supposed for the Characters of Theophrastus was in fact nearly that of a similar book in modern times, Earle's *Microcosmographie*. In the notice 'To the Reader Gentile or Gentle' Earle says: 'I haue for once aduentur'd to playe the Midwife's part, helping to bring forth these Infants into the World, which the Father would haue smoothered: who hauing left them lapt vp in loose Sheets, as soon as his Fancy was deliuered of them, written especially for his Priuate Recreation, to passe away the time in the

But whatever view may be held regarding the origin of the book, on one point there can be no doubt; as we possess it, it bears the marks of a later hand. This hand is seen in the proem, in the clauses added at the end of certain chapters, and probably in some of the definitions. The common consent of critics has long pronounced the proem spurious. Theophrastus is made to say in it that he is about to record the experience of ninety years and nine—a startling statement, made apparently in the belief that his great age would be most impressive if it were put just short of the century. Diogenes says that Theophrastus died at eighty-five. The assertion in the proem has, indeed, thus much of internal evidence in its favour—that some of the sentiments found in that composition are strongly suggestive of second childhood. 'Often before now,' says the writer, 'have I applied my thoughts to the puzzling question—one, probably, which will puzzle me for ever—why it is that, while all Greece lies under the same sky, and all the Greeks are educated alike, it has befallen us to have characters variously constituted.' It is not of great moment to inquire why the proem promises descriptions of good as well as of bad men. There may have been a vague tradition that the book once included sketches of virtues corresponding to those of the vices; or this may have been the private opinion of the literary forger. Accordingly he wrote such a preface as he conceived that the book might, in its complete state, have had[1].

Traces of a later hand. The proem.

Six chapters[2] end with clauses which are not only feeble in themselves, but are foreign to the style of the Characters. It is now generally believed that they were added by some one who could not perceive that the quiet humour of the descriptions was spoilt by hortatory comments. One only of the

Clauses.

Country, and by the forcible request of Friends drawne from him; Yet passing seuerally from hand to hand in written Copies, grew at length to be a prety number in a little Volume; and among so many sundry dispersed Transcripts, some very imperfect and surreptitious had like to haue past the Presse, if the Author had not vsed speedy meanes of prevention.'

[1] Petersen has used the undoubted spuriousness of the proem as an argument against the original unity of the book. The forger added it, he thinks, 'ut speciem hae unitatis haberent laciniae.' I abstained above (pp. 8 ff.) from using this argument, because it seemed to me two-edged. Suppose that, in the forger's time, it was known that the Characters *had* once formed a single book, and that this book had had a proem, which was no longer extant. The desire of restoring it would have been motive enough for the forgery

[2] In this ed., nos V (usually I), XVI (VI), XVIII (III), XX (VIII), XXI (XXVIII), XXX (XXIX).

ORIGIN OF THE BOOK

number—the paragraph added to the sketch of the Newsmaker—has a faint tinge of the manner of Theophrastus; but it betrays itself by its general tone, and especially by the opening and concluding sentences. Another case—the brief addition to the chapter on φιλοπονηρία—might admit of doubt; but this again will be condemned if the test of general style is applied.

The spurious element in the Definitions cannot be so easily
The Definitions separated; for, even if the text were always certain, the fitness of the definition to the subject, which has generally been made a principal test of authenticity, is a question on which opinions differ endlessly. We will not venture to do more than state our impression that some of the definitions stand just, some nearly, as Theophrastus wrote them, that some have been mutilated more seriously; and that a few have been added by a later hand to chapters which the author had perhaps left without any definition.

If it is asked when and by whom the proem and clauses were
Date and author of the interpolations. probably added, Petersen's conjecture appears very probable,—that they are due to a rhetorician of the second or third century of the Christian era. He supposes that the same person extracted the Characters from the Περὶ Ἠθῶν, and therefore places him earlier than Diogenes Laertius (circ. 210 A.D.), to whom they were known as forming a separate book. But, if the Characters are not supposed to be extracts, it is unimportant whether the interpolator lived before or after that writer. The age of the Ptolemies, and the second and third Christian centuries, are known to have been periods in which literary frauds were common. An Alexandrian forger of the earlier period, however, would probably have done his work more neatly and more cautiously than the author of the proem; and it seems more likely that he should be assigned to the later period. It is quite possible that he may have been a rhetorician, since the study of the leading types of character, ἤθη, was so much used in the rhetorical schools; but this likelihood is hardly much strengthened by the fact which Petersen notices, that all the MSS which contain the Characters contain also rhetorical writings. What is spurious in the definitions can hardly be attributed to any one man, but must have come in gradually.

It has already been said that the order of the Characters, as they
Arrangement of the Characters. follow each other in the manuscripts, shows no attempt at method; and it has been suggested how this order may have arisen. To the reader it is intolerably inconvenient. Many of the Characters are separated from each other

by differences so fine that they cannot easily be distinguished unless they are placed side by side. But the usual arrangement, instead of helping such comparison, makes it as difficult as possible. The chapters have been thoroughly shuffled. Those on Flattery and on Complaisance are respectively nos 2 and 5; those on Garrulity and Loquacity, 3 and 7; those on Penuriousness, Meanness, and Avarice, 10, 22, and 30; and so throughout. Thus a person who reads the Characters consecutively is troubled with a sense that the same traits are perpetually recurring; but cannot, unless he often pauses and turns back, keep their several combinations clearly before him. In an edition published in 1852, Mr Sheppard made an effort to remedy the evil. He combined the Characters into eight groups, having regard to the general principle which he recognised as common to each group. This was a great improvement. His classification seems to us, however, liable to one objection. It is *too* scientific. In the endeavour to connect a group of characters by the principle which is their common root, he has sometimes overlooked strong resemblances which lie on the surface, and which, in sketches like these, form the practically important affinities. For instance, he classes Arrogance with Boasting, Petty Ambition, and Late-learning, because deep down in all these may be found Egotism; but Surliness with Grumbling, Distrustfulness, and Evilspeaking, because at the root of these is an 'organic moroseness of temper.' But—to pass over the question whether these ground principles are right—has not Surliness, as described by Theophrastus, so much in common with Arrogance that each will be understood better if viewed by the light of the other?

Sheppard's arrangement.

The arrangement which we have ourselves adopted is less ambitious. It does not seek to carry generalisation higher than the small groups into which the Characters obviously fall, and aims merely at placing these in a practically convenient order. Three objects have been kept in view. (1) The juxtaposition of Characters closely akin, e.g. Penuriousness, Meanness, Avarice. (2) The juxtaposition of such as present a direct contrast, e.g. the Oligarch and the Patron of Rascals; the Ironical Man and the Boaster. (3) General continuity, as far as anything of the kind can be obtained. For example, Irony being from one point of view allied to Arrogance, the Ironical man serves to break the transition from the Arrogant man, who precedes, to the Boaster who follows him. In the same way the Late-learner bridges the chasm between Petty Ambition and Unseasonableness. The Stupid Man forms a sort of link between the Offensive Man (the dull neglecter of his person) and the Boor. The Grumbler, with his murmurs against all the world, conducts us from the Evilspeaker to the Distrustful Man, who 'presumes that all men are unjust.' In two places only are there absolute breaks, viz. after Avarice and after Superstition; for Surliness has to Complaisance the affinity of contrast. To prevent any inconvenience in referring to other editions, the usual numbering is given side by side with our own in the list of the Characters.

II.

THEOPHRASTUS AND SOME OF HIS IMITATORS.

THE sketches of Theophrastus form perhaps the earliest extant example of a kind of writing which has been popular ever since, and which, in modern Europe especially, has an immense literature of its own. Even an outline of the history of character-writing in its chief developements would require more space and much wider knowledge than are at our command. But it may not be uninteresting briefly to compare Theophrastus with one or two of the modern writers who have taken him as their master, or who resemble him in the form of their work. The chief, or among the chief, of these are Hall, Earle, Overbury, and La Bruyère.

The method of Theophrastus is to consider a quality as embodied in a representative man, and to describe it by a simple enumeration of actions which this man will do. Classes or types of character can thus be sketched in bold, clear outline. But fine portraiture is not possible under such conditions. The subtler parts of character are scarcely the same in any two men; and a portrait which is to give only those traits which are common to a class cannot be at the same time the accurate and intimate likeness of an individual. Again, these subtler characteristics are seen not so much in particular actions as in the relations of one action to another; and, if minute inferences from these are to be sure, the induction must be large. A novelist is able to develope tolerably complete theories of character because he takes a long series of connected actions. But even then bare recital is not sufficient; the less obvious relations between different parts of conduct need to be interpreted for ordinary readers. In a first-rate novel the characters are left to speak as much as possible for themselves; but, when there is risk of their meaning being missed or only half-seen, help is given by comment; and, as they are gradually worked out, there is from time to time a pause in which whole stages of developement are reviewed. In the hands of a master this is perhaps the highest form of character-drawing. If it is contrasted with sketches

Style of Theophrastus.

such as those of Theophrastus, it will be seen more clearly how and why these are rudimentary. Here we have a bare enumeration of actions not necessarily connected.

Yet this style, if incompatible with work of the highest kind, has excellences proper to it; and in attaining these Theophrastus seems to have been successful. First of them, perhaps, is definiteness. Illustrations from social life are so apt to be vague that it is important for the author to start with a very clear conception of the character which he means to draw, and to take care that the outlines do not become hazy. They will inevitably become so, unless he chooses incidents in which the quality to be exemplified is not only present but predominant. In this respect Theophrastus will, if closely studied, be found usually accurate. Thus the Penurious, Mean, and Avaricious men are described without any confusion of the ideas distinctive of each, and without the special significance of their respective actions being lost in the strong general resemblance. The same clearness of conception will be seen on comparing the portraits of the Garrulous and Loquacious men. The only instance of a certain vagueness seems to us to be the chapter on Unpleasantness, but this, very likely, is only because we have not got the right point of view.

The next essential in a sketch of this sort seems to be that it should combine, as far as may be, generality with individuality. It must be characteristic of a class, and must at the same time be so lively as to set before us a particular man whom we can see. Here, again, Theophrastus seems very good. He hits the mean between abstract statement and details which might suit this or that person, but which would rob the picture of its generic interest. He effects this, indeed, at the cost of subtlety; but this is a necessity of the style. In a style less cramping, an English writer has reached this special excellence in a far higher degree than Theophrastus did, or perhaps any one who ever lived. One of the most striking things in the 'Book of Snobs' and in some of the 'Sketches and Travels in London' is the length to which individualisation has been carried without spoiling the claims of the personages to be typical.

Lastly, a book like the Characters ought to have humour. As no direct comment is admitted, the facts must be presented in such a light and (as far as possible) in such a connection that they shall comment upon themselves. Theophrastus does not fail here, though, as a rule, his humour is somewhat broad. The best examples of it are, in our opinion, the Chapters on the Newsmaker and on the Boastful Man.

Modern Character-writers. The Latin translation of the Characters by Casaubon, published in 1592, and his commentary which appeared seven years later, probably gave an impulse to the taste among scholars for this kind of writing; though it was not unknown before[1]. The seventeenth century in England was especially rich in it. There was, in one particular, a rough analogy between the literature of that century in England and the Greek literature of the age of Theophrastus; both were marked by the reaction from creating to analysing[2], and in both ethical analysis was a favourite subject. Fifty-six 'characters' or books of characters, published between the years 1605 and 1700, are enumerated by Dr Bliss[3] in his edition of Earle; and at a later time he had increased this list fourfold. The book of Theophrastus may fairly be considered as the parent of all these; for in the earliest of them which became popular it is expressly cited as the model.

Hall. Hall's 'Characterismes of Vertues and Vices' was published in 1608. In the 'Proeme' to the First Book he says:—'I have heere done it as I could, following that ancient Master of Moralitie, who thought this the fittest taske for the ninetie-and-ninth yeere of his age.'[4] It will be seen presently how often Hall was indebted in details to Theophrastus; but the broad differences are far more striking.

In the first place, Hall's method differs from that of his Greek exemplar in this important respect, in which he seems to have set the fashion to the English school. He does not merely describe certain actions proper to a character, but comments upon it in general terms; aiming at epigram, pointed expressions, lively images. For example, Theophrastus begins—'The Flatterer is a person who will say as he walks with another, "Do you observe how people are looking at you?"

---

[1] Rimbault, in the Introduction to his edition of Overbury (p. 11), mentions 'two small tracts descriptive of the characters of rogues and knaves—"The Fraternitye of Vacabondes," 1565; and "A Caveat for Common Cursetors vulgarely called Vagabones, set forth by Thomas Harman," 1567.'

[2] The general intellectual characteristics of the period early in which Theophrastus lived are thus described by Heyne, in an essay *de genio seculi Ptolemaeorum*, printed in his *Opuscula* (1 3). 'Legere litus, radere humum pennis dixeris, non facile alto se committere aut sublime ferri Nullus itaque vehementior impetus, quo animus legentis iucunde impellatur ac perturbetur, nulla inventorum fecunditas aut sententiarum copia, aut numerosa oratio, quae omnia a divino illo spiritu incalescentibus adesse solent. Limpidos et amoenos rivulos per prata properare videas, non magnum ac vastum flumen devolvi.'

[3] Quoted by Arber in the Introduction to his edition of Earle's *Microcosmographie*, in the English Reprints, p. 7.

[4] See p. 18.

etc.; and the chapter is throughout a simple narrative of his sayings and doings. Hall:—'The Flatterer is bleareyed to ill, and cannot see vices; and his tongue walks euer in one tracke of unjust praises, and can no more tell how to discommend than to speake true...His Art is nothing but delightfull cozenage, whose rules are smoothing and garded with periurie . Like that subtle fish, he turnes himselfe into the colour of every stone...He is the moth of liberal mens coats, the earewig of the mightie, the bane of Courts, a friend and a slave to the trencher, and good for nothing but to be a factor for the Diuell.' The prevalent taste for strained conceits found ample scope in delineations of character such as these. Hall is, however, less affected and wearisome in this way than some of his successors. The discursive element bears a large proportion to the descriptive, but does not overpower it.

He is further distinguished from Theophrastus by a gravity both of subject and of manner. The qualities described by the Greek writer are for the most part rather ridiculous than repulsive; the Evilspeaker is the most seriously odious person whom he has portrayed. But among the vices described by Hall are Hypocrisy, Profanity, Envy. Among the representatives of 'vertues' are the Wise man, the Faithful, the Truly-noble. The blame and the praise awarded to these are uttered with an earnestness, often with a fervour, in which the voice of the preacher is heard above that of the essayist. To judge him on the evidence of this book alone, Hall was a man of warm disposition, of much tender and noble feeling; ingenious, but not very subtle; and with no especial qualification for his task beyond a fancy fertile in illustration. His language would at times rise into something like the stately music of Milton's prose, did not the love of petty conceits too soon dwarf it and drag it down. This, for instance, in the portrait of the Wise Man:

'His free discourse runnes backe to the ages past, and recouers euents out of memory, and then preuenteth Tyme in flying forward to future things; and comparing one with the other can giue a verdict well-neere propheticall : wherein his conjectures are better than another's judgements.'

And this in the Faithful character :

'The celestiall spirits do not scorne his company, yea his service. Hee deales in these worldly affaires as a stranger, and hath his heart euer at home . without a written warrant hee dare doe nothing, and with it, anything. His warre is perpetuall, without truce, without intermission; and his victorie certaine : hee meets with the infernall powers, and tramples them vnder feet. The shield that he euer beares before him can neither be missed nor pierced: if his hand be wounded, yet his heart is safe: he is often tripped, seldome foiled; and if sometimes foiled, neuer vanquished.'

This talent for rhetoric sometimes carries Hall beyond the bounds of just description. But the commonest blemish of his style is a straining after antithesis. Thus the disregard of the Faithful man for his irreligious parents is called a 'holy carelessness.'

Lastly, there is one example in Hall of an innovation upon the plan of Theophrastus, which later character-writers made more largely. In 'the Good Magistrate' he describes the representative, not merely of certain moral qualities, but of the qualities proper for a certain office. By far the greater part of Overbury's and Earle's sketches are of this kind, treating of the characteristics of a certain station or calling: e.g. 'An Ostler': 'A Pyrate': 'An Elder Brother': 'A Sexton.' Overbury has in some instances pushed this style to the extreme of grotesqueness, as in his character of A Drunken Dutchman Resident in England.

With these differences of plan, method, and tone Hall is yet a real disciple of Theophrastus. Every sketch contains passages in which the concise narrative manner of the Greek writer is closely copied. The chapters on the Busiebodie and on the Slothfull Man are perhaps the best instances. Besides this general imitation, a great number of particular touches have been borrowed. One or two examples will suffice to show how directly they have been taken.—

THEOPHRASTUS.	HALL.
The Flatterer.	*The Flatterer.*
The Flatterer is a person who will say as he walks with another, 'Do you observe how people are looking at you?'	When hee walks with his friend hee sweares to him that no man els is looked at.
The Penurious Man.	*The Covetous.*
When a servant has broken a pot or a plate, he will take the value out of his rations.	If his servant breake but an earthen dish for want of light, hee abates it out of his quarters wages.
The Officious Man.	*The Busie-bodie.*
He will undertake to show the path, and after all be unable to find the way.	This man will also thrust himself forward to be the guide of the way he knowes not.
The Distrustful Man.	*The Distrustfull*
The Distrustful Man is one who, having sent his slave to market, will send another to ascertain what price he gave	When hee hath committed a message to his seruant, he sends a second after him to listen how it is deliuered.

Overbury. Sir Thomas Overbury's 'Characters or Witty Descriptions of the Properties of Sundry Persons' was published in 1614[1]. Out of eighty sketches only ten can be reckoned as descriptive of intrinsic character. The rest are concerned with such peculiarities as are brought out by certain occupations or positions in life. These are curious as illustrating manners, of which Overbury was a quick observer, and which he could represent with lively skill. For the delineation of character in the proper sense he had little talent. Tricks of behaviour and speech caught his eye; but his reflections are generally trivial, and he had not a fine perception of moral differences. Thus in his chapter on A Proud Man he has confused the characteristics of Haughtiness and Vanity, which could hardly exist in such a union as he depicts. Hall, whose acuteness was not his strongest point, shows oftener and with less effort an insight into the springs of action. The elaborate quaintness of Overbury's language and his faculty for pointed expression render this defect more conspicuous. The novelty of the manner is frequently out of proportion to the originality of the idea. His thoughts seem overdressed, and this, together with the sometimes coarse vehemence of the satire, often gives a vulgar air to his writing. Hallam pronounces the 'Faire and happy Milk-mayd' the best of his characters. It is very pretty, but somewhat too conventional; and to us there seems to be more true poetry in the similar picture of the Franklin. It would seem as if country life in its humbler phases had had a peculiar attraction for Overbury; that his sympathy was not extended to squires is shown by the portrait of the Country Gentleman.

A touch in his description of A Covetous Man suggests that he had made a minute study of Hall. 'He neuer spends candle but at Christmas...in hope that his seruants will breake glasses *for want of light*, which they doubly pay for in their wages.' Compare Hall's, 'If his servant breake but an earthen dish *for want of light*, he abates it out of his quarters wages.' Whether he had read Theophrastus or not is less certain. In two places there are curious but not conclusive resemblances:—

---

[1] The 'Characters' were attached to his poem of *A Wife, now a Widdowe*. The date 1614 is given by Arber, Introd. to Earle's *Microcosmographie*, p. 8, and by Rimbault in his Introd. to Overbury's Works, p. 13....Rimbault says that with the exception of two small tracts of 1565 and 1567, 'Overbury claims the distinction of being the *earliest* writer of Characters which this country can boast' (*ib* p. 11). He overlooks Hall, who came between in 1608.

THEOPHRASTUS.	OVERBURY.
The Penurious Man.	*A Covetous Man.*
He is apt also to enforce the right of distraining.	If he euer pray, it is that some one may breake his day, that the beloued forfeiture may be obtained.
The Arrogant Man.	*A Proud Man.*
He will not permit himself to give any man the first greeting.	He never salutes first.

A more interesting comparison is suggested by Earle's '*Microcosmographie, or a Piece of the World Discovered.*'

Earle. The book contains seventy-eight characters, fifty-four of which appeared in 1628, twenty-three in the following year, and one in 1633. The name of the author was never formally announced, but it was known at the time that he was John Earle, then a Fellow of Merton College, Oxford. He was in his twenty-eighth year when the first instalment of the Characters was published in 1628. Of the whole number, about thirty are properly ethical; the rest are of the same class as those which compose seven-eighths of Overbury's work, and in which the persons are viewed not as possessors of certain qualities but as players of certain parts in life. Earle is not so thoroughly at home with men of all sorts and conditions as Overbury, who had probably seen far more of the world; nor are his reflections mingled so largely as those of Hall with bits of picturesque narrative which point their own moral. But as an analyst of human nature he is immeasurably superior to either. Theophrastus, whose severely simple plan allowed little scope for subtlety, must also yield to him in fine delineation. Earle was not merely ingenious, but had a special gift for the study of character, his humour is of a thoughtful kind which goes beneath peculiarities of the surface to their origin in a bent or warp of the mind, for which it seeks to account; and so, while Hall and Overbury describe traits which are recognised as true and remark smartly upon them, Earle helps us to see why they are there, and gives us a sense of comprehending the whole character better. Thus, speaking of the way in which the flatterer ministers to his patron's self-approbation, Hall says:—

Conscience hath no greater adversarie; for when she is about to play her iust part of accusation, he stops her mouth with good termes and well-neere strangleth her with shifts.

This is a lively expression of the fact, but does not get beyond it. Earle contrives at once to state and to account for it:—

He is one neuer chides you, but for your vertues, as, You are too good, too honest, too religious; when his chiding may seeme but the earnester commendation, and yet would faine chide you out of them too: *for your vice is the thing he has use of*, and wherein you may best use him, and hee is neuer more active than in the worst diligences.

Of the relation of flattery to friendship, Hall says:—

Flatterie is nothing but false friendship, fawning hypocrisie, dishonest ciuilitie, base merchandize of words, a plausible discord of the heart and lips.

These ingenious phrases do nothing towards defining wherein the contrast between the flatterer and the friend consists. Earle brings out clearly a particular point of the contrast:—

His looke, conuersation, companie, and all the outwardnesse of friendshippe (are) more pleasing by odds, for a true friend dare take the liberty to bee sometimes offensiue; whereas he is a great deale more cowardly, and will not let the least hold goe, for feare of losing you.

In his chapter on the Male-Content, Hall makes this general remark upon the character:—

Nothing dislikes him but the present: for what hee condemned while it was, once past hee magnifies, and striues to recall it out of the iawes of Time.

This, after all, tells us nothing that we did not know before. Earle, describing a Discontented man, makes an observation which throws a real light on one of the causes by which such a temper is commonly produced:—

He considered not the nature of the world till he felt it, and all blowes fall on him heauier, because they light not first on his expectation.

Overbury's sketch of a Vaine-glorious Coward in Command, and Earle's of a Coward, both dwell chiefly on the bluster under which Cowardice seeks to hide itself. The bearing of the coward in society is thus described by Overbury.—

No man can worse define betweene pride and noble courtesie: he that salutes him not so farre as a pistoll carries level, gives him the disgust or affront, chuse you whether.

Earle places this same arrogance in a far more amusing and instructive light:—

Wonderfull exceptious and cholerick where he sees men are loth to giue him occasion, and you cannot pacify him better than by quarrelling with him.... Men fall out with him of purpose to get courtesies from him, and be brib'd againe to a reconcilement.

A general comparison of Earle with the other two English writers would show that as a rule he has deeper feeling, more acuteness, a finer humour. An instance of what we mean by his deeper feeling occurs at the end of the chapter on a Plaine Country Fellow.

For Death hee is neuer troubled, *and if hee get in but his Haruest before*, let it come when it wil he cares not.

This shows more sympathy with the man's inner life than would be found in Hall or Overbury. Good examples of his humour and sagacity are these remarks on the Insolent Man :—

> He is one that lookes on all men as if he were very angry, but especially on those of his acquaintance, whom hee beates off with a surlier distance, as men apt to mistake him because they haue known him. And for this cause he knowes not you, till you haue told him your name, which *he thinkes he has heard, but forgot*, and with much adoe seems to recouer.. . No vice drawes with it a more generall hostility, and makes men readier to search into his faults, and of them, his beginning: and no tale so vnlikely but is willingly heard of him, and beleeu'd.

And these on the Suspitious or Iealous Man :—

> He is a fellow commonly guilty of some weaknesses, which he might conceale if hee were carelesse: Now his over-diligence to hide them, makes men pry the more. Howsoever hee imagines you have found him, and it shall goe hard but you must abuse him whether you wil or no.

A close comparison of Earle with Theophrastus would be unfair to both, since the styles in which they respectively excelled were distinct. But if it could be doubted that Earle, a distinguished classical scholar, had studied the Greek Characters then recently made popular by Casaubon, two passages would place it beyond a question :—

THEOPHRASTUS.	EARLE.
The Avaricious Man.	*A Sordid Rich Man*
It is just like him, too, when he is paying a debt of thirty minas, to withhold four drachmas.	Hee loues to pay short a shilling or two in a great sum, and is glad to gaine that, when he can no more.
The Boor.	*A Plaine Country Fellow.*
He shows surprise and wonder at nothing else, but will stand still and gaze when he sees an ox or an ass or a goat in the streets.	His mind is not much distracted with obiects· but if a goode fat Cowe come in his way, he stands dumbe and astonisht, and though his haste be neuer so great, will fixe here halfe an houre's contemplation.

La Bruyère. La Bruyère published in 1688[1] 'Les Caractères, ou les Moeurs de ce Siècle,' with a translation of the Characters of Theophrastus prefixed to it. He is generally reckoned as the chief modern imitator of Theophrastus; but though, like Hall, he acknowledges the Greek writer as his master, he is not his disciple in the same sense. He borrows from him the conception and the title,

---

[1] The permission to print the book was obtained by the printer Oct. 8, 1687; the book was published March 10, 1688, according to M. Servois in his edition of La Bruyère in the series Les Grands Ecrivains de la France, vol. I p. 91.

but not the method of his work. The 'Characters' of La Bruyère are a series of essays on the manners of the day. Each of them treats some large subject in a discursive style; one is 'de la société,' another 'du mérite personnel,' another 'de la ville,' and so forth. These essays are here and there illustrated with sketches of representative men, which may, indeed, be compared with the characters of Theophrastus, but are slighter and more hastily drawn. Many of them are said to have been portraits of the author's contemporaries; and the desire of making an unmistakeable personal allusion seems to have been often stronger than that of illustrating principles. Among the best are Arsène, in the essay 'Des Ouvrages de l'Esprit,'—the gloomy genius who belongs to a mutual-admiration society;—Phédon, in the 'Des Biens de Fortune,'—the ostentatiously humble, but sinister man,—and Cydias, in the 'De la Société,'—the suggestive talker by profession.

The freer plan of La Bruyère's work, and the more diversified society from which he drew his materials, enabled him to give it an interest far more varied than the Characters of Theophrastus can claim. Hallam's decision that 'the Greek writer, with no contemptible degree of merit, has been incomparably surpassed by his imitator,'[1] is in this sense just; but it must be remembered that the two works cannot be regarded as performances competing in the same line of excellence. Each has its merit, and that of La Bruyère is in perhaps the higher walk; but for this very reason a direct rivalry is impossible.

The French version of Theophrastus is spirited, but is for the most part little more than a paraphrase; and shows that La Bruyère's conception of a translator's duties was as loose as his knowledge of Greek appears to have been imperfect[2]. The great success, however,

---

[1] Introduction to the *Literature of Europe*, part IV, ch. 4, § 52.

[2] In the Character of ὀψιμαθία (D'Une Tardive Instruction, no. VIII in our Translation) the words καὶ παρὰ τοῦ υἱοῦ μανθάνειν τὸ ἐπὶ δόρυ καὶ ἐπὶ ἀσπίδα καὶ ἐπ' οὐράν are thus rendered.—'Il apprende de son propre fils les évolutions qu'il faut faire dans les rangs à droit ou à gauche, *le maniement des armes, et quel est l'usage à la guerre de la lance et du bouclier.*' La Bruyère did not see that τὸ ἐπὶ δόρυ, 'Right Wheel,' etc., was already translated by 'évolutions—à droit,' etc.; and added the italicised words to express what he thought to be the meaning of the Greek, 'that which concerns the spear and shield'; thus translating it twice over, and the second time wrongly. M. Servois, his latest editor, observes (p. 86, note 1), that no version which La Bruyère can have had before him can have suggested this blunder. it must have been his own. Again in the chapter on ἀπιστία (De la Défiance, c. XXIII in our translation), after the words μάλιστα μὲν μὴ δοῦναι, where the vulgate has a lacuna since supplied by the Vatican MS, he inserts in his text a translation of *three distinct* conjectures made by Casaubon for the purpose of filling the gap. He did not see, or did not care, that they were proposed as alternatives.

of his book, which in six years went through eight editions, did more than anything before or since to make the name of Theophrastus popular. Imitations were numerous. One of these, *Le Théophraste Moderne*, attracted some notice on account of a curious mystification of which it was the subject. A pamphlet entitled 'Sentimens Critiques sur les Caractères de Théophraste de Monsieur de la Bruyère,' appeared in 1701; in which that work was reviewed in company with the 'Modern Theophrastus,' but far more severely than the latter. In the same year was published 'l'Apologie de Monsieur de la Bruyère'; the anonymous author of this defence took no notice, however, of the criticisms upon the 'Modern Theophrastus.' It was presently known that the 'Modern Theophrastus,' the Criticism, and the Reply, were by the same person, Brillon, a lawyer. He had done himself the honour of attacking his own book in the society of La Bruyère's; but had taken care that it should not sustain such damage as to require the services of an apologist[1].

[1] The story is told by M. Servois in his introduction to the *Caractères*, p. 99.

ΘΕΟΦΡΑΣΤΟΥ ΧΑΡΑΚΤΗΡΕΣ
THE CHARACTERS OF THEOPHRASTUS

THE CHARACTERS

In the Order of the MSS.		In this Edition.	PAGE	In Alphabetical Order.		PAGE
Εἰρωνεία	I	... V	... 50	Ἀγροικία		84
Κολακεία	II	.. I	... 38	Ἀδολεσχία		100
Ἀδολεσχία	III	.. XVIII	... 100	Ἀηδία		78
Ἀγροικία	IV	... XIV	... 84	Αἰσχροκέρδεια		128
Ἀρέσκεια	V	... II	... 42	Ἀκαιρία		74
Ἀπόνοια	VI	... XVI	... 92	Ἀλαζονεία		54
Λαλιά	VII	... XIX	... 102	Ἀναισθησία		82
Λογοποιΐα	VIII	... XX	... 106	Ἀναισχυντία		88
Ἀναισχυντία	IX	... XV	88	Ἀνελευθερία		124
Μικρολογία	X	... XXIV	... 118	Ἀπιστία		116
Βδελυρία	XI	... XVII	... 96	Ἀπόνοια		92
Ἀκαιρία	XII	... IX	... 74	Ἀρέσκεια		42
Περιεργία	XIII	... X	... 76	Αὐθάδεια		44
Ἀναισθησία	XIV	... XIII	.. 82	Βδελυρία		96
Αὐθάδεια	XV	... III	... 44	Δειλία		134
Δεισιδαιμονία	XVI	.. XXVIII	. 138	Δεισιδαιμονία		138
Μεμψιμοιρία	XVII	... XXII	. 114	Δυσχέρεια		80
Ἀπιστία	XVIII	... XXIII	... 116	Εἰρωνεία		50
Δυσχέρεια	XIX	.. XII	... 80	Κακολογία		110
Ἀηδία	XX	... XI	.. 78	Κολακεία		38
Μικροφιλοτιμία	XXI	.. VII	... 60	Λαλιά		102
Ἀνελευθερία	XXII	... XXV	... 124	Λογοποιΐα		106
Ἀλαζονεία	XXIII	... VI	... 54	Μεμψιμοιρία		114
Ὑπερηφανία	XXIV	IV	... 48	Μικρολογία		118
Δειλία	XXV	.. XXVII	. 134	Μικροφιλοτιμία		60
Ὀλιγαρχία	XXVI	. XXIX	... 148	Ὀλιγαρχία		148
Ὀψιμαθία	XXVII	... VIII	... 70	Ὀψιμαθία		70
Κακολογία	XXVIII	... XXI	... 110	Περιεργία		76
Φιλοπονηρία	XXIX	... XXX	... 154	Ὑπερηφανία		48
Αἰσχροκέρδεια	XXX	... XXVI	... 128	Φιλοπονηρία		154

THE CHARACTERS

In the Order adopted in the present Edition. See page 20 f.

				PAGE
THE FLATTERER	I	3 usually II	......	39
THE COMPLAISANT MAN	II	V		43
THE SURLY MAN	III	XV	......	45
THE ARROGANT MAN	IV	XXIV	......	49
THE IRONICAL MAN	V	I	......	51
THE BOASTFUL MAN	VI	XXIII	......	55
THE MAN OF PETTY AMBITION	VII	XXI	......	61
THE LATE-LEARNER	VIII	XXVII	......	71
THE UNSEASONABLE MAN	IX	XII	......	75
THE OFFICIOUS MAN	X	XIII	......	77
THE UNPLEASANT MAN	XI	XX	......	79
THE OFFENSIVE MAN	XII	XIX	......	81
THE STUPID MAN	XIII	XIV	......	83
THE BOOR	XIV	IV	......	85
THE SHAMELESS MAN	XV	IX	......	89
THE RECKLESS MAN	XVI	VI	......	93
THE GROSS MAN	XVII	XI	......	97
THE GARRULOUS MAN	XVIII	VII	......	101
THE LOQUACIOUS MAN	XIX	VII	......	103
THE NEWSMAKER	XX	VIII	......	107
THE EVIL-SPEAKER	XXI	XXVIII	......	111
THE GRUMBLER	XXII	XVII	......	115
THE DISTRUSTFUL MAN	XXIII	XVIII	......	117
THE PENURIOUS MAN	XXIV	X	......	119
THE MEAN MAN	XXV	XXII	......	125
THE AVARICIOUS MAN	XXVI	XXX	......	129
THE COWARD	XXVII	XXV	......	135
THE SUPERSTITIOUS MAN	XXVIII	XVI	......	139
THE OLIGARCH	XXIX	XXVI	......	149
THE PATRON OF RASCALS	XXX	XXIX	......	155

36   ΠΡΟΟΙΜΙΟΝ

[προοίμιον

ἤδη μὲν καὶ πρότερον πολλάκις ἐπιστήσας τὴν διάνοιαν
ἐθαύμασα, ἴσως δὲ οὐδὲ παύσομαι θαυμάζων, τί γὰρ δήποτε,
τῆς Ἑλλάδος ὑπὸ τὸν αὐτὸν ἀέρα κειμένης καὶ πάντων τῶν
Ἑλλήνων ὁμοίως παιδευομένων, συμβέβηκεν ἡμῖν οὐ τὴν
5 αὐτὴν τάξιν τῶν τρόπων ἔχειν. ἐγὼ γάρ, ὦ Πολύκλεις,
συνθεωρήσας ἐκ πολλοῦ χρόνου τὴν ἀνθρωπίνην φύσιν
καὶ βεβιωκὼς ἔτη ἐνενήκοντα ἐννέα, ἔτι δὲ ὡμιληκὼς πολλαῖς
τε καὶ παντοδαπαῖς φύσεσι καὶ παρατεθεαμένος ἐξ ἀκριβείας
πολλῆς τούς τε ἀγαθοὺς τῶν ἀνθρώπων καὶ τοὺς φαύλους,
10 ὑπέλαβον δεῖν συγγράψαι, ἃ ἑκάτεροι αὐτῶν ἐπιτηδεύουσιν
ἐν τῷ βίῳ. ἐκθήσω δέ σοι κατὰ γένος, ὅσα τε τυγχάνει
γένη τρόπων τούτοις προσκείμενα καὶ ὃν τρόπον τῇ
οἰκονομίᾳ χρῶνται· ὑπολαμβάνω γάρ, ὦ Πολύκλεις, τοὺς
υἱεῖς ἡμῶν βελτίους ἔσεσθαι, καταλειφθέντων αὐτοῖς ὑπο-
15 μνημάτων τοιούτων, οἷς παραδείγμασι χρώμενοι αἱρήσονται
τοῖς εὐσχημονεστάτοις συνεῖναί τε καὶ ὁμιλεῖν, ὅπως μὴ
καταδεέστεροι ὦσιν αὐτῶν. τρέψομαι δὲ ἤδη ἐπὶ τὸν
λόγον· σὸν δὲ παρακολουθῆσαί τε καὶ εἰδῆσαι, εἰ ὀρθῶς
λέγω. πρῶτον μὲν οὖν ποιήσομαι τὸν λόγον ἀπὸ τῶν

---

1. **Often before now &c.**] Since the criticism of C. G. Sonntag, published in 1787, on this proem, there has been no doubt among scholars of its spuriousness. The fatuous remark with which it begins, the sensational statement as to the writer's age, and the general feebleness of the whole production betray a clumsy forger. Petersen's conjecture (p. 62) that he probably was not a dweller in Greece seems likely enough. See *Introd.* p 18.

6. **ninety years and nine**] Diogenes (v, 40) says that Theophrastus died at 85. This, as Zeller says (*Philosoph. der Gr.* Part II, sect. 2, p. 641), is a good deal more probable than the statement here. The only confirmation of the latter is Jerome's assertion (*Ep.* 34 *ad Nepotian.* iv b) that Theophrastus lived to 107: but even there another reading is 'Themistoclem'

8 f. **both the good and the worthless**

[PROEM

Often before now have I applied my thoughts to the puzzling question—one, probably, which will puzzle me for ever—why it is that, while all Greece lies under the same sky and all the Greeks are educated alike, it has befallen us to have characters variously constituted. For a long time, Polycles, I have been 5 a student of human nature; I have lived ninety years and nine; I have associated, too, with many and diverse natures; and, having observed side by side, with great closeness, both the good and the worthless among men, I conceived that I ought to write a book about the practices in life of either sort. 10

I will describe to you, class by class, the several kinds of conduct which characterise them and the mode in which they administer their affairs; for I conceive, Polycles, that our sons will be the better if such memorials are bequeathed to them, using which as examples they shall choose to live and consort 15 with men of the fairest lives, in order that they may not fall short of them.

And now I will turn to my narrative; be it your part to come along with it and to see if I speak rightly. In the first place, then, I will commence my account with those who have studied 20

---

among men] The author of the proem goes on to say that he will describe *both* sorts. There may have been, in his time, a tradition that the book had once contained descriptions of virtues as well as vices, or this may have been his own opinion; accordingly he writes such a preface as he conceived that the book in its complete state might have had. Petersen, believing the Characters to be extracts from the large work περὶ ἠθῶν, suggests that the extracter may have begun with the intention of selecting descriptions of virtues also. See *Introd.* p 18.

11 **class by class**] κατὰ γένος. Schneider and Ussing understand these words rightly, but strangely say that the promise is not fulfilled, since the Characters, as they have come to us, are not arranged 'in any certain order.' But κατὰ γένος means only that several classes, γένη, of characters are to be described, one by one; not necessarily in any particular order. Ast, on the other hand, is wrong, I think, in taking κατὰ γένος to mean 'generically,' *generatim*, 'ita ut non singulos vel certos quosdam homines exhibeam, sed hominum mores in universum exprimam' This would surely be γενικῶς.

38   ΚΟΛΑΚΕΙΑC Α'

20 τὴν εἰρωνείαν ἐζηλωκότων, ἀφεὶς τὸ προοιμιάζεσθαι καὶ
πολλὰ περὶ τοῦ πράγματος λέγειν· καὶ ἄρξομαι πρῶτον
ἀπὸ τῆς εἰρωνείας καὶ ὁριοῦμαι αὐτήν· εἶθ᾽ οὕτως τὸν
εἴρωνα διέξειμι, ποῖός τίς ἐστι καὶ εἰς τίνα τρόπον κατενή-
νεκται· καὶ τὰ ἄλλα δὴ τῶν παθημάτων, ὥσπερ ὑπεθέμην,
25 πειράσομαι κατὰ γένος φανερὰ καθιστάναι.]

κολακείας α'.

τὴν δὲ κολακείαν ὑπολάβοι ἄν τις ὁμιλίαν αἰσχρὰν εἶναι,
συμφέρουσαν δὲ τῷ κολακεύοντι, τὸν δὲ κόλακα τοιοῦτόν
τινα, ὥστε πορευόμενον ἅμα εἰπεῖν· ἐνθυμῇ ὡς ἀποβλέπουσι
πρὸς σὲ οἱ ἄνθρωποι; τοῦτο οὐδενὶ τῶν ἐν τῇ πόλει γίνεται
5 πλὴν ἢ σοί· ηὐδοκίμεις χθὲς ἐν τῇ στοᾷ· πλειόνων γὰρ
ἢ τριάκοντα ἀνθρώπων καθημένων καὶ ἐμπεσόντος λόγου,
τίς εἴη βέλτιστος, ἀπ᾽ αὐτοῦ ἀρξαμένους πάντας ἐπὶ τὸ ὄνομα
αὐτοῦ κατενεχθῆναι· καὶ ἄλλα τοιαῦτα λέγων ἀπὸ τοῦ ἱματίου
ἀφελεῖν κροκύδα, καὶ ἐάν τι πρὸς τὸ τρίχωμα τῆς κεφαλῆς
10 ὑπὸ πνεύματος προσενεχθῇ ἄχυρον, καρφολογῆσαι, καὶ

---

1. **Flattery**] The Definition is defective. It describes the manner in which Flattery affects the interests of the person who practises it; but does not say what it is in respect to the person who is its object, viz. a desire to please.

After describing the man who conducts himself in society as he ought to do, and observing that for this mean there is no name, Aristotle says (*Eth. Nic.* IV 6): 'Of those who try to give pleasure, he who with no further motive aims at being pleasant is Complaisant (ἄρεσκος, see c. II); he who does so in order that advantage may accrue to him *in respect of money or anything that money procures* is a Flatterer: while he who is peevish about everything is (as has been said) Cross (δύσκολος—the αὐθάδης of Theophrastus, c. III) and Quarrelsome.'

The notion conveyed by the term κολακεία is not precisely what we usually mean by 'flattery,' but something coarser. It meant a sort of extravagant toadyism, practised, not as a fine art, but simply as an industry—as a recognised method of obtaining a livelihood. This tone is unconsciously illustrated by Athenaeus when, in his reminiscences of eminent Flatterers (VI, pp. 248—260), he speaks of 'Cheirisophus, the flatterer of Dionysius,' 'Callicrates, the flatterer of Ptolemy,' 'Anaxarchus, one of the flatterers of Alexander.' These men had, as it were, been preferred to permanent posts. The remark (Ath. VI, p. 248 § 53) that the κόλαξ 'is not far from the Parasite' is true in so far as material benefit—especially in the form of entertainment—was the object of both. But the κόλαξ claimed this in right of a supposed personal devotion, the Parasite rather in virtue of his power

Irony[1], dispensing with preface or many words about the matter. I will begin with Irony and define it, next I will set forth, in like manner, the nature of the Ironical man, and of the character into which he has drifted; and then I will try, as I proposed, to make the other affections of the mind plain, each after its kind.]

I (II). THE FLATTERER.

Flattery may be considered as a mode of companionship degrading but profitable to him who flatters.

The Flatterer is a person who will say as he walks with another, 'Do you observe how people are looking at you? This happens to no man in Athens but you. A compliment was paid to you yesterday in the Porch. More than thirty persons were sitting there; the question was started, Who is our foremost man? Everyone mentioned you first, and ended by coming back to your name.' With these and the like words, he will remove a morsel of wool from his patron's coat; or, if a speck of chaff has been laid on the other's hair by the wind, he will

---

[1] The Chapter on Irony (V in this ed.) stands first in the traditional order.

---

to amuse. [The literary development of the type is the subject of a paper by Otto Ribbeck in the *Abhandlungen* of the Leipzig Academy, IX, 1883.)

6. **the Porch**] i.e. the στοὰ ποικίλη, the Porch of Paintings a piazza, not attached to any building, standing at the N.E. corner of the market-place. It was furnished with stone benches, and afforded the kind of shelter for conversation and exercise needed in a warmer climate. Of the paintings on its walls the most famous were Micon's fresco of Theseus and the Amazons, and a fresco of Marathon by Polygnotus. In front stood a row of bronze statues, among which Pausanias (about 180 A.D) mentions those of Solon and Seleucus —Two other piazzas of the same kind stood in the Market-place; (1) the Royal Porch, where the 'king' Archon held his court, on the S W. side;

and (2) the Porch of Freedom, probably to the E of it—so called from a statue of Zeus Eleutherios.

10. **a morsel of wool**] Suidas gives κροκύδας ἀφαιρεῖν: '*to pick off shreds*,' as a proverb for those 'who will do anything for the sake of flattery.' (The proverb is found in a fragment of Aristophanes, 657) Hesychius explains the word κροκυλεγμός—'the picking off of shreds in the manner of a flatterer.' According to Plutarch, Valeria, Sulla's last wife, first attracted his notice at the theatre by the attention of removing a thread from his cloak (*Sulla*, c. 35). Ovid attributes a like flattery to the skilful lover (*Amor.* III 2, 41).—

Ah, while I speak, one small speck here doth rest—
Away, base atom, from that snowy breast!

ΚΟΛΑΚΕΙΑΣ Α'

ἐπιγελάσας δὲ εἰπεῖν· ὁρᾷς; ὅτι δυοῖν σοι ἡμερῶν οὐκ ἐντετύχηκα, πολιῶν ἔσχηκας τὸν πώγωνα μεστόν, καίπερ, εἴ τις καὶ ἄλλος, ἔχεις πρὸς τὰ ἔτη μέλαιναν τὴν τρίχα· καὶ λέγοντος δὲ αὐτοῦ τι τοὺς ἄλλους σιωπᾶν κελεῦσαι, καὶ
15 ἐπαινέσαι δὲ ἀκούοντος, καὶ ἐπισημήνασθαι δέ, εἰ παύεται, ὀρθῶς· καὶ σκώψαντι ψυχρῶς ἐπιγελάσαι τό τε ἱμάτιον ὦσαι εἰς τὸ στόμα ὡς δὴ οὐ δυνάμενος κατασχεῖν τὸν γέλωτα· καὶ τοὺς ἀπαντῶντας ἐπιστῆναι κελεῦσαι, ἕως ἂν αὐτὸς παρέλθῃ· καὶ τοῖς παιδίοις μῆλα καὶ ἀπίους πριάμενος
20 εἰσενέγκας δοῦναι ὁρῶντος αὐτοῦ, καὶ φιλήσας δὲ εἰπεῖν· χρηστοῦ πατρὸς νεόττια· καὶ συνωνούμενος δὲ κρηπῖδας τὸν πόδα φῆσαι εἶναι εὐρυθμότερον τοῦ ὑποδήματος· καὶ πορευομένου πρός τινα τῶν φίλων προδραμὼν εἰπεῖν ὅτι πρὸς σὲ ἔρχεται, καὶ ἀναστρέψας, ὅτι προήγγελκα. ἀμέλει δὲ καὶ τὰ
25 ἐκ γυναικείας ἀγορᾶς διακονῆσαι δυνατὸς ἀπνευστί· καὶ τῶν ἑστιωμένων πρῶτος ἐπαινέσαι τὸν οἶνον, καὶ παρακείμενος εἰπεῖν· ὡς μαλακῶς ἐσθίεις· καὶ ἄρας τι τῶν ἀπὸ τῆς τραπέζης φῆσαι· τουτὶ ἄρα ὡς χρηστόν ἐστι· καὶ ἐρωτῆσαι, μὴ ῥιγοῖ, καὶ εἰ ἐπιβάλλεσθαι βούλεται, καὶ ἔτι ταῦτα λέγων
30 περιστεῖλαι αὐτόν· καὶ μὴν πρὸς τὸ οὖς προσκύπτων διαψιθυρίζειν, καὶ εἰς ἐκεῖνον ἀποβλέπων τοῖς ἄλλοις λαλεῖν· καὶ τοῦ παιδὸς ἐν τῷ θεάτρῳ ἀφελόμενος τὰ προσκεφάλαια αὐτὸς ὑποστρῶσαι· καὶ τὴν οἰκίαν φῆσαι εὖ ἠρχιτεκτονῆ-

---

13. **white hairs**] So in the *Knights*, where Kleon and his rival are bidding against each other for the favour of Demus (v 906):—'*Kl* And I will pluck out your grey hairs and make you young again'

17. **laugh at a frigid joke**] Compare Athenaeus VI, p. 249 § 55.—'The same authority (one Hegesander) relates that Cheirisophus, the flatterer of Dionysius, seeing his patron laughing with some acquaintances—(he was too far from them to hear the conversation)—laughed too. When Dionysius asked him why he was laughing when he could not hear what was said, he answered, "My confidence in yon assures me that the remark was amusing".'

20. **his Honour**] αὐτός, *ipse*, 'the master', said especially of the head of a household or of a school. See the *Clouds* (v 218): '*Strepsiades*. Pray, now, who is this person suspended in a basket? *Disciple* It is himself. *S*. And who is "himself"? *D*. Socrates.'

23. **assists at the purchase of slippers**] The κρηπίς was probably a kind of half-shoe, covering the fore part of the foot, and strapped on at the heels. The ordinary Greek foot-covering, the

pick it off; adding with a laugh, 'Do you see? Because I have not met you for two days, you have had your beard full of white hairs; although no one has darker hair for his years than you.' Then he will request the company to be silent while the great man is speaking, and will praise him, too, in his hearing, and mark his approbation at a pause with 'True', or he will laugh at a frigid joke, and stuff his cloak into his mouth as if he could not repress his amusement. He will request those whom he meets to stand still until 'his Honour' has passed. He will buy apples and pears, and bring them in and give to the children in the father's presence; adding, with kisses, 'Chicks of a good father.' Also, when he assists at the purchase of slippers, he will declare that the foot is more shapely than the shoe. If his patron is approaching a friend, he will run forward and say, 'He is coming to you'; and then, turning back, 'I have announced you.' He is just the person, too, who can run errands to the women's market without drawing breath. He is the first of the guests to praise the wine; and to say, as he reclines next the host, 'How delicate is your fare!' and (taking up something from the table) 'Now this—how excellent it is!' He will ask his friend if he is cold, and if he would like to put on something more; and, before the words are spoken, will wrap him up. Moreover he will lean towards his ear and whisper with him; or will glance at him as he talks to the rest of the company. He will take the cushions from the slave in the theatre, and spread them on the seat with his own hands. He will say that

---

hypodema, was a sandal bound under the foot; the 'sandalion,' a sandal with a small upper leather across the toe, but covering less of the fore part of the foot than the 'crepis': the 'embas' was the shoe proper. See Becker's Exc. to sc. XI of the *Charicles*.

28. **the women's market**] Mentioned again in c. XXV as the place from which a female slave is hired. Nothing is certainly known about it. Becker (*Char.* Exc. to sc. IV) shows that it probably does not mean 'the market frequented by women,' since at Athens freewomen never, and female slaves rarely, marketed.

He suggests that it may have been (1) a market in which the sellers were women: (2) a market in which articles chiefly for female use were sold. (So Pollux, X 18, on a passage of Menander, 456 Kock.)—Ussing prefers to suppose that it was (3) the place where slave-girls were sold or hired. The word δυνατός in the text seems to imply that the mission was discreditable.

29. **to praise the wine**] Thus Horace's host Nasidienus had invited Nomentanus to dinner in order that he might call attention 'to anything which was escaping notice' (*Sat.* II 8, 25).

36. **the cushions**] As the seats in the

σθαι, καὶ τὸν ἀγρὸν εὖ πεφυτεῦσθαι, καὶ τὴν εἰκόνα ὁμοίαν
35 εἶναι.
[καὶ τὸ κεφάλαιον τὸν κόλακα ἔστι θεάσασθαι πάντα καὶ
λέγοντα καὶ πράττοντα οἷς χαριεῖσθαι ὑπολαμβάνει.]

ἀρεσκείας β'.

ἡ δὲ ἀρέσκειά ἐστι μὲν, ὡς ὅρῳ περιλαβεῖν, ἔντευξις οὐκ
ἐπὶ τῷ βελτίστῳ ἡδονῆς παρασκευαστική, ὁ δὲ ἄρεσκος
ἀμέλει τοιοῦτός τις οἷος πόρρωθεν προσαγορεύσας καὶ ἄνδρα
κράτιστον εἰπὼν καὶ θαυμάσας ἱκανῶς, ἀμφοτέραις ταῖς χερσὶ
5 μὴ ἀφιέναι, καὶ μικρὸν προπέμψας καὶ ἐρωτήσας, πότε αὐτὸν
ὄψεται, ἔτι ἐπαινῶν ἀπαλλάττεσθαι· καὶ παρακληθεὶς δὲ
πρὸς δίαιταν μὴ μόνον, ᾧ πάρεστι, βούλεσθαι ἀρέσκειν,
ἀλλὰ καὶ τῷ ἀντιδίκῳ, ἵνα κοινὸς εἶναι δοκῇ· καὶ τοὺς ξένους

theatre were merely semicircular tiers of rock-hewn ledges, those who desired to be comfortable brought their own cushions. Kleon's rival in the *Knights* pities Demus for the discomforts of the Pnyx —'He (Kleon) does not care how uneasily you sit on the rocks. How different from me, who have had this'—(producing a cushion) —'stitched up as a present for you' (v 783). Aeschines (*in Ctes.* p. 64 § 76) alleges in proof of the servility of Demosthenes to Macedon that, when Philip's envoys were introduced to the Ecclesia, he ushered them to the place of honour, 'and arranged cushions and spread purple draperies.' Ovid says (*Art Am.* I 160)'—

Small things take triflers men have owed a place
To smoothing cushions with a dexterous grace

39. **his portrait**] The word εἰκών here is probably to be understood, not of a painting, but of a portrait-statue or bust. In Diog. Laert. V 52 the execution of the 'portrait' of Nicomachus for which Theophrastus left directions in his will is assigned to Praxiteles the sculptor. (Flattering references to the 'house' and the 'portrait' are satirised in Lucian's *Imagines*, c. 6 and c. 20.)

1. **Complaisance**] The word rendered 'mode of address'—ἔντευξις—occurs again in the same sense in the Defin. to c. XI. It is not equivalent to ὁμιλία, but narrower in meaning, denoting chiefly the manner of accosting: see Athen. VI p. 256 § 16, 'Their (the flatterers') mode of address (ἔντευξις) is so artistic, so plausible towards all men.'

The Flatterer, according to Aristotle, flatters for money or what money buys: the Complaisant man 'aims at being pleasant with no further object' (μὴ δι' ἄλλο τι). This is a fault (1) because to combat the wishes of others is sometimes a duty to them or to oneself· thus Aristotle's Perfectly-behaved man is one who will occasionally 'make difficulties' (δυσχεραίνειν) for either reason or both. *Eth. Nic.* IV 6. (2) Because the primary object of the Complaisant man is, not that others may be pleased, but that he may be pleasant. He desires popularity, either

ns patron's house is well built, that his land is well planted, and that his portrait is like.

[In short the Flatterer may be observed saying and doing all 40 things by which he conceives that he will gain favour.]

II (V). THE COMPLAISANT MAN.

Complaisance may be defined as a mode of address calculated to give pleasure, but not with the best tendency.

The Complaisant man is very much the kind of person who will hail one afar off with 'my dear fellow'; and, after a large display of respect, seize and hold one by both hands. He will 5 attend you a little way, and ask *when* he is to see you, and will take his leave with a compliment upon his lips. Also, when he is called in to an arbitration, he will seek to please, not only his principal, but the adversary as well, in order that he may be

---

from mere vanity, or for the sake of influence. When, therefore, he is said to aim at being pleasant 'without any *further* object,' this does not exclude *a* selfish object. To be thought pleasant is itself the object which he most covets. He is unmercenary, as contrasted with the Flatterer: but he is not disinterested.

In the pair of portraits which Theophrastus has drawn two salient points of difference may be noted. (1) The Flatterer treats his patron as an admired superior, for whom he displays devotion, but whom it would be impertinent to assure of his goodwill. The Complaisant man treats his associate as an equal for whom he has a warm friendship. (2) The Flatterer, who desires material benefits, is constant to a once-found patron; partly because ripe intimacy is essential to complete success, and partly because he is unwilling to relinquish a certainty. The Complaisant man, on the other hand, desires to be on creditably cordial terms with as large a number of persons as possible.

8. to an arbitration] The system of Arbitration at Athens served in some degree to mitigate the Athenian passion for lawsuits—it being understood that 'the arbitrator looks to equity, as the judge to the law' (Ar. *Rhet.* I 13). Arbitrators were of two kinds: (1) Public (these consisted of all Athenian citizens in the sixtieth year of their age,—the last year of military service, Aristotle's *Constitution of Athens*, c. 53). A public arbitrator could try any civil cause, if the complainant preferred that course to going before a jury. Or a particular question of fact involved in a civil cause was sometimes referred to them. (2) Private: chosen to settle a dispute by mutual agreement between the parties. In this case there were usually three arbitrators. Two of these were considered as advocates respectively of the two disputants. The third sat as umpire (Demosth. *in Neaer* p 1360 § 45). Here the Complaisant man is one of the advocates. In c. IV the Arrogant man is the umpire.

44 ΑΥΘΑΔΕΙΑC Γ'

δὲ εἰπεῖν ὡς δικαιότερα λέγουσι τῶν πολιτῶν· καὶ κεκλη-
10 μένος δὲ ἐπὶ δεῖπνον κελεῦσαι καλέσαι τὰ παιδία τὸν
ἑστιῶντα, καὶ εἰσιόντα φῆσαι σύκου ὁμοιότερα εἶναι τῷ
πατρί, καὶ προσαγαγόμενος φιλῆσαι καὶ παρ' αὑτὸν καθ-
ίστασθαι· καὶ τοῖς μὲν συμπαίζειν αὐτὸς λέγων ἀσκός,
πέλεκυς, τὰ δὲ ἐπὶ τῆς γαστρὸς ἐᾶν καθεύδειν ἅμα θλιβόμενος.

αὐθαδείας γ'.

ἡ δὲ αὐθάδειά ἐστιν ἀπήνεια ὁμιλίας ἐν λόγοις, ὁ δὲ
αὐθάδης τοιοῦτός τις οἷος ἐρωτηθείς, ὁ δεῖνα ποῦ ἐστιν· εἰπεῖν·
πράγματά μοι μὴ πάρεχε· καὶ προσαγορευθεὶς μὴ ἀντι-

10 **that foreigners speak more justly**] This may be understood merely of general conversation. There were, however, two occasions on which this tendency might find special scope. The mercantile contracts (σύμβολα) between the Greek republics provided for the hearing, in the defendant's city, of lawsuits arising out of commerce. In such an action tried at Athens the foreigner would therefore always be the complainant; and the Complaisant juror may be conceived as warmly sympathising with his grievance. Again, when foreign envoys made a representation or a demand before the Ecclesia, the Complaisant citizen would ostentatiously support their claim.

In this instance the man whose sole aim is to please voluntarily offends the sentiment of the majority for the sake of conciliating a small minority. This might at first sight appear inconsistent with his character. But it is, in fact, perfectly true to it. The Complaisant man believes that the regard of any individual can be purchased outright by certain ignoble civilities Once bought, it is his property; and, on his principle that friendships are to be counted, not weighed, his next object is to secure the regard of some one else. His citizens are always with him; but if the 'foreigners' are to be enrolled among his acquaintance, this must be done while they are at Athens.

12 **to send for the children**] The doom of seclusion under which the Women's Apartment lay does not seem to have extended in its full rigour to the nursery. Children, or at least young boys, were sometimes guests in the dining-room see Lucian's *Dream*, c. 11: 'Come you, too, Micyllus, and dine with us: I will send my boy to dine in the Women's Apartments, that there may be room for you.' But when young people came to table they *sat*; to recline was the privilege of their elders. See Xenophon's *Sympos.* I 12, 'Autolycus' (a boy old enough to have won the pancratium, i e about 14) 'sat beside his father; the other guests reclined as usual.'

(13. **as like their father as figs**] Herondas VI 60, οὐ δ' ἂν σῦκον εἰκάσαι σύκῳ ἔχοις ἂν οὕτω)

14. **and kiss them**] The Flatterer, when *he* wished to pay his court to the children, felt it necessary to present them with fruit. This illustrates the distinction referred to in the first note to this chapter. As the Flatterer had voluntarily assumed a quasi-menial position, he could not ex-

THE SURLY MAN. III (XV)

deemed impartial. He will say, too, that foreigners speak more justly than his fellow-citizens. Then, when he is asked to dinner, he will request the host to send for the children; and will say of them, when they come in, that they are as like their father as figs; and will draw them towards him, and kiss them, and establish them at his side,—playing with some of them, and himself saying 'Wineskin,' 'Hatchet,' and permitting others to go to sleep upon him, to his anguish.

III (XV). THE SURLY MAN.

Surliness is discourtesy in words.

The Surly man is one who, when asked where so-and-so is, will say, 'Don't bother me', or, when spoken to, will not reply.

---

pect, like the Complaisant man, that his mere good-humour with the children should gratify their father.

16. 'Wineskin'—'Hatchet'] Some child's-game, of which nothing is known. It may have consisted, for instance, in one of the players bringing down his hand edgewise ('hatchet') on the other's clenched fist, before he could snatch it away. That the words are not names which the guest calls the children—as they have usually been explained—is clear from the αὐτός in the text, which shows that the children said them too. Casaubon's theory that the 'wineskin' and 'hatchet' were little toys (περιδέραια) hung round the children's necks, which the guest takes up and names successively, supposes the children to be infants.

1. Surliness] The Definition is imperfect; for the person described here is discourteous not in words only but in deeds; as when he refuses to sing. Probably the composer of the Definition wished to convey the idea that the Surly man is rough on the surface only, but often kindly beneath it: e.g. he gives money to his friend in difficulties, though with a rude speech.

The conception of αὐθάδεια presented here illustrates a general characteristic of these sketches, of which c. XII furnishes perhaps the best example. A word originally of large meaning is considered in that special sense to which social usage had narrowed it. Αὐθάδης is properly 'one who pleases himself'; the word might, and did, express every shade of self-will, from the stubbornness of a Prometheus to the caprice of a coquette. But Theophrastus—in accordance, probably, with the usage of his day—limits it to one special case. His αὐθάδης is the man of morose, unsociable manners; apt to make rude speeches and to be generally ungracious, tenacious, above all things, of his independence, to the extent of grudging homage to the gods; but capable of doing kindnesses, though in a rude way. We know from other sources that the word had come to be used in this special sense—of a certain manner in society; but the quality of this manner is variously described. Already in Euripides (*Medea*, 223) the αὐθάδης is one who is 'harsh to his fellow-citizens, from want of culture' (πικρὸς . ἀμαθίας ὕπο). The author of the *Magna Moralia* (prob later than Aristotle, Grant, Vol. I, Essay I, p. 14)

46 ΑΥΘΑΔΕΙΑΣ Γ′

προσειπεῖν· καὶ πωλῶν τι μὴ λέγειν τοῖς ὠνουμένοις, πόσου
5 ἂν ἀποδοῖτο, ἀλλ' ἐρωτᾶν, τί εὑρίσκει· καὶ τοῖς τιμῶσι καὶ
πέμπουσιν εἰς τὰς ἑορτὰς εἰπεῖν, ὅτι οὐκ ἂν γένοιτο διδο-
μένων· καὶ οὐκ ἔχειν συγγνώμην οὔτε τῷ χρώσαντι αὐτὸν
ἀκουσίως οὔτε τῷ ὤσαντι οὔτε τῷ ἐμβάντι· καὶ φίλῳ δὲ
ἔρανον κελεύσαντι εἰσενεγκεῖν εἰπών, ὅτι οὐκ ἂν δοίη, ὕστερον
10 ἥκειν φέρων καὶ λέγειν ὅτι ἀπόλλυσι καὶ τοῦτο τὸ ἀργύριον·
καὶ προσπταίσας ἐν τῇ ὁδῷ δεινὸς καταράσασθαι τῷ λίθῳ·
καὶ ἀναμεῖναι οὐκ ἂν ὑπομεῖναι πολὺν χρόνον οὐδένα· καὶ
οὔτε ᾆσαι οὔτε ῥῆσιν εἰπεῖν οὔτε ὀρχήσασθαι ἂν ἐθελῆσαι·
δεινὸς δὲ καὶ τοῖς θεοῖς μὴ ἐπεύχεσθαι.

---

describes the αὐθάδης very much as he is described here—'one who will not associate or converse with any man' (I 28). Eudemus, contemporary with Theophrastus, identifies the αὐθάδης with the δύσκολος, or Cross man, of Aristotle, the opposite of the κόλαξ and ἄρεσκος (*Eth. Nic.* IV 6, 9), describing him as 'regulating his life with no respect to others (μηδὲν πρὸς ἕτερον ζῶν), but *contemptuous*' (*Eth. Eudem.* III 7, 4). This element of 'contempt' becomes the distinctive feature of αὐθάδεια in the analysis given of it by Philodemus of Gadara, a contemporary of Cicero:—' The so-called Surly man (ὁ αὐθάδης λεγόμενος) seems to be compounded of conceit (οἴησις), arrogance (ὑπερηφανία), and contemptuousness (ὑπεροψία).' (*De Vitiis* X, col. XVI, 39 ed. Ussing.) That is, he thinks too highly of himself (conceit), too meanly of others (contempt), and acts upon his estimate (arrogance). Philodemus adds this example:—Sharing a bath with another person, the Surly man will order hot (or cold) water without previously consulting his associate.

Now this is what the Arrogant man of Theophrastus (c. IV) would do; but not what his Surly man would do; and it may be proper to point out the main differences between them as conceived by him.

1. The Surly man acts chiefly from a desire to be left alone; though, as proud men are also reserved, he often seems to act from pride. The Arrogant man acts from a desire to enforce the recognition of a fancied superiority. 2. The Surly man repels advances, but does not take liberties. The Arrogant man does both.

6. **with their compliments**] Xen. *Cyrop.* VIII 4, 4: 'Also, when he had occasion to commend any of his domestics, he used to *compliment* them with presents from his table' (ἐτίμα ἀπὸ τῆς τραπέζης).

7. **at feast-tide**] The great festivals were occasions not only of public sacrifice but of private sacrifices in every house. Portions (μερίδες) of the flesh were often sent to those friends who were not present at the dinner given after the sacrifice (note on c. XV, 5). Thus, when the Discontented man receives such a present (c. XXII) he complains that it is a poor substitute for an invitation to the dinner. See Ar. *Acharn.* 1048: '*Slave*. Dicaeopolis! *D.* Whom have we here? *Sl.* A bridegroom has sent you this flesh from the wedding feast.' Plutarch mentions this among the attentions by which Antigonus Gonatas sought to conciliate the founder of the Achaean League: 'Whenever he held a sacrifice at Corinth he

THE SURLY MAN. III (XV)

If he has anything for sale, instead of informing the buyers at what price he is prepared to sell it, he will ask them what he is to get for it. Those who send him presents with their compliments at feast-tide are told that he 'will not touch' their offerings. He cannot forgive a person who has besmirched him by accident, or pushed him, or trodden upon his foot. Then, if a friend asks him for a subscription, he will say that he cannot give one; but will come with it by and by, and remark that he is losing this money also. When he stumbles in the street he is apt to swear at the stone. He will not endure to wait long for anyone; nor will he consent to sing, or to recite, or to dance. He is apt also not to pray to the gods.

---

used to send portions of the flesh to Aratus at Sicyon' (*Arat.* c. 15). The Pitcher-feast (the second day of the Anthesteria) was especially an occasion for such offerings: see note on c. XXVI, 31.

10. **for a subscription**] See note on c. V, 14.

14. **nor will he consent to sing**] i.e., to take his turn in the σκόλιον, or 'catch,' which the company are singing over their wine. Each guest, though not in regular order, usually sang a short stanza or verse. In Athenaeus (XV, p. 695 § 50) the first singer gives an alcaic stanza on the dangers of the sea; the second takes him up with a quatrain in the style of a nursery rhyme; the third, fourth, fifth and sixth then go through the stanzas on Harmodius and Aristogeiton. —In the *Clouds*, Pheidippides incenses his father by acting as the αὐθάδης does here. 'First I requested him to take the lyre, and sing a song of Simonides, the Shearing of the Ram; but he quickly objected that to play the lyre and sing at dessert was an old-fashioned custom' (vv 1355 ff.).

14 **to recite**] ῥῆσις meant especially a speech from a tragedy. Demosthenes gives as instances of ῥήσεις the prologue of the *Hecuba* and the Messenger's speech from an unknown play (*de Coron.* p. 315 § 267, cf. Ar. *Wasps*, 580). The declamation of such a passage seems to have been accepted at entertainments as a substitute for a song. Thus, when Pheidippides haughtily refuses to sing, his father requests him 'at least to take the myrtle branch and say something from Aeschylus'; and finally 'he chanted a speech (ᾖσε ῥῆσιν) from Euripides' (*Clouds*, 1371). Aeschines speaks of his rival 'telling the Senate a long story about the young Alexander—how he played the lyre to us over our wine, declaimed some speeches, and sang see-saw catches (ἀντικρούσεις) with another youth' (*in Timarch.* p. 24 § 160).

14. **to dance**] See note on c IX, 21.

15. **not to pray to the gods**] This touch alone momentarily lifts the αὐθάδης of Theophrastus from his petty sullenness into something of that more tragic obstinacy which the old poets associated with αὐθάδεια. In the *Prometheus Vinctus* αὐθάδης is the word used to describe, on the one hand, the stubborn patience of the sufferer,—on the other, the inflexible resolve of Zeus (vv. 928, 985). It was αὐθάδεια, stubborn self-reliance, says Plutarch (*Crass* 19), which prevented Crassus from recalling an ill-omened speech which had excited the superstitious fears of his men: see note on c. XIII, 21 f. In this, its sterner sense, αὐθάδης would exactly describe Virgil's *contemptor divom Mezentius*.

ὑπερηφανίας δ΄.

ἔστι δὲ ἡ ὑπερηφανία καταφρόνησίς τις πλὴν αὑτοῦ τῶν ἄλλων, ὁ δὲ ὑπερήφανος τοιόσδε τις οἷος τῷ σπεύδοντι ἀπὸ δείπνου ἐντεύξεσθαι φάσκειν ἐν τῷ περιπατεῖν· καὶ εὖ ποιήσας μεμνῆσθαι φάσκειν· καὶ βαδίζων ἐν ταῖς ὁδοῖς
5 τὰς διαίτας κρίνειν τοῖς ἐπιτρέψασι· καὶ χειροτονούμενος ἐξόμνυσθαι τὰς ἀρχάς, οὐ φάσκων σχολάζειν· καὶ προσελθεῖν πρότερος οὐδενὶ θελῆσαι. καὶ τοὺς πωλοῦντάς τι καὶ μισθουμένους δεινὸς κελεῦσαι ἥκειν πρὸς αὐτὸν ἅμ᾽ ἡμέρᾳ· καὶ ἐν ταῖς ὁδοῖς πορευόμενος μὴ λαλεῖν τοῖς ἐντυγχάνουσι,

---

1. **Arrogance**] The relation of Arrogance, as treated by Theophrastus, to Surliness has been spoken of in note 1 to c. III. In regard to Aristotle's system, Arrogance is a species of what he terms χαυνότης, Vanity or Inflation—the opposite extreme being Mean-spiritedness, and the middle-state Lofty-mindedness A remark which Aristotle makes in speaking of these qualities is worthy of attention— viz. that the Vain man *may* possess the same things (e g. ability, wealth, etc) which go to justify the Lofty-minded man's claim to high consideration; but the Vain man's claim is invalid on moral grounds. 'Those who possess these advantages *without virtue* are neither entitled to deem themselves worthy of great things, nor are they properly called Lofty-minded. . They mimic the Lofty-minded man, while they do not resemble him,— i.e. they do so in such things as they can; the actions which are according to virtue they, of course, cannot do; and at the same time they look down upon others. Now the Lofty-minded man looks down upon others justly (for he judges truly); but most people do so at random' (*Eth. Nic.* IV 3, 20).

Casaubon considers the Arrogance described here as related, not only to Surliness, but to Boastfulness (c. VI). But Boastfulness and Petty Ambition (c. VII) are referable to a principle distinct from that of Arrogance,—the desire, namely, of honour, as distinguished from opinion concerning one's own worthiness for honour.

3. **he will see him after dinner**] The Ironical man acts, from a different motive, in the same way: see note on c V, 10.

3. **when he is taking his walk**] Plut. *Thes.* c. 35: 'Some say that he stumbled and fell accidentally, while taking his walk, as usual, after dinner' The young Autolycus, in Xenophon's *Symposium*, leaves the party early 'to take his walk' (εἰς περίπατον. IX 1). Zeus, in Lucian's *Zeus Tragoedus*, says to the other gods,— 'We were entertained in the Peiraeus— as many of us, that is, as Mnesitheus invited to the sacrifice. Then, after the libation, you went your various ways, as it pleased you, but I—for it was not very late—went back to the town to take my evening stroll (τὸ δειλινόν) in the Cerameicus' (c. 15) (The plaintiff, in the speech of Demosthenes *Against Conon*, p 1258 § 7, was taking his usual evening walk in the market-place with a friend, when he was assaulted by the defendant.)

4. **to recollect benefits which he has**

IV (XXIV). THE ARROGANT MAN.

Arrogance is a certain scorn for all the world beside oneself.
The Arrogant man is one who will say to a person who is in a hurry that he will see him after dinner when he is taking his walk. He will profess to recollect benefits which he has conferred. As he saunters in the streets, he will decide cases for those who have made him their referee. When he is nominated to public offices, he will protest his inability to accept them, alleging that he is too busy. He will not permit himself to give any man the first greeting. He is apt to order persons who have anything to sell, or who wish to hire anything from him, to come to him at daybreak. When he walks in the streets, he will

---

conferred] i e he will remind others in a patronizing manner that he has placed them under obligations; which may or may not be true, for the ambiguous φάσκειν, 'to allege,' leaves it doubtful. This trait illustrates the difference between Arrogance and Lofty-mindedness. It is characteristic of the Lofty-minded man, as Aristotle observes, to *remember* whom he has benefited (*Eth. Nic.* IV 3, 25). The Arrogant man (who is a bad imitation of the Lofty-minded, *ib.* 21) does not only remember,—he proclaims that he remembers

6. who have made him their referee] See note on c. II, 8.

6. when he is nominated to public offices] Almost all public officers (including the archons) were appointed by lot; others—as the ten Generals and all ambassadors—by show of hands in the Ecclesia. The suffrages of the people have nominated the Arrogant man to an office of the latter kind; but, as the appointment is invalid without his acceptance of office, the present tense is used, and he *is* said to be 'in process of being elected' (χειροτονούμενος). Instead of accepting, he makes an oath before the Ecclesia that he cannot serve; assigning, not a definite reason, such as illness or want of means, but the vague one that he

is 'too busy.' See Demosth. *de Fals. Legat.* p. 379 § 124, where the brother of Aeschines takes a physician with him to the assembly, and makes oath of his brother's inability to serve on an embassy. From the version of this incident given by Aeschines, we learn a detail—viz. that an oath of this kind could not be made before the Senate, but only before the Ecclesia (Aeschin. *de Falsa Legat.* p. 40 § 95).

9. the first greeting] The first χαῖρε was expected, of course, to come from the inferior. Micyllus, in Lucian's *Dream* (c. 14), thus describes his meeting with an acquaintance who had suddenly grown rich : 'The other day I saw him approaching, and said "Hail, O Simon" But he, indignant: "Servant, desire that needy person not to clip (κατασμικρύνειν) my name. My name is not Simon, but Simonides".'

11. when he walks in the streets] Athenian criticism on demeanour in the streets appears to have been severe. Athenaeus quotes two verses of Alexis—

Nothing, in my opinion, is so low
As walking out of just time in the streets:

(ἀρρύθμως: Ath. I, p. 21 § 38). In the speech against Pantaenetus (Dem. *adv. P.* p. 982) it is anticipated that he may say of the defendant—'Nicobulus is an

J. T.

10 κάτω κεκυφώς, ὅταν δὲ αὐτῷ δόξῃ, ἄνω πάλιν· καὶ ἑστιῶν
τοὺς φίλους αὐτὸς μὴ συνδειπνεῖν ἀλλὰ τῶν ὑφ' αὐτόν τινι
συντάξαι αὐτῶν ἐπιμελεῖσθαι· καὶ προαποστέλλειν δέ, ἐπὰν
πορεύηται, τὸν ἐροῦντα ὅτι προσέρχεται· καὶ οὔτε ἐπ' ἀλει-
φόμενον αὐτὸν οὔτε λουόμενον οὔτε ἐσθίοντα ἐᾶσαι ἂν
15 εἰσελθεῖν. ἀμέλει δὲ καὶ λογιζόμενος πρός τινα τῷ παιδὶ
συντάξαι τὰς ψήφους διωθεῖν καὶ κεφάλαιον ποιήσαντι
γράψαι αὐτῷ εἰς λόγον· καὶ ἐπιστέλλων μὴ γράφειν ὅτι
χαρίζοιο ἄν μοι, ἀλλ' ὅτι βούλομαι γενέσθαι, καὶ ἀπέσταλκα
πρός σε ληψομένους, καὶ ὅπως ἄλλως μὴ ἔσται, καὶ τὴν
20 ταχίστην.

εἰρωνείας ε'.

ἡ μὲν οὖν εἰρωνεία δόξειεν ἂν εἶναι, ὡς τύπῳ λαβεῖν,
προσποίησις ἐπὶ χεῖρον πράξεων καὶ λόγων, ὁ δὲ εἴρων

unpopular man; he walks fast, talks loud, and carries a walking-stick' (the stick implying an affectation of Spartanism; note on c. VII, 20); and after contrasting his own moral worth with that of the plaintiff, Nicobulus adds: 'Such, Pantaenetus, am I who walk quick, and such are you who walk composedly' (ἀτρέμας). Aeschines is described 'walking through the market-place with his cloak down to his heels, stepping as high as Pythocles'—(another orator of the Macedonian party)—Demosth. *de Fals. Legat.* p. 442 § 314. Plato expressly mentions 'walking quietly (ἡσυχῇ) in the streets' as a mark of σωφροσύνη: *Charmid.* p. 159 B.

17. **when he is anointing himself, or bathing**] The exclusion of a visitor at such a time scarcely reaches the modern idea of Arrogance. But this is a good illustration of that hostility to domestic privacy which was bred in the citizens of a Greek republic at once by the temper of their race, by the physical conditions of their life, and (not least) by democratic sentiment. The first symptom in Pausanias of a transition to Persian manners was that 'he began to make himself difficult of access' (Thuc. I 130). Menelaus, in Euripides, reproaches Agamemnon with having become, on his accession to power, 'hard for his friends to approach, keeping within bolted doors and seldom seen' (ἔσω κλῄθρων σπάνιος, *Iph. Aul.* 344). Agesilaus stole away the influence of Lysander because the latter 'affected a haughty reserve (ἐσεμνύνετο), being difficult of access, while the former delighted to be accessible to all' (Xen. *Ages.* 9, 2); and Plutarch, contrasting the same persons, describes the one as 'popular' (δημοτικός), the other as 'vulgar' (φορτικός: Plut. *Ages.* 7, 2: 8, 4).

19. **push the counters apart**] A difficulty has arisen concerning some item of the account. Instead of allowing the groups of counters on the counting-board to remain stationary until this difficulty has been settled, the Arrogant man desires his slave to break up the groups

THE IRONICAL MAN. V (I).

not speak to those whom he meets, keeping his head bent down, or at other times, when so it pleases him, erect. If he entertains his friends, he will not dine with them himself, but will appoint a subordinate to preside. As soon as he sets out on a journey, he will send some one forward to say that he is coming. He is not likely to admit a visitor when he is anointing himself, or bathing, or at table. It is quite in his manner, too, when he is reckoning with any one, to bid his slave push the counters apart, set down the total, and charge it to the other's account. In writing a letter, he will not say 'I should be much obliged,' but 'I wish it to be thus and thus'; or 'I have sent to you for' this or that; or 'You will attend to this strictly'; or 'Without a moment's delay.'

V (I). THE IRONICAL MAN.

Irony, roughly defined, would seem to be an affectation of the worse in word or deed.

(διωθεῖν)—to form the counters in a line at the foot of the board, representing the total as it *now* stands—and to make out a bill accordingly. Compare note on c. XIII, 3.

20. **in writing a letter**] Philodemus describes the Surly man (whom he considers as a variety of the Arrogant, see note on c. III, 1) as 'one who in writing a letter will not add "Hail" at the beginning, or "Farewell" (ἔρρωσο) at the end' (*De Vitiis* x, col. xvii 25 ed. Ussing).

1. **Irony**] It is defined here as 'an affectation of the worse,' literally 'on the side of worse' (ἐπὶ χεῖρον), i.e. of self-depreciation. Aristotle (*Eth. Nic.* II 7) defines Irony as προσποίησις ἐπὶ τὸ ἔλαττον, 'pretence on the side of less,' i.e. conscious understating (or underacting) of the truth; and in the *Eudemian Ethics* (III 7) the Ironical man is described as ἐπὶ τὰ χείρω καθ' αὑτοῦ ψευδόμενος, 'misrepresenting himself for the worse.' Both passages have contributed to the definition in the text; the latter supplying ἐπὶ τὸ χεῖρον (instead of ἔλαττον), the former προσποίησις. From their fusion results a phrase which is faulty and inexact, but of which the general meaning is clear

This sketch forms a remarkable chapter in the history of the word Irony; first, because of the restricted sense in which it is already employed by a pupil of Aristotle; and secondly because the conception, while thus narrowed, seems also to have become indistinct.

It is necessary to recall the sense in which Irony is understood by Aristotle (*Eth. Nic.* IV 7 §§ 2 ff.). 'It seems to be the tendency of the Boastful man to lay claim to creditable things, either when they do not belong to him, or in a greater degree than they belong to him. The Ironical man, on the contrary, tends to disclaim or to depreciate things which do belong to him. The intermediate character, being (so to say) "matter-of-fact" (αὐθέκαστος) is truthful in his life and in his speech, confessing the attributes which are his, and neither exaggerating nor

ΕΙΡΩΝΕΙΑϹ Ε'

τοιοῦτός τις οἷος προσελθὼν τοῖς ἐχθροῖς ἐθέλειν λαλεῖν, οὐ
μισεῖν· καὶ ἐπαινεῖν παρόντας, οἷς ἐπέθετο λάθρα, καὶ τούτοις
5 συλλυπεῖσθαι ἡττωμένοις· καὶ συγγνώμην δὲ ἔχειν τοῖς
αὑτὸν κακῶς λέγουσι καὶ ἐπὶ τοῖς καθ' ἑαυτοῦ λεγομένοις·
καὶ πρὸς τοὺς ἀδικουμένους καὶ ἀγανακτοῦντας πράως δια-
λέγεσθαι· καὶ τοῖς ἐντυγχάνειν κατὰ σπουδὴν βουλομένοις
προστάξαι ἐπανελθεῖν· καὶ μηδὲν ὧν πράττει ὁμολογῆσαι
10 ἀλλὰ φῆσαι βουλεύεσθαι· καὶ προσποιήσασθαι ἄρτι παρα-
γεγονέναι καὶ ὀψὲ γενέσθαι αὐτὸν καὶ μαλακισθῆναι· καὶ
πρὸς τοὺς δανειζομένους καὶ ἐρανίζοντας <ὡς ἀργύριον οὐκ
ἔχει· καὶ πωλῶν λέγειν> ὡς οὐ πωλεῖ, καὶ μὴ πωλῶν φῆσαι
πωλεῖν· καὶ ἀκούσας τι μὴ προσποιεῖσθαι, καὶ ἰδὼν φῆσαι

---

extenuating them... Ironical persons, leaning to understatement, impress one as being more refined in character; for they seem to speak with a view, not to advantage, but to avoiding pomposity And moreover it is *creditable* things which such persons especially disclaim; as, for example, did Socrates.' The general characteristic of the Ironical man is, then, that he holds in reserve, for whatever purpose, something of his available power. This purpose may be an earnest dialectic one, like that of Socrates. Or it may be to avoid ostentation or check impertinence; as Aristotle's Lofty-minded man is 'ironical' to the common crowd (*Eth. N.* IV 3, 28). Or the purpose may be merely playful; as Anacharsis in Lucian says that the Athenians were reputed 'ironical' in conversation (*Anach* c 15).

Theophrastus has in most of his portraits embodied those traits which are generic to the character described. His Flatterer, his Avaricious man, his Boaster are fairly representative of the classes who flatter, hoard, or boast. But his picture of the Ironical man, judged by his master's standard, is strikingly inadequate. He does not show us the man whose habit it is—either in earnest or in jest, now for the discomfiture of pretence, now for the friendly insinuation of reproof or praise—to keep on the inside edge of the truth. He describes merely a person who takes a cynical pleasure in misleading or inconveniencing others by the concealment of his real feelings and intentions.

But not only is the conception of this portrait narrow; it is also unfaithful to the essence of the quality portrayed by Plato and defined by Aristotle. True Irony is a masked battery, a screen assisting the more effective use of a real power which it veils. But the person described by Theophrastus appears to deceive for the sake of deceiving; no touch in the picture suggests that he has any meaning or purpose in reserve. His irony resembles rather a curtain on the stage, with nothing behind it but the mechanism which sustains the illusion. Again, when he is described as expressing incredulity and cautioning another person against too ready belief, this is a misplaced characteristic. The ironical and the sceptical mind have, perhaps, much in common; but the avowal, as distinguished from the insinuation, of unbelief is not a trait of Irony.

The characters of Theophrastus are essentially popular, interpreting the notions currently attached in society to certain epithets. In the present instance this fact, while lessening the author's respon-

THE IRONICAL MAN. V (I)

The Ironical Man is one who goes up to his enemies, and volunteers to chat with them, instead of showing hatred. He will praise to their faces those whom he attacked behind their backs, and will sympathise with them in their defeats. He will show forgiveness to his revilers, and excuse things said against him; and he will talk blandly to persons who are smarting under a wrong. When people wish to see him in a hurry, he will desire them to call again. He will never confess to anything that he is doing, but will always say that he is thinking about it. He will pretend that he has 'just arrived,' or that he 'was too late,' or that he 'was unwell.' To applicants for a loan or a subscription he will say that he has no money; when he has anything for sale, he will deny that he means to sell; or, when he does *not* mean to sell, he will pretend that he does. Hearing,

---

sibility for the defects of his portrait, heightens the significance of these defects themselves. It shows that a word most flexibly and delicately expressive, a word contrived to include, without confounding, innumerable shades of grave or playful tone, had scarcely passed into currency when it was debased. Already in the time of Aristotle's pupil 'irony' is popularly understood in a sense almost wholly bad, and the fine precision of the term has been lost. (In his note on *Eth. N.* IV 7 § 3 Sir A. Grant has noticed this swift decay.)

The definition speaks of 'words and deeds': but this sketch supplies no true example of practical irony. As in verbal irony there is a contrast between the thought and the expression, so in practical there must be a contrast between the apparent and the real character of the action: as when Timon (to borrow an illustration from Bp Thirlwall's famous essay) gave the thieves gold to ruin them. (The definition is regarded as spurious by Gomperz in the *Sitzungsberichte* of the Vienna Academy, 1889 The character of the εἴρων is discussed by Ribbeck in the *Rheinisches Museum*, XXXI (1876) 381—400.)

6. **in their defeats**] when they are defeated in lawsuits for this meaning of ἡττᾶσθαι see cc. XVII, 10, XXX, 5.

10. **to call again**] This resembles a trait ascribed to the Arrogant man (c. IV). But the Arrogant man puts off his visitor for the sake of asserting his own consequence; the Ironical man, merely because it is of his character to be evasive. The caller presses, perhaps, for a definite answer to some proposal which he has already made. The Ironical man (who has made up his mind, but enjoys mystification) replies—'I am afraid that I have not quite decided...Could you call tomorrow?'

12. **he will pretend that he has 'just arrived'**] I understand this and the next two clauses as being the reasons which the Ironical man alleges for his ignorance of what has been passing in the world. He is in a company where some one asks him—'Have you heard what happened at A's house?' He replies (knowing the facts, but wishing to elicit the speaker's view of them) 'I have only just returned to town,' or 'I came too late for it,' or 'I have been ill for the last few days' That μαλακισθῆναι refers to *illness*, seems certain from c. X, where ὁ μαλακιζόμενος is 'the invalid.'

14. **a subscription**] ἔρανος—such as

ΑΛΑΖΟΝΕΙΑC Ϛ'

15 μὴ ἑωρακέναι, καὶ ὁμολογήσας μὴ μεμνῆσθαι· καὶ τὰ μὲν σκέψεσθαι φάσκειν, τὰ δὲ οὐκ εἰδέναι, τὰ δὲ θαυμάζειν, τὰ δ' ἤδη ποτὲ καὶ αὐτὸς οὕτω διαλογίσασθαι. καὶ τὸ ὅλον δεινὸς τῷ τοιούτῳ τρόπῳ τοῦ λόγου χρῆσθαι· οὐ πιστεύω· οὐχ ὑπολαμβάνω· ἐκπλήττομαι· καὶ λέγειν ἑαυτὸν ἑτέρου
20 ἀκηκοέναι, καὶ μὴν οὐ ταῦτα πρὸς ἐμὲ διεξῄει· παράδοξόν μοι τὸ πρᾶγμα· ἄλλῳ τινὶ λέγε· ὅπως δὲ σοὶ ἀπιστήσω ἢ ἐκείνου καταγνῶ ἀποροῦμαι· ἀλλ' ὅρα μὴ σὺ θᾶττον πιστεύεις.

[τοιαύτας φωνὰς καὶ πλοκὰς καὶ παλιλλογίας εὑρεῖν ἔστι τοῦ εἴρωνος. τὰ δὴ τῶν ἠθῶν μὴ ἁπλᾶ ἀλλ' ἐπίβουλα
25 φυλάττεσθαι μᾶλλον δεῖ ἢ τοὺς ἔχεις.]

ἀλαζονείας Ϛ'.

ἀμέλει δὲ ἡ ἀλαζονεία δόξειεν ἂν εἶναι προσποίησις ἀγαθῶν οὐκ ὄντων, ὁ δὲ ἀλαζὼν τοιοῦτός τις οἷος ἐν τῷ

---

was made for a man in difficulties by his friends. Compare cc III, VI, XXV. It was usually understood that such assistance was a loan: see c. XXII. There were also at Athens regularly organized societies which, as well as the subscriptions paid to them, were called ἔρανοι. These seem to have been partly dining-clubs, partly associations for mutual relief in case of need. Demosthenes (*in Meid.* p. 574 § 184) alludes to both sorts of 'subscription'—that which was raised privately on occasion among friends, and that which was paid to a club. He is insisting on the practical value of a good character:—'I believe that all men in the course of their lives *pay in subscriptions* for their own benefit—not those merely (1) *which individuals raise*, or (2) *for which collecting officers* (πληρωταί) *are appointed*, but others also. For instance—we have among us a man considerate, humane, merciful to many: to such a man it is right that like measure should be meted by all, if ever he come to want or into peril of the law.' This custom of the ἔρανος furnishes a favourite metaphor to the orators. e g. Dem. *in Aristog.* 1 p. 776 § 22: 'Everything that each man among us does by the injunction of the law is his contribution (ἔρανος) as a citizen of the commonwealth.'

1. **Boastfulness**] ἀλαζονεία is with Aristotle the fault, in respect to truth, on the side of excess, as 'irony' on the side of defect; and the ἀλαζών is one 'who lays claim to creditable things which do not belong to him, or in a greater degree than they belong to him' (*Eth. N.* IV 7). It is remarked in that chapter that 'those who boast *for the sake of reputation* lay claim to things for which men are praised or congratulated; those who boast *for the sake of gain*, to things which are available to others, and of which the non-possession may escape notice, to the character, for instance, of a clever seer or doctor.' The ἀλαζών of Theophrastus belongs to the former class; and accordingly pretends to wealth, generosity, etc. Aristotle further

THE BOASTFUL MAN. VI (XXIII)

he will affect not to have heard, seeing, not to have seen; if he has made an admission, he will say that he does not remember it. Sometimes he has 'been considering the question'; sometimes he does 'not know'; sometimes he is 'surprised'; sometimes it is 'the very conclusion' at which he 'once arrived' himself. And, in general, he is very apt to use this kind of phrase: 'I do not believe it'; 'I do not understand it'; 'I am astonished.' Or he will say that he has heard it from some one else: 'This, however, was not the story that he told me.' 'The thing surprises me', 'Don't tell *me*'; 'I do not know how I am to disbelieve you, or to condemn him'; 'Take care that you are not too credulous.'

[Such the speeches, such the doublings and retractions to which the Ironical man will resort. Disingenuous and designing characters are in truth to be shunned more carefully than vipers.]

VI (XXIII). THE BOASTFUL MAN.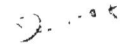

Boastfulness would seem to be, in fact, pretension to advantages which one does not possess.

---

remarks that '*irony*' may be pushed into ἀλαζονεία, 'as in the case of the Spartan style of dress; foi both excess and extreme defects are in the nature of boastfulness.' The delineation of Theophrastus does not touch this more subtle form of the quality; and his ἀλαζών will therefore be adequately rendered by 'boastful,' as Menander's was by the Latin *gloriosus* (Plaut. *Mil. Glor.* II 1, 18).

'Boastful,' however, does not seem to be a perfect rendering for ἀλαζών in its most general sense. 'Boastful' implies pretension of a more direct, explicit kind than is necessarily intended by the Greek word; which included many more artistic forms of self-assertion. Thus a fashionable soothsayer might have been termed ἀλαζών; but would not be described in English as 'boastful.' Perhaps 'Swaggerer,' in the extended sense in which it is sometimes heard now, would convey the general notion of the word more faithfully. The simpler and more usual rendering, 'boastful,' has, however, been preferred here, since it was adequate to the occasion; and also because 'Swaggerer,' in its proper sense as applied to demeanour, answers more nearly to the Greek σαλακών (Ar. *Rhet.* II xvi).

The Aristotelian contrast between Irony and Boastfulness is not effectively maintained in the two sketches of Theophrastus; partly because the Irony of Theophrastus is not that of Aristotle (see note on c. V, 1); partly because the relation of the Boastful man to truth is, for the purpose of this sketch, less important than the motive of his actions, viz. a desire of reputation. In this he resembles the man of Petty Ambition (c. VII), but with a difference:—the latter places

56   ΑΛΑΖΟΝΕΙΑϹ Ϛ´

δείγματι ἑστηκὼς διηγεῖσθαι ξένοις ὡς πολλὰ χρήματα αὐτῷ
ἐστιν ἐν τῇ θαλάττῃ· καὶ περὶ τῆς ἐργασίας τῆς δανειστικῆς
5 διεξιέναι, ἡλίκη, καὶ αὐτὸς ὅσα εἴληφε καὶ ἀπολώλεκε· καὶ
ἅμα ταῦτα πλεθρίζων πέμπειν τὸ παιδάριον ἐπὶ τὴν τράπεζαν,
δραχμῆς αὐτῷ κειμένης. καὶ συνοδοιπόρου δὲ ἀπολαύσας ἐν
τῇ ὁδῷ, δεινὸς λέγειν ὡς μετ᾽ Ἀλεξάνδρου ἐστρατεύσατο, καὶ
ὡς αὐτῷ εἶχε, καὶ ὅσα λιθοκόλλητα ποτήρια ἐκόμισε· καὶ
10 περὶ τῶν τεχνιτῶν τῶν ἐν τῇ Ἀσίᾳ, ὅτι βελτίους εἰσὶ τῶν ἐν
τῇ Εὐρώπῃ, ἀμφισβητῆσαι· καὶ ταῦτα δὴ φῆσαι, οὐδαμοῦ
ἐκ τῆς πόλεως ἀποδεδημηκώς· καὶ γράμματα δὲ εἰπεῖν ὡς
πάρεστι παρ᾽ Ἀντιπάτρου τριττὰ δή, λέγοντα παραγίνεσθαι

---

honour in trifles; the Boaster pretends to things which a majority of men do, in fact, honour. (The character has been discussed in Ribbeck's *Alazon*, Leipzig, 1882.)

3. **in the bazaar**] The bazaar, δεῖγμα, where merchants displayed samples of their wares, was on the shore of the Peiraeus, where there were other places of business, e g. the Corn Market (ἀλφιτόπωλις στοά, Ar. *Eccl.* 682) That it was close to the quays appears from Xenophon's account of the descent made upon the Peiraeus by Teleutias in 389 B.C.: 'Some of his men, too, sprang ashore into the bazaar, and, seizing some merchants and skippers, carried them on board' (*Hellen* V 1, 21). Compare Lysias *frag.* 45 § 7: 'As he could not walk, they carried him on the sofa to the bazaar, and showed him in that state to many Athenians and foreigners.'—On the reading διαζεύγματι, see *Crit App.*

4. **the great sums which he has at sea**] Money lent on bottomry (ναυτικόν) was lost to the lender in case of disaster to the ship· 'the contract (συγγραφῶν) providing, as is the invariable rule, for the repayment of the money *in case of the ship coming safe into harbour*' (Dem. *adv. Zenoth.* p. 863 § 5). Hence the rate of interest was high· Dem *adv. Polycl.* p. 1212 § 17 speaks of ναυτικὸν ἐπόγδοον, i.e. money thus lent at 12⅜ per cent. Cf. Xen.

Vect. III 9, ' He gets, as on bottomry, about 20 per cent.' (ἐπίπεμπτον αὐτῷ γίγνεται).

5. **money-lending business**] The bankers (τραπεζῖται) who kept the tables in the market-place were generally money-lenders (δανεισταί) too, but money-lending was also carried on, both on a great and on a small scale, as a distinct business. Alciphro's *Letters* relate some of the bitter experiences of countrymen in their dealings with ·the town usurers.' A fisherman who requires a new net has recourse to such help. 'Then that shrivelled Chremes, with contracted brows, who eyes all men like a wild bull, enamoured, perhaps, of my boat, relaxed his severe, unsmiling face; lifted his eyes; smiled softly on me, and professed himself ready to do me any service.. .But when, the time having come, he demanded back principal and interest without allowing one day's grace, I recognised my old friend whom I remembered sitting at the Diomeian gate,—the possessor of the crooked stick, the enemy of all men, Chremes of Phyle.' He sells his wife's necklace to ' Pasion the banker,'—pays the usurer—and vows 'never again to go to one of the city money-lenders, though he should be worn to a shadow with hunger first ' (Alc. III 3).

10. **with Alexander**] On the reading Εὐάνδρου, see *Crit. App.* VI 8 —Compare the strain in which the Miles Gloriosus of

THE BOASTFUL MAN. VI (XXIII)

The Boastful Man is one who will stand in the bazaar talking to foreigners of the great sums which he has at sea; he will discourse of the vastness of his money-lending business, and the extent of his personal gains and losses; and, while thus drawing the long-bow, will send his boy to the bank, where he keeps—tenpence. He loves, also, to impose upon his companion by the road with a story of how he served with Alexander, and on what terms he was with him, and what a number of gemmed cups he brought home, contending, too, that the Asiatic artists are superior to those of Europe; and all this when he has never been anywhere out of Attica. Then he will say that a letter has come from Antipater—'this is the

---

Plautus (Menander's Ἀλαζών) boasts of his exploits in Asia (Act I Sc 1, etc.).

11. **gemmed cups**] Compare Juvenal v 37 ff.:—'Ifi Virro's own hands are beakers on which the tears of the Sun-maidens have stiffened, and saucers embossed with beryl. *You* are not trusted with gold—or, when it is given to you, a sentinel is planted on the spot, to count the gems and watch your sharp nails. Excuse him; there is a fine and admired jasper there; for Virro, like many, shifts from his fingers to his cups those gems which the successful rival of jealous Iarbas used to put on the outside of his scabbard.' Golden cups inlaid with gems (φιάλαι λιθοκόλλητοι χρυσαῖ) are mentioned among the presents made to a favourite by the Persian king, Athen. II p. 48 § 31

13. **when he has never been anywhere out of Attica**] For ἡ πόλις, meaning, not Athens merely, but Athens with her territory, Attica, compare Ar. *Peace* 250: '*Poseidon.* Woe to thee, Sicily! How wilt thou, too, perish!—*Trygaeus.* How that poor country (πόλις) will be carded to shreds!' So 'seagirt cities' for 'islands' Aesch. *Eum.* 77.—So far from having seen the wonders of the East, the boaster has not even crossed Cithaeron or passed the Isthmus. The Athenian feeling against unnecessary travel receives intense expression in Plato's *Laws* (XII p. 950 A):—'It is the tendency of intercourse between cities to mix manners of the most various kinds, strangers inoculating each other with new-fangled notions (καινοτομίας ἐμποιούντων). Now this is likely to inflict upon a community well-governed under proper laws an injury more serious than any other; but to the majority of cities, as living under laws in no wise good, it is of no consequence that they are contaminated by welcoming strangers among themselves, and by flaunting forth (ἐπικωμάζοντας) in their own turn to other cities, whenever any man, young or old, takes a fancy for going abroad in any way or on any occasion.' It is then proposed (p. 950 D): 'In the first place, let no one *under forty years of age* be permitted to go abroad on any pretence whatever. Next, let absence from Athens *on private affairs* be permitted to no man: on public business, to heralds, embassies, and perhaps to some sacred missions.' Absence on military service is, of course, excepted. In the *Crito*, Socrates imagines the laws complimenting him on having never once left Attica on any *private* business (p. 52 B).

14. **Antipater**] The reference is probably to that period (322—319 B.C.) during which Antipater was absolute master of Athens. When Alexander went to Asia in 334 B.C. Antipater was left regent of Macedonia; and on the king's death in 323 he was reappointed to that

αὐτὸν εἰς Μακεδονίαν, καὶ διδομένης αὐτῷ ἐξαγωγῆς ξύλων
15 ἀτελοῦς, ὅτι ἀπείρηται, ὅπως μηδ᾽ ὑφ᾽ ἑνὸς συκοφαντηθῇ
περαιτέρω φίλος ὢν πλεῖν ἢ προσήκει Μακεδόσι· καὶ ἐν τῇ
σιτοδείᾳ δὲ ὡς πλείω ἢ πέντε τάλαντα αὐτῷ γένοιτο τὰ ἀνα-
λώματα διδόντι τοῖς ἀπόροις τῶν πολιτῶν· ἀνανεύειν γὰρ
οὐ δύνασθαι. καὶ ἀγνώτων δὲ παρακαθημένων κελεῦσαι
20 θεῖναι τὰς ψήφους ἕνα αὐτῶν, καὶ ποσῶν καθ᾽ ἑξακοσίας καὶ
κατὰ μνᾶν καὶ προστιθεὶς πιθανῶς ἑκάστοις τούτων ὀνόματα
ποιῆσαι καὶ δέκα τάλαντα· καὶ τοῦτο φῆσαι εἰσενηνέχθαι
εἰς ἐράνους αὐτῷ, καὶ τὰς τριηραρχίας εἰπεῖν ὅτι οὐ τίθησιν
οὐδὲ τὰς λειτουργίας ὅσας λελειτούργηκε· καὶ προσ-
25 ελθὼν δὲ τοὺς ἵππους τοὺς ἀγαθοὺς τοῖς πωλοῦσι προσ-

post. A league of the Greek States, headed by Athens, was formed against him; and the Lamian war ensued. This was terminated by the Macedonian victory at Crannon in the autumn of 322. Athens, now helpless, accepted Antipater's terms; 12,000 of the poorer citizens were deported,—the richer remnant being little more than 9000; the leaders of the patriotic party, including Demosthenes and Hyperides, were banished; and a Macedonian garrison was quartered in the Peiraeus. In the following year (321) Antipater succeeded Perdiccas as supreme regent, and thus became actual head of the whole Macedonian empire. He died in the first half of 319, bequeathing the regency to Polyperchon. See c. xx, where there is a reference to the latter half of 319 B C (In the interval between the end of the Lamian war in October 322 and the death of Antipater in the first half of 319, Antipater was in Macedonia on three occasions only.—(1) late in 322, when his daughter was married to Craterus; (2) at the end of the winter, between the Aetolian war and the Asiatic expedition; and (3) between his return from Asia, early in 320, and his death. It was only on this last occasion that he stayed long enough in Macedonia to make it possible for the ἀλαζών to pretend that he had received three invitations from Antipater. See Cichorius in the Leipzig edition, p lvi f.)

16. privilege of exporting timber] from Macedonia, the great timber-market of Greece, to Athens Xen. *Hellen.* VI 1, 11 'Holding Macedonia, the country from which the Athenians import their timber, we shall of course be in a position to build many more ships than they can.' Compare the pseudo-Demosth Speech 'On the Treaty with Alexander,' p. 219 § 28 (in reference to Alexander having asked leave to have some boats built at the Peiraeus): 'Of course it cannot be said that timber for shipbuilding is plentiful at Athens and has failed in Macedonia,— the country which supplies it on the cheapest terms to any foreigners who require it.' When Brasidas took Amphipolis in 424 B.C. one of the causes of the alarm at Athens was that that city was useful 'in sending them timber for ship building' (Thuc. IV 108).

16. free of duty] i.e. free of the Macedonian duty upon exports. It is improbable that Antipater would have interfered to remit the Athenian tax (two-per-cent, πεντηκοστή, Boeckh *P.E.* III 4) on imports: besides this would have been called εἰσαγωγή, rather than ἐξαγωγή, ἀτελής. Compare Andocides *de Reditu* p. 21 § 11: 'I supplied your army at Samos

THE BOASTFUL MAN. VI (XXIII)

third'—requiring his presence in Macedonia; and that, though he was offered the privilege of exporting timber free of duty, he has declined it, that no person whatever may be able to traduce him further for being more friendly than is becoming with Macedonia. He will state, too, that in the famine his outlay came to more than five talents in presents to the distressed citizens; ('he never could say No';) and actually, although the persons sitting near him are strangers, he will request one of them to set up the counters; when, reckoning by sums of six hundred drachmas or of a mina, and plausibly assigning names to each of these, he will make a total of as many as ten talents. This, he will say, was what he contributed in the way of charities; adding that he does not count any of the trierarchies or public services which he has performed. Also he will go up to the sellers of the best horses, and pretend that he desires to

---

—the Four Hundred having already seized the government here—with spars for oars, as Archelaus (king of Macedon 413—399 B.C.) was a family friend of mine, and allowed me to cut down and export as many as I pleased.'

19. that no person whatever may be able to traduce him further] He alleges, as his motive for declining the offer, his wish to avoid the denunciations of informers, who might accuse him of having too close relations with the Macedonian government. As Athens was at this time absolutely subject to Antipater, who had taken vigorous measures to clear it of all but Macedonian partisans, these fears may appear strange. But a fact noticed by Plutarch shows that, heavy as was the yoke, enough of public spirit was stirring beneath it to cause at least a general impatience. In 319 B.C.—three years after the introduction of the Macedonian garrison—the Athenians were importuning (ἐνοχλούντων) Phocion to intercede with Antipater for its removal (Plut. *Phoc.* c. 30). In such a state of the public mind the reception of special favours from the regent might well be a dangerous distinction.

19. (in the famine] Probably that of 330—326 B.C. Cp Dem., Or. 34 § 39, and A. Schaefer, *Dem. u. s Zeit*, III 295^2.)

20. in presents to the distressed citizens] On these charities, ἔρανοι, see note on c. V, 14.

23. to set up the counters] See note on c. IV, 19.

23. reckoning by sums of six hundred drachmas] 100 drachmas = 1 mina: 60 minas = 1 talent. The boastful man first states that he has given 'more than five talents' (about £1200) in charity He then proceeds to verify his statement. Taking the counting-board, he arranges the counters in small groups to represent the items—' 600 drachmas (= 6 minas, about £24) to A; one mina, £4, to B'; and so forth. When at last the items are cast up, they make a total of more than £2400, instead of £1200, and it becomes evident that his first estimate was prompted by excessive modesty.

27. trierarchies or public services] See note on c. XXIX, 26

29. the best horses] At Athens horses were in a special sense what Aeschylus calls them—'ornaments of wealth' (*P V.* 474). The keeping of

ποιήσασθαι ὠνητιᾶν· καὶ ἐπὶ τὰς κλίνας ἐλθὼν ἱματισμὸν ζητῆσαι εἰς δύο τάλαντα, καὶ τῷ παιδὶ μάχεσθαι ὅτι τὸ χρυσίον οὐκ ἔχων αὐτῷ ἀκολουθεῖ· καὶ ἐν μισθωτῇ οἰκίᾳ οἰκῶν φῆσαι ταύτην εἶναι τὴν πατρῴαν πρὸς τὸν μὴ εἰδότα, 30 καὶ ὅτι μέλλει πωλεῖν αὐτὴν διὰ τὸ ἐλάττω εἶναι αὐτῷ πρὸς τὰς ξενοδοχίας.

μικροφιλοτιμίας ζ'.

ἡ δὲ μικροφιλοτιμία δόξειεν ἂν εἶναι ὄρεξις τιμῆς ἀνελεύθερος, ὁ δὲ μικροφιλότιμος τοιοῦτός τις οἷος σπουδάσαι ἐπὶ δεῖπνον κληθεὶς παρ' αὐτὸν τὸν καλέσαντα κατακείμενος δειπνῆσαι· καὶ τὸν υἱὸν ἀποκεῖραι ἀγαγὼν εἰς Δελφούς· καὶ

horses, especially for the great contests, seems to have been regarded as in a manner a duty which was incumbent upon rich men—their proper contribution to the public splendour. See Demosth. *adv. Phaenipp.* p. 1046 § 14: 'In one thing only can Phaenippus the defendant be proved to have shown public spirit towards you, judges: he is a good and spirited owner of horses (ἱππoτρόφος... φιλότιμος)'—where the irony does not disturb the fact that, in the popular view, this *was* public spirit. Compare Xen. *Hipparch.* I 12: '(you may win over parents) by explaining this to them,—that their sons will be forced to keep horses, if not by you, by their fortune; but that, if they begin to ride under your auspices, you will deter them from giving extravagant or mad (μανικῶν) prices for horses.' Miltiades was 'of a house which kept four-horse chariots' (for the contests: Her. VI 35). Some of the good breeds were branded in the flank (ἐν ἰσχίοις, Anacr. 28, 2). The 'samphoras' and 'koppatias' (marked with the old letters san ⟩ and koppa ϙ) are known from the *Clouds* 23, 122: and Strabo mentions a 'wolf' brand in Italy (V 1, 9) The 'koppatias' of Pheidippides cost 12 minas, about £48 (*Clouds* 23) the same sum is the value of a horse in Lysias *de maled.* p. 133 § 10 In the speech of Isaeus *de Dicaeog. hered.* the rival claimant is taunted thus: 'You have never possessed a horse worth more than 3 minas' (£12: p. 55 § 43).

30 **the upholstery mart**] In that part of the market-place where the frames (κλῖναι) of couches and beds were sold, the coverlets, rugs, pillows—everything included in the term ἱματισμός, 'bedding'—could probably be bought too. Luxurious drapery for couches was a specially eastern luxury; thus, when Artaxerxes sent Themistocles 'a silver-footed bed and costly coverings,' he sent therewith 'a person to strew them; observing that the Greeks did not understand bed-making' (οὐκ ἐπίστασθαι ὑποστρωννύειν, Athen. II p. 48 § 31). In the *Frogs* (V 544) 'coverlets from Miletus' are mentioned; the same which are said in the *Georgics* to be 'of great price' (III 306). It was specially noted as a sign of the degeneracy of Spartan manners when they began 'to use coverings for their couches of the present large size and costly workmanship, superbly embroidered; so that some of the guests invited shrank

buy; or, visiting the upholstery mart, he will ask to see draperies to the value of two talents, and quarrel with his slave for having come out without gold. When he is living in a hired house he will say (to any one who does not know better) that it is the family mansion; but that he means to sell it, as he finds it too small for his entertainments.

VII (XXI). THE MAN OF PETTY AMBITION.

Petty Ambition would seem to be a mean craving for distinction.

The man of Petty Ambition is one who, when asked to dinner, will be anxious to be placed next to the host at table. He will take his son away to Delphi to have his hair cut. He

---

from resting their elbows on the cushions' (Athen. IV p. 142 § 20).

1. **Petty Ambition**] Compare with this character what Aristotle says of the χαῦνοι, or Vain (*Eth. N.* IV 3).—'They set themselves off with dress and outward show (σχήματι) and the like, and wish their advantages to be manifest, and talk about them, as if they expected to receive honour by means of these things.' But the μικροφιλότιμος does not necessarily, like the χαῦνος, overrate *himself*; he only overrates those things on which he founds his claim to honour. In ostentation, again, he resembles the ἀλαζών. But *he* places honour in the trifles which he really possesses; the ἀλαζών, in greater things which he does not possess. If some editors had not maintained that part of this chapter suits the ἄρεσκος (see *Crit. App* VII 1), it would have seemed needless to point out the wide difference between the characters. The complaisant man desires to be popular for what he is; the μικροφιλότιμος, to be admired for what he has.

4. **placed next to the host**] Plutarch says (*Quaest. Conv.* I 3, 1):—'Different places (at table) are honourable with different nations....With the Greeks, the first. With the Romans, the last place on the middle couch, which they call the consular.' Here, as the context shows, 'the first' place, said to be that of honour among the Greeks, must mean the first on the first couch; and if Plutarch and Theophrastus are to be reconciled, it must be supposed that the host was second on the first couch. In Plato's *Symposium*, however, Agathon, the host, is placed on the last or lowest couch,— ἔσχατος κατακείμενος (p. 175 C); as the Roman host was usually *summus in imo* (though in Hor. S 2, 8, 20 *medius in imo*). Probably there was no invariable custom.—Contests for precedence at table supply Lucian with some good touches. See the *Dialogues of the gods* c. 13 '*Zeus*. Cease, Asclepius and Heracles, quarrelling like men These things are unseemly and improper at the dinner-table of the gods. *Heracles.* But Zeus, would you have this druggist recline at table above me? *Zeus.* Cease, I repeat, and do not disturb our party Heracles, you may well allow Asclepius to take precedence of you. He died first.'

5. **to Delphi to have his hair cut**] On completing his 16th year (Bekker, *Anecd.* 255) an Athenian boy became technically

ΜΙΚΡΟΦΙΛΟΤΙΜΙΑC Ζ'

5 ἐπιμεληθῆναι δὲ ὅπως αὐτῷ ὁ ἀκόλουθος Αἰθίοψ ἔσται· καὶ ἀποδιδοὺς μνᾶν ἀργυρίου καινὸν ποιῆσαι ἀποδοῦναι· καὶ πλειστάκις δὲ ἀποκείρασθαι καὶ τοὺς ὀδόντας λευκοὺς ἔχειν· καὶ τὰ ἱμάτια δὲ χρηστὰ μεταβάλλεσθαι καὶ χρίσματι ἀλείφεσθαι· καὶ τῆς μὲν ἀγορᾶς πρὸς τὰς τραπέζας προσ-
10 φοιτᾶν, τῶν δὲ γυμνασίων ἐν τούτοις διατρίβειν οὗ ἂν ἔφηβοι γυμνάζωνται, τοῦ δὲ θεάτρου καθῆσθαι, ὅταν ᾖ θέα, πλησίον τῶν στρατηγῶν· καὶ ἀγοράζειν αὐτῷ μὲν μηδὲν, ξένοις δὲ ἐπιστάλματα εἰς Βυζάντιον ἁλμάδας καὶ Λακωνικὰς κύνας εἰς Κύζικον καὶ μέλι Ὑμήττιον εἰς Ῥόδον, καὶ ταῦτα

'a youth,' ἔφηβος (though the δοκιμασία on his *formal* enrolment among the ἔφηβοι did not take place till the 18th year)[1]. His long hair was then cut off, and a lock dedicated (usually) to some river-god,—as Orestes, in Aeschylus, offers his to the Inachus (*Cho.* 6); the first-fruits of the living body being thus symbolically offered to water, 'nourisher of youth' (κουροτρόφος). Athen. XI p. 495 § 88· 'Youths about to cut off the lock offer to Heracles a large cup filled with wine, which they call Oinisteria; and, having poured a libation, give it to the company to drink.' The old custom was to offer the lock to Apollo at Delphi —a place especially suitable to the rite in its inner meaning, since the abundance of *water* there was probably the chief reason for which Delphi was chosen as the central seat of worship (Curtius *Hist. Gr.* bk II c. 4). Compare Plut. *Thes.* c. 5 'It being at that time still the custom that those who were passing out of boyhood into youth should go to Delphi and offer to the god a lock of their hair, Theseus went thither; and from him they say that a spot is still called the Thesea.'

6. **an Aethiopian**] The intercourse with the East then recently opened by Alexander's expedition had brought back slaves into fashion. Compare Alciphro's *Letters* (which refer to this period) II 2, 5: 'From that moment he has not ceased sending me every kind of luxury,—dresses, gold ornaments, maids, footmen, Indians male and female.' In the *Rhetorica ad Herennium* (prob. of Cicero's age) the pretender to wealth directs his slave to borrow an Aethiopian, and come for him to the baths (IV 50, 63).

8. **his hair cut very frequently**] See note on c. XXIV, 27.

10. **anoint himself with unguent**] Instead of using (at the baths or the gymnasium) plain olive-oil, he uses a thick perfumed unguent, χρίσμα. See Xen. *Anab.* IV 4, 13: 'Abundant material for unguent (χρῖμα) was found in the place, which they used instead of olive-oil (ἀντ' ἐλαίου). It was obtained from hog's lard, sesame, bitter almonds, and terebinths. The latter supplied also a liquid perfume (μύρον).'—In Xenophon's *Symposium* II 3 the host proposes after dinner to send for μύρον. Socrates objects, observing that 'the olive-oil used in the gymnasia' is the only one which it befits a *man* to use.

11. **the bankers' tables**] A fashionable lounge. Plat. *Apol.* p. 17 C: 'Do not be surprised' (Socrates says) 'if you hear me defending myself in the same terms which I am wont to use in the market-place at the bankers' tables, where most of you have heard me.' Plutarch *de Garrul.* § 21 gives examples of the three kinds of reply which may be made to the question 'Is Socrates at home?' (1) The necessary; as 'Not at home.'

[1] Cp Aristotle's *Constitution of Athens*, c. 42

THE MAN OF PETTY AMBITION. VII (XXI) 63

will be careful, too, that his attendant shall be an Aethiopian: and, when he pays a mina, he will cause the slave to pay the sum in new coin. Also he will have his hair cut very frequently, and will keep his teeth white; he will change his clothes, too, while still good; and will anoint himself with unguent. In the market-place he will frequent the bankers' tables; in the gymnasia he will haunt those places where the young men take exercise; in the theatre, when there is a representation, he will sit near the Generals. For himself he will buy nothing, but will make purchases on commission for foreign friends—pickled olives to go to Byzantium, Laconian hounds for Cyzicus, Hymettian

(2) The polite; as 'Not at home; he is at the bankers' tables.' (3) The superfluous; as 'Not at home. He is at the bankers' tables, awaiting some Ionian strangers, for whom'—etc. etc.

12. **where the young men take exercise**] Besides the palaestras or wrestling-schools, Athens had at this time three large gymnasia, provided with wrestling-rooms, baths, grounds for running and javelin practice, etc.—the Lyceum, the Cynosarges, and the Academy. These were open to persons of all ages; but separate parts were assigned to adults (i.e. persons above 20), ephebi (18—20), and boys. The ephebeum was a large hall with seats placed round it, opening off the colonnade which ran round the great court of the gymnasium. Here the best performances would generally be seen, and here, consequently, the man of petty ambition would find himself where he always desired to be—in the most popular resort.

13. **near the Generals**] In the *Birds* (794) Aristophanes mentions τὸ βουλευτικόν, 'the senatorial places' in the theatre near the orchestra; and in the *Wasps* (575) the Strategi of that day are described as sticklers for their 'places of honour.' But it would seem that the seats for high officials were not very definitely marked off. See Demosth. *in Meid.* p. 572 § 178, where the πάρεδρος or coadjutor of the archon lays hands upon a person who 'was taking possession of a place' (θέαν καταλαμβάνοντος) and attempts to expel him from the theatre. The incident shows that the public had access to the immediate neighbourhood of the official seats. In Plato's time a place in the 'orchestra-circle' could be obtained for 'a drachma at the most' (10*d*.: *Apol.* p. 26 E). Compare Hor. *Ep.* I 1, 67·

Grow rich, grow rich by fair means or by all,
And view sad Pupius from a nearer stall.

16. **Laconian hounds**] A small breed of red dog (*fulvus* Laco, Hor. *Epod.* 6, 5), which the ancients supposed to have been got by a cross with a fox (Arist. *H. A.* VIII 27). Pindar (*frag.* 73) speaks of 'the Laconian hounds, in chasing wild beasts keenest of all things that move', Sophocles (*Aj.* 8) gives them the epithet 'true-scenting'; Virgil praises 'Sparta's swift small hounds' (*Georg.* III 405). Compare the *Midsummer Night's Dream* IV, 1, 'My hounds are bred out of the Spartan kind .A cry more tunable Was never holla'd to nor cheered with horn In Crete, in Sparta, nor in Thessaly.'

16 **Cyzicus**] in Mysia on the Propontis; once a dependency of Athens. The treaty of Antalcidas (387 B.C.) gave it, with the other towns of Asia, to the Persian king. At the death of Alexander it fell under the government of Leonnatus; and on his death in 322 under that of Antigonus.

ΜΙΚΡΟΦΙΛΟΤΙΜΙΑΣ Ζ'

15 ποιῶν τοῖς ἐν τῇ πόλει διηγεῖσθαι. ἀμέλει δὲ καὶ πίθηκον θρέψαι δεινὸς καὶ τίτυρον κτήσασθαι καὶ Σικελικὰς περιστερὰς καὶ δορκαδείους ἀστραγάλους καὶ Θουριακὰς τῶν στρογγύλων ληκύθους καὶ βακτηρίας τῶν σκολιῶν ἐκ Λακεδαίμονος καὶ αὐλαίαν ἔχουσαν Πέρσας ἐνυφασμένους καὶ
20 αὐλίδιον παλαιστριαῖον κόνιν ἔχον καὶ σφαιριστήριον, καὶ τοῦτο περιϊὼν χρῆσαι τοῖς φιλοσόφοις, τοῖς σοφισταῖς, τοῖς ὁπλομάχοις, τοῖς ἁρμονικοῖς ἐπιδείκνυσθαι· καὶ αὐτὸς ἐν ταῖς

---

19. **a satyr ape**] a kind of short-tailed ape, to which the Greeks gave the name of *tityrus*. The *Tityri*, mythical companions of Dionysus, are sometimes identified with, sometimes distinguished from the Satyrs. There was also a kind of ape called σάτυρος (Ael. *H.A.* 16, 21: Plin. *H.N.* IV VIII 54, etc.): whether it was the same as the *tityrus*, does not appear. (In the Leipzig edition of 1897 it is suggested that the *tityrus* may have been a kind of bird, mentioned in Hesychius. But its identification as 'a short-tailed ape' is supported by *Scholia* in the Paris MS B and in the Munich Epitome, doubtless derived from a similar *scholium* on Theocritus (Diels, *Theophrastea*, pp. 15, 18).)

19. **Sicilian doves**] Philemon, the comic poet (circ. 330 B.C), praises Sicily, among other things, for its doves (Athen XIV p 658 § 76). And Nicander (circ 160 B.C.) is quoted in Athen. IX p 395 § 51 as saying, 'keep wheat-fed pigeons in thy house, or doves of Sicily, whom neither hawk nor falcon vexes.'

19. **deer-horn dice**] The ἀστράγαλοι mentioned here (*tali*) were numbered on four sides, the other two being round: the κύβοι (*tesserae*) on all six. Astragali, as the name implies, were properly knuckle-bones; here they are of the horn of the gazelle (δορκάς). In Athen. V p 194 § 22 it is said that the capricious temper of Antiochus Epiphanes used to show itself in the unequal value of his presents:—'to some he would give deer-horn dice,—to others, dates,—to others, gold.' In Lucian *Amor.* c. 16 a disconsolate lover amuses himself by throwing (to obtain an omen) 'four dice of the horn of the African gazelle (Λιβυκῆς δορκός).' ('Deer-horn dice' are included in an inventory of the temple of Asclepius for 339—8 B.C., *Corp. Inscr. Att.* II 766, 23.)

19. **Thurian vases**] 'Thurian' vases are not mentioned elsewhere The peculiar shape meant by στρογγύλος is explained by the description of an olive-jar in Appuleius *Flor.* I 9, 35 as 'onion-shaped' (*lenticulari forma*), 'round and squat' (*pressula rotunditate*=στρογγύλος).

20. **walking-sticks with the true Laconian curve**] The custom of carrying a walking-stick seems to have been regarded at Athens as especially Spartan. In the *Ecclesiasusae* (74) the women provide themselves with 'Laconian walking-sticks and men's dresses.' The fashion must have been common; for the invalid in the speech of Lysias (*de Inval* p. 169 § 12) speaks of himself as 'using two walking-sticks, while *other people* use one.' The painter Parrhasius—a contemporary of Lysias—who affected personal splendour, is described as 'leaning on a cane studded with gold rings' (Athen. XII p. 543 § 62). In Demosth. *adv. Pant.* p. 982, however, 'carrying a walking-stick' is mentioned as an offensive trait; either as suggesting an affectation of Spartanism, or as a mark of dandyism: see note on c. IV, 11.

21. **a curtain**] a piece of tapestry hung on the walls of his dining-room. The tapestry which fell at the dinner-

THE MAN OF PETTY AMBITION. VII (XXI)

honey for Rhodes; and will talk thereof to people at Athens. Also he is very much the person to keep a monkey; to get a satyr ape, Sicilian doves, deerhorn dice, Thurian vases of the approved rotundity, walking-sticks with the true Laconian curve, and a curtain with Persians embroidered upon it. He will have a little court provided with an arena for wrestling and a ball-alley, and will go about lending it to philosophers, sophists, drill-sergeants, musicians, for their displays; at which he himself

---

party of Nasidienus, and showered dust upon the table, was probably hung on the walls: Hor. *S.* II 8, 54. Horace speaks of 'the dinners of *poor* men without tapestries or purple'· *Od.* III 29, 14.—The subject of the embroidery is a victory of Greeks over Persians, as the Painted Porch at Athens (c. 1 l. 6) was 'frescoed with the trowsered Medes'; and as, in the Roman theatre (Virg. *Geo.* III 25), 'Wrought on the gorgeous curtain, Britons rise.'

22. a little court provided with an arena] Xen. *de Rep Athen.* II 10: 'Rich men have in some cases *private gymnasia* and baths with dressing-rooms.'

22. ball-alley] Various games with the hand-ball were popular in Greece; and a public gymnasium probably always included a σφαιριστήριον. Horace tells us that he used to play 'the three-cornered game' (of catching the ball) before taking the bath. *S.* I 6, 126.

23. to philosophers] for a conversazione, such as in the *Protagoras* takes place at the house of Callias; where Socrates finds Protagoras pacing the colonnades with his 'sacred band' (χορός) of disciples. Hippias and Prodicus are also there,—the latter quartered, so full is the house, in a store-room (*Prot.* p. 315 D). Plato's Callias is, in this respect, very much what the μικροφιλότιμος aspires to be. The arcades surrounding the court of a public gymnasium were fitted with seats (ἐξέδραι) and large semicircular benches (ἡμικύκλια) 'where philosophers, rhetoricians, and literary men in general could sit and converse' (Vitr. V 11, 2).

23. to sophists] i.e. to professors of rhetoric. As rhetoric was the most important branch of the encyclopaedic practical education which the 'sophists' professed to give, the term 'sophist' came to be more and more nearly identified with 'rhetorician', until, under the Empire, it appears as its recognised synonym. Thus the rhetorician Libanius (circ. 340 A.D.) is expressly styled 'the Sophist.' —The miniature gymnasium was lent to the philosopher for a conversazione, it is lent to the 'sophist' for a formal declamation, or for one of those continuous florid expositions in which these professors loved to indulge. Compare Juv. VII 39.

If to declaim is your aspiring bent,
Your patron's dingiest premises are lent.

24. drill-sergeants] who gave lessons in the use of the arms carried by the hoplite, i.e. the pike (δόρυ), the short sword, and the large oblong shield (ὅπλον). Thus they were not mere fencing-masters, but, like the Roman *campidoctores*, drill-sergeants. The scene of Plato's *Laches* is laid at the place where one of these men had just been displaying his dexterity (ἐπιδεικνύμενον, p. 171 E); and the professional teaching of drill for money is there, as in the *Euthydemus* p. 272 D, spoken of as something new. Athenaeus quotes a statement that 'scientific fence under arms' (ὁπλομαχίας μαθήσεις) was first taught by one Dameas of Mantinea (IV p 154 § 4). Compare Plut *an seni ger. s. resp.* c. 18 p. 793 D: 'We do not leave our bodies absolutely without exercise when we can no longer use spades or

J. T.

ΜΙΚΡΟΦΙΛΟΤΙΜΙΑΣ Ζ'

ἐπιδείξεσιν ὕστερον ἐπεισιέναι ἐπὶ <τῷ εἰπεῖν τὸν ἕτερον>
τῶν θεωμένων πρὸς τὸν ἕτερον ὅτι τούτου ἐστὶν ἡ παλαίστρα·
25 καὶ βοῦν θύσας τὸ προμετωπίδιον ἀπαντικρὺ τῆς εἰσόδου
προσπατταλῶσαι, στέμμασι μεγάλοις περιδήσας, ὅπως οἱ
εἰσιόντες ἴδωσιν ὅτι βοῦν ἔθυσε· καὶ πομπεύσας μετὰ τῶν
ἱππέων τὰ μὲν ἄλλα πάντα δοῦναι τῷ παιδὶ ἀπενεγκεῖν
οἴκαδε, ἀναβαλόμενος δὲ θοἰμάτιον ἐν τοῖς μύωψι κατὰ τὴν
30 ἀγορὰν περιπατεῖν. καὶ κολοιῷ δὲ ἔνδον τρεφομένῳ δεινὸς
κλιμάκιον πρίασθαι καὶ ἀσπίδιον χαλκοῦν ποιῆσαι, ὃ ἔχων
ἐπὶ τοῦ κλιμακίου ὁ κολοιὸς πηδήσεται· καὶ κυναρίου δὲ
Μελιταίου τελευτήσαντος αὐτῷ μνῆμα καὶ στηλίδιον ποιήσας
ἐπιγράψαι ΚΛΑΔΟΣ ΜΕΛΙΤΑΙΟΣ· καὶ ἀναθεὶς δακτύλιον

jumping-weights (ἁλτῆρες, to give an impetus), or throw the quoit, or *fight under arms* (ὁπλομαχεῖν). To the Greek States, which (except Sparta) had only a militia subject to little constant discipline, the professional drill-sergeants would be useful: comp. note on c. x, 9.

24. **musicians**] Stratonicus, a contemporary of Theophrastus, is said to have been the first who made the advance from the playing of the cithara without any accompaniment (ψιλὴ κιθάρισις) to symphony (πολυχορδία), and took pupils in concerted music (ἁρμονικῶν), and constructed a score (διάγραμμα): Athen VIII p. 352 § 46. We ought probably to understand ἁρμονικοί here of this symphony-playing—then a novelty.

28. **the skin of the forehead**] For the meaning of the Greek word, see Her. VII 70 'They had upon their heads the *forehead-skins* (προμετωπίδια) of horses, *flayed off* with the ears and mane.' The skin of the victim's forehead is hung up, with garlands round it, over the doorway leading from the vestibule (πρόθυρον) into the court of the house. (In later writers it is called βουκράνιον, a term adopted in modern archaeological literature. The skin of the forehead is included in the cut reproduced on p. 175 of the Leipzig edition from Conze's *Archaologische Untersuchungen auf Samothrake*, I pl. 62) Compare, for the form of the ostentation, Ar *Acharnians* 989: 'He has thrown out these feathers before his door as a sample of his fare' (i e to inform passers-by that he has had game for dinner).

30. **a procession of the knights**] The 1200 knights, commanded by the two Hipparchs and by the ten Phylarchs of the tribes, paraded publicly on several occasions. These occasions were chiefly of three classes: (1) the great festivals, especially the Panathenaea, to which the Chorus of Knights in Aristophanes allude, saying that their fathers were 'worthy of the *robe*' (*Kn.* 566): and the Dionysia, Xen. *Hipparch.* 3 § 2. (2) Certain periodical reviews, held, according to Xenophon, in four places,—in the grounds of the Lyceum, in the grounds of the Academy; in the hippodrome; and at the port of Phalerum: Xen. *Hipp.* 3, 1. (3) Special occasions of public rejoicing or mourning, when the goddess on the acropolis was to be thanked or entreated —The Roman Knights had but one annual ceremony corresponding to this; the *transvectio*, on the ides of July, to the temple of Castor in the forum from the temple of Mars without the wall.

32 **putting on his cloak**] In the procession a mantle (χλαμύς), instead of

THE MAN OF PETTY AMBITION. VII (XXI)

will appear upon the scene rather late, in order that the spectators may say one to another, 'This is the owner of the palaestra.' When he has sacrificed an ox, he will nail up the skin of the forehead, wreathed with large garlands, opposite the entrance, in order that those who come in may see that he has sacrificed an ox. When he has been taking part in a procession of the knights, he will give the rest of his accoutrements to his slave to carry home; but, after putting on his cloak, will walk about the market-place in his spurs. He is apt, also, to buy a little ladder for his domestic jackdaw, and to make a little brass shield, wherewith the jackdaw shall hop upon the ladder. Or if his little Melitean dog has died, he will put up a little memorial slab, with the inscription, A SCION OF MELITA. If he

the ordinary cloak, was probably worn,—'purple and embroidered' acc. to the Schol. on Ar. *Knights* 566; as the Roman Knights paraded in the *trabea* or toga with purple stripes. The μικροφιλότιμος does not shock public taste by walking about in this. He resumes his ordinary cloak (ἱμάτιον), and leaves the clinking of his spurs to hint the circumstance of which he is vain. (Originally only a single spur was used, Xenophon, *de re equestri*, 8, 5. The text is the earliest authority for two.)

(34 f. **a little brass shield, wherewith the jackdaw shall hop upon the ladder**] On p 166 of the Leipzig edition there is a reproduction of a painting on a vase at Athens, Collignon's Catalogue, no 566, representing a small crested bird, with its wing protected by a round shield The note on p 168 mentions a gem, with a crane on the point of climbing a ladder)

36. **his little Melitean dog**] Plin. *H. N.* III 26: 'Next comes Corcyra, called Melaena (the Black), between which and Illyricum is Melita, from which Callimachus (circ. 280 B C) states that the little "Melitean" dogs take their name' The Black Corcyra is now Curzola; and this Melita is the long, narrow island S.E. of it, now called Meleda, in N. lat. 42, close to the eastern shore of the Adriatic. On these islands see Sir G Wilkinson's *Dalmatia and Montenegro*, I p. 257. This old account preserved by Pliny is more to be trusted than Strabo's (VI 2) remark that Malta was the home of the breed,—a natural guess. 'Melitean' dogs had all the privileges of the modern lap-dog. In Lucian *de merced. cond.* § 34, a lady requests a philosopher to carry 'Myrrhine': 'It was absurd to see the little dog peeping out of his cloak just under his chin, and barking in her small voice (such is the Melitean breed), and licking the philosopher's beard.' One of Alciphro's *Letters* expresses a slave's terror at the accidental poisoning of 'Plangon, the little Melitean dog which we keep as a tame pet for the mistress' (III 22). (A vase-painting in the *Annali dell' Instituto*, 1852 T, reproduced in Edmonds and Austen's edition, p. 30, exhibits an Athenian youth taking a walk with his dog in front of him. Above the dog is the inscription, Μελιταίε.)

(36 f. **a little memorial slab**] In the *Anthologia Palatina*, VII 211, we have the epitaph of a 'Melitean' dog Several Greek inscriptions on pet-dogs are cited by Mr E. L. Hicks in the *Journal of Hellenic Studies*, III 130 f, where it is suggested that we should either make Κλάδος the name of the dog, or alter it into κάλλος. On p. 165 of the Leipzig edition we have a reproduction of a Lycian tablet carved with the figure of a small dog seated above his epitaph)

37. **a scion of Melita**] The master

68   ΜΙΚΡΟΦΙΛΟΤΙΜΙΑC Ζ´

35 χαλκοῦν ἐν τῷ Ἀσκληπιοῦ τοῦτον ἐκτρίβειν στιλπνῶν καὶ
ἀλείφων ὁσημέραι. ἀμέλει δὲ καὶ συνδιοικήσασθαι παρὰ
τῶν πρυτάνεων ὅπως ἀπαγγείλῃ τῷ δήμῳ τὰ ἱερά, καὶ παρα-
σκευασάμενος λαμπρὸν ἱμάτιον καὶ ἐστεφανωμένος παρελθὼν
εἰπεῖν· ὦ ἄνδρες Ἀθηναῖοι, ἐθύομεν οἱ πρυτάνεις τῇ μητρὶ
40 τῶν θεῶν τὰ ἱερὰ ἄξια καὶ καλά· καὶ ὑμεῖς δέχεσθε τὰ
ἀγαθά· καὶ ταῦτα ἀπαγγείλας ἀπιὼν διηγήσασθαι οἴκαδε τῇ
αὑτοῦ γυναικί, ὡς καθ᾽ ὑπερβολὴν εὐημερεῖ.

desires to proclaim that his dog was of the choice Melitean breed, and this he does in a characteristically high-flown phrase. Compare with κλάδος the poetical use of ἔρνος, θάλος, ὄζος, πτόρθος. On the conjecture καλός for κλάδος, see *Crit.App.*

38. **a brass ring**] Probably one of those which were worn as amulets, and which were supposed to have a protecting, or, for the sick, a healing virtue. The invalid, having recovered, dedicates to Asclepius the ring which, by the god's blessing, has helped to cure him. Compare Ar. *Plutus* 881: '*Informer.* Where have you got this cloak? *Just Man.* I do not care for you, for I wear this ring which I bought from Eudemus for tenpence *Inf.* But there is no charm against an informer's bite.' Clemens Alex. *Strom.* I p 334 B: 'Execestus the tyrant of the Phocians used to wear two charmed rings (γεγοητευμένους), and could discern from their clink against each other the right moments for action. He died, however, by the hand of an assassin; though not before the clink had warned him, as saith Aristotle in his Polity of the Phocians' (Hicks, *l.c.*, 133, notices the rings of gold and iron in a treasure-list of the Parthenon, 398 B.C. It has, however, been suggested that we should here accept the proposal to alter δακτύλιον into δάκτυλον, the votive offering of a bronze representation of a finger being specially appropriate in a 'temple of Asclepius.' Such fingers are actually mentioned in an inventory of the Asclepieum at Athens. See *Crit. App.*

A votive finger found in Cyprus is figured in Schreiber's *Atlas*, XV 11.)

38. **in the temple of Asclepius**] The Athenian Asclepieum stood on the slope of the Acropolis at the s.w. corner: Paus. I 21, 4. Plutarch, inquiring why the Roman temples of Aesculapius are always outside the city walls, observes that 'the Greeks have their temples of Asclepius placed on open and tolerably high ground; and that his great Hellenic shrine —that at Epidaurus—was at some distance from the town' (*Quaest. Rom.* § 94 p. 286 D). This circumstance may have assisted the efficacy which a brief sojourn at the god's temple was supposed to have for invalids. Paus. II 27, 6 3.

39. **daily burnishings and oilings**] The μικροφιλότιμος, having dedicated a ring which, like that in Aristophanes (see n. 38), is worth perhaps tenpence, visits the temple daily in order to see that it is kept in a state creditable to the donor.

40. **from the presidents of the Senate**] Public sacrifices on behalf of the state were frequently offered by the Senate of Five-Hundred, the members of the presiding section (πρυτάνεις) conducting the ceremony. The place was probably either the Prytaneum adjoining the Senate-House on the north side, or the Metroum (temple of the Mother of the gods) on its south side. That the occasions were frequent appears from Antipho *de choreut* p. 146 § 45, where the duty of 'conducting rites (ἱεροποιεῖν) and sacrificing on behalf of the democracy' is spoken of as one which the

has dedicated a brass ring in the temple of Asclepius, he will wear it to a wire with daily burnishings and oilings. It is just like him, too, to obtain from the presidents of the Senate by private arrangement the privilege of reporting the sacrifice to the people; when, having provided himself with a smart white cloak and put on a wreath, he will come forward and say: 'Athenians! we, the presidents of the Senate, have been sacrificing to the Mother of the Gods meetly and auspiciously, receive ye her good gifts!' Having made this announcement he will go home to his wife and declare that he is supremely fortunate

---

prytanis had *repeatedly* performed during his five weeks of office.

41. the privilege of reporting the sacrifice] The more formal and systematic state-religion of Rome restricted the privilege of reporting the auspices (*nuntiatio*) to the magistrate who presided when they were taken; or to the augur who acted as his deputy. Here the μικροφιλότιμος obtains it as a personal favour; but, as appears from his address to the people, he was at least one of the fifty presidents of the Senate. (Hicks, *l. c.*, 135 f, points out that the public decrees of Athens, 'from the middle of the fourth century onwards, are full of μικροφιλοτιμία'; and that, in the inscriptions after 300 B.C., 'instead of the national concerns of Greece, we have reports of how such and such officials have performed certain sacrifices' 'The political importance of the prytanes' (or 'presidents of the Senate') 'having declined before the days of Theophrastus, it was natural that more prominence should be given to their religious functions.' 'Special mention is made of their Report of the favourable nature of their sacrifices.' 'In the time of Theophrastus, these Reports were taken as a matter of course.' But 'there were already individuals who were glad to make' them 'an occasion of personal parade,' *ib* 138—140)

42 a smart white cloak and wreath] Aesch. *in Ctes.* p. 46 § 77 (speaking of the joy shown by Demosthenes at the death of Philip): 'Though his daughter was but a week dead, before he had mourned for her or discharged the fitting rites, he put on a garland, clad himself in white, and proceeded to offer burnt sacrifice.'

45. to the Mother of the Gods] In her temple on the east side of the Marketplace, immediately south of the Senate-House. Here were kept the graven tablets of the laws (Lycurg. *in Leocr.* p. 156 § 66) and the original drafts of the decrees of the Ecclesia (Aesch. *in Ctes.* p. 80 § 187). Athenio (afterwards leader of the Servile war) is said to have stolen some of these αὐτόγραφα from the Metroum during a popular tumult (Ath. V p. 214 § 53). (See also Pausanias I 3, 5, with Frazer's note.)

46. receive ye her good gifts] A regular formula. See no. 54 of the προοίμια, or exordia for public speeches, ascribed (though improbably) to Demosthenes.—'Our (senatorial) province has been duly discharged for you. We have sacrificed to Zeus the Saviour, to Athene, and to Victory, and these sacrifices have been fair and prosperous for you. We have sacrificed also to Persuasion and to the Mother of the Gods and to Apollo; and here also the sacrifices were favourable. Receive, therefore, these blessings at the hands of the gods.'

ΟΨΙΜΑΘΙΑΣ Η΄

ὀψιμαθίας η΄.

ἡ δὲ ὀψιμαθία φιλοπονία δόξειεν ἂν εἶναι ὑπὲρ τὴν ἡλικίαν, ὁ δὲ ὀψιμαθὴς τοιοῦτός τις οἷος ῥήσεις μανθάνειν ἑξήκοντα ἔτη γεγονὼς καὶ ταύτας λέγων παρὰ πότον ἐπιλανθάνεσθαι· καὶ παρὰ τοῦ υἱοῦ μανθάνειν τὸ ἐπὶ δόρυ καὶ ἐπὶ
5 ἀσπίδα καὶ ἐπ' οὐράν· καὶ εἰς ἡρῷα συμβάλλεσθαι τοῖς μειρακίοις λαμπάδα τρέχειν. ἀμέλει δὲ κἄν που κληθῇ εἰς Ἡράκλειον, ῥίψας τὸ ἱμάτιον τὸν βοῦν αἴρειν ἵνα τραχηλίσῃ·

1. **Late-learning**] The man described here is one who, from whatever cause, was prevented in his youth from acquiring those accomplishments which were included in the Greek idea of a liberal education, and which belonged to one or other of its two higher branches,—'music' and 'gymnastics.' He comes in later life into the society of people with whom his early education places him at a disadvantage; and a sense of this makes him ambitious to repair the defect. Instead, however, of taking up self-culture at the point and in the branches which mature years prescribe, he falls into the error of M. Jourdain. He attempts to start afresh; to acquire, by sudden application, things which must be learned early and gradually; and which, even if they could be learned to good purpose now, demand more time than a man ought to spend in sacrificing to the graces.

Just as, in the man of Petty Ambition, the love of honour is made mean by a low estimate of what is honourable, so in the Late-Learner the desire γηράσκειν πολλὰ διδασκόμενος is made absurd by a wrong choice of studies. The best point in the character is its respect for culture, the weakest, its pride in accomplishments which seem precious because they have long been admired from a distance.

These were the ideas ordinarily conveyed by the word ὀψιμαθής,—a term analogous, from one point of view, to 'pedant.' Timaeus called Aristotle ὀψι-μαθῆ σοφιστήν, 'a pedantic sophist,' for presuming to criticise the Locrian polity (Polyb. XII 9, 4). Gellius notes the tendency to bring in new or obsolete words in writing and speaking as 'a vice of late-learning, which the Greeks call ὀψιμαθία' (XI 7, 3). 'You know how insolent,' says Cicero, 'are late-learners' (*Fam.* IX 20, 2). In ridiculing the taste for interlarding Latin with Greek, Horace himself sets an example of abstinence, by paraphrasing into *seri studiorum* the term for which his own language supplied no equivalent (*S.* 1, 10, 21)

3 **passages for recitation**] See note on c. III, 5.

5. '**Right Wheel**,' '**Left Wheel**'] To turn towards the right was to turn 'towards the spear-hand'; to the left, 'towards the shield-hand' (or, for cavalry, ἐπὶ ἡνίαν, 'towards the bridle-hand'). Thus Xen. *Cyr.* VII 5, 6, μετεβάλοντο ἐπ' ἀσπίδα, 'they wheeled to the left.' Xenophon often uses the phrases in reference to *slantwise* marching: e.g ἐπὶ δόρυ ἡγεῖσθαι, to lead one's men *on* their own right (*Anab.* IV 3, 26). See his *Lacon. Resp.* 11, 8: 'The Lacedaemonians do with the greatest ease even those things which drill-sergeants consider most difficult. When they are marching in column (ἐπὶ κέρως), one section (ἐνωμοτία) of a company is, of course, behind another Now if, at such a moment, the enemy appear in front in phalanx, the word is passed to the commander of each section

VIII (XXVII). THE LATE-LEARNER.

Late-learning would seem to mean the pursuit of exercises for which one is too old.

The Late-Learner is one who will study passages for recitation when he is sixty, and break down in repeating them over his wine. He will take lessons from his son in 'Right Wheel,' 'Left Wheel,' 'Right-about-face.' At the festivals of heroes he will match himself against the boys for a torch-race; nay, it is just like him, if haply he is invited to a temple of Heracles, to throw off his cloak and seize the ox in order to bend its neck

---

to form in front, coming up upon the left (εἰς μέτωπον παρ' ἀσπίδα καθίστασθαι).'

6. at the festivals of heroes] Because no festival common to all the heroes is mentioned by Greek writers, this allusion has been treated as obscure. But each of the heroes had his own festival. Such were the Theseia at Athens, the Aiaceia at Aegina, the Aianteia at Salamis, the Diocleia at Megara. The terms in which Thucydides mentions the honour paid to Brasidas at Amphipolis imply that an annual festival, ἑορτή, was always celebrated in memory of a canonised hero (v 11). In Plutarch's *praecepta de ger. resp.* c. 15 § 7 a man is spoken of as 'giving the banquet in some festival at a hero's tomb' (ἡρῷα δειπνῶν ἐπιταφίου τινός); and probably, where tradition pointed to the grave,—as in the case of Eurystheus, buried at Pallene near Athens, Eur. *Her.* 1031,—the festival would be held there. Compare the honours paid by Alexander to the tomb of Achilles at Sigeum, Arrian I 11.

7. for a torch-race] The most probable account of the torch-race is that it was contested by two or more parallel chains of runners; along each a torch was passed; and the runners of that chain which carried its torch most quickly to the goal were collectively the winners. The length of the course at the great festivals was about half-a-mile. True to his principle of beginning at the beginning, the Late-Learner does not compete with the ἔφηβοι, but enters for the boys' race. (Torch-races were held, not only at the Panathenaea and the festivals of Hephaestus and Prometheus, but also at those held in honour of heroes. These last continued throughout the night, *Corp. Inscr. Att.* II add. n. 453 b, ἡρῴοις. παννυχίδας συνετέλεσεν. The Ephebi took part in such races at the Theseia and Aianteia, *Corp. Inscr. Att.* I 466, 9, τὰς λαμπάδας ἔδραμον τοῖς τε Θησείοις κτλ., *Ephemeris*, 1860, n. 4097, 52 f, τὸν ἀγῶνα τῶν Αἰαντείων τήν τε πομπὴν συνέπεμψαν τῷ Αἴαντι, ἔδραμον δὲ καὶ τὴν λαμπάδα)

8. to a temple of Heracles] Small chapels or shrines of Heracles were probably numerous in Attica,—his worship being associated with that of Theseus. See Plut. *Thes.* 35 'Theseus, on his release (from Hades, by Heracles), returned to Athens; and all those sacred enclosures (τεμένη) which were formerly his, and which had been set apart for him by the city, he consecrated to Heracles, and called, instead of Thesea, Heraclea.' The same legend is given by Euripides, *H. F.* 1327, where these sanctuaries are spoken of as existing 'throughout the land' (πανταχοῦ χθονός). Heracles had also an altar in the outer Cerameicus: Paus. I 30 § 1.

9 **seize the ox**] The ὀψιμαθής has been invited by a friend to assist at a sacrifice. Eager to display his strength,

καὶ προσανατρίβεσθαι εἰσιὼν εἰς τὰς παλαίστρας· καὶ ἐν
τοῖς θαύμασι τρία ἢ τέτταρα πληρώματα ὑπομένειν τὰ
10 ᾄσματα ἐκμανθάνων· καὶ τελούμενος τῷ Σαβαζίῳ σπεῦσαι,
ὅπως καλλιστεύσῃ παρὰ τῷ ἱερεῖ· καὶ εἰς ἀγρὸν ἐφ᾽ ἵππου
ἀλλοτρίου κατοχούμενος ἅμα μελετᾶν ἱππάζεσθαι, καὶ πεσὼν
τὴν κεφαλὴν κατεαγέναι· καὶ ἐν δεκάταις συνάγειν τοὺς μεθ᾽
αὑτοῦ συναυλήσοντας· καὶ μακρὸν ἀνδριάντα παίζειν πρὸς
15 τὸν ἑαυτοῦ ἀκόλουθον· καὶ διατοξεύεσθαι καὶ διακοντίζεσθαι
τῷ τῶν παίδων παιδαγωγῷ καὶ ἅμα μανθάνειν παρ᾽ αὐτοῦ
<κελεύειν> ὡς ἂν καὶ ἐκείνου μὴ ἐπισταμένου· καὶ ὡς
παλαίων δ᾽ ἐν τῷ βαλανείῳ πυκνὰ ἕδραν στρέφειν, ὅπως πε-

---

he throws off his cloak and seizes the head of the victim,—drawing it back so as to expose the throat to the knife. So *Il.* 1 459, 'they drew back the head and cut the throat' (ἀνέρυσαν καὶ ἔσφαξαν). The word τραχηλίζω was used of a wrestler seizing his adversary by the throat, and bearing back his head: Plut. *de curios* 12, 'See the athlete with his neck in the grip of a boy' (τραχηλιζό-μενον).—There is no special fitness in the sacrifice of the ox to Heracles; it was the ordinary victim at a sacrifice of the more costly kind: see c. VII, 27. A bull was probably the peculiar victim in the worship of Heracles and Theseus,—the two bull-slayers of legend; and it was also one of the three animals (suovetaurilia) offered to the heroes generally: see Diod. IV 39.

10 **palaestras**] He scorns the promiscuous company at the gymnasia, and goes to the palaestras, the regular wrestling schools: see note on c. XIX, 16.

11. **at a conjuror's performance**] See note on c XVI, 6. The conjuror's entertainment is here varied by songs. It has been proposed, but needlessly, to read θεάμασι, i e 'stage plays.'

13. **Sabazius**] On this character of Dionysus see note on c. XXVIII, 9.

13. **to acquit himself best**] In the Speech *de Corona* Aeschines is described as assisting his mother in the mystic ceremonial by which she professed to purge guilt; instructing the candidates when to rise from their knees, and prescribing the formula which they were to recite (p 313 § 259). The candidate for initiation in the rites of Sabazius is anxious to be perfect in a lesson of this kind.

16. **on a tenth-day festival**] On the tenth day after birth a child received its name, the parents holding a sacrifice (δεκάτην θύειν) and entertaining their friends. Peisthetaerus in the *Birds* replies to the begging poet who pretends that he has *long* sung the praises of the new Cloud-city, 'Have I not this very moment held its tenth-day festival, and named it like a child?' One of the objects of entertaining a large company on this occasion was similar to that which was served by the wedding-feast—viz. to secure witnesses in case the legitimacy of the child should afterwards be disputed: see Demosth. *Adv. Boeot. de nom.* p. 1001 § 22, Isaeus *de Pyrrhi her.* p. 45 § 70.

17. **to play the flute with him**] The ὀψιμαθής aims at distinction in the two especially liberal branches of Greek education; gymnastics and music. The Roman feeling (under the Republic at least) that there was something unmanly in being skilful on a musical instrument was very different from the Greek. Aristotle speaks of such skill as 'worthy of a free man, and honourable' (ἐλευθέριον καὶ καλήν: *Polit.* VIII 3). In Plato's *Laws*

THE LATE-LEARNER. VIII (XXVII) 73

back. He will go into the palaestras and try an encounter; at 10 a conjuror's performance he will sit out three or four audiences, trying to learn the songs by heart; and, when he is initiated into the rites of Sabazius, he will be eager to acquit himself best in the eyes of the priest. Riding into the country on another's horse, he will practise his horsemanship by the way, and, falling, 15 will break his head. On a tenth-day festival he will assemble persons to play the flute with him. He will play at *tableaux vivants* with his footman; and will have matches at archery and javelin-throwing with his children's attendant, whom he exhorts, at the same time, to learn from *him*,—as if the other knew 20 nothing about it either. At the bath he will wriggle frequently, as if wrestling, in order that he may appear educated; and, when

---

it is recommended that a boy should have music lessons from the age of thirteen to that of sixteen (p. 809 E).

17. **play at tableaux vivants**] Nothing whatever is known as to the nature of the amusement called μακρὸν ἀνδριάντα παίζειν: nor is the text certain: see *Crit. App.* Ast proposed to read παίειν: 'he will fence at a tall dummy'—the ἀνδριάς serving the purpose of the wooden post at which Roman swordmasters taught their pupils to cut and thrust: 'Who has not seen the wounds of the post?' Juv. VI 247. As this exercise could scarcely be competitive, Ast wished to transfer τὸν αὑτοῦ ἀκόλουθον to the next clause. Coray read μικρὸν ἀνδριάντα πιέζειν: 'he will press a statuette between his hands (to harden them)' This curious interpretation was suggested by a passage in Diog. Laert. (VI 23), which says of Diogenes the cynic that, to harden his frame, he used 'to roll on smooth sand in summer, and in winter to embrace statues covered with snow.'

18. **archery and javelin-throwing**] Both these were among the exercises of the gymnasium; but they were esteemed in very different degrees. Archery was not a subject of contest at the great festivals; and the bowmen of Greek armies in historical times were usually of an inferior social grade; at Athens, Scythian slaves, at Sparta, Helots (Xen. *Hellen.* IV 5). Javelin-throwing, on the other hand, was one of the five exercises of the pentathlum at the great contests, and was therefore systematically practised from boyhood One of Antiphon's speeches turns on a case of a boy having accidentally shot another 'while practising the javelin with his fellows at the gymnasium' (*Tetral.* II 3 § 3).

20. **to learn from him**] Compare Plutarch *de fort. Alex.* II c. 1: 'Philip, also, was in these things (jealousy of professional artists) smaller and more puerile than his true self, because his accomplishments had come late (ὑπ' ὀψιμαθίας). Thus they say that when he was once wrangling with a harper about the execution of a passage, and fancied that he was confuting him, the man smiled quietly and answered, "Far from you, O king, be the degradation of understanding these things better than me"'

21. **at the bath**] See note on c. XIV 28.

(21 **he will wriggle frequently**] The term ἑδροστρόφοι is applied to wrestlers in Theocritus XXIV 109)

22. **that he may appear educated**] The popular Greek ideal of a good education is expressed in Plato's *Theages* p. 122 E: 'Did not your father have you educated in the same things in which

74 ΑΚΑΙΡΙΑC Θ΄

παιδεῦσθαι δοκῇ· καὶ ὅταν ὦσι πλησίον γυναῖκες μελετᾶν
20 ὀρχεῖσθαι αὐτὸς αὑτῷ τερετίζων.

ἀκαιρίας θ΄.

ἡ μὲν οὖν ἀκαιρία ἐστὶν ἐπίτευξις λυποῦσα τοὺς ἐν-
τυγχάνοντας, ὁ δὲ ἄκαιρος τοιοῦτός τις οἷος ἀσχολουμένῳ
προσελθὼν ἀνακοινοῦσθαι· καὶ πρὸς τὴν αὑτοῦ ἐρωμένην
κωμάζειν πυρέττουσαν· καὶ δίκην ὠφληκότι ἐγγύης προσ-
5 ελθὼν κελεῦσαι αὐτὸν ἀναδέξασθαι· καὶ μαρτυρήσων παρεῖναι τοῦ πράγματος ἤδη κεκριμένου· καὶ κεκλημένος εἰς
γάμους τοῦ γυναικείου γένους κατηγορεῖν· καὶ ἐκ μακρᾶς
ὁδοῦ ἥκοντας ἄρτι παρακαλεῖν εἰς περίπατον. δεινὸς δὲ καὶ
προσάγειν ὠνητὴν πλείω διδόντα ἤδη πεπρακότι· καὶ ἀκη-
10 κοότας καὶ μεμαθηκότας ἀνίστασθαι ἐξ ἀρχῆς διδάσκων·

all other gentlemen's sons (οἱ τῶν καλῶν κἀγαθῶν υἱεῖς) are educated—for instance, letters, harp-playing, wrestling, and other exercises?' Arist. *Polit.* VIII 3, 'There are chiefly four branches of education—letters, gymnastics, music, and (in some cases) painting ..for painting, also, seems useful in enabling one to judge better of artists' work.' It is interesting to compare the popular with the higher Greek conception of 'the educated man' Aristotle says (*Eth* IV 1, 3) that to the consideration of every subject may be brought two valuable things—first, special knowledge (ἐπιστήμη), and secondly, 'a sort of educatedness' (οἷον παιδεία τις). The man of special knowledge is the arbiter of fact; the 'educated' man is the critic of method. So in Plato's *Erastae* (p. 135 D) it is said that the philosopher is able, as becomes 'a freeborn and educated man,' to follow the statements of the special artist (δημιουργός) better than the general company can; and Socrates observes that this makes the man of culture, like the pentathlete, 'a sort of second-best all round' (ὑπακρόν τινα περὶ πάντα: p. 136 A).

(23. **practise dancing steps**] A terra-cotta from Myrina representing the typical old-man of Attic comedy, dancing and throwing kisses with his right hand, is reproduced in the Leipzig edition, p. 228, from the original in Vienna.)

1. **Unseasonableness**] This, in its general sense, includes another character described by Theophrastus,—that of περιεργία, Officiousness. But between Unseasonableness in its strict sense and Officiousness there are two points of difference. The unseasonable man does the wrong thing at the wrong time; the mistake of the officious man consists either in doing a thing (in itself opportune) too well, or in undertaking it when it is beyond his power. The officious man always acts with a kind purpose, and has his attention habitually directed to the needs of others: the unseasonable man blunders chiefly through thinking too exclusively of himself.

THE UNSEASONABLE MAN. IX (XII)   75

women are near, he will practise dancing-steps, warbling his own accompaniment.

IX (XII).   THE UNSEASONABLE MAN.

Unseasonableness consists in a chance meeting disagreeable to those who meet.

The Unseasonable man is one who will go up to a busy person, and open his heart to him. He will serenade his mistress when she has a fever. He will address himself to a man who has been cast in a surety-suit, and request him to become his security. He will come to give evidence when the trial is over. When he is asked to a wedding, he will inveigh against womankind. He will propose a walk to those who have just come off a long journey. He has a knack, also, of bringing a higher bidder to him who has already found his market. He loves to rise and go through a long story to those who have

---

4. **serenade**] The 'comastes' was not always the midnight reveller armed with 'flambeaux and levers and bows that threaten the barred doors' (Hor. *Od.* III 26, 6). Sometimes he is merely the prototype of the modern serenader. Such is the 'comastes' in Theocritus (III 1); such the player of the 'quavering flute' against whom Horace warns Asterie (*Od.* III 7, 20). Compare Lucian *Marin. Dial.* I 4. '*Galatea.* Polyphemus is quite musical too. *Doris.* Oh, Galatea! We heard him singing when he went to serenade you the other day' (ὁπότε ἐκώμασε πρώην ἐπί σε).

6. **cast in a surety-suit**] Sureties were required by Athenian law in two cases chiefly: (1) in public causes, for the appearance of the accused on the day of trial. If he failed to appear, his surety became liable to the penalty for contempt of court; and, in consideration of the risk run, the surety was allowed to hold the bailee in confinement till the day for his appearance (Xen. *Hellen.* I 7, 35, ἐδέθησαν ὑπὸ τῶν ἐγγυησαμένων). (2) In public and certain private causes, surety was taken for the satisfaction of the judicial award. If the principal made default, his surety was liable for the money, and was sued in a 'surety-suit' (ἐγγύης δίκη). But this responsibility was limited to one year from the time when the principal's liability was incurred (Dem. *adv. Apat* p 901).

8. **he will inveigh against womankind**] He does this in their presence; for the wedding-feast was the one entertainment in which Greek manners permitted respectable women to take part. Plato proposed that the statutable wedding-party should consist of twenty persons, ten of either sex (*Laws* VI p 775 A). At the wedding-feast described by Lucian, the women, with the bride, are placed on one side of the table, the male guests on the other (*Symp.* cc 8 ff). (At the same feast, a tirade against marriage was received with laughter because it was unseasonable, ὡς οὐκ ἐν καιρῷ λεγομένοις)

καὶ πρόθυμος δὲ ἐπιμεληθῆναι ἃ μὴ βούλεταί τις γενέσθαι
αἰσχύνεται δὲ ἀπείπασθαι· καὶ θύοντας καὶ ἀναλίσκοντας
ἥκειν τόκον ἀπαιτήσων· καὶ μαστιγουμένου οἰκέτου παρ-
εστὼς διηγεῖσθαι ὅτι καὶ αὐτοῦ ποτε παῖς οὕτω πληγὰς
15 λαβὼν ἀπήγξατο· καὶ παρὼν διαίτῃ συγκρούειν, ἀμφοτέρων
βουλομένων διαλύεσθαι· καὶ ὀρχησόμενος ἅψασθαι ἑτέρου
μηδέπω μεθύοντος.

περιεργίας ί.

ἀμέλει περιεργία δόξειεν ἂν εἶναι προσποίησίς τις λόγων
καὶ πράξεων μετ᾽ εὐνοίας, ὁ δὲ περίεργος τοιοῦτός τις οἷος
ἐπαγγέλλεσθαι ἀναστάς, ἃ μὴ δυνήσεται· καὶ ὁμολογου-
μένου τοῦ πράγματος δικαίου εἶναι ἐνστὰς ἐλεγχθῆναι· καὶ
5 πλεῖον δὲ ἐπαναγκάσαι τὸν παῖδα κεράσαι, ἢ ὅσον δύνανται
οἱ παρόντες ἐκπιεῖν· καὶ διείργειν τοὺς μαχομένους, καὶ οὓς
οὐ γινώσκει· καὶ ἀτραποῦ ἡγήσασθαι, εἶτα μὴ δύνασθαι
εὑρεῖν, οὗ πορεύεται· καὶ τὸν στρατηγὸν προσελθὼν ἐρωτῆσαι, πότε μέλλει παρατάττεσθαι, καὶ τί μετὰ τὴν αὔριον

15. **and incurring expense**] Since, after a sacrifice, it was usual to entertain friends: see note on c. XV, 5.

19. **assisting at an arbitration**] As an advocate of one of the two parties: see note on c. II, 8.

21 **who is not yet drunk**] The Roman 'nemo saltat sobrius' implied that dancing was altogether incompatible with the dignity of a freeborn man. This was not the Greek feeling. The remark in the text only means that dancing, the ultimate expression of joy, is absurd when a man dances in cold blood. Cf. Athen. XIV p. 629 —'Well says Damon the Athenian that songs and dances must come when the soul is at all stirred. Liberal and beautiful souls impart the same qualities to their dances and songs; souls of the opposite kind, the opposite. Wherefore also the saying of Cleisthenes the despot of Sicyon was witty, and the sign of a cultivated understanding. Having seen, as they say, one of his daughter's suitors dance in a vulgar manner—it was Hippocleides the Athenian —he said that "he had danced off his marriage"; deeming, as it seems, that the soul of the man resembled his dancing.' (Cf. Her. VI 129.)

1. **Officiousness**] The desire to please, either by rendering an extraordinary service or by performing an ordinary one unusually well, is present in every act ascribed to this character. 'Officiousness' therefore seems to render it better than the more literal 'Overbusiness,' which is too harsh. The distinction between ἀρέσκεια and περιεργία scarcely needs to be pointed out; the good-will in the latter

THE OFFICIOUS MAN. X (XIII)

heard it and know it by heart; he is zealous, too, in charging himself with offices which one would rather not have done, but is ashamed to decline. When people are sacrificing and incurring expense, he will come to demand his interest. If he is present at the flogging of a slave, he will relate how a slave of his own was once beaten in the same way—and hanged himself; or, assisting at an arbitration, he will persist in embroiling the parties when they both wish to be reconciled. And, when he is minded to dance, he will seize upon another person who is not yet drunk.

X (XIII). THE OFFICIOUS MAN.

Officiousness would seem to be, in fact, a well-meaning presumption in word or deed.

The Officious man is one who will rise and promise things beyond his power; and who, when an arrangement is admitted to be just, will oppose it, and be refuted. He will insist, too, on the slave mixing more wine than the company can finish, he will separate combatants, even those whom he does not know, he will undertake to show the path, and after all be unable to find his way. Also he will go up to his commanding officer, and ask when he means to give battle, and what is to be his order

---

case is honest, not affected, and the exaggeration is due simply to an error of judgment. Compare note on c. IX, 1.

6. mixing more wine] The wine and the water were usually mixed together in the bowl, and thence poured into the cups of the guests. (The οἰνοχόος was the ladler-out of the wine; and οἰνοχόη was the ladle used for that purpose.) Athenaeus however quotes a poet who had written on the subject, and from whom it appears that this was not always the case: 'No man' says Xenophanes 'would in mixing his glass first pour in the wine: the water comes first, and the wine on top of it' (Ath. XI p. 782, § 18).

9. his commanding officer] Here we have the undisciplined zeal, as in c. XXVII the uncontrollable terror, of a badly-trained militiaman. Touches like these well illustrate the character of the Athenian military force—one which it shared with that of every Greek state except Sparta. Xenophon says with truth that the Spartans alone were 'true artists in war; the other Greeks, hasty amateurs (αὐτοσχεδιασταί) in campaigning' (*Lac. Polit.* 13, 5).

10. when he means to give battle] Compare Plutarch *Demetr.* c. 28: 'It is said that when Demetrius was a boy he asked his father (Antigonus) when they were to march. Antigonus replied in anger: "Are you miserable lest *you* should be the only person who does not hear the trumpet?"'

10. what is to be his order] The

ΑΗΔΙΑC ΙΑ'

10 παραγγέλλει· καὶ ἀπαγορεύοντος τοῦ ἰατροῦ ὅπως μὴ δώσει οἶνον τῷ μαλακιζομένῳ, φήσας βούλεσθαι διάπειραν λαμβάνειν εὖ ποτίσαι τὸν κακῶς ἔχοντα· καὶ γυναικὸς δὲ τελευτησάσης ἐπιγράψαι ἐπὶ τὸ μνῆμα τοῦ τε ἀνδρὸς αὐτῆς καὶ τοῦ πατρὸς καὶ τῆς μητρὸς καὶ αὐτῆς τῆς γυναικὸς
15 τοὔνομα καὶ ποδαπή ἐστι, καὶ προσεπιγράψαι, ὅτι οὗτοι πάντες χρηστοὶ ἦσαν· καὶ ὀμνύναι μέλλων εἰπεῖν πρὸς τοὺς παρεστηκότας, ὅτι καὶ πρότερον πολλάκις ὀμώμοκα.

ἀηδίας ιαʹ.

ἔστιν ἡ ἀηδία, ὡς ὅρῳ λαβεῖν, ἔντευξις λύπης ποιητικὴ ἄνευ βλάβης, ὁ δὲ ἀηδὴς τοιοῦτός τις οἷος ἐγείρειν ἄρτι καθεύδοντα εἰσελθών, ἵνα αὐτῷ λαλῇ· καὶ ἀνάγεσθαι δὴ μέλλοντας κωλύειν, καὶ προσελθὼν δεῖσθαι ἐπισχεῖν, ἕως ἂν

---

present tense implies in Greek a certain obsequiousness which makes the indiscreet zeal more absurd.—παραγγέλλειν 'to pass the word,' which the commander gives to his lieutenants and they to their subalterns. The περίεργος must be supposed to be a brigadier commanding (as 'taxiarch') the infantry or (as 'phylarch') the cavalry of his tribe.

14. **a deceased woman's tombstone**] Casaubon doubted whether γυναικός meant the man's own wife; but, to say nothing of the fact that her husband is mentioned among those who *were* estimable, this would have been τῆς γυναικός or τῆς αὑτοῦ γυναικός: see XVIII, XXIII, XXIV, XXVIII. Some relative of the περίεργος is meant, whose funeral it devolved upon him to superintend.

14. **the name of her husband**] It may be inferred from this passage that it was usual at the time to write upon a woman's tomb merely her own name,—with perhaps that of her husband, if she had been married, or of her father, but not both. There is a very evident emphasis upon γυναικός: the strangeness of the fuller inscription consists in the fact that the tomb is a *woman's*. The same feeling which placed a woman's glory in the absolute silence of her life (Thuc II 45) may have suggested—what, indeed, it made inevitable—that her tombstone should say little. Plato was legislating for his own sex only, when he permitted tombstones to record 'the praises of the deceased in not more than four heroic verses' (*Laws* XV p. 958 E). Pausanias notices it as *peculiar* at Sicyon that 'they add no inscription, but after simply stating the name of the deceased, without intimating his descent (οὐ πατρόθεν ὑπειπόντες), bid 'Farewell to the dead' (II 7, 3). (The tombstone of a native Athenian woman was usually inscribed with 'her own name and the name of her *father* and his deme. If, however, she were married, her husband's name and deme were always given ..In no case do we find the name of the woman's *mother* given, as it is by the Officious man. Neither is he right, in the case of an

for the day after tomorrow. When the doctor forbids him to give wine to the invalid, he will say that he wishes to try an experiment, and will drench the sick man. Also he will inscribe upon a deceased woman's tombstone the name of her husband, of her father, and of her mother, as well as her own, with the place of her birth; recording further that 'All these were Estimable Persons.' And when he is about to take an oath he will say to the bystanders, 'This is by no means the first that I have taken.'

XI (XX). THE UNPLEASANT MAN.

Unpleasantness may be defined as a mode of address which gives harmless annoyance.

The Unpleasant man is one who will come in and awake a person who has just gone to sleep, in order to chat with him. He will detain people who are on the very point of sailing; indeed he will go up to them and request them to wait until he

---

Attic woman, in naming her birth-place.' Phrases like χρηστοὶ πάντες are not found on *Attic* tombstones; E. L. Hicks, in *Journal of Hellenic Studies*, iii 141–3.)

(18. **this is by no means the first that I have taken**] Similarly, in a fragment of Menander, 569:—

'Glycera, what mean these tears, I swear to you,
I, who have sworn full many a time before')

1. **Unpleasantness**] The epithet 'harmless' (ἄνευ βλάβης) with which the 'annoyance' given by the character is qualified, seems merely an attempt by the composer of the Definition to indicate that λύπη, 'pain,' is not to be understood in a material sense. Thus the Shameless man, for instance, does not merely offend the taste, but sometimes inflicts positive damage, βλάβη,—as on the butcher from whom he steals tripe. The Unpleasant man on the other hand —says the Definition—is annoying in an aesthetic sense only.

The outlines of this Character are not firmly drawn; the traits which it includes do not seem distinctly referable to any one dominant moral quality: it is altogether a slight sketch, put together from observations and impressions which have not been thoroughly sorted or analysed. It has elements in common with at least three characters which are elsewhere treated separately and fully:—1. The Unpleasant man is *unseasonable*. He disturbs a friend's sleep that he may talk to him, and keeps a ship waiting while he takes a walk. 2. He is *boastful*; as when he speaks of his cistern and of his cook. 3. He is *gross*, i.e. a coarse jester; as in the question which he addresses to his mother.

No one of these tendencies is strongly marked; but they are so blended as to form a whole which would, in English phrase, be most nearly described by Ill-breeding; meaning thereby a want of tact which is not accidental, but is due to a defect, natural or engendered, in sure good-feeling

5 περιπατήση· καὶ τὸ παιδίον τῆς τίτθης ἀφελόμενος, μασώμενος σιτίζειν αὐτὸς καὶ ὑποκορίζεσθαι ποππύζων καὶ
πανούργιον τοῦ πάππου καλῶν· καὶ ἐρωτῆσαι δὲ δεινὸς
ἐναντίον τῶν οἰκείων· εἰπέ, μάμμη, ὅτ' ὤδινες καὶ ἔτικτές με,
ποία τις ἡμέρα; καὶ <λέγειν> ὅτι ψυχρὸν ὕδωρ ἐστὶ παρ'
10 αὐτῷ λακκαῖον, καὶ ὡς κῆπος λάχανα πολλὰ ἔχων καὶ ἁπαλά,
καὶ μάγειρος εὖ τὸ ὄψον σκευάζων· καὶ ὅτι ἡ οἰκία αὐτοῦ
πανδοκεῖόν ἐστι· μεστὴ γὰρ ἀεί· καὶ τοὺς φίλους αὐτοῦ
εἶναι τὸν τετρημένον πίθον· εὖ ποιῶν γὰρ αὐτοὺς οὐ δύνασθαι ἐμπλῆσαι· καὶ ξενίζων δὲ δεῖξαι τὸν παράσιτον αὐτοῦ,
15 ποῖός τις ἐστι, τῷ συνδειπνοῦντι· καὶ παρακαλῶν δὲ ἐπὶ τοῦ
ποτηρίου, εἰπεῖν ὅτι τὸ τέρψον τοὺς παρόντας παρεσκεύασται.

δυσχερείας ιβ'.

ἔστιν ἡ δυσχέρεια ἀθεραπευσία σώματος λύπης παρασκευαστική, ὁ δὲ δυσχερὴς τοιοῦτός τις οἷος λέπραν ἔχων
καὶ ἀλφὸν καὶ τοὺς ὄνυχας μεγάλους περιπατεῖν καὶ φῆσαι
ταῦτα εἶναι αὐτῷ συγγενικὰ ἀρρωστήματα· ἔχειν γὰρ αὐτὰ
5 καὶ τὸν πατέρα καὶ τὸν πάππον, καὶ οὐκ εἶναι ῥᾴδιον αὐτοῦ

(7. **take his child from the nurse**] A terra-cotta, probably from Tanagra, in the British Museum represents an old man fondling an infant. It is reproduced on p 157 of the Leipzig edition)

12. **cistern-water**] The remark is ἀηδές as being boastful; and perhaps also as suggesting thin potations. The female legislator in the *Ecclesiasusae* (154) proposes 'that no publican be allowed to construct cisterns in the wine-shops' Athenaeus tells a story—preserved by a brother dramatist—of Diphilus. The comic poet is dining out, and compliments his host upon the coolness of the wine —

'Your cistern must be admirably cool'
'Yes, we take pains to ice it—with your prologues'
(Ath XIII p. 580 § 43)

15. **the pierced cask**] In Lucian's *Dialogues of the Dead* (XI 4) the shades of two philosophers converse mournfully on the uselessness of instilling truths into minds which have no power to retain them —'It was just the case of those daughters of Danaus, for ever refilling the sieve-like cask.'

16. **will show off the qualities of his parasite**] He draws attention, at his own table, to the appetite of his parasite,—incites him to buffoonery,—and, in short, displays him as one of his possessions. The abject condition of the professional Athenian parasite is vividly set forth in Alciphro's *Letters*,—who, in this as in other things, seems to have drawn upon the poets of the Middle and New Comedy. The parasite is described as ever hesitating between two evils—on the one hand, gaunt hunger—on the

has taken a stroll. He will take his child from the nurse, and
feed it from his own mouth, and chirp endearments to it, calling
it 'papa's little rascal.' He is apt, also, to ask before his relations, 'Tell me, mammy,—when you were bringing me into
the world, how went the time?' He will say that he has
cool cistern-water at his house, and a garden with many fine
vegetables, and a cook who understands dressed dishes. His
house, he will say, is a perfect inn—always crammed; and his
friends are like the pierced cask—he can never fill them with
his benefits. Also, when he entertains, he will show off the
qualities of his parasite to his guest; and will say, too, in an
encouraging tone over the wine, that the amusement of the
company has been provided for.

XII (XIX). THE OFFENSIVE MAN.

Offensiveness is distressing neglect of the person.

The Offensive man is one who will go about with a scrofulous
or leprous affection, or with his nails overgrown, and say that
these are hereditary complaints with him; his father had them,
and his grandfather, and it is not easy to be smuggled into *his*

---

other, not indignities merely, but blows, cuffs, all manner of ill-usage from his patron and his patron's guests (III 6, 7, 49). His position is unbearable: he thinks of taking to the road with a band of brigands who lie in wait at the Scironian rocks for travellers to Corinth; he attempts small parts at the theatre, and implores his brother parasites to come and applaud; he even tries country life; but it is in vain, he always relapses into the old dilemma between starvation and maltreatment (III 70, 71). The parasite in Plautus and Terence holds, if not a higher, at least a safer position.

The word 'parasite' is said to occur in a *bad* sense first in a fragment of Araros ('Αραρώς) the son of Aristophanes, whose first piece, acc. to Suidas, was acted in Ol. 101 (376—372 B C.. Meineke, *Frag. Com. Gr.* I 343, III 273; Kock, II 215). In older times 'parasite' was a term of honour, meaning a person appointed to assist the magistrates in celebrating sacrificial feasts, and otherwise called σύνθοινος: Athen. p. 234 § 26.

1. **Offensiveness**] The appropriation of the word δυσχέρεια to the special sense which it bears here is remarkable. It is perhaps the strongest example of a characteristic common in some degree to all these sketches—that they treat general terms simply in reference to the particular meaning, however arbitrary, which the social usage of the day had fixed upon them see c III, note 1. It may be accidental, but seems worthy of notice, that twice in the *Philoctetes* of Sophocles δυσχέρεια is used precisely in the sense to which it is restricted here—when the sufferer speaks of the annoyance which his malady must cause to those with whom he sails: vv. 473, 900.

J. T.

82 ΑΝΑΙϹΘΗϹΙΑϹ ΙΓ'

εἰς τὸ γένος ὑποβάλλεσθαι...καὶ ἐλαίῳ σαπρῷ ἐν βαλανείῳ χρώμενος χρίεσθαι· καὶ χιτωνίσκον παχὺν καὶ ἱμάτιον σφόδρα λεπτὸν καὶ κηλίδων μεστὸν ἀναβαλόμενος εἰς ἀγορὰν ἐξελθεῖν.

ἀναισθησίας ιγ'.

ἔστι δὲ ἡ ἀναισθησία, ὡς ὅρῳ εἰπεῖν, βραδυτὴς ψυχῆς ἐν λόγοις καὶ πράξεσιν, ὁ δὲ ἀναίσθητος τοιοῦτός τις οἷος λογισάμενος ταῖς ψήφοις καὶ κεφάλαιον ποιήσας ἐρωτᾶν τὸν παρακαθήμενον, τί γίνεται; καὶ δίκην φεύγων καὶ ταύτην
5 εἰσιέναι μέλλων, ἐπιλαθόμενος εἰς ἀγρὸν πορεύεσθαι· καὶ θεωρῶν ἐν τῷ θεάτρῳ μόνος καταλείπεσθαι καθεύδων· καὶ λαβών <τι> καὶ ἀποθεὶς αὐτὸς τοῦτο ζητεῖν καὶ μὴ δύνασθαι εὑρεῖν· καὶ ἀπαγγέλλοντος αὐτῷ ὅτι τετελεύτηκέ τις αὐτοῦ τῶν φίλων, ἵνα παραγένηται, σκυθρωπάσας καὶ δακρύσας εἰπεῖν·
10 ἀγαθῇ τύχῃ. δεινὸς δὲ καὶ ἀπολαμβάνων ἀργύριον ὀφειλόμενον μάρτυρας παραλαβεῖν· καὶ χειμῶνος ὄντος μάχεσθαι

---

6. **rancid oil**] Compare Juvenal v 88:—

Your humbler sauceboats know the grosser oil
Which came in whernes from Jugurtha's soil,
Which helps the Moor to bathe in peace at Rome,
And guards his countrymen from snakes at home.

7. **a thick tunic**] He wears the lightest summer mantle over such a tunic as is worn only in winter. Aristophanes in the *Birds* (714) speaks of the time when—

The swallow brings us news,
'Tis time to sell the winter cloak and buy the summer blouse:

and Horace of the man who wears—

In June a cape, a jersey when it snows.

(*Epp* 1 xi 18)

1. **Stupidity**] In *Eth. N.* II 7 Aristotle observes that there is no proper name for those who care too little about pleasure; but proposes to call them *insensible* (ἀναίσθητοι). The word is used here in a general meaning, of one whose 'perceptions' are slow. All the phases of this slowness described by Theophrastus have a common characteristic,—inattention to the immediate present. It is because the ἀναίσθητος is seldom thinking of what he is doing at the moment that his actions leave no stamp upon his memory, and that he forgets an engagement just formed. For the same reason, when social pressure hurries him into speaking or acting on the instant, he is apt to say or do mechanically something which does not suit the occasion.

3. **after doing a sum**] In c VI it is said of the Boastful man that, when sitting in a public place among strangers, he will ask one of them to 'set up the counters' (θεῖναι τὰς ψήφους) in order to verify a boast which he has made. These

THE STUPID MAN. XIII (XIV)

family...He will use rancid oil to anoint himself at the bath; and will go forth into the market-place wearing a thick tunic, and a very light cloak, covered with stains.

XIII (XIV). THE STUPID MAN.

Stupidity may be defined as mental slowness in speech and action.

The Stupid man is one who, after doing a sum and setting down the total, will ask the person sitting next him 'What does it come to?' When he is defendant in an action, and it is about to come on, he will forget it and go into the country; when he is a spectator in the theatre, he will be left behind slumbering in solitude. If he has been given anything, and has put it away himself, he will look for it and be unable to find it. When the death of a friend is announced to him, in order that he may come to the house, his face will grow dark—tears will come into his eyes—and he will say 'Heaven be praised!' He is apt, too, when he receives payment of a debt, to call witnesses; and in winter-time to quarrel with his slave for not having bought

---

two passages seem to show that people sometimes carried about a 'ready reckoner' in the shape of a small ciphering-board (ἀβάκιον), like that used by an arithmetic master (calculator) at Rome: Mart. x 62, 4.—See note on c. IV, 19.

5. **when he is defendant in an action**] The preliminary investigation of the case before the archon is over; a day has been appointed for it to come before a court; but, before this day (ἡ κυρία τοῦ νόμου, Dem. *Meid.* p. 544 § 93) arrives, the Stupid man forgets the whole matter, and leaves Athens. The consequence is that judgment goes against him by default.

10. **in order that he may come to the house**] The duty of a relative or friend was not merely to attend the funeral (ἐκφορά); he was also expected to visit the house at least once while the corpse was laid out (πρόθεσις). Not to take part in the 'mourning' (τὸ κῆδος) then made, was thought unfeeling neglect: Isocr. *Aegin.* p. 390. See Demosth. *adv. Macart.* p. 1071 § 64, 'These female relations he invites both to be present at the laying out of the dead, and to follow him to the grave.' Plut. *de Consol. ad Ux.* c. 3, 'This also is mentioned with surprise by those who visited the house (οἱ παραγενόμενοι, i.e. during the πρόθεσις), that you have not put on mourning nor was there any show of splendour or pomp about the burial.' So in the *Andria* (106) I 1, 79, the mourner *often* (*frequens*) visits the house of death.

13. **call witnesses**] as if he were *making*, instead of receiving, a payment. Compare Dem. *in Phorm.* p. 915 § 30, 'I suppose you all know that (these men) borrow with few witnesses, but call many when they pay.'

84 ΑΓΡΟΙΚΙΑΣ ΙΔ'

τῷ παιδί, ὅτι σικύους οὐκ ἠγόρασε· καὶ τὰ παιδία ἑαυτοῦ
παλαίειν ἀναγκάζων καὶ τροχάζειν εἰς κόπους ἐμβάλλειν·
καὶ ἐν ἀγρῷ αὐτὸς φακῆν ἕψων δὶς ἅλας εἰς τὴν χύτραν
15 ἐμβαλὼν ἄβρωτον ποιῆσαι· καὶ ὕοντος τοῦ Διὸς εἰπεῖν, ἡδύ
γε τῶν ἄστρων ὄζει, ὅτε δὴ οἱ ἄλλοι λέγουσι τῆς γῆς· καὶ
λέγοντός τινος, πόσους οἴει κατὰ τὰς ἱερὰς πύλας ἐξενεχθῆναι
νεκρούς; πρὸς τοῦτον εἰπεῖν· ὅσοι ἐμοὶ καὶ σοὶ γένοιντο.

ἀγροικίας ιδ'.

ἡ δὲ ἀγροικία δόξειεν ἂν εἶναι ἀμαθία ἀσχήμων, ὁ δὲ

---

15. **cucumbers**] In the *Peace* (1001) Trygaeus prays 'that the marketplace may be full of good things—large garlic, *early* cucumbers, apples, pomegranates.' But the Stupid man forgets that it is not even spring yet.

15. **make his children wrestle**] Through mere dull inadvertence he incites his children to continue their violent exercise long after signs of fatigue have begun to appear. Athletics filled a large place in the life of a Greek; but his instinct for moderation in this as in other things is often marked. See Plato's *Erastae* p. 133 E (where Socrates wants to show that polymathy is not philosophy), 'Pray, now, do you consider that in the gymnasia heavy work (φιλοπονία) is athleticism (φιλογυμναστία)?' Aristotle says that gymnastic science is the knowledge of the *moderate* in toil: *Eth. N.* I 6, 4.

15. **and run races**] Eur. *Medea* 46, 'Here come in my children from their races'—ἐκ τρόχων, where a variant is ἐκ τροχῶν (τροχός) 'from their hoops.' Mr Sheppard understands τροχάζειν here of trundling hoops; but elsewhere the word always means to run races. (It is equivalent to τρέχειν in Xenophon, *Cyrop.* II 4, 3, *Anab* VII 3, 46, *Hellen.* VII 2, 22.) An anonymous critic suggested τροχίζειν: but this (though supported by the analogy of σφαιρίζειν) does not occur in the sense of 'driving a hoop.' Probably the word for that would have been κρικηλατεῖν, or perhaps τροχηλατεῖν,—certainly not τροχιάζειν, as Ast suggests.

18 **when it is raining**] The point concealed under the corrupt text is probably of the kind which the most intelligible of the restorations affords. The ἀναίσθητος makes one of his *verbal* blunders. Ussing supposes the general sense to have been: 'When it rains, he praises the fine weather, and does things which can be done only when it is fine.' But probably even the ἀναίσθητος, if (for instance) he went out to dig, would discover that the weather was unpropitious

21. **the Sacred Gate**] Sulla, in 86 B.C., broke into Athens by levelling 'that part of the wall which is between the Peiraic and the Sacred Gate'; and the ensuing massacre in the neighbourhood of the agora 'spread over the whole Cerameicus within the Dipylum' (Plut. *Sulla* 14). The Dipylum (superseding the Thriasian Gate) was on the N W. side of Athens; the Peiraic was on the S W., the Sacred Gate was probably between them, and was so called because it led (as did also the Dipylum) to the Sacred Road to Eleusis. Now the Outer Cerameicus, upon which the Sacred Gate,

cucumbers; and to make his children wrestle and run races until he has exhausted them. If he is cooking a leek himself in the country, he will put salt into the pot twice, and make it uneatable. When it is raining, he will observe 'Well, the smell from the sky is delicious' (when others of course say 'from the earth'); or, if he is asked 'How many corpses do you suppose have been carried out at the Sacred Gate?' he will reply, 'I only wish that you or I had as many.'

XIV (IV). THE BOOR.

Boorishness would seem to be ignorance offending against propriety.

---

as well as the Dipylum, would thus open, was the cemetery for those who were honoured with public burial. See the *Birds*, 395:—'The Cerameicus shall receive us: for, in order that we may have a public funeral, we will tell the Generals that we died in battle with the enemy in Birdland.'—For a discussion of the conjecture Ἡρίας πύλας, see *Critical Appendix*.

21. **I only wish that you or I had as many**] The Stupid man, in absence of mind, answers as if he had been asked (for instance) 'How many minas do you suppose that Glaucon is worth?' Thus inadvertently he speaks words of fearful omen, for he associates *death* with himself and with his questioner by a *wish*. For a precisely similar instance of ἀναισθησία betrayed into δυσφημία, see Plutarch *Crass*. 19: 'And from Crassus himself, as he was addressing the soldiers, fell an utterance which agitated and appalled them. He directed them to break down the bridge over the river, *in order that no one might return*. And whereas he ought, when he perceived the strangeness (ἀτοπίαν—a euphemism) of the phrase, to have recalled and explained it to those whom his words had terrified, he neglected through obstinacy to do so.'—For the form of the expression ὅσοι ἐμοὶ γένοιντο, cf. Theocr. xvi 19, αὐτῷ μοί τι γένοιτο, 'give me pelf for myself.'

1. **Boorishness**] The sense of ἀμαθία in the Definition is illustrated by Eur. *Med.* 223, 'harsh to his fellow-citizens from *want of culture*' (ἀμαθίας ὕπο).

The selection of the Rustic as a definite type is remarkable. Small as Attica was, the demarcation between town and country life was sharply drawn. As Athens grew in wealth, the richer part, indeed, of the country population were more and more attracted to it; and Isocrates, speaking in 380 B.C., can already contrast his own time with the days when 'the houses and establishments in the country were handsomer than those within the walls, and when many of the citizens did not even come to town for the festivals' (*Areop.* p. 150 § 52). But there remained a frugal farmer-class, strongly conservative of the old simplicity, totally strange to the life of the city, and rarely—in some cases, never—visiting it. A vivid picture of this class—probably derived in part from the Greek comic dramatists—is given in the *Letters* of Alciphro, of which the imaginary writers belong to the age of Theophrastus. The temptations which beset the rustic on his visits to Athens are forcibly described. A farmer sends in his son to sell wood and barley; the young

ΑΓΡΟΙΚΙΑС ΙΔ'

ἄγροικος τοιοῦτός τις οἷος κυκεῶνα πιὼν εἰς ἐκκλησίαν
πορεύεσθαι· καὶ τὸ μύρον φάσκειν οὐδὲν τοῦ θύμου ἥδιον
ὄζειν· καὶ μείζω τοῦ ποδὸς τὰ ὑποδήματα φορεῖν· καὶ μεγάλῃ
5 τῇ φωνῇ λαλεῖν· καὶ τοῖς μὲν φίλοις καὶ οἰκείοις ἀπιστεῖν,
πρὸς δὲ τοὺς αὑτοῦ οἰκέτας ἀνακοινοῦσθαι περὶ τῶν μεγί-
στων· καὶ τοῖς παρ' αὐτῷ ἐργαζομένοις μισθωτοῖς ἐν ἀγρῷ
πάντα τὰ ἀπὸ τῆς ἐκκλησίας διηγεῖσθαι· καὶ ἀναβεβλημένος
ἄνω τοῦ γόνατος καθιζάνειν· καὶ ἐπ' ἄλλῳ μὲν μηδενὶ μήτε
10 θαυμάζειν μήτε ἐκπλήττεσθαι ἐν ταῖς ὁδοῖς, ὅταν δὲ ἴδῃ βοῦν
ἢ ὄνον ἢ τράγον, ἑστηκὼς θεωρεῖν. καὶ προαιρῶν δέ τι ἐκ
τοῦ ταμιείου δεινὸς φαγεῖν· καὶ ζωρότερον πιεῖν· καὶ ἀλέσαι
μετὰ τῆς σιτοποιοῦ τοῖς ἔνδον πᾶσι καὶ αὑτῷ τὰ ἐπιτήδεια·
καὶ ἀριστῶν δὲ ἅμα τοῖς ὑποζυγίοις ἐμβαλεῖν· καὶ κόψαντος

man sees a philosopher at the Academy, and to his father's dismay comes back a Cynic (III 40). Another, having been sent in to buy earthenware, is betrayed into a ruinous carouse; a third, after disposing of his figs and nuts, goes to the theatre, and is thrown into ecstasies of wonder and terror by a conjuror (III 17, 20). The rareness of such visits is also marked. In one letter a young Attic farmer requests a neighbour to be his guide in *a first* visit to Athens; he longs to see 'what this thing may be which they call town' (III 31). In another, a son implores his mother to 'come and see the splendours of the town before her dying day'; for, though distant but a few hours' journey, she has never seen them (III 39).

It was from the intellectual, quite as much as from the aesthetic side, that an Athenian viewed Rusticity. Aristotle calls the man incapable of a joke—the opposite extreme to the Buffoon—ἄγροικος, a Rustic; and, when he afterwards changes his word, it is only to substitute for it another (ἄγριος) which expresses in a still stronger form the result of living too much in the country. The sketch which Theophrastus gives us is so far defective that it contrasts rusticity, not with town intelligence, but merely with town elegance.

3. **a posset**] The κυκεών (a favourite dish with the Attic peasant, Aristoph. *Peace*, 1169) was a sort of thick posset, made with wine, barley-meal, grated cheese, and honey, and sometimes flavoured with thyme. The rustic carries the fragrance on his breath into the Ecclesia

5. **his shoes too large for his feet**] In the *Knights* (317) Cleon is accused of having sold bad shoe-leather 'to the country people'; so that 'before they had worn the shoes a day, they were too large by a couple of spans.' Compare Hor. *Sat.* I 3, 30, 'He may be laughed at because he is shaved in a somewhat rustic fashion—because his toga falls to his heels—because the loose shoe will hardly cling to his foot'—Cf note on c. I, 23.

6. **talks confidentially to his own servants**] Greek manners, unlike Roman, permitted familiarity with slaves. After telling a story to illustrate the fear in which a Roman slave stood of his master, Plutarch adds,—'but the Attic slave will tell his master, as he digs, the terms of the

THE BOOR. XIV (IV)

The Boor is one who, having drunk a posset, will go into the Ecclesia. He vows that thyme smells sweeter than any perfume; he wears his shoes too large for his feet; he talks in a loud voice. He distrusts his friends and relatives, but talks confidentially to his own servants on the most important matters; and recounts all the news from the Ecclesia to the hired labourers working on his land. Wearing a cloak which does not reach the knee, he will sit down. He shows surprise and wonder at nothing else, but will stand still and gaze when he sees an ox or an ass or a goat in the streets. He is apt also to take things out of the store-room and eat them; and to drink his wine rather strong. He will help the bakery-maid to grind the corn for the use of the household and for his own; he will eat his breakfast while he shakes down hay for his beasts of burden; he will answer

---

last Convention; so perfect is their familiarity' (*de Garrul.* 18). Xenophon says — 'We have given to our slaves the right to talk like equals (ἰσηγορία) with freemen, just as to resident-aliens the right of so talking with citizens', and he explains the indulgence by the fact that in a naval State, which requires the personal service of its citizens, the industries must be in the hands of the slaves, who will grow rich, and must then be kept in good humour (*de republ. Ath.* I 12).—The Rustic's rusticity consists, then, not in conversing with his slaves, but in conversing with them on important matters, which, with a surly reserve, he withholds from his own family.

8. **hired labourers**] Slavery did not altogether swamp the labour-market. Poor men, chiefly foreigners, found employment as artisans, farm-labourers, or domestics: see Plat. *Rep* 371. Lysis, in Plato's dialogue, says that his father's chariot was driven at the games by a *hired* charioteer (*Lys*. p. 208 E), while the groom mentioned in the same passage is a *slave*. The shrine of Eurysaces in the market-place is mentioned by Pollux as the place at which 'those who ply for hire used to congregate.'

11. **when he sees an ox or an ass or a goat**] Compare Earle's Character of a Plaine Country Fellow:—'His mind is not much distracted with objects; but if a good fat Cowe come in his way, he stands dumbe and astonisht, and though his haste be never so great, will fixe here halfe an houres contemplation'

13. **drink his wine rather strong**] Temperate drinkers always put more water than wine into the bowl. Five parts of water to two of wine appears to have been a favourite mixture (Athen. x p. 426 § 28). In a fragment of one of the comedies of Eupolis the Wine-God is thus greeted on his appearance—

Hail, Dionysus: are you 'Five-and-two'?

Hesiod (*Op*. 594) recommends three parts of water to one of wine,—the mixture which in Horace (*Od*. III 8, 13) the Graces are said to approve. As to stronger compounds, a poet in Athenaeus (II p 36 § 2) says—

Half-wine half-water is a maddening drink,
Wine without water brings paralysis.

The Spartan Cleomenes was supposed to have gone mad through having learned from the Scythians to drink wine *neat* (Her. VI 84).

88 ΑΝΑΙΣΧΥΝΤΙΑΣ ΙΕ΄

15 τὴν θύραν ὑπακοῦσαι αὐτός, καὶ τὸν κύνα προσκαλεσάμενος καὶ ἐπιλαβόμενος τοῦ ῥύγχους εἰπεῖν· οὗτος φυλάττει τὸ χωρίον καὶ τὴν οἰκίαν· καὶ τὸ ἀργύριον δὲ παρά του λαμβάνων ἀποδοκιμάζειν, λίαν λέγων λευρὸν εἶναι, καὶ ἕτερον ἅμα ἀλλάττεσθαι· καὶ ἐὰν τὸ ἄροτρον χρήσῃ ἢ κόφινον
20 ἢ δρέπανον ἢ θύλακον, ταῦτα τῆς νυκτὸς <ἀπαιτεῖν> κατὰ ἀγρυπνίαν ἀναμιμνησκόμενος· καὶ εἰς ἄστυ καταβαίνων ἐρωτῆσαι τὸν ἀπαντῶντα πόσου ἦσαν αἱ διφθέραι καὶ τὸ τάριχος, καὶ εἰ σήμερον ὁ ἄρχων νουμηνίαν ἄγει· καὶ εἰπεῖν εὐθὺς ὅτι βούλεται καταβὰς ἀποκείρασθαι καὶ τῆς αὐτῆς
25 ὁδοῦ παριὼν κομίσασθαι παρ᾽ Ἀρχίου τοῦ ταρίχους· καὶ ἐν βαλανείῳ δὲ ᾆσαι καὶ εἰς τὰ ὑποδήματα δὲ ἥλους ἐγκροῦσαι.

ἀναισχυντίας ιε΄.

ἡ δὲ ἀναισχυντία ἐστὶ μέν, ὡς ὁρῷ λαβεῖν, καταφρόνησις

---

17. **the dog**] The house-dog which kept watch in the hall. In Ar. *Lysist.* 1213 the servant at the door warns importunate visitors to 'beware of the dog.' The arrival of a welcome guest is thus described in some verses quoted by Athenaeus (1 p. 3 § 4):—

First, the hall-porter is all smiles—the dog
Wags a pleased tail—and some one hastes to set
A chair, unhidden.

21. **if he has lent his plough**] It is impossible not to be struck by the frequent allusions in these sketches to loans between neighbours of things used in housekeeping or farming. Thus the Penurious man (XXIV) is one who 'forbids his wife to lend salt, or a lamp-wick, or cummin, or verjuice, or meal for sacrifice, or garlands, or cakes'; cf. cc. XV, XXIII, XXVI. Such touches remind us that the social life of Attica was, in the best sense, homely; and of the saying of Pericles, that Athenians understood φιλοκαλεῖν μετ᾽ εὐτελείας. Compare Xenophon *Mem.* II 2, 12. 'Well,' said Socrates, 'and do you not wish to be on good terms with your neighbour, that he may give you a light for your fire when you want one?'

24. **hides**] διφθέραι were sometimes worn by country people. A rustic in the *Clouds* (72) is described as 'clad in leather, driving in his goats from Phelleus.' (We may also compare, in the first scene of Menander's *Epitrepontes*, ὦ κάκιστ᾽ ἀπολούμενοι, | δίκας λέγοντες περιπατεῖτε, διφθέρας | ἔχοντες.)

25. **the New Moon**] The first of the (lunar) month was fair-day at Athens. Ar. *Wasps* 171, 'I want to sell my ass; for it is new moon': *Knights* 43, 'this man bought a slave at the last new moon.' A public sacrifice, at which the archon presided, was held on the acropolis on this day. Demosth. *Aristog.* I p. 800 (urging the jury to be true to their oaths), 'How (else), when you go up to the acropolis at the new moon, can you pray the

a knock at the door himself, and call the dog to him, and take hold of his nose, saying 'This fellow looks after the place and the house.' When he is given a piece of money, he will reject it, saying that it is too smooth, and thereupon will take another instead; and, if he has lent his plough, or a basket or sickle or bag, and remembers it as he lies awake, he will ask it back in the middle of the night. On his way down to Athens he will ask the first man that he meets how hides and salt-fish were selling, and whether the archon celebrates the New Moon to-day; adding immediately that he means to have his hair cut when he gets to town, and at the same visit to bring some salt-fish from Archias as he goes by. He will also sing at the bath; and will drive nails into his shoes.

XV (IX). THE SHAMELESS MAN

Shamelessness may be defined as neglect of reputation for the sake of base gain.

---

gods to bless Athens and to bless each one of you?'

28. **salt-fish**] As fresh fish was the favourite delicacy at Athens, so salt-fish was the cheapest and commonest food. While Dicaeopolis, in the *Acharnians*, having made peace for himself, is preparing to dine on pheasants and thrushes, Lamachus ruefully provides himself with the fare of a campaigner—onions and salt-fish (*Ach.* 1100). There were shops expressly for its sale in the market-place (c. XVI), and it was also sold at the city-gates (Ar. *Knights* 1246). Cargoes of salted thunnies, mackerel, etc., were imported from the Hellespont and the Euxine: Athen. III p. 116 § 85.

28. **will sing at the bath**] At the public baths, no less than in the streets or at the theatres, manners were on their trial. The term 'Tribalhans,' which Demosthenes uses in the general sense of 'roysterers,' meant especially, according to one old lexicon, *those who behave with ill-breeding at the baths*. The Shameless man (XV), the Offensive man (XII), and the Late-learner (VIII) all make the baths a place for the display of their characters. The Rustic sings in mere gaiety of spirit. Horace complains of more deliberate offenders:—'Some recite their works in the forum; not a few at the bath' (*Sat.* I 4, 75): and Martial says of an irrepressible reciter—'I fly to the baths—you still buzz at my ear' (III 44, 12). Seneca too reckons among the nuisances of those resorts 'the man who likes to hear his own voice' (Ep. 56). One of the temptations may have been the vaulted roof.

1. **Shamelessness**] The clause in the Definition—'for the sake of base gain'—is significant. It is the key, as will presently be explained, to the special and limited sense in which Theophrastus considers Shamelessness. Compare the pseudo-Platonic *Definitions* p. 416: 'Shamelessness is a state of mind tolerant of ignominy for the sake of gain.'

Shamelessness in its general sense—

ΑΝΑΙΣΧΥΝΤΙΑΣ ΙΕ'

δόξης αἰσχροῦ ἕνεκα κέρδους, ὁ δὲ ἀναίσχυντος τοιοῦτος οἷος πρῶτον μέν, ὃν ἀποστερεῖ, πρὸς τοῦτον ἀπελθὼν δανείζεσθαι· εἶτα θύσας τοῖς θεοῖς αὐτὸς μὲν δειπνεῖν παρ' ἑτέρῳ, τὰ δὲ κρέα ἀποτιθέναι ἁλσὶ πάσας· καὶ προσκαλεσάμενος τὸν ἀκόλουθον δοῦναι ἀπὸ τῆς τραπέζης ἄρτον καὶ κρέας ἄρας, καὶ εἰπεῖν ἀκουόντων πάντων· εὐωχοῦ, τιμιώτατε· καὶ ὀψωνῶν δὲ ὑπομιμνῄσκειν τὸν κρεωπώλην εἴ τι χρήσιμος αὐτῷ γέγονε, καὶ ἑστηκὼς πρὸς τῷ σταθμῷ μάλιστα μὲν κρέας, εἰ δὲ μή, ὀστοῦν εἰς τὸν ζωμὸν ἐμβαλεῖν· καὶ ἐὰν μὲν λάβῃ, εὖ ἔχει, εἰ δὲ μή, ἁρπάσας ἀπὸ τῆς τραπέζης χολίκιον ἅμα γελῶν ἀπαλλάττεσθαι· καὶ ξένοις δὲ αὐτοῦ θέαν ἀγοράσας μὴ δοὺς τὸ μέρος θεωρεῖν, ἄγειν δὲ καὶ τοὺς υἱεῖς εἰς τὴν

'the not-shrinking from doing disgraceful things' (*Eth. N.* IV 9)—comprehends three characters described by Theophrastus: 1. Shamelessness (ἀναισχυντία) in his special sense: 2. Recklessness or the Abandoned character (ἀπόνοια): 3. Grossness (βδελυρία). We will attempt to discriminate these; having regard, not to the ideas which the terms might or ought to convey, but merely to the positive sense in which Theophrastus has used them.

(1) His Shameless man, then,—whom it will be convenient to distinguish as the man of Shrewd Effrontery—is one who is restrained by no scruple from committing those small injustices for which there is a practical impunity. He is not at war with society; he does not outrage it by any grave misdemeanour, or even by any eccentricity so violent that a brazen jocularity cannot carry it off. The strength of his genius lies in this,—that, while he is habitually guilty of sharp practice in his dealings with the world, and while he knows that the world knows it, he is able to suppress every trace of consciousness that he is not generally respected and beloved. The first trait given by Theophrastus is the most expressive. He dines out at a time when he was socially bound to be dispensing instead of receiving hospitality. But, instead of betraying embarrassment, he gaily assumes the licence of a privileged and especially popular guest.

(2) The Reckless or Abandoned man (ἀπονενοημένος) is also shameless. But, whereas the man of Shrewd Effrontery represses, for the sake of gain, an instinct of shame probably feeble from the first, the Reckless man has fiercely cast off a sense of shame which may once have been fine. The breach between him and his self-respect is complete and irreconcilable, transforming his whole character, and driving him into grotesque forms of self-insult. The man of Shrewd Effrontery is on good terms with the world; the Reckless man is a social outcast.

(3) The Gross man differs from the other two chiefly in this,—that he stands morally on a higher, aesthetically on a lower level. He does 'shameless' things neither, like the man of Shrewd Effrontery, with a view to advantage, nor, like the Reckless man, in a sort of desperation; but naturally, with the relish of a coarse nature for monstrous jests, which seem to him the more humorous if they extort signs of disgust. But, if he is in more violently bad taste, he is less immoral than the other two; for his offences are less voluntary, and, on the whole, of

THE SHAMELESS MAN. XV (IX)

The Shameless man is one who, in the first place, will go and borrow from the creditor whose money he is withholding. Then, when he has been sacrificing to the gods, he will put away the salted remains, and will himself dine out; and, calling up his attendant, will give him bread and meat taken from the table, saying in the hearing of all, 'Feast, most worshipful.' In marketing, again, he will remind the butcher of any service which he may have rendered him; and, standing near the scales, will throw in some meat, if he can, or else a bone for his soup; if he gets it, it is well; if not, he will snatch up a piece of tripe from the counter, and go off laughing. Again, when he has taken places at the theatre for his foreign visitors, he will see the performance without paying his own share, and will bring

---

a lighter kind He does not defraud his neighbour, like the man of Shrewd Effrontery; nor, like the Reckless man, leave his mother to starve

5. when he has been sacrificing] As in Homeric, so in later times, a sacrifice was usually followed by a feast. Thus, in one of Antipho's speeches, a man has a sacrifice to perform to Zeus Ctesius in the Peiraeus: he makes it the occasion of giving a farewell dinner to a friend who is about to sail (*de Venef.* § 16). The sacrifice in honour of any domestic event, e.g. the naming of a child, or an athletic victory (δεκάτην, νικητήρια θύειν) —always implied the entertaining of friends. After public sacrifices, in like manner, the people were feasted (Isaeus *de Astyph. hered.* § 21), a regular portion of bread and meat being given to each person (Plut. *Symp.* II 10, 7). To hold a sacrifice without giving a dinner would have been thought inhospitable, to dine out on the same day, shameless

6. calling up his attendant] A Roman custom allowed the guest to hand to his slave, stationed behind him, delicacies which he wished to reserve for use at home see Athen. IV p. 128 § 2, where, at an elaborate wedding-banquet, the slaves in attendance on their masters carry baskets, which are soon filled. But on ordinary occasions it was thought ill-bred to use this privilege. see Lucian's *Symp.* c. 2, *Hermot.* c. 2; Martial II 37. And there is no proof that the custom was tolerated at all by earlier Greek manners: at Rome it may have been connected in origin with the client's dole. Here the Shameless man is of course represented as taking an unusual liberty. A similar trait is mentioned of the Avaricious man, who, at a club-dinner, asks for a dish for his slaves (c XXVI).

8. in marketing] See note on c. XVII, 12.

13. when he has taken places at the theatre] Having his house full of guests, perhaps at one of the festivals, he takes a certain number of places for a series of performances at the theatre. His visitors pay for the tickets; but, on the first day, he contrives to go himself in the place of one of them; and, emboldened by success, brings on the second day his children and their 'pedagogue' in the room of others. Similarly the Avaricious man (c. XXVI) 'seizes the opportunity of taking his boys to the play, when the lessees of the theatre grant free admission.' The ordinary price of admission was two obols,—rather more than 3d,—which the State furnished to poor people at the festivals. Foreigners probably had to take their places through citizens; and foreign women at least seem to have been

ΑΠΟΝΟΙΑΣ ΙϚ'

ὑστεραίαν καὶ τὸν παιδαγωγόν· καὶ ὅσα ἐωνημένος ἄξιά τις
15 φέρει, μεταδοῦναι κελεῦσαι καὶ αὐτῷ· καὶ ἐπὶ τὴν ἀλλοτρίαν
οἰκίαν ἐλθὼν δανείζεσθαι κριθὰς, ποτὲ δὲ ἄχυρον, καὶ ταῦτα
χρήσαντας ἀναγκάσαι ἀποφέρειν πρὸς αὐτόν. δεινὸς δὲ καὶ
πρὸς τὰ χαλκεῖα τὰ ἐν τῷ βαλανείῳ προσελθὼν καὶ βάψας
ἀρύταιναν βοῶντος τοῦ βαλανέως αὐτὸς αὑτοῦ καταχέασθαι,
20 καὶ εἰπεῖν ὅτι λέλουται, κᾆτα ἀπιὼν, οὐδεμία σοὶ χάρις.

ἀπονοίας ιϛ'.

ἡ δὲ ἀπόνοιά ἐστιν ὑπομονὴ αἰσχρῶν ἔργων τε καὶ λόγων,
ὁ δὲ ἀπονενοημένος τοιοῦτός τις οἷος ὀμόσαι ταχύ, κακῶς
ἀκοῦσαι καὶ λοιδορηθῆναι δυνάμενος, τῷ ἤθει ἀγοραῖός τις
καὶ ἀνασεσυρμένος καὶ παντοποιός· ἀμέλει δυνατὸς καὶ
5 ὀρχεῖσθαι νήφων τὸν κόρδακα καὶ προσωπεῖον οὐκ μὴ ἔχων ἐν
κωμικῷ χορῷ· καὶ ἐν θαύμασι δὲ τοὺς χαλκοῦς ἐκλέγειν καθ'

---

restricted to a particular part of the house. In a fragment of Alexis the women complain, 'we have to sit at the theatre in the back rows, as if we were foreigners' (ξέναι· Alex. *frag.* 25, 1 Meineke)

18. **and borrow barley**] See note on c. XIV, 21

20. **the coppers in the baths**] for heating the water. A shower-bath was sometimes taken by having water dashed over the head; and this office was performed by the bathman. See Plat. *Rep.* I p. 344 D, 'Thrasymachus now thought of going, after having, like a bathman, dashed his discourse over our ears in a full torrent.' The Shameless man does this for himself, and thus finds a pretext for depriving the attendant of his fee. (ἐμαυτῷ βαλανεύσω was a proverbial phrase for doing a thing for oneself. Zenobius III 58.)

1. **Recklessness**] On the difference between this character and those which precede and follow it, see c. XV, note 1. The term ἀπονενοημένος contrasts a former with an actual state; before a man can be desperate he must have hoped. The Definition fails to mark this; but the Character marks it throughout. It is the picture of a person who has gone from bad to worse, until he retains just so much remembrance of a more respectable self as serves to give him a frantic pleasure in insulting his own dignity. He is ready to be *even* a crier or a cook; a statement which shows how advantageous is the original position supposed for the now Reckless man. The ideas conventionally attached to the words ἀπόνοια, ἀπονενοημένος will be seen from pseudo-Demosth. *in Aristog.* I p. 780 § 32: 'Do you not see that in his policy there is no calculation, no restraining sense of honour (αἰδώς), but that *recklessness* (ἀπόνοια) is its guide? Or rather, his policy *is* utter recklessness,—that worst of evils to the man upon whom it comes, a thing terrible and cruel to all,—to the State, intolerable. For the reckless man (ὁ ἀπονενοημένος) has given himself up,—has no care for the safety which calcula-

THE RECKLESS MAN. XVI (VI)

his sons, too, and their attendant the next day. When anyone secures a good bargain, he will ask to be given part in it. He will go to another man's house and borrow barley, or sometimes bran; and moreover will insist upon the lenders delivering it at his door. He is apt, also, to go up to the coppers in the baths,— 20 to plunge the ladle in, amid the cries of the bath-man,—and to souse himself; saying that he has had his bath, and then, as he departs,—'No thanks to you!'

XVI (VI). THE RECKLESS MAN.

Recklessness is tolerance of shame in word and deed.

The Reckless man is one who will lightly take an oath, being proof against abuse, and capable of giving it; in character a coarse fellow, defiant of decency, ready to do anything; just the person to dance the cordax, sober and without a mask, in 5 a comic chorus. At a conjuror's performance, too, he will collect

---

tion can ensure,—and prospers, if he does prosper, against expectation and against probability.' Plutarch makes callousness to ill repute the essence of ἀπόνοια (*Alcib.* 13, 4).

3. **being proof against abuse, and capable of giving it**] The aor. λοιδορηθῆναι is here, as in Demosthenes, deponent, having an active sense, 'to revile': see *Crit. App.* The Reckless man cannot only listen unmoved to reproaches (κακῶς ἀκοῦσαι), but can retort them.

5. **to dance the cordax**] The author of the *Clouds*, taking credit to himself for the propriety of his muse, instances some things which she has eschewed. Among these it is specified that she has 'never mocked bald men, nor danced the cordax' (540).

5. **sober**] Cf. Demosth. *Olynth.* II p. 23 § 19: 'The rest of (Philip's) court consists of brigands and flatterers and such-like persons, capable of dancing, *when intoxicated*, dances which I would rather not name to you.'

5. **without a mask**] Demosth. *de Falsa Legat.* p. 433 § 287: 'men at the very sight of whom you would cry out— the blackguard Nicias and the execrable Curebion, who plays comic parts in the procession without the mask' (i.e. at the Dionysia). Observe the article: *the* (indispensable) mask.

6. **at a conjuror's performance**] Jugglers, puppet-showmen and the like travelled about to the fairs and festivals at towns. Plutarch compares persons who circulate absurd opinions to men 'dragging about a sort of conjuror's apparatus and booth (πυλαίαν) on their backs' (*de fac. Lunae* 8). In Plato's *Republic* (VII p. 514 B) the wall over which the prisoners in the cave see images flit is compared to the 'screens which conjurors set between themselves and the spectators, over which they show their tricks.' Sometimes they were allowed to perform in theatres (Athen. I p 19 § 16: Alciphr. III 20). The tricks were of the established type—bringing fire out of the mouth (Athen. IV p. 129

94 ΑΠΟΝΟΙΑΣ ΙϚ'

ἕκαστον παριών, καὶ μάχεσθαι τοῖς τὸ σύμβολον φέρουσι
καὶ προῖκα θεωρεῖν ἀξιοῦσι· δεινὸς δὲ καὶ πανδοκεῦσαι καὶ
τελωνῆσαι καὶ μηδεμίαν ἐργασίαν αἰσχρὰν ἀποδοκιμάσαι,
10 ἀλλὰ κηρύττειν, μαγειρεύειν, κυβεύειν, τὴν μητέρα μὴ τρέφειν, ἀπάγεσθαι κλοπῆς, τὸ δεσμωτήριον πλείω χρόνον
οἰκεῖν ἢ τὴν αὑτοῦ οἰκίαν. καὶ τούτων δ' ἂν εἶναι δόξειε τῶν
περιϊσταμένων τοὺς ὄχλους καὶ προσκαλούντων, μεγάλῃ τῇ
φωνῇ καὶ παρερρωγυίᾳ λοιδορουμένων καὶ διαλεγομένων

§ 3), swallowing knives (Plut. *Lyc.* 19), making pebbles pass from one cup to another, or producing them from the mouth or ears of a spectator (Alciphr. III 20). (Cp ἐν τοῖς θαύμασιν in Xenophon, *Symposium*, II 1, and Isocr. XV 213.)

8. the free-pass] τὸ σύμβολον appears to mean a token or ticket given by the conjuror to his friends, or paid for, before the performance commenced. Compare Ar. *Plut.* 278, 'why do you not go?—Charon offers you your ticket' (τὸ σύμβολον δίδωσι)—with allusion to the tickets given to jurymen when they entered court, and on presenting which they received their pay. (See Aristotle's *Constitution of Athens*, col. 32, 14 and 37, 2, and figs. 4 and 5 in Frontispiece, ed. Sandys.)

9. an inn-keeper] The unpopularity of inn-keepers arose partly, no doubt, from the general feeling in ancient Greece against taking money for hospitality; but they were also infamous, as a class, for extortion. See a curious passage in Plato's *Laws*, XI p. 918 D: 'On this account (eagerness for gain) all the lines of life connected with retail trade, commerce, inn-keeping, have fallen under suspicion and become utterly disreputable...A man opens lodgings, for the sake of trade, in a lonely place, a long way from anywhere. He receives bewildered travellers in barely tolerable quarters, or affords warmth, quiet, and rest in his close rooms to people driven in by angry storms. And then, after receiving them as friends, he does not provide them with hospitable entertainment in accordance with that reception,

but *holds them to ransom*,—like captive enemies whom he has got into his clutches,—on the most exorbitant, unjust, rascally terms. It is these offences, and others like them, shamefully common in all such callings, which have brought discredit upon such ministration to men's need.' But though it was discreditable to keep, it was not so to frequent an inn. The Athenian ambassadors to Philip stay at inns (Dem. *de F. Legat.* p. 272); and Dionysus in the *Frogs* (114) inquires which are the best inns on the road to Hades.

9 a tax-farmer] Andocides *de Myst.* p. 17 § 133:—'Agyrrhius became chief-farmer of the two-per-cent. tax two years ago, buying it for thirty talents; and had for his partners the whole set who muster under the white-poplar' (the spot at Athens where the tax-contracts were sold); '*you know what they are like.*'

10. a crier's] The Homeric 'herald' was also ambassador, 'messenger of Zeus and men' (*Il.* I 334); his office was sacred and his person inviolable. The house of the Heralds at Athens were the priestly representatives of this bygone dignity. But the modern 'herald'—the crier who made proclamation in the Ecclesia or in the market-place—seems to have been on a level with the Roman *praeco.* Speaking of the shifts to which poor poets are reduced, Juvenal says: 'Others have not thought it too low or base to become criers' (VII 5).

11. a cook's] The meals of an Athenian household were usually prepared by the female slaves; only on

the pence, going along from man to man, and wrangling with those who have the free-pass, and claim to see the show for nothing. He is apt, also, to become an inn-keeper or a tax-farmer; he will decline no sort of disreputable trade, a crier's, a cook's; he will gamble, and neglect to maintain his mother; he will be arrested for theft, and spend more time in prison than in his own house.

And he would seem, too, to be one of these persons who collect and call crowds about them, ranting in a loud cracked voice and haranguing them; meanwhile some will approach, and

---

special occasions was a man-cook hired from one of the shops in the market-place in which the business of professed cook was combined with that of butcher. When Aristippus was reproached with employing a professional orator in a lawsuit, 'Well,' he answered, 'and, when I give a dinner-party, I hire a cook' (Diog. II 72). The earliest mention of a mancook as part of the establishment is said by Athenaeus to have occurred in a writer who lived about 280 B.C : Athen. XIV p. 658 § 22. Commenting upon the luxury brought in at Rome by the Asiatic conquests, Livy says: 'Then it was that the cook, esteemed and treated by the ancients *as the vilest of slaves*, began to be prized' (XXXIX 6).

11. **he will gamble**] Aeschines *in Timarch*. p. 8 § 53 : 'He spent his days in a gambling-house, where the fighting-stage (τηλία, a board with a ring chalked upon it) is set out, and they match fighting-cocks, and play at dice.' Alciphr. III 54 : 'Perhaps you will ask me why I am crying, or how I came to have my head broken, or why this flowered cloak of mine is torn to tatters? I won at dice. Would that I never had! What business had I to match my weak self against sturdy young men? No sooner had I swept all the stakes on the table towards me, and broken their bank, than they made a general rush at me. Some pounded me with their fists, others used stones, others tore my clothes. I clung fast to my money, determined to die rather than give up to them any part of my winnings. Well, for a time, I made a good fight of it, standing the showers of blows, resisting the wrenching fingers, and sitting still like a Spartan who is being flogged on Orthia's altar. At last, however, I grew faint, and allowed the ruffians to take their plunder.'

11. **will neglect to maintain his mother**] Loss of civil rights was the legal penalty for proved neglect of parents Aeschin. *in Timarch*. p. 4 § 28. 'And whom did our lawgiver condemn to silence (in the Ecclesia)? Evil livers. And where does he make this clear? 'Let there be' he says 'a scrutiny of the public speakers, in case there be any speaker in the Ecclesia who is a striker of his father or mother, or who neglects to maintain them or to give them a home.' Solon, however, enacted that 'no son should be compelled to maintain a father who failed to have him taught some trade' (Plut. *Sol* 22).

12. **will be arrested for theft**] The Greek term ἀπάγεσθαι implies that the man is caught in the fact and taken at once before the Commissioners of Police ('the Eleven'). According to the letter of Athenian law in the time of Demosthenes, theft was a capital crime in three cases : (1) theft to the value of more than 50 drachmas, or about £2 : (2) theft to the value of more than 10 drachmas (8s.) from the gymnasia, the baths, or the ports: (3) theft of anything by night (Dem. *in Timocr*. p. 736 § 113).

15 πρὸς αὐτούς· καὶ μεταξὺ οἱ μὲν προσίασιν, οἱ δὲ ἀπίασι πρὶν ἀκοῦσαι αὐτοῦ, ἀλλὰ τοῖς μὲν τὴν ἀρχὴν, τοῖς δὲ συλλαβὴν, τοῖς δὲ μέρος τοῦ πράγματος λέγει, οὐκ ἄλλως θεωρεῖσθαι ἀξιῶν τὴν ἀπόνοιαν αὐτοῦ ἢ ὅταν ᾖ πανήγυρις. ἱκανὸς δὲ καὶ δίκας τὰς μὲν φεύγειν, τὰς δὲ διώκειν, τὰς δὲ
20 ἐξόμνυσθαι, ταῖς δὲ παρεῖναι, ἔχων ἐχῖνον ἐν τῷ προκολπίῳ καὶ ὁρμαθοὺς γραμματιδίων ἐν ταῖς χερσίν· καὶ οὐκ ἀποδοκιμάζειν δὲ οὐδὲ καπήλων ἀγοραίων στρατηγεῖν, καὶ εὐθὺς τούτοις δανείζειν, καὶ τῆς δραχμῆς τόκον τρία ἡμιωβόλια τῆς ἡμέρας πράττεσθαι, καὶ ἐφοδεύειν τὰ μαγειρεῖα, τὰ
25 ἰχθυοπώλια, τὰ ταριχοπώλια, καὶ τοὺς τόκους ἀπὸ τοῦ ἐμπολήματος εἰς τὴν γνάθον ἐκλέγειν.

[ἐργώδεις δέ εἰσιν οἱ τὸ στόμα εὔλυτον ἔχοντες εἰς λοιδορίαν καὶ φθεγγόμενοι μεγάλῃ τῇ φωνῇ, ὡς συνηχεῖν αὐτοῖς τὴν ἀγορὰν καὶ τὰ ἐργαστήρια.]

βδελυρίας ιζ'.

οὐ χαλεπὸν δέ ἐστι τὴν βδελυρίαν διορίσασθαι· ἔστι

20. **some public gathering**] πανήγυρις is a word of general meaning. He chooses for his displays a time when Athens is full; either a market-day or a festival. As the great festivals were occasions of buying and selling, πανήγυρις seems, at least in later Greek, to have meant especially the *fair* coincident with a festival: see Paus. X 32, 9 (describing a festival in Phocis): 'On the last of the three days they *hold a fair* (πανηγυρίζουσι), selling slaves, and, indeed, all beasts of burden.'

22. **excusing himself on oath**] He is concerned with law-suits in one of three capacities,—as defendant, as plaintiff, or as witness. In the last case he sometimes attends the courts, bringing a mass of papers; but he sometimes makes oath that he knows nothing of the matter. This was ἐξόμνυσθαι. Those who, when cited, refused either to give evidence or to take this oath, were liable to a fine of 1000 drachmas. Demosth. *in Neaer.* p. 1354: 'I call Hipparchus himself before you. I will compel him to give evidence, or to excuse himself on oath according to law.'

23. **in the breast of his cloak**] which was worn deep, and served as a bag or purse. Theocritus says, speaking of the niggardly spirit of the age, 'Everyone keeps his hand in the bosom of his robe' (i e. guards his pockets closely: XVI 17).

25. **to be a captain of market-place hucksters**] i.e. to be patron and subsidizer of the retail-traders (κάπηλοι) who kept taverns and eatinghouses in the marketplace, and who were, as a class, in bad repute. He lends them small sums with which to carry on their business, and goes the round of their shops to levy his

others go away without hearing him out; but to some he gives the first chapter of his story, to others an epitome, to others a fragment; and the time which he chooses for parading his recklessness is always when there is some public gathering. Great is he, too, in lawsuits, now as defendant, now as prosecutor; sometimes excusing himself on oath, sometimes attending the court with a box of papers in the breast of his cloak and satchels of note-books in his hands. He will not disdain either to be a captain of market-place hucksters, but will readily lend them money, exacting, as interest upon ten-pence, two-pence half-penny a day; and will make the round of the cook-shops, the fishmongers, the fish-picklers, thrusting into his cheek the interest which he levies on their gains

[These are troublesome persons, for their tongues are easily set wagging abusively; and they talk in so loud a voice that the market-place and the workshops resound with them.]

XVII (XI). The Gross Man.

Grossness is not difficult to define; it is obtrusive and objectionable pleasantry.

---

interest. He has himself been described as ἀγοραῖός τις. See *Crit. App*

26. **two-pence half-penny a day**] The drachma = 6 obols: this is therefore 25 per cent. a day. Compare Plaut *Epid.* I 1, 5: 'He actually borrowed this money from a usurer at Thebes on daily interest,—a sesterce for every silver mina.' Taking the mina at rather more than £4, and the sesterce at 2*d.*, this would be about 74 per cent. a year. Menippus, the Cynic, 'was a money-lender by the day, and was called the day-lender' (ἡμεροδανειστής: Diog. VI 99).

27. **the cook-shops**] Isocrates implies that in his time the shops of this kind in the market-place had a better class of customers than formerly: for he says that *then* 'no decent servant, even, would have thought of eating and drinking in a tavern' (*Areop.* p. 149 § 49). See, however, the story in Plutarch *Demosth.* 60.— 'Diogenes once saw in a tavern Demosthenes—who was ashamed and shrank back "The more you shrink back," he said, "the more you will be in the tavern."'

28. **thrusting into his cheek**] Ar. *Eccl.* 818: 'I had been selling grapes, and came back with my cheek full of copper coins.'

29. **the interest on their gains**] ἀπὸ τοῦ ἐμπολήματος, 'out of their receipts from what they sell,' ἐμπολᾶν meaning not merely 'to buy,' but 'to gain by traffic.' Isaeus *de Hagn. hered.* p. 88 § 43. 'Besides these he left furniture, cattle, barley, wine, fruit, by which they made (ἐνεπόλησαν) 4900 drachmas.'

32. **the workshops**] See note on c. XVII, 15.

1. **Grossness**] βδελυρός, in its graver sense, was nearly equivalent to Black-

γὰρ παιδιὰ ἐπιφανὴς καὶ ἐπονείδιστος, ὁ δὲ βδελυρὸς τοιοῦτος οἷος ἀπαντήσας γυναιξὶν ἐλευθέραις <ἀσχημονεῖν>· καὶ ἐν θεάτρῳ κροτεῖν ὅταν οἱ ἄλλοι παύωνται, καὶ συρίττειν
5 οὓς ἡδέως θεωροῦσιν οἱ λοιποί· καὶ πληθούσης τῆς ἀγορᾶς προσελθὼν πρὸς τὰ κάρυα ἢ τὰ μύρτα ἢ τὰ ἀκρόδρυα ἑστηκὼς τραγηματίζεσθαι, ἅμα τῷ πωλοῦντι προσλαλῶν· καὶ καλέσαι δὲ τῶν παριόντων ὀνομαστί τινα, ᾧ μὴ συνήθης ἐστί· καὶ σπεύδοντας δέ που ὁρῶν περιμεῖναι κελεῦσαι· καὶ
10 ἡττημένῳ δὲ μεγάλην δίκην ἀπιόντι ἀπὸ τοῦ δικαστηρίου προσελθεῖν καὶ συνησθῆναι· καὶ ὀψωνεῖν ἑαυτῷ καὶ αὐλητρίδας μισθοῦσθαι, καὶ δεικνύειν δὲ τοῖς ἀπαντῶσι τὰ ὠψωνημένα καὶ παρακαλεῖν ἐπὶ ταῦτα· καὶ διηγεῖσθαι προστὰς πρὸς κουρεῖον ἢ μυροπώλιον ὅτι μεθύσκεσθαι
15 μέλλει· καὶ εἰς ὀρνιθοσκόπου τῆς μητρὸς ἐξελθούσης

guard. But it was used also in a lighter sense, to describe that kind of coarse buffoon whom Aristotle calls βωμολόχος (*Eth. N.* II 7, 13). See Plato's *Republic* p. 338 D, where Thrasymachus says, in reference to his opponent having used what he considers an extravagantly unfair illustration, βδελυρὸς εἶ, ὦ Σώκρατες,—'Socrates, you are a buffoon.' In this sketch the graver and lighter meanings are blended; but the latter predominates. It is impossible to find an exact equivalent in English. 'Buffoon' has acquired too polite associations. 'Blackguard' is, on the whole, too grave for the character intended here. 'Gross' appears least inadequate. It does not, indeed, interpret the humorous side of the character; but then neither does its Greek original,—the humorous sense attached to βδελυρός being conventional.

4. **hiss the actors**] A demonstrative Athenian audience did not always confine themselves to hissing. Demosthenes, taunting Aeschines with his ill-success on the stage, remarks that the tragic contests in which he used to take part were 'contests for his life,' from which he frequently came off 'with wounds' (*de Coron.* p. 314); i.e. he was pelted. Again, *de Fals. Legat.* p. 449 'When he played the woes of Thyestes and the Trojan war, you drove him off the boards with your hisses, and *all but stoned him to death*' Lucian describes an impersonation of Ajax so vivid that 'the whole house went mad at once along with Ajax,—they danced, shouted, tore off their clothes' (*de Salt.* 83)

5. **when the market-place is full**] 'Full market' was an expression for the hours from about 9 A.M. to noon. See Her. IV 181 (speaking of a spring in the oasis of Ammon): 'through the hour of dawn it is warm; at full market colder; noon comes, and it is intensely cold.' Again, III 104: '(the Indians) have the sun hottest in the early morning,—not, like others, at noon, but from sunrise to the breaking-up of market' (i.e. midday, when people went home to a siesta. see note on c. XXIV, 28).

6. **myrtleberries**] a favourite delicacy at dessert. Athenians, according to a poet in Athenaeus (XIV p. 652 D), 'sing the praises of myrtleberries, of honey, of the portals of the acropolis, and fourthly of dried figs.'

THE GROSS MAN. XVII (XI)

The Gross man is one who will insult freeborn women; who, in a theatre, will applaud when others cease, and hiss the actors who please the rest of the spectators. When the market-place is full, he will go up to the place where nuts or myrtleberries or fruits are sold, and stand munching while he chatters to the seller. Then he will call by name to a passer-by with whom he is not familiar; or, if he chance to see persons in a hurry, he will cry 'stop'; or he will go up to a man who has lost a great law-suit and is leaving the court, and will congratulate him. He will do his own marketing, and hire flute-players; moreover he will show to everyone who meets him the provisions that he has bought, with an invitation to come and eat them; and will explain, as he stands at the door of a barber's or perfumer's shop, that he means to get drunk. His mother having gone out to the soothsayer's, he will use words of evil omen; or, when

---

9 f. **will cry ' stop ']** Terence alludes to this as a well-worn practical joke: *Phormio* v vi. 7: '*Antipho.* Hi, Geta! *Geta* (who is running in the opposite direction). There you go again. Is there anything new or wonderful in being called back when one has set out running?'

11 f. **he will do his own marketing]** The ordinary practice, except among the very poor, was to send a slave to market: see (for a somewhat earlier period) Xen. *Mem.* I 5, 2: 'Would we take a present of such (a worthless slave) to be our attendant or our marketer?' It is observable that in these Characters the persons, besides the βδελυρός, who are named as marketing for themselves are the Shameless man (c. XV) and the Penurious man (c. XXIV); others have their provisions bought by slaves (cc. XIII, XXIII). At the fishmarket, however, where the chief dainty was contended for, gourmands seem to have watched their own interests: Aesch. *in Tim.* p. 9 § 65, 'who is there among you who has not been to the fishmarket and seen what sums these people spend?' Alexis vividly describes a citizen haggling with a fishmonger for a pair of mullets (*frag.* XII 2 Meineke).

15. **a barber's or perfumer's shop]** Lysias *de inval.* p 170 § 20: 'Each man has his favourite lounge, one frequents a perfumer's shop, another a barber's, another a shoemaker's, and so forth; the most popular establishments being those nearest the market-place.' Pseudo-Demosth. *in Arist.* I p. 786 (describing an unsociable person), 'He never frequents any of the barbers' or perfumers' shops in the town, or indeed any of the workshops.'

17. **to the soothsayer's]** Some persons invoked assistance of this kind in very small domestic difficulties See c. XXVIII: 'If a mouse gnaws through a meal-bag, he will go to the expounder of sacred law' Nicias, according to Plutarch, kept a prophet (μάντις) at his house, whom he used to consult 'ostensibly about public affairs; but chiefly, in fact, about his private concerns, and especially about silver-mines' (*Nic.* c 4).

17. **will use words of evil omen]** His mother is seeking a revelation of the will of the gods; to utter, at such a moment, words which will offend them, is not only to thwart her prayer, but to expose her to their anger. To 'blaspheme,' in the Greek sense, was not merely to speak *against* the gods, but to speak, when they were

βλασφημῆσαι· καὶ εὐχομένων καὶ σπενδόντων ἐκβαλεῖν τὸ
ποτήριον καὶ γελάσαι, ὥσπερ ἀστεῖόν τι πεποιηκώς· καὶ
αὐλούμενος δὲ κροτεῖν ταῖς χερσὶ μόνος τῶν ἄλλων καὶ
συντερετίζειν καὶ ἐπιτιμᾶν τῇ αὐλητρίδι, τί οὐ ταχὺ παύ-
20 σαιτο· καὶ ἀποπτύσαι δὲ βουλόμενος ὑπὲρ τῆς τραπέζης,
προσπτύσαι τῷ οἰνοχόῳ.

ἀδολεσχίας ιη΄.

ἡ δὲ ἀδολεσχία ἐστὶ μὲν διήγησις λόγων μακρῶν καὶ
ἀπροβουλεύτων· ὁ δὲ ἀδολέσχης τοιοῦτός ἐστιν οἷος, ὃν μὴ
γινώσκει, τούτῳ παρακαθεζόμενος πλησίον πρῶτον μὲν τῆς
αὐτοῦ γυναικὸς εἰπεῖν ἐγκώμιον· εἶτα, ὃ τῆς νυκτὸς εἶδεν
5 ἐνύπνιον, τοῦτο διηγήσασθαι· εἶθ᾽ ὧν εἶχεν ἐπὶ τῷ δείπνῳ
τὰ καθ᾽ ἕκαστα διεξελθεῖν· εἶτα δὴ προχωροῦντος τοῦ πράγματος λέγειν, ὡς πολὺ πονηρότεροί εἰσιν οἱ νῦν ἄνθρωποι
τῶν ἀρχαίων· καὶ ὡς ἄξιοι γεγόνασιν οἱ πυροὶ ἐν τῇ ἀγορᾷ·
καὶ ὡς πολλοὶ ἐπιδημοῦσι ξένοι· καὶ τὴν θάλατταν ἐκ Διονυ-
10 σίων πλόϊμον εἶναι· καὶ εἰ ποιήσειεν ὁ Ζεὺς ὕδωρ πλεῖον, τὰ

---

deemed present, as at a sacrifice, of any dismal subject, distasteful to the bright and gracious visitants. Clytaemnestra complains that the *lamentations* of Electra prevent her from sacrificing to the gods; Philoctetes is left on Lemnos because his cries of pain make offerings and libations unavailing (Soph. *El.* 632, *Phil.* 8). See the striking passage in Plato's *Laws* (VII p. 800 B): 'Suppose, I say, that when a sacrifice had been performed and the victims duly burnt, some individual, the man's son or perhaps brother, standing near the altar and oblations, should break into all manner of ill-omened words—should we not say that his utterances would cast a gloom—a sense of whispered and foreshadowed evil—upon his father and upon all his house?'

18 **will drop his cup**] A bad omen, —what the Romans called *caducum auspicium*. When Crassus was on his fatal march into Armenia,—a march discouraged by many omens,—a sacrifice was held soon after crossing the Euphrates; when the augur handed to Crassus the liver of the victim, *he dropped it.* 'Then, seeing that all present were deeply troubled, he said, smiling, "Such is old age, but at all events no arms shall be dropped"' (Plut. *Crass.* 19).

1. **Garrulity**] The epithet 'ill-considered' in the Definition embodies the distinction drawn by Theophrastus between Garrulity and Loquacity. It is a difference, not of quantity, but of quality. The Loquacious man is possibly able; he is certainly ambitious; it is his tendency to treat a subject in a large manner, with copious, if not always apt, illustration.

people are praying and pouring libations, he will drop his cup, and laugh as if he had done something clever. Also, when the flute is being played to him, he alone of all the company will 20 beat time with his hands, and trill an accompaniment; and will reprove the player, asking why she did not stop sooner. And, when he desires to spit, he will spit across the table at the cupbearer.

XVIII (III). THE GARRULOUS MAN.

Garrulity is the discoursing of much and ill-considered talk.

The Garrulous Man is one who will sit down beside a person whom he does not know, and first pronounce a panegyric on his own wife; then relate his dream of last night; then go through in detail what he has had for dinner Then, warming to the 5 work, he will remark that the men of the present day are greatly inferior to the ancients; and how cheap wheat has become in the market; and what a number of foreigners are in town, and that the sea is navigable after the Dionysia; and that, if Zeus

---

The Garrulous man is necessarily weak; talking is, with him, not an ambition, nor exactly a pleasure, but rather an acquired physical need; and, being neither inventive nor logical, he can neither rise out of the tritest topics nor pursue any one of these. Loquacity wearies, Garrulity irritates; the one—as Theophrastus says—induces sleep; the other, fever.

The specimen of Garrulity given in this chapter seems not inartistic. It is characteristic, as has been said, of the Garrulous man that he is incapable of pursuing a subject,—his remarks being either wholly unconnected, or connected by an inadequate link, the chain in the latter case being seldom long. Now the discourse in the text shows both the absolute and the feebly-disguised solution of continuity. The topics are:—(1) His wife; suggesting his dream upon the bed of which she is the partner. (2) His dinner (absolute change of subject). (3) The Inferiority of the moderns (do).

(4) The Cheapness of wheat in the marketplace (do.); suggesting (i) the Strangers seen there; who suggest (ii) the Dionysia, for which they may have come; and this (iii) the Navigable Season; leading to (iv) the Crops, and (v) his own Farmingplans, which remind him of (vi) the Difficulty of living, and (vii) the Goodfortune of Damippus, who could afford so great a torch at the Mysteries; these suggest (viii) Temples generally, especially the Odeum.—(5) His indisposition yesterday (absolute change of subject). 'Yesterday' suggests (i) To-day, and what day of the Month it is; which suggests the Calendar generally, and so (ii) the Festivals which are its landmarks.

9. after the Dionysia] i.e. the 'great' Dionysia. The four festivals of Dionysus fell in four successive months: (1) The 'Rural' in December; (2) the 'Lenaea' in January; (3) the 'Anthesteria' in February; (4) the 'great' or 'city'

ἐν τῇ γῇ βελτίω ἔσεσθαι· καὶ ὅτι ἀγρὸν εἰς νέωτα γεωργήσει·
καὶ ὡς χαλεπόν ἐστι τὸ ζῆν· καὶ ὡς Δάμιππος μυστηρίοις
μεγίστην δᾷδα ἔστησε· καὶ πόσοι εἰσὶ κίονες τοῦ Ὠιδείου;
καὶ χθὲς ἤμεσα· καὶ τίς ἐστιν ἡμέρα σήμερον; καὶ ὡς
15 Βοηδρομιῶνος μέν ἐστι τὰ μυστήρια, Πυανεψιῶνος δὲ Ἀπατούρια, Ποσειδεῶνος δὲ τὰ κατ' ἀγροὺς Διονύσια· κἂν
ὑπομένῃ τις αὐτὸν, μὴ ἀφίστασθαι.
[παρασείσαντα δὴ δεῖ τοὺς τοιούτους τῶν ἀνθρώπων καὶ
διαράμενον ἀπαλλάττεσθαι, ὅστις ἀπύρετος βούλεται εἶναι·
20 ἔργον γὰρ συναρκεῖσθαι τοῖς μήτε σπουδὴν μήτε σχολὴν
διαγινώσκουσιν.]

λαλιᾶς ιθ'.

ἡ δὲ λαλιά, εἴ τις αὐτὴν ὁρίζεσθαι βούλοιτο, εἶναι ἂν

Dionysia in March. About this time sets in the northern etesian; followed each day, after the sunset lull, by the south-breeze now called the 'embates.' 'Never, except in the short winter season, is there any uncertain irregularity in wind and weather; the commencement of the fair season—the safe months, as the ancients called it—brings with it an immutable law followed by the winds in the entire archipelago; every morning the north-wind arises from the coasts of Thrace, and passes over the whole island-sea' (Curtius, *Hist. Gr.* trans. Ward I p. 13 f.). With it came the merchants 'flying over the sea in spring-time like birds of passage to all foreign cities' (Plato *Laws* XII p. 952 E). It was the special pride of Athens that, unlike some other cities, she excluded no foreigner, not even enemies, from anything which she could teach or show (Thuc. II 39).

12. **set up a very large torch at the Mysteries**] The Lesser Mysteries of Demeter were celebrated at Athens at the end of February; the Greater at Eleusis at the end of September. These lasted nine days. On the fifth, a procession of the fully-initiated (ἐπόπται) and of those initiated in the Lesser rites (μύσται) walked from Athens to Eleusis, carrying torches, and led by the torch-bearer (δᾳδοῦχος). They remained there two days; on the sixth night the mystae became epoptae; next day they returned to Athens. It seems probable that, on the evening of the fifth or 'torch' day, there was at Athens a sort of illumination, when those who did not go to Eleusis burned torches before their doors. These torches symbolised the search of Demeter for Persephone; precisely as the lamps burnt at the night-festival (λυχνοκαΐα) at Sais symbolised the search of Isis for Osiris, and were burnt throughout Egypt on that night before the houses of those who could not attend the festival (Her. II 62). (The text probably refers to the custom of setting up large sculptured representations of torches in front of temples. Examples of these may be seen in reliefs from Samothrace, in coins of Cyzicus and Megara, and at Eleusis itself (Studniczka on p. 24 of the Leipzig edition). A 'coin of Megara showing Demeter lighting a colossal torch' is re-

THE LOQUACIOUS MAN. XIX (VII)

would send more rain, the crops would be better; and that he will work his land next year; and how hard it is to live; and that Damippus set up a very large torch at the Mysteries; and 'How many columns has the Odeum?'; and that yesterday he was unwell; and 'What is the day of the month?'; and that the Mysteries are in Boëdromion, the Apaturia in Pyanepsion, the rural Dionysia in Poseideon. Nor, if he is tolerated, will he ever desist.

[He who would not have a fever must shake off such persons, and thrust them aside, and make his escape. It is hard to bear with those who cannot discern between the time to trifle and the time to work.]

XIX (VII). THE LOQUACIOUS MAN.

Loquacity, if one should wish to define it, would seem to be an incontinence of talk.

---

produced on p. 4 of Edmonds and Austen's edition from the original in the British Museum, *Cat. of Coins, Att. &c.*, XXII 3.)

13. **the Odeum**] or 'Music-hall' Athens had three such buildings: (1) the Odeum near the fountain 'Enneakrounos' (Paus. 1 8 § 6, 10 § 1); older, according to Hesychius, than the theatre of Dionysus. On one occasion three thousand hoplites were called together in it: Xen. *Hellen.* II 4 § 9. It was apparently a semi-circular building, arranged on the general plan of a Greek theatre, except that it was roofed for the sake of sound. (2) The Odeum of Pericles, which is probably the one meant here; built about 440 B.C. at the S E corner of the acropolis. The form was round. It had a pointed roof, said to be in imitation of the tent of Xerxes; in the interior 'many seats *and columns*' (Plut *Per.* 13). (3) The Odeum built about 150 A D. at the S.W. corner of the acropolis by Herodes Atticus, and called after his wife the 'Odeum of Regilla.' It was the largest in Greece, the interior diameter being about 240 ft (Paus. VII

20 § 3).

15. **the Apaturia**] Between the Mysteries in September, and the 'Rural' or local celebrations of the Dionysia in December, fell in October the Apaturia; a festival kept in nearly all Ionic cities, and having for its objects (1) the recognition of a common descent from Ion, and, through him, from his father Apollo, whom Ionians worshipped as Apollo Patroüs; (2) the maintenance of the ties of clanship subordinate to this common tie; children being then enrolled in their father's 'phratria.'—Ephesus and Colophon alone, whose inhabitants claimed to be the purest Ionians, were forbidden by a religious scruple to celebrate it (Her. 1 147).

1. **Loquacity**] It is well defined as '*incontinence* (ἀκρασία) of talk'; for, while Garrulity drops its unconnected remarks with dull persistence, Loquacity is fluent and eager. Compare Ar *Frogs* 838 'a mouth unbridled—*intemperate* (ἀκρατές)—of which the gates stand ever wide.'—See note on c. XVIII, 1

ΛΑΛΙΑС ΙΘ'

δόξειεν ἀκρασία τοῦ λόγου, ὁ δὲ λάλος τοιοῦτός τις οἷος τῷ
ἐντυγχάνοντι εἰπεῖν, ἂν ὁτιοῦν πρὸς αὐτὸν φθέγξηται, ὅτι
οὐδὲν λέγει, καὶ ὅτι αὐτὸς πάντα οἶδε, καί, ἂν ἀκούῃ αὐτοῦ,
5 μαθήσεται· καὶ μεταξὺ δὲ ἀποκρινομένῳ ὑποβάλλειν, εἶπας
σύ; μὴ ἐπιλάθῃ ὃ μέλλεις λέγειν· καὶ εὖ γε, ὅτι με ὑπέμνη-
σας· καὶ τὸ λαλεῖν ὡς χρήσιμόν που· καὶ ὃ παρέλιπον·
καὶ ταχύ γε συνῆκας τὸ πρᾶγμα· καὶ πάλαι σε παρετήρουν,
εἰ ἐπὶ τὸ αὐτὸ ἐμοὶ κατενεχθήσει· καὶ ἑτέρας ἀρχὰς τοιαύτας
10 πορίσασθαι, ὥστε μηδὲ ἀναπνεῦσαι τὸν ἐντυγχάνοντα. καὶ
ὅταν γε τοὺς καθ' ἕνα ἀπογυιώσῃ, δεινὸς καὶ ἐπὶ τοὺς ἀθρόους
καὶ συνεστηκότας πορευθῆναι καὶ φυγεῖν ποιῆσαι μεταξὺ
χρηματίζοντας· καὶ εἰς τὰ διδασκαλεῖα δὲ καὶ εἰς τὰς παλαί-
στρας εἰσιὼν κωλύειν τοὺς παῖδας προμανθάνειν, τοσαῦτα
15 προσλαλῶν τοῖς παιδοτρίβαις καὶ διδασκάλοις. καὶ τοὺς
ἀπιέναι φάσκοντας δεινὸς προπέμψαι καὶ ἀποκαταστῆσαι
εἰς τὴν οἰκίαν· καὶ πυθόμενος τὰ τῆς ἐκκλησίας ἀπαγγέλ-
λειν, καὶ προσδιηγήσασθαι δὲ καὶ τὴν ἐπ' Ἀριστοφῶντός
ποτε γενομένην [τοῦ ῥήτορος] μάχην καὶ τὴν Λακεδαιμονίων

7. **Do you tell me so? don't forget, &c.**] i.e. 'You astonish me: take care that you do not involve yourself in a self-contradiction.' See *Crit. App.*

16. **he will go into the schools**] Aeschines (*in Timarch.* p. 2 § 12) quotes an ancient law providing for the strict privacy of schools. 'Let it not be lawful for those above the age of boys to enter (the schools) while the boys are there, except for the son, brother, or son-in-law of the master; and, if anyone enter contrary to this rule, let him be punished with death.' The very terms, however, in which Aeschines refers to this ordinance as embodying the *old* feeling on the subject imply that it had become obsolete.

16. **the palaestras**] here in the strict sense—schools of wrestling and boxing. 'Gymnasium' properly meant a place of more general resort and of more various resources, including grounds for running and archery, javelin-ranges, baths, &c.—Physical education probably began very early. Plato recommends that the distinctive discipline for boys and for girls should begin at six years of age—that of a boy with lessons in riding and in the use of the bow, javelin, and sling; 'letters' are to come at the age of ten (*Laws* VII p. 794 C). Aristotle thought that the active training of mind *and body* might begin at the seventh year (*Politics* VII 17).

20. **the news from the Ecclesia**] On the text see *Crit. App.* The meaning probably is that, on the breaking up of the Ecclesia, the λάλος obtains a summary of the debate from some one who was there, and retails it to others. At the time when these Characters were probably written, the number of Athenian citizens, i.e. of persons privileged to attend the Ecclesia, was comparatively small. The following measure had been

THE LOQUACIOUS MAN. XIX (VII)

The Loquacious Man is one who will say to those whom he meets, if they speak a word to him, that they are quite wrong, and that *he* knows all about it, and that, if they listen to him, they will learn; then, while one is answering him, he will put in, 'Do you tell me so?—don't forget what you are going to say'; or 'Thanks for reminding me'; or 'How much one gets from a little talk, to be sure!'; or 'By-the-bye'—; or 'Yes! you have seen it in a moment', or 'I have been watching you all along to see if you would come to the same conclusion as I did'; and other such cues will he make for himself, so that his victim has not even breathing-time. Aye, and when he has prostrated a few lonely stragglers, he is apt to march next upon large, compact bodies, and to rout them in the midst of their occupations. Indeed, he will go into the schools and the palaestras, and hinder the boys from getting on with their lessons, by chattering at this rate to the trainers and masters. When people say that they are going, he loves to escort them, and to see them safe into their houses. On learning the news from the Ecclesia, he hastens to report it; and to relate, in addition, the old story of the battle in Aristophon [the orator]'s year, and of the

---

taken by Antipater in 322:—'Out of 21,000 qualified citizens of Athens, all those who did not possess property to the amount of 2000 drachmae were condemned to disfranchisement and deportation. The number below this prescribed qualification, who came under the penalty, was 12,000, or three-fifths of the whole. They were set aside as turbulent, noisy democrats; the 9000 richest citizens, the 'party of order,' were left in exclusive possession, not only of the citizenship, but of the city' (Grote c. xcv). The great mass of the population could, at such a time, learn the proceedings of the Ecclesia only by hearsay.

22. **the battle in Aristophon's year**] The battle of Megalopolis in Arcadia, where a Lacedaemonian army was defeated by Antipater, regent of Macedonia during the absence of Alexander. This event is placed by Mr Grote (c. xcv) in 330 B.C., Ol. CXII 3, in which year Aristo-

phon was archon (Clinton, *Fast. Hellen.*). This is the usual explanation of the reference, and probably the right one. Mr Clinton, indeed, places the battle of Megalopolis about Sept. 331 B.C.; and inclines to the view of Casaubon that 'the battle in Aristophon's year' means the contest between Demosthenes and Aeschines in 330 B.C., when the latter spoke his oration *Against Ctesiphon*, and the former replied in the speech *On the Crown*. Were not Casaubon's proposed change of τοῦ ῥήτορος to τῶν ῥητόρων a violent one, this ingenious view would have some probability. But it seems impossible that, without the help of τῶν ῥητόρων, μάχη could bear such a sense. The words τοῦ ῥήτορος are now usually bracketed as spurious. They were added by one who confused the Aristophon who was archon in 330 B.C., and who is otherwise unknown, either with (1) Aristophon of Azenia, who

106   ΛΟΓΟΠΟΙΙΑΣ Κ'

20 ἐπὶ Λυσάνδρου, καὶ οὕς ποτε λόγους αὐτὸς εἶπας εὐδοκίμησεν ἐν τῷ δήμῳ, καὶ κατὰ τῶν πληθῶν γε ἅμα διηγούμενος κατηγορίαν παρεμβαλεῖν, ὥστε τοὺς ἀκούοντας ἤτοι ἐπιλαθέσθαι ἢ νυστάξαι ἢ μεταξὺ καταλιπόντας ἀπαλλάττεσθαι· καὶ συνδικάζων δὲ κωλῦσαι κρῖναι, καὶ συνθεωρῶν θεάσα-
25 σθαι, καὶ συνδειπνῶν φαγεῖν, λέγων ὅτι χαλεπὸν τῷ λάλῳ ἐστὶ σιωπᾶν, καὶ ὡς ἐν ὑγρῷ ἐστιν ἡ γλῶττα, καὶ ὅτι οὐκ ἂν σιωπήσειεν, οὐδ' εἰ τῶν χελιδόνων δόξειεν ἂν εἶναι λαλίστερος· καὶ σκωπτόμενος ὑπομεῖναι καὶ ὑπὸ τῶν αὐτοῦ παιδίων, ὅταν αὐτὸν ἤδη καθεύδειν βουλόμενα κελεύῃ λέ-
30 γοντα· πάππα, λάλει τι ἡμῖν, ὅπως ἂν ἡμᾶς ὕπνος λάβῃ.

λογοποιίας κ'.

ἡ δὲ λογοποιία ἐστὶ σύνθεσις ψευδῶν λόγων καὶ πράξεων ὧν βούλεται ὁ λογοποιῶν, ὁ δὲ λογοποιὸς τοιοῦτός τις οἷος ἀπαντήσας τῷ φίλῳ εὐθὺς καταβαλὼν τὸ ἦθος καὶ μειδιάσας ἐρωτῆσαι· πόθεν σύ, καὶ λέγεις τί; τί ἔχεις περὶ τοῦδε
5 εἰπεῖν καινόν; καὶ ἐπιβαλὼν ἐρωτᾶν, μὴ λέγεταί τι καινότερον; καὶ μὴν ἀγαθά γέ ἐστι τὰ λεγόμενα· καὶ οὐκ ἐάσας

---

was dead in 330 B.C., Aesch *in Ctes* § 139; or with (2) Aristophon of Collytus, also dead then; compare Dem. *de Cor.* §§ 162 and 75. Both were distinguished as politicians and speakers.

23. **the Lacedaemonian victory**] This is usually understood of Aegospotami, 405 B C. and there was no other battle 'in the time of Lysander' of sufficient importance to have been alluded to in this way. If the clause is genuine, the Loquacious man for once seems to degenerate into Garrulity. The comparatively recent battle of Megalopolis (330 B.C.) may have had some real connexion with the political questions just discussed in the Ecclesia; but why he should go on to speak of an event so remote as the fight at Aegospotami,—

unless because this was a battle also, and one in which the fortune went the other way,—does not appear. See *Crit. App.*

32 **a greater chatterer than a swallow**] Dionysus in the *Frogs* (93) describes the swarms of chattering poetasters as 'colleges of swallows.' Virgil, too, calls the swallows 'garrulous' (*Geo.* IV 307). There were other proverbs for loquacity: see Alexis in Athen. IV p. 133 § 10:—

Not tailed cicada, jay, or nightingale,
Not turtle-dove or grasshopper can match
Thy chattering.

1. **Newsmaking**] The character described here is that of a maker, not merely a monger, of news. A deliberate impostor, not merely a reckless gossip, is the subject of the portrait. He 'assumes

THE NEWSMAKER. XX (VIII)

Lacedaemonian victory in Lysander's time; also of the speech for which he himself once got glory in the Assembly; and he will throw in some abuse of 'the masses,' too, in the course of his narrative; so that the hearers will either forget what it was about, or fall into a doze, or desert him in the middle and make their escape. Then, on a jury, he will hinder his fellows from coming to a verdict, at a theatre from seeing the play, at a dinner-party, from eating; saying that 'it is hard for a chatterer to be silent,' and that this tongue *will* run, and that he could not hold it, though he should be thought a greater chatterer than a swallow. Nay, he will endure to be the butt of his own children, when, drowsy at last, they make their request to him in these terms—'Papa, chatter to us, that we may fall asleep!'

XX (VIII). THE NEWSMAKER.

Newsmaking is the framing of fictitious sayings and doings at the pleasure of him who makes news.

The Newsmaker is a person who, when he meets his friend, will assume a demure air, and ask with a smile—'Where are *you* from, and what are your tidings? What news have you to give about this affair?' And then he will reiterate the question—'Is anything fresh rumoured? Well certainly these are glorious

---

a demure air' that he may seem the more assured of his intelligence, he is careful to quote 'such authorities that no one can possibly lay hold upon them'; he makes 'plausible' comments upon his own story. It is the studied artifice implied in these touches which distinguishes him from the mere retailer, or even embellisher, of idle rumours, such as the 'scurra' in Plautus, who knows 'what Juno said to Jupiter' (*Trinum.* I 2, 171). At Athens more than in other cities the desire of news was a passion; other cities had their newsmongers; at Athens an exceptional demand produced the Newsmaker. (Cf. Lysias, *Or.* XXII 14, (τὰς συμφορὰς τὰς ὑμετέρας) λογοποιοῦσιν κτλ., Dem. *Phil* I p 54 § 49, ἀνοητότατοι γὰρ εἰσιν οἱ λογοποιοῦντες, and Juvenal, VI 407—412)

(7. **Is anything fresh rumoured?**] Dem. *Phil.* I p. 43 § 10:—'Or tell me, do ye like walking about and asking one another.—is there any news? Why, could there be greater news (γένοιτ' ἂν τι καινότερον;) than that a Macedonian is subduing Athenians and directing the affairs of Greece?' Acts xvii 21 —'For all the Athenians and strangers which were there spent their time in nothing else, but either to tell, or to hear some new thing,' τι καινότερον)

108 ΛΟΓΟΠΟΙΙΑC Κ'

ἀποκρίνασθαι εἰπεῖν· τί λέγεις; οὐδὲν ἀκήκοας; δοκῶ μοί
σε εὐωχήσειν καινῶν λόγων· καὶ ἔστιν αὐτῷ ἢ στρατιώτης
ἢ παῖς Ἀστείου τοῦ αὐλητοῦ ἢ Λύκων ὁ ἐργολάβος παρα-
10 γεγονὼς ἐξ αὐτῆς τῆς μάχης, οὗ φησιν ἀκηκοέναι· αἱ μὲν
οὖν ἀναφοραὶ τῶν λόγων τοιαῦταί εἰσιν αὐτοῦ, ὧν οὐδεὶς ἂν
ἔχοι ἐπιλαβέσθαι· διηγεῖται δέ, τούτους φάσκων λέγειν,
ὡς Πολυπέρχων καὶ ὁ βασιλεὺς μάχῃ νενίκηκε, καὶ Κάσσανδρος ἐζώγρηται· καὶ ἂν εἴπῃ τις αὐτῷ, σὺ δὲ ταῦτα
15 πιστεύεις; φήσει, τὸ πρᾶγμα βοᾶσθαι γὰρ ἐν τῇ πόλει, καὶ
τὸν λόγον ἐπεντείνειν, καὶ πάντας συμφωνεῖν, ταὐτὰ γὰρ
λέγειν περὶ τῆς μάχης· καὶ πολὺν τὸν ζωμὸν γεγονέναι·
εἶναι δὲ αὐτῷ καὶ σημεῖον τὰ πρόσωπα τῶν ἐν τοῖς πράγ-
μασιν· ὁρᾶν γὰρ αὐτῶν πάντων μεταβεβληκότα· λέγει δ',
20 ὡς καὶ παρακήκοε παρὰ τούτοις κρυπτόμενόν τινα ἐν οἰκίᾳ

11. **Asteius the fluteplayer**] Asteius is supposed to be with the army. If it were only for festal purposes, musicians would always be found in a Greek camp. Fluteplayers, in particular, may have been there for two special purposes—as part of the military band, since Dorians, at least, like Asiatics (Her. I 17) usually marched to battle to the sound of the flute (Plut. *Lyc.* 21)—and also with a view to sacrifices, at which the flute was sometimes played (Ar. *Peace* 952).

11. **Lycon the contractor**] The term ἐργολάβος included all who undertook work by contract; e.g. it might be applied to the sculptor who took an order for statues. In 316 Cassander was besieging Pydna. He had sent for 'weapons and engines of all kinds' (Diod. XIX 36); he had blockaded the city, and 'carried a palisade from sea to sea' (*ib.* 49). The 'contractor' may have been concerned with the works of the siege. (*Puto ea aetate notum magis, quam nobilem, Athenis fuisse Lyconem istum,* Casaubon.)

15. **Polyperchon and the king**] (Polyperchon is the form found in contemporary inscriptions, e.g. *Corp. Inscr. Att.* II 723, in the Paris MS B, and in the Munich Epitome of this passage of Theophrastus Cp. Niese's *Geschichte der griech. und mak. Staaten,* i 234 n. I. The time referred to is probably the latter half of 319 B.C., Ol. CXV 2) The discussion as to the date may be elucidated by the following table of events:—

323 B.C. Death of Alexander the Great (in the first half of June). Philip Arrhidaeus, the imbecile half-brother of Alexander, is declared king, a share in the sovereignty being reserved for the unborn child of Alexander by Roxana. A regent is appointed to govern for Philip Arrhidaeus. The child of Roxana (Alexander IV) is born in the same year.

319. Death of the regent Antipater (in the first half of the year). He is described as still alive in c VI. He bequeaths his office, with the guardianship of the joint kings, Philip Arrhidaeus and Alexander IV, to Polyperchon, one of Alexander's generals. Cassander, son of Antipater, disappointed of the regency, goes to war with Polyperchon. Athens presently declares for Cassander. At the same time Eurydice, wife of Philip Arrhidaeus, resolves to throw off the authority of the regent. Roxana flies with her young son

tidings!' Then, without allowing the other to answer, he will go on—'What say you? You have heard nothing? I flatter myself that I can treat you to some news'; and he has a soldier, or a slave of Asteius the fluteplayer, or Lycon the contractor, just arrived from the field of battle, from whom he says that he has heard of it. In fact the authorities for his statements are always such that no one can possibly lay hold upon them. Quoting these, he relates how Polyperchon and the king have won the battle, and Cassander has been taken alive; and, if anyone says to him, ' But do you believe this?'—'Why,' he will answer, 'the town rings with it! The report grows firmer and firmer— everyone is agreed—they all give the same account of the battle'; adding that the hash has been dreadful; and that he can tell it, too, from the faces of the Government—he observes that they have all changed countenance He speaks also of having heard privately that the authorities have a man hid in a house who

---

Alexander IV to Aeacides, king of Epeirus.

317. Polyperchon invades Macedonia with Aeacides, accompanied by Olympias, mother of Alexander the Great. Eurydice is defeated. She and her husband Philip Arrhidaeus are put to death.

316. Cassander goes to Macedonia and besieges Pydna, into which Olympias has thrown herself with Roxana and Alexander IV. Aeacides and Polyperchon are prevented from succouring Pydna by the defection of their troops (Diod. XIX 36). The town falls; Cassander puts Olympias to death, and imprisons Alexander, with his mother Roxana, in Amphipolis.

(It has been a matter of dispute whether 'the king' in the text is the young Alexander IV or Philip Arrhidaeus. Schwarz and Jebb declared in favour of the former. Jebb supposed that the Newsmaker's story belonged to the year 316, while Cassander was advancing to the siege of Pydna (l. 11). At that time Philip Arrhidaeus had been put to death, and Polyperchon was endeavouring to aid Alexander IV. The latter was accordingly identified as 'the king' in conjunction with whom Polyperchon had 'won the battle.' But, in 316, Alexander IV was only a boy of seven, and it is unnatural to describe him as 'winning a battle' at that age. Other considerations point to 319 as the true date and to Philip Arrhidaeus as 'the king' This identification was suggested by Casaubon, who was followed by Ast, Ussing, and Cichorius. As successor of his half-brother, Alexander the Great, he reigned from 323 to 317 under the regency of Perdikkas and Antipater and (on the death of Antipater in the first half of 319) under that of Polyperchon. In the second half of 319 he was supported by Polyperchon, and it was not until the last few months of his life that he was opposed by him. See the discussion by Cichorius on pp. LIX f of the Leipzig edition)

20 the hash has been dreadful] τὸν ζωμόν, lit. 'the broth,'—the carnage. The introduction of this phrase seems happily characteristic. A spirited metaphor is convenient to the utterer of a fiction.

(21. the Government] Phocion and the oligarchical party of 319 B C)

ἤδη πέμπτην ἡμέραν ἥκοντα ἐκ Μακεδονίας, ὃς πάντα ταῦτα οἶδε· καὶ ταῦτα πάντα διεξιών, πῶς οἴεσθε; πιθανῶς σχετλιάζει λέγων· δυστυχὴς Κάσσανδρος· ὦ ταλαίπωρος· ἐνθυμεῖ τὸ τῆς τύχης; ἀλλ᾿ οὖν ἰσχυρός γε γενόμενος...· καὶ δεῖ δ᾿ αὐτὸ σὲ μόνον εἰδέναι· πᾶσι δὲ τοῖς ἐν τῇ πόλει προσδεδράμηκε λέγων.

[τῶν τοιούτων ἀνθρώπων τεθαύμακα τί ποτε βούλονται λογοποιοῦντες· οὐ γὰρ μόνον ψεύδονται ἀλλὰ καὶ ἀλυσιτελῶς ἀπαλλάττουσι· πολλάκις γὰρ αὐτῶν οἱ μὲν ἐν τοῖς βαλανείοις περιστάσεις ποιούμενοι τὰ ἱμάτια ἀποβεβλήκασιν, οἱ δ᾿ ἐν τῇ στοᾷ πεζομαχίᾳ καὶ ναυμαχίᾳ νικῶντες ἐρήμους δίκας ὠφλήκασιν· εἰσὶ δ᾿ οἳ καὶ πόλεις τῷ λόγῳ κατὰ κράτος αἱροῦντες παρεδειπνήθησαν. πάνυ δὴ ταλαίπωρον αὐτῶν ἐστι τὸ ἐπιτήδευμα· ποίᾳ γὰρ ἐν στοᾷ, ποίῳ δὲ ἐργαστηρίῳ, ποίῳ δὲ μέρει τῆς ἀγορᾶς οὐ διημερεύουσιν ἀπαυδᾶν ποιοῦντες τοὺς ἀκούοντας οὕτως καὶ καταπονοῦντες ταῖς ψευδολογίαις;]

κακολογίας κα΄.

ἔστι δὲ ἡ κακολογία ἀγωγὴ τῆς ψυχῆς εἰς τὸ χεῖρον ἐν λόγοις, ὁ δὲ κακολόγος τοιόσδε τις οἷος ἐρωτηθείς, ὁ δεῖνα τίς ἐστιν; εἰπεῖν καθάπερ οἱ γενεαλογοῦντες· πρῶτον ἀπὸ τοῦ γένους αὐτοῦ ἄρξομαι. τούτου ὁ μὲν πατὴρ ἐξ ἀρχῆς

(27. **he was a strong man once**] Cassander was destitute of men and money when he fled to the Macedonian court, early in 319. But he soon succeeded in winning the support of Ptolemy, Antigonus and Lysimachus, and thus getting the harbours of Athens under his control, and forming a large fleet, so that during the same year he was able to confront Polyperchon with a considerable force. Cf. p. 73 of the Leipzig edition)

35. **the Porch**] See note on c. I, 6

37. **what workshop**] See note on c. XVII, 15.

1. **Evil-speaking**] This character differs from all the others drawn by Theophrastus in being seriously odious. Still, the κακολόγος described here is too eager and outspoken to be a detractor of the most vicious kind. 'The sting of ill-temper'—as the last sentence of the chapter phrases it—makes him petulant and bitter; but this very petulance has a comic side. He reminds us more of

THE EVIL-SPEAKER. XXI (XXVIII)

came just five days ago from Macedonia, and who knows it all. And in narrating all this—only think!—he will be plausibly pathetic, saying 'Unlucky Cassander! Poor fellow! Do you see what fortune is? Well, well, he was a strong man once...': adding 'No one but you must know this'—when he has run up to everybody in town with the news.

[It is a standing puzzle to me what object such men can have in their inventions; for, besides telling falsehoods, they incur positive loss. Often have cloaks been lost by those of them who draw groups round them at the baths; often has judgment gone by default against those who were winning battles or sea-fights in the Porch; and some there are who, while mounting the imaginary breach, have missed their dinner. Their manner of life is indeed most miserable. What porch is there, what workshop, what part of the market-place which they do not haunt all day long, exhausting the patience of their hearers in this way, and wearying them to death with their fictions?]

XXI (XXVIII). THE EVIL-SPEAKER.

The habit of Evil-speaking is a bent of the mind towards putting things in the worst light.

The Evil-speaker is one who, when asked who so-and-so is, will reply, in the style of genealogists, 'I will begin with his parentage. This person's father was originally called Sosias;

Mrs Candour than of Iago.—For the word ἀγωγή in the Definition see *Crit. App.*

4. **in the style of genealogists**] whose study was a very popular one in Greece. Hesiod's *Theogony* and the *Genealogies* of Hecataeus (in which the myths and family legends were treated historically) may be taken as representative instances of the early Greek taste for tracing pedigree In Plato's *Cratylus* there is a sarcasm on this taste,—so far, at least, as it concerned the immortals. After observing that Zeus was the son of Cronos, Cronos of Ouranos, Socrates regrets that he does not remember 'the pedigree given by Hesiod, and whom he states to have been the remoter ancestors of these persons.' (p. 396 c.) Compare Plut. *de Curios*. c. 2 (people neglect their own concerns, while) 'they trace the descent of others, showing that their neighbour's grandfather was a Syrian and his grandmother a Thracian.'

5. **Sosias**] a Thracian name, Xen. *Vect.* 4, 14. In the *Wasps*, and in Terence's *Hecyra*, it is the name of a slave; in the *Andria*, of a freedman. The man is said to have changed his original name, which bewrayed a barbarian origin, first for that of Sosistratus, suggestive of gallant ancestors, then for

ΚΑΚΟΛΟΓΙΑΣ ΚΑ'

Σωσίας ἐκαλεῖτο, ἐγένετο δ' ἐν τοῖς στρατιώταις Σωσίστρατος· ἐπειδὴ δὲ εἰς τοὺς δημότας ἐνεγράφη, <Σωσίδημος>. ἡ μέντοι μήτηρ εὐγενὴς Θρᾷττά ἐστι· καλεῖται γοῦν ἡ ψυχὴ <Κορινθιακῶς>· τὰς δὲ τοιαύτας φασὶν ἐν τῇ πατρίδι εὐγενεῖς εἶναι· αὐτὸς δὲ οὗτος, ὡς ἐκ τοιούτων γεγονώς, κακὸς καὶ μαστιγίας. καὶ ἱκανὸς δὲ πρός τινα εἰπεῖν· ἐγὼ δήπου τὰ τοιαῦτα οἶδα, ὑπὲρ ὧν οὐ πλανᾷ πρὸς ἐμὲ καὶ τούτους διεξιών· αὗται αἱ γυναῖκες ἐκ τῆς ὁδοῦ τοὺς παριόντας συναρπάζουσι· καὶ οἰκία τις αὕτη τὰ σκέλη ἠρκυῖα· οὐ γὰρ οὖν λῆρός ἐστι τὸ λεγόμενον, ἀλλ' ὥσπερ κύνες αἱ γυναῖκες ἐν ταῖς ὁδοῖς συνέρχονται· καὶ τὸ ὅλον ἀνδρολάλοι τινές, καὶ αὐταὶ ἐπὶ θύραν τὴν αὔλειον ὑπακούουσι. ἀμέλει δὲ καὶ κακῶς λεγόντων ἑτέρων συνεπιλαμβάνεσθαι εἰπών· ἐγὼ δὲ τοῦτον τὸν ἄνθρωπον πλέον πάντων μεμίσηκα· καὶ γὰρ εἰδεχθής τις ἀπὸ τοῦ προσώπου ἐστίν, ἡ δὲ πονηρία οὐδενὶ ὁμοία· σημεῖον δέ· τῇ γὰρ αὑτοῦ γυναικὶ τάλαντα εἰσενεγκαμένῃ προῖκα ἕξ, ἐξ ἧς παιδίον αὐτῷ γέγονε, τρεῖς χαλκοῦς εἰς ὄψον δίδωσι, καὶ τῷ ψυχρῷ λούεσθαι ἀναγκάζει τῇ τοῦ Ποσειδῶνος ἡμέρᾳ. καὶ συγκαθήμενος δεινὸς περὶ τοῦ

that of Sosidemus, which speaks still more eloquently of a descent from Athenian patriots. Compare Lucian's *Timon* c. 21, where the sudden inheritor of wealth is transformed 'from the sometime Pyrrhias or Dromo or Tibius, into Megacles or Megabyzus or Protarchus.' And so, in the *Dream*, c. 14, Simon, on becoming rich, dilates into Simonides.

6. **in the ranks**] This need not mean more than that he had served among the mercenaries of Athens. Hired troops had long formed by far the larger proportion of her military force; thus 10,000 mercenaries (ξένοι) and only 4000 citizens go to Olynthus (Dem. *de F. Legat.* § 266). In the allied Greek army which met Philip at Chaeronea there were altogether 17,000 mercenaries (*de Cor.* § 237). Thrace, the country of Sosias, furnished Athens with cavalry and peltasts in the Peloponnesian war (Thuc. II 29). But the κακολόγος probably means to hint that Sosias had been a Thracian *slave*—enrolled among the city-guard of public slaves (τοξόται), who, in time of war, were sometimes called into the field: see Boeckh *P. E.* bk II c. 11.

6. **Sosistratus**] A name illustrious in Sicilian history. The best-known Sosistratus was tyrant of Syracuse for a short time before the accession of Agathocles in 317 B.C.

6 f. **when he was enrolled in his deme**] A man was an Athenian citizen either (1) as the son of parents both of whom were citizens,—ἐξ ἀστοῦ καὶ ἐξ ἀστῆς γεγονώς: or (2) by adoption,—ποιήσει πολίτης, Dem. *adv. Lept.* p. 466 § 30. In the latter case he was, upon adoption, enrolled in an assigned deme.

in the ranks he came to rank as Sosistratus; and, when he was enrolled in his deme, as Sosidemus. His mother, I may add, is a noble damsel of Thrace—at least she is called 'my life' in the language of Corinth—and they say that such ladies are esteemed noble in their own country. Our friend himself, as might be expected from his parentage, is—a rascally scoundrel.' He is very fond, also, of saying to one: 'Of course—*I* understand that sort of thing; you do not err in your way of describing it to our friends and me. These women snatch the passers-by out of the very street...That is a house which has not the best of characters...Really there *is* something in that proverb about the women...In short, they have a trick of gossiping with men,—and they answer the hall-door themselves.'

It is just like him, too, when others are speaking evil, to join in:—'And *I* hate that man above all men. He *looks* a scoundrel—it is written on his face; and his baseness—it defies description. Here is a proof—he allows his wife, who brought him six talents of dowry and has borne him a child, three farthings for the luxuries of the table; and makes her wash with cold water on Poseidon's day.' When he is sitting with

A person who, not being a citizen in either of these ways, had his name on the list of a deme, was liable to a ξενίας γραφή. A case of fraudulent registration is mentioned in Dem. *adv. Leoch.* p. 1091. To guard against frauds, every register was periodically revised, and doubtful claims were voted upon (διαψή-φισις, *argum.* Dem. *adv. Eubul.*).

8. **a noble damsel of Thrace**] See Plat. *Theaet.* p 175 D, where it is said that mental clumsiness 'does not excite the ridicule *of Thracian maidservants or of any other uneducated person*, for they do not perceive it' Again, *ib.* p. 174 A, the Θρᾷττα is the type of an uncouth barbarian. 'Thratta,' like Syra, occurs as a proper name, Dem. *in Neaer.* p. 1357.

9. **in the language of Corinth**] See *Crit. App*

18. **they answer the hall-door themselves**] Describing the consternation produced at Athens by the news of Chaeronea, Lycurgus says—'Freeborn women might be seen *at the doors of houses*, scared, stricken with dismay,. *a sight unworthy of themselves and of the city*' (*in Leocr.* p. 153 § 40).

24. **for the luxuries of the table**] εἰς ὄψον. He provides his wife with *necessary* food, i.e. σῖτος, bread; everything beyond this,—meat, fish, etc., ὄψον—she has to find out of her allowance. Aristophanes mentions among the established customs of Athenian wives that of 'marketing surreptitiously on their own account' (αὑταῖς παροψωνεῖν, *Eccl* 666)

24. **makes her wash with cold water**] The warm bath—denounced in the *Clouds* (423 B C) as a novel luxury—was already in Xenophon's time regarded as an almost necessary comfort, see *Mem.* III 13, 3. The penurious husband grudges the cost of this cheap luxury.

25. **on Poseidon's day**] Probably the great day of the Poseidonia,—a festival ranked by Athenaeus with the Eleusinia

ΜΕΜΨΙΜΟΙΡΙΑϹ ΚΒ'

ἀναστάντος εἰπεῖν, καὶ ἀρχήν γε εἰληφὼς μὴ ἀποσχέσθαι
25 μηδὲ τοὺς οἰκείους αὐτοῦ λοιδορῆσαι· καὶ πλεῖστα περὶ τῶν
φίλων καὶ οἰκείων κακὰ εἰπεῖν καὶ περὶ τῶν τετελευτηκότων,
κακῶς λέγειν ἀποκαλῶν παρρησίαν καὶ δημοκρατίαν καὶ
ἐλευθερίαν καὶ τῶν ἐν τῷ βίῳ ἥδιστα τοῦτο ποιῶν.
[οὕτως ὁ τῆς δυσκολίας ἐρεθισμὸς μανικοὺς καὶ ἐξεστη-
30 κότας ἀνθρώπους τοῖς ἤθεσι ποιεῖ.]

μεμψιμοιρίας κβ'.

ἔστιν ἡ μεμψιμοιρία ἐπιτίμησις παρὰ τὸ προσῆκον τῶν
δεδομένων, ὁ δὲ μεμψίμοιρος τοιόσδε τις οἷος, ἀποστείλαντος
μερίδα τοῦ φίλου, εἰπεῖν πρὸς τὸν φέροντα· ἐφθόνησάς μοι
τοῦ ζωμοῦ καὶ τοῦ οἰναρίου, οὐκ ἐπὶ δεῖπνον καλέσας. καὶ
5 τῷ Διὶ ἀγανακτεῖν, οὐ διότι οὐχ ὕει, ἀλλὰ διότι ὕστερον·
καὶ εὑρὼν ἐν τῇ ὁδῷ βαλλάντιον εἰπεῖν· ἀλλ' οὐ θησαυρὸν
εὕρηκα οὐδέποτε· καὶ πριάμενος ἀνδράποδον ἄξιον καὶ
πολλὰ δεηθεὶς τοῦ πωλοῦντος, θαυμάζω, εἰπεῖν, εἴ τι ὑγιὲς
οὕτω ἄξιον ἐώνημαι· καὶ πρὸς τὸν εὐαγγελιζόμενον ὅτι υἱός
10 σοι γέγονεν, εἰπεῖν ὅτι ἂν προσθῇς καὶ τῆς οὐσίας τὸ ἥμισυ

as a great gathering, πανήγυρις (XII p. 500). As the Anthesteria and the Lenaea were respectively held in the months of the same name, it is probable that the Poseidonia fell in Poseideon,—the month answering to the latter half of December and the first half of January. Offerings to Poseidon on the 8th day of that month are mentioned in the *Corp. Inscr. Gr.* I 523 (Michel's *Recueil*, No 692). 'On Poseidon's day,' then, means merely 'in the depth of winter'

33. **the character of insanity and frenzy**] Because a bitterness so extreme against others, and such reckless impiety as that of blaspheming the dead, imply a mind which the gods have afflicted. As moderation, σωφροσύνη, was the first of virtues to a Greek, so the sense which he gave to μανικός was large. It included every violent sin against the principle of human humility (τὸ κατ' ἄνθρωπον φρονεῖν),—e.g. excessive railing at one's neighbours. See Plato *Symp.* p. 173 D, where it appears that a bitterly censorious person had acquired the nickname of μανικός. Cambyses, in his daring impieties, exactly fulfilled the Greek conception of μανία· see Her. III 29, 33.

1. **Grumbling**] Discontent, in its general sense, includes the quality which Theophrastus describes here, and which may be rendered 'Grumbling.' Discontent is either active or passive; but usage has given a predominance to the active sense of the word. When a man is said to be 'discontented,' it is usually implied that he feels a restless desire to improve

THE GRUMBLER. XXII (XVII)

others, he loves to criticise one who has just left the circle; nay, if he has found an occasion, he will not abstain from abusing his own relations. Indeed, he will say all manner of injurious things of his friends and relatives, and of the dead; misnaming slander 'plain speaking,' 'republican candour,' 'independence,' and making it the chief pleasure of his life.

[Thus can the sting of ill temper produce in men the character of insanity and frenzy.]

XXII (XVII). THE GRUMBLER.

Grumbling is undue censure of one's portion.

The Grumbler is one who, when his friend has sent him a present from his table, will say to the bearer, 'You grudged me my soup and my poor wine, or you would have asked me to dinner.' He will be annoyed with Zeus, not for not raining, but for raining too late; and, if he finds a purse on the road, 'Ah,' he will say, 'but I have never found a treasure!' When he has bought a slave cheap after much coaxing of the seller, 'It is strange,' he will remark, 'if I have got a sound lot, such a bargain.' To one who brings him the good news, 'A son is born to you,' he will reply, 'If you add that I have lost half my

---

his position. The Grumbler, on the other hand, represents only the passive form of discontent. Dissatisfied with all persons and things, he yet makes no effort to remove the causes of his dissatisfaction, which is in itself a source of gloomy pleasure. As the Discontented man (in the special sense) is generally one who is striving to rise, the Grumbler is often one whose fortunes have declined. Theophrastus has lightly marked this when he describes the friends of the Grumbler as raising a subscription for him. 'All men whose affairs go wrong,' says Hegio in the *Adelphoe*, 'are somehow prone to suspicions,—prone to take everything as a slight.' The Grumbler entertains that presumption that 'all men are unjust' which, in a more earnest form, constitutes the Distrustful character (c. XXIII). But, unlike the Distrustful man, he does not entertain it so seriously as to take secret counsel with it; it is with him rather a trick of speech, bred by despondency; and, instead of prompting him to guard against wrongs, finds vent merely in protestations that he has been wronged.

2 f. **sent him a present from his table**] See note on c. III, 6.

7 **never found a treasure**] See note on c. XXVI, 18.

10. **brings — the good news, 'A son is born to you'**] In Lucian's *Charon* (c. 17) Hermes, acting as guide to the ferryman of Hades in a holiday visit to earth, points out to him a man 'who is rejoicing because his wife has borne to him *a male child*, and is feasting his friends on the occasion.'

116 ΑΠΙΣΤΙΑC ΚΓ'

ἄπεστιν, ἀληθῆ ἐρεῖς· καὶ δίκην νικήσας καὶ λαβὼν πάσας
τὰς ψήφους, ἐγκαλεῖν τῷ γράψαντι τὸν λόγον ὡς πολλὰ
παραλελοιπότι τῶν δικαίων· καὶ ἐράνου εἰσενεχθέντος παρὰ
τῶν φίλων καὶ φήσαντός τινος, ἱλαρὸς ἴσθι, καὶ πῶς; εἰπεῖν·
15 ὅτε δεῖ τἀργύριον ἀποδοῦναι ἑκάστῳ καὶ χωρὶς τούτων χάριν
ὀφείλειν ὡς εὐηργετημένον;

ἀπιστίας κγ'.

ἔστιν ἀμέλει ἀπιστία ὑπόληψίς τις ἀδικίας κατὰ πάντων,
ὁ δὲ ἄπιστος τοιοῦτός τις οἷος ἀποστείλας τὸν παῖδα ὀψωνή-
σοντα ἕτερον παῖδα πέμπειν πευσόμενον πόσου ἐπρίατο·
καὶ φέρειν αὐτὸς τὸ ἀργύριον καὶ κατὰ στάδιον καθίζων
5 ἀριθμεῖν πόσον ἐστί· καὶ τὴν γυναῖκα τὴν αὑτοῦ ἐρωτᾶν
κατακείμενος, εἰ κέκλεικε τὴν κιβωτόν, καὶ εἰ σεσήμανται τὸ
κυλικούχιον, καὶ εἰ ὁ μοχλὸς εἰς τὴν θύραν τὴν αὐλείαν ἐμ-

13. **by a unanimous verdict**] No slight triumph where there were 500 jurors, or perhaps twice or three times that number. If the defendant in an action gained more than four-fifths of the votes, the plaintiff was fined; the unanimity, on a large Athenian jury, of even four-fifths being considered to imply a case so triumphantly clear that the other side deserved to be punished for presumably vexatious proceedings.

13. **the composer of his speech**] Antipho (born in 480 B.C.) is said to have been the first professional λογογράφος,—i e. writer, for money, of speeches which his employers delivered in court. Lysias, Isocrates and (in early life) Demosthenes were among the great orators who exercised this profession—despised, like that of the sophists, chiefly because it was paid. Contrasting the career of Demosthenes with the undeniable respectability of his father, Aeschines says·—'The trierarch appeared changed into a speech-writer—so ludicrously did he belie his father's antecedents' (*in Ctes.* p. 78 § 173). Demosthenes retorts the accusation —'Well, he applies to others the contemptuous names of speech-writer and sophist, and attempts to deride them, yet he himself will be proved liable to these charges. *Now* are not *you* a speech-writer, and a vile one?' (*de F. Legat.* p. 418 § 246). In the *Phaedrus* we find that a like taunt was addressed to Lysias (p. 257 c).—Cf. note on c. XXX, 16.

1. **Distrustfulness**] Speaking of the general characteristics of elderly men, Aristotle says:—'They are ill-disposed (κακοήθεις); for an ill-disposition consists in putting the worst construction upon everything. They are also prone to sinister suspicions (καχύποπτοι), through their distrustfulness (ἀπιστίαν); and distrustful, through experience' In this passage of Aristotle Distrustfulness has its most general sense, denoting merely reluctance to take things on credit. Out

THE DISTRUSTFUL MAN. XXIII (XVIII)

property, you will speak the truth.' When he has won a lawsuit by a unanimous verdict, he will find fault with the composer of his speech for having left out several of the points in his case. If a subscription has been raised for him by his friends, and someone says to him 'Cheer up!'—'Cheer up?' he will answer; 'when I have to refund his money to every man, and to be grateful besides, as if I had been done a service!'

XXIII (XVIII). THE DISTRUSTFUL MAN.

Distrustfulness is a presumption that all men are unjust.

The Distrustful man is one who, having sent his slave to market, will send another to ascertain what price he gave. He will carry his money himself, and sit down every two-hundred yards to count it. ⟨He will ask his wife in bed if she has locked the wardrobe, and if the cupboard has been sealed, and the bolt

---

of this, when carried too far, springs a fault, κακοήθεια,—a tendency to construe unfavourably all the actions and motives of others. κακοήθεια, again, has a special form, καχυποψία; that is, excessive distrust of the actions and motives of others as they affect one's self. Now the ἀπιστία described by Theophrastus is not the general ἀπιστία of Aristotle. It is not even coextensive with κακοήθεια. It is that form which καχυποψία takes in a mind rather weak and mean than malicious. Hence the Distrustful man of Theophrastus presents an outward resemblance to his Penurious man, insomuch that one of the traits of the latter has been transferred by many editors to the former (see *Crit. App.* XXIII, 11). Many of their actions are, indeed, formally identical; the difference lies in the motives and consequent moral significance.

2. **having sent his slave to market]** See note on c. XVII, 11 f

4. **will carry his money himself]** The Distrustful man can, as we see below, afford a slave to attend him in his walks; but he does not allow this slave, as was usual, to carry the purse. Compare c. VI, where the Boaster chides his attendant for having come out without gold. So probably in c. VII: 'when he pays a mina, he will cause (the slave) to pay the sum in new coin.'

6. **if the cupboard has been sealed]** This was done with wax called ῥύποι, Ar. *Lys.* 1200 Doors, when sealed, were not usually locked, the object being merely that the master might know if they had been tampered with. Diogenes has a story of a person who used to seal up his store-room and then throw the signet-ring in through a slit in the door. His servants, discovering this, used to break open the store-room, seal it up again, and throw back the ring (IV 8 § 59). The wives in the *Thesmophoriazusae* complain that forged signet-rings no longer secure their escape from their sealed apartments, their husbands now carry *worm-wood* seals (θριπήδεστα σφραγίδια),—mottled in imitation of worm-eaten wood, so that the task of making exact copies would be endless (v. 427)

118 ΜΙΚΡΟΛΟΓΙΑC ΚΔ'

βέβληται, καὶ ἂν ἐκείνη φῇ, μηδὲν ἧττον αὐτὸς ἀναστὰς
γυμνὸς ἐκ τῶν στρωμάτων καὶ ἀνυπόδητος τὸν λύχνον ἅψας
10 ταῦτα πάντα περιδραμὼν ἐπισκέψασθαι καὶ οὕτω μόλις
ὕπνου τυγχάνειν· καὶ τοὺς ὀφείλοντας αὐτῷ ἀργύριον μετὰ
μαρτύρων ἀπαιτεῖν τοὺς τόκους, ὅπως μὴ δύνωνται ἔξαρνοι
γενέσθαι· καὶ τὸ ἱμάτιον δὲ ἐκδοῦναι δεινός, οὐχ ὃς βέλτιστα
ἐργάσεται, ἀλλ' ὅταν ᾖ ἄξιος ἐγγυητὴς τοῦ γναφέως· καὶ
15 ὅταν ἥκῃ τις αἰτησόμενος ἐκπώματα, μάλιστα μὲν μὴ δοῦναι,
ἂν δ' ἄρα τις οἰκεῖος ᾖ καὶ ἀναγκαῖος, μόνον οὐ πυρώσας
καὶ στήσας καὶ σχεδὸν ἐγγυητὴν λαβὼν χρῆσαι· καὶ τὸν
παῖδα δὲ ἀκολουθοῦντα κελεύειν αὐτοῦ ὄπισθεν μὴ βαδίζειν
ἀλλ' ἔμπροσθεν, ἵνα φυλάττηται αὐτόν, μὴ ἐν τῇ ὁδῷ ἀπο-
20 δράσῃ· καὶ τοῖς εἰληφόσι τι παρ' αὐτοῦ καὶ λέγουσι, πόσου;
κατάθου· οὐ γὰρ σχολάζω πω πέμπειν, <εἰπεῖν·> μηδὲν πραγ-
ματεύου· ἐγὼ γάρ, ἂν σὺ μὴ σχολάσῃς, συνακολουθήσω.

μικρολογίας κδ'.

ἡ δὲ μικρολογία ἐστὶ φειδωλία τοῦ διαφόρου ὑπὲρ τὸν

11. **in the presence of witnesses**] Some understand 'the same persons who originally witnessed the loan.' But this seems a needless refinement. The Distrustful man brings witnesses simply in order that, if his creditor repudiates the debt, the fact of the repudiation may be established. His remedy is then easy, for he has of course preserved evidence of the loan.

12. **to send his cloak to be cleaned**] See note on c. XXV, 18.

14. **security for the fuller**] He prefers the workman, whether skilful or not, who can find a friend to go bail in a satisfactory amount for the due return of the cloak.

14. **to ask the loan of cups**] Pieces of gold or silver plate were often lent between neighbours for the table or for a sacrifice (compare note on c XIV, 21). Athenaeus tells a story of a pretentious host whose table was covered with plate borrowed among his friends, and who bragged of his readiness 'to break all these things and get new ones.' A guest observed, 'then you will destroy every man's own' (XIII p. 585) See the *Rhetorica ad Herennium* IV 50 (a pretender to wealth has brought some guests home to dinner): 'He had charged his slave Sannio to borrow plate, couch-coverings, servants; and the fellow, who was not without shrewdness, had mustered a very fair show. Our hero brings home his guests—observing that he has lent his "largest" house to a friend for a wedding. The slave whispers that the plate is wanted back—(in fact the lender had felt extremely uneasy). "Go to!"

put upon the hall-door; and, if the reply is 'Yes,' not the less will he forsake the blankets, and light the lamp and run about shirtless and shoeless to inspect all these matters, and barely thus find sleep.) He will demand his interest from his creditors in the presence of witnesses, to prevent the possibility of their repudiating the debt He is apt also to send his cloak to be cleaned, not to the best workman, but wherever he finds sterling security for the fuller. When anyone comes to ask the loan of cups, he will, if possible, refuse; but, if perchance it is an intimate friend or a relation, he will almost assay the cups in the fire, and weigh them, and do everything but take security, before he lends them. Also he will order his slave, when he attends him, to walk in front and not behind, as a precaution against his running away in the street. To persons who have bought something of him and say, 'How much is it? Enter it in your books, for I am too busy to send the money yet,'—he will reply: 'Do not trouble yourself; if you are not at leisure, I will accompany you.'

XXIV (X). The Penurious Man.

Penuriousness is too strict attention to profit and loss.

---

quoth he, "I have lent him my house—given him my servants—and now he wants my plate! Well, though I have guests, he shall have a loan of it. We will enjoy ourselves off Samian earthenware"'

16. **he will almost assay the cups in the fire**] His unwillingness to lend them is so extreme that he seems as if he wished solemnly to prove the fineness of the metal and to register the weight, and then to take formal securities, before parting with his cups. See *Crit App.*

18. **his slave, when he attends him**] Citizens of the richer class were usually attended by a slave when they went out: see cc. IV, VI, VII. On the other hand, it is a mark of arrogance in Meidias that he is attended by '*three or four* slaves' (Dem. *in Meid.* § 158).

20. **to persons who have bought something of him**] On the text, see *Crit. App.* The meaning appears to be as follows:—The buyer has no money with him, and says that he cannot *immediately* send it by a servant from his house, as he has business to transact before going home. He therefore requests the seller to make a memorandum of the amount. The distrustful seller's suspicions are aroused. 'Do not take the trouble of sending a servant with the money' he says; 'if you have business to do, I will accompany you to the places which you must visit, and then go home with you and receive the money myself'

1. **Penuriousness**] 'There seem to be several modes of Illiberality (ἀνελευθερίας). For whereas it consists in two things,—defect in giving and excess in taking,—it is not present in its entirety to all, but is sometimes divided; so that

ΜΙΚΡΟΛΟΓΙΑΣ ΚΔ'

καιρόν, ὁ δὲ μικρολόγος τοιοῦτός τις οἷος ἐν τῷ μηνὶ ἡμιω-
βόλιον ἀπαιτεῖν ἐλθὼν ἐπὶ τὴν οἰκίαν· καὶ συσσιτῶν ἀριθμεῖν τὰς κύλικας, πόσας ἕκαστος πέπωκε, καὶ ἀπάρχεσθαι
5 ἐλάχιστον τῇ Ἀρτέμιδι τῶν συνδειπνούντων· καὶ ὅσα μικροῦ
τις πριάμενος λογίζεται πάντα φάσκειν εἶναι ἄγαν· καὶ
οἰκέτου χύτραν ἢ λοπάδα κατάξαντος εἰσπρᾶξαι ἀπὸ τῶν
ἐπιτηδείων· καὶ τῆς γυναικὸς ἐκβαλούσης τρίχαλκον οἷος
μεταφέρειν τὰ σκεύη καὶ τὰς κλίνας καὶ τὰς κιβωτοὺς καὶ
10 διφᾶν τὰ καλύμματα· καὶ ἐάν τι πωλῇ, τοσούτου ἀποδόσθαι,
ὥστε μὴ λυσιτελεῖν τῷ πριαμένῳ· καὶ οὐκ ἂν ἐᾶσαι οὔτε
συκοτραγῆσαι ἐκ τοῦ αὐτοῦ κήπου οὔτε διὰ τοῦ αὐτοῦ ἀγροῦ
πορευθῆναι οὔτε ἐλάαν ἢ φοίνικα τῶν χαμαὶ κειμένων

---

some men exceed in taking, and others fall short in giving' (Ar. *Eth. N.* IV 1). The Love of Money is considered by Theophrastus in the twofold aspect indicated by Aristotle. The sketches of the Penurious and of the Mean man portray it chiefly as a defect in giving, that of the Avaricious man, as an excess in taking.

(1) The Penurious man, or Reckoner-of-trifles, answers to that class of the illiberal whom Aristotle describes as 'stingy' (φειδωλοί), 'close-fisted' (γλισχροί), 'skin-flints' (κίμβικες). He is minutely and consistently economical. He enforces his own rights to the uttermost; the rights of others he barely satisfies, but does not invade. He may even act from a certain sense of fairness, and from fear of being compelled to do something shameful (*Eth. N.* IV 1). His fault is not necessarily more than that of misjudging the degree of economy which it is his duty to practise.

(2) The Mean man (ἀνελεύθερος) of Theophrastus answers nearly to the Shabby man (μικροπρεπής) of Aristotle (*Eth. N.* IV 2). The distinctive thing about him is the disproportion between his economies and his fortunes. He is a trierarch, and borrows the steersman's rugs. He gives a large wedding-feast, and grudges food to the servants. Yet, like the Penurious man, though he treats others shabbily, he does not defraud them.

(3) The Avaricious man (αἰσχροκερδής Ar. *Eth. N.* IV 1) 'takes whence he ought not, and more than he ought.' He cheats everyone: he sells watered wine to his friends, and gives short measure to his slaves. As described by Theophrastus, he includes the other two characters. Thus, like the μικρολόγος, he sets too little bread on the table; and, like the ἀνελεύθερος, he shirks giving a wedding-present.

2. **while the month is current]** Interest on money was at Athens often reckoned by the month. Thus 10 per cent. per annum was usually called 'five-obol interest'—i.e. the payment of five obols for the use of 600 (one mina) *monthly*. The last day of the month—for which the Penurious man refuses to wait—was pay-day. Strepsiades in the *Clouds*, deploring his son's extravagance, says: 'and *I* am in despair when I see the moon drawing the month out of its teens; the interest grows apace' (v. 16). Again (v. 1130):—'and then, that day which of all I most dread and abhor and detest—*then* comes the last of the month (ἕνη τε καὶ νέα). Everyone of my creditors

THE PENURIOUS MAN. XXIV (X)

The Penurious man is one who, while the month is current, will come to one's house and ask for a half-obol. When he is at table with others, he will count how many cups each of them has drunk; and will pour a smaller libation to Artemis than any of the company. Whenever a person has made a good bargain for him and charges him with it, he will say that it is too dear. When a servant has broken a jug or a plate, he will take the value out of his rations; or, if his wife has dropped a three-farthing piece, he is capable of moving the furniture and the sofas and the wardrobes, and of rummaging in the curtains. If he has anything to sell, he will dispose of it at such a price that the buyer shall have no profit. He is not likely to let one eat a fig from his garden, or walk through his land, or pick up one

vows that he will commence an action and beggar me.'

5. **a smaller libation to Artemis**] This probably refers to a banquet given during a festival of Artemis. See Plut. *de Glor. Athen.* 7: 'The Athenians have consecrated to Artemis the 16th day of Munychion (April—May) on which, while they were conquering at Salamis, she shone on them full-orbed.' Plutarch also mentions (*de Herod. malig.* 26) that before the battle of Marathon the Athenians had vowed to Artemis of the Chase (Agrotera) as many kids as they should slay barbarians. The number of the slain proved countless; they compounded therefore with the goddess by decreeing to sacrifice 500 kids yearly The Marathon-day was Boëdromion 6th (late in September). The allusion in the text may be either to the spring or to the autumn festival. The only divinities to whom it is known that libations were *ordinarily* made at dinner were (1) the Good Genius, ἀγαθὸς δαίμων, (2) the Zeus and Hera, Teleioi of marriage, (3) the Heroes, (4) Zeus Soter.

7. **and charges him with it**] For λογίζεται=*imputat*, see Ar. *Plutus* 381: 'Oh well, *I do* believe (Heaven knows!) that you would spend three minas in a friendly way, and charge me with twelve'

(τρεῖς μνᾶς ἀναλώσας λογίσασθαι δώδεκα). So Arist. *Oecon.* II 34.

8. **broken a jug**] Dionysus, in the *Frogs*, thus describes the spirit of the age: '*Now* every Athenian when he comes home screams to his servants, "Where is that jug?" "Who has eaten off the sardine's head?" "The bowl that I bought last year is no more!"' (v. 980).

9. **out of his rations**] A quart (choenix) of meal a-day, with figs and olives, and a little wine and vinegar, seem to have formed the ordinary rations of a Greek slave. To replace, out of these, even a jug, must have required prudence. In the *Phormio* of Terence Davus complains of the iniquitous fashion which compels his fellow-servant Geta to make a present to the bride of his master's son. 'What he, poor fellow, has saved up with difficulty, ounce by ounce, out of his rations, defrauding his appetite, she will snatch at one swoop, little reckoning with what pains it has been hoarded' (I i 9).

(9f. **a three-farthing piece**] τρίχαλκον, short for τριημιτεταρτημόριον, a very small silver coin worth three χαλκοῖ, or three-eighths of an obol)

13 f. **eat a fig from his garden**] Compare Plato's *Laws* VIII p. 844 E.

ΜΙΚΡΟΛΟΓΙΑC ΚΔ'

ἀνελέσθαι· καὶ τοὺς ὅρους δὲ ἐπισκοπεῖσθαι ὁσημέραι εἰ
15 διαμένουσιν οἱ αὐτοί. δεινὸς δὲ καὶ ὑπερημερίαν πρᾶξαι
καὶ τόκον τόκου ἀπαιτῆσαι· καὶ ἑστιῶν τοὺς δημότας μικρὰ
τὰ κρέα κόψας παραθεῖναι· καὶ ὀψωνῶν μηδὲν πριάμενος
εἰσελθεῖν· καὶ ἀπαγορεῦσαι τῇ γυναικὶ μήτε ἅλας χρῆσαι
μήτε ἐλλύχνιον μήτε κύμινον μήτε ὀρίγανον μήτε οὐλὰς
20 μήτε στέμματα μήτε θυλήματα, ἀλλὰ λέγειν, ὅτι τὰ μικρὰ
ταῦτα πολλά ἐστι τοῦ ἐνιαυτοῦ. καὶ τὸ ὅλον δὲ τῶν μικρο-
λόγων καὶ τὰς ἀργυροθήκας ἔστιν ἰδεῖν εὐρωτιώσας καὶ κλεῖς
ἰωμένας, καὶ αὐτοὺς δὲ φοροῦντας ἐλάττω τῶν μηρῶν τὰ
ἱμάτια, καὶ ἐκ ληκυθίων μικρῶν πάνυ ἀλειφομένους, καὶ
25 ἐν χρῷ κειρομένους, καὶ τὸ μέσον τῆς ἡμέρας ὑπολυομένους,

'If a stranger, having come into Attica, desire to eat the ripe fruit as he passes along the roads, let him pluck the garden-fruit (τῆς γενναίας ὀπώρας, see Ast) without payment and as a guest-gift,—one attendant being also privileged; but of the "wild" fruit, as it is called, let the law restrain our visitors from partaking.' (In contrast to the illiberality of the Penurious man, we have the generosity of Cimon, 'who had no fences to any of his estates, so that anyone who pleased could help himself to the fruit,' Aristotle's *Constitution of Athens*, c. 27)

15 f. **inspect his boundaries**] The boundary-line between farms was usually marked by large stones or slabs (ὅροι). (When the land was mortgaged, the fact was inscribed on these slabs; cf. Solon in Aristotle's *Constitution of Athens*, c. 12, with Sandys' note, p. 45 f.) The Roman *termini* were sometimes stones, sometimes wooden posts. Ovid exhorts the god of boundaries not to allow dishonest encroachments (*Fasti* II 677).—

To wheedling neighbours lend not thou an ear,
Lest mortals above Jove thou seem to fear;
But, whether plough or harrow graze the line,
Cry ' *There* is your field—*this*, I think, is mine.'

17 **to enforce the right of distraining**] ὑπερημερίαν πρᾶξαι When, in a civil action, the court ordered the payment of money or the delivery of property, a day was named on or before which the order should be obeyed. The defaulter became liable, as ὑπερήμερος, to an execution in his house (ἐνεχυράζεσθαι). The same was the case when a loan, or interest upon a loan, had become overdue (Ar *Clouds* 34). But to exercise the right of distraining, except in the last resort, seems to have been thought harsh. See the speech of Demosthenes against Euergus. A trierarch had obtained an order of the Senate for the delivery of certain ship-furniture which a citizen, bound to furnish it, had withheld. The term fixed by the order has expired; the need is urgent. Yet the claimant 'allows some days to elapse,' and only when all remonstrances have failed *threatens* to distrain (p. 1149) For another instance see Demosth. *in Meid.* p. 540.

17 f. **to exact compound interest**] The rates of interest in Greece were high, ranging ordinarily from 10 to 30 or 40 per cent. To exact compound interest was thought extortionate. Ar. *Clouds* 1115: 'A plague on you obol-weighers, you and your "principal" and your "interest upon interest."' In Lucian's *Auction of Careers* (πρᾶσις βίων)—where various lots in life are described and praised by eminent representatives—the

THE PENURIOUS MAN. XXIV (X) 123

of the olives or dates that lie on the ground; and he will inspect his boundaries day by day to see if they remain the same. He is apt, also, to enforce the right of distraining, and to exact compound interest. When he feasts the men of his parish, the cutlets set before them will be small; when he markets, he will come in having bought nothing. And he will forbid his wife to lend salt, or a lamp-wick, or cummin, or verjuice, or meal for sacrifice, or garlands, or cakes; saying that these trifles come to much in the year. Then, in general, it may be noticed that the money-boxes of the penurious are mouldy, and the keys rusty; that they themselves wear their cloaks scarcely reaching to the thigh; that they anoint themselves with very small oil-flasks; that they have their hair cut close; that they take off their

Stoic Chrysippus defends the combination of philosophy with usury:—'Yes, the wise man, indeed, is the only man whom it can become to lend. .Aye, and *he will not take simple interest merely, like the rest of the world*, but fresh interest upon that' (c. 23).

18. **when he feasts the men of his parish**] Every Athenian citizen was a member (1) by descent, of one of the ten tribes formed by Cleisthenes, and (2) of one of the three *phratriae* or clans into which each tribe was divided, (3) according to his place of residence, of one of the demes or parishes—not necessarily contiguous—which each tribe comprised. Fellow-tribesmen (φυλέται), fellow-clansmen (φράτορες), and fellow-parishioners (δημόται) had common sacrifices and banquets. A festival of tribesmen is mentioned in Demosth. *in Meid.* § 156: a festival of clansmen below in c. XXVI. The dinner of fellow-parishioners mentioned here is probably one of those which followed a sacrifice, and which were given by certain members of the deme in rotation. The Mean man performs this duty shabbily —Compare a fragment from the Χείρων of Cratinus (the younger) in Meineke, p. 515: 'After many a year I have come home from the wars—found out with difficulty my kinsmen, clansmen, demesmen—*and been enrolled upon their mess-list*' (εἰς τὸ κυλικεῖον ἐνεγράφην— 'their side-board': the schol. explains it συμπόσιον).

19. **when he markets**] See note on c. XVII, 11 f.

21. **to lend salt**] See note on c. XIV, 21.

21 f. **meal—garlands—cakes**] Barley-meal, mixed with salt, was strewn before the sacrifice on the victim's head. Garlands were worn by the sacrificers, and sometimes placed on the victim. Cakes were burnt on the altar. At the sacrifice in the *Peace* (v. 1041), the thighs of the victim are first laid on the fire; the entrails and the cakes (θυλήματα) are then placed upon them.

25. **scarcely reaching to the thigh**] Athenian fashion seems to have been fastidious in regard to the length of the cloak. The wearing of 'short cloaks' is mentioned in the *Protagoras* among those things which mark an affectation of Spartan austerity (p. 342 C); and in c XIV, 9 we have seen that it is a mark of rusticity. On the other hand the arrogant Aeschines is described ' walking through the market-place with his cloak drooping to his ankles' (Dem. *de F. Legat.* § 314).

27. **have their hair cut close**] In order that it may be a long time before it is necessary to have it cut again. The

124   ΑΝΕΛΕΥΘΕΡΙΑС ΚΕ'

καὶ πρὸς τοὺς γναφεῖς διατεινομένους, ὅπως τὸ ἱμάτιον αὐτοῖς ἕξει πολλὴν γῆν, ἵνα μὴ ῥυπαίνηται ταχύ.

ἀνελευθερίας κε'.

ἡ δὲ ἀνελευθερία ἐστὶ περιουσία τις ἀφιλοτιμίας ἐς δαπάνην ἔχουσα, ὁ δὲ ἀνελεύθερος τοιοῦτός τις οἷος νικήσας τραγῳδοῖς ταινίαν ξυλίνην ἀναθεῖναι τῷ Διονύσῳ, ἐπιγραψάμενος αὐτοῦ τὸ ὄνομα· καὶ, ἐπιδόσεων γινομένων, ἐκ τοῦ
5 δήμου ἀναστὰς σιωπῇ ἐκ τοῦ μέσου ἀπελθεῖν· καὶ ἐκδιδοὺς

philosophers in the *Clouds* are described as 'clever, sensible men, not one of whom —so economical are they—was ever known to have his hair cut' (v. 834). Close-clipped hair was, at Athens, properly a mark of mourning. Thus Theramenes, when, after Arginusae, he wished to excite a feeling against the generals, hired men to appear at the Apaturia in black clothes 'with their hair cut close' (ἐν χρῷ κεκαρμένους) 'that they might seem to be relatives of the lost' (Xen. *Hellen.* I 7, 8). At Sparta, however, it was the ordinary fashion; and so, for a time, the Penurious man's hair would be in keeping with his Spartan-like cloak.

28. **in the middle of the day**] when people went home to the noontide siesta—as Horace did, at the same hour, to his luncheon and his 'rest in the house' (*domesticus otior*, Sat I 6, 128) The Penurious man seizes the opportunity of sparing his shoes by taking them off during this interval of seclusion Compare the *Lysistrata* v. 418. A shoe pinches, and this order is given to the shoemaker.—'*Come at noon*, and ease it.'

29. **the fuller**] See note on c. xxv, 18.

1. **Meanness**] See note on c. XXIV, 1.

3 f. **when he has gained the prize in a tragic contest**] Not as the poet, but as the choregus who brought out the tragedy, and for whom its success was considered a distinction hardly less than for the author.

4. **will dedicate a wooden scroll**] The duties of the choregia consisted in finding maintenance and instruction for the chorus (in tragedy, usually of 15 persons) as long as they were in training; and in providing the dresses and equipments for the performance. Lysias speaks of two such choregiae costing together about £200 (*de bon. Aristoph.* § 42), and of another which cost about £120 (ἀπολ. δωροδ. § 161). The Mean man, like Aristotle's μικροπρεπής, 'after a great expenditure mars the honour of it for a trifle' (*Eth N.* IV 2) Instead of offering in the temple of Dionysus, or displaying in some public place, the bronze tripod which was awarded to a successful choregus, he dedicates merely a narrow tablet of wood, carved to resemble a scroll, and thus records his victory in the cheapest possible way.—Isaeus numbers among the private adorners of Athens 'those who had offered in the temple of Dionysus the tripods which they had gained as victorious choregi' (*de Dicaeog. hered.* p 113); and Plutarch says that Nicias had presented to the temple a shrine (νεώς) on which these tripods were placed (*Vit. Nic.* 3). Before the time of Theo-

THE MEAN MAN. XXV (XXII)

shoes in the middle of the day; and that they are urgent with the fuller to let their cloak have plenty of earth, in order that it may not soon be soiled. 30

XXV (XXII). THE MEAN MAN.

Meanness is an excessive indifference to honour where expense is concerned.

The Mean man is one who, when he has gained the prize in a tragic contest, will dedicate a wooden scroll to Dionysus, having had it inscribed with his own name. When subscrip- 5 tions for the treasury are being made, he will rise in silence from his place in the Ecclesia, and go out from the midst. When he is celebrating his daughter's marriage, he will sell

---

phrastus a more costly fashion had come in—that of placing the prize-tripod in a small shrine built specially for it, either in the precincts of the Theatre or in the 'Street of Tripods' (Paus. I 20) on the east side of the Acropolis. One such monument remains,—that of Lysicrates, choregus in 335 B.C. The site of the chapel dedicated in 320 B.C. by the choregus Thrasyllus (Paus. I 21) is still marked by a cave above the theatre on the south side of the Acropolis. Contrasted with this new practice, the Mean man's conduct would seem still meaner than it would have done at an earlier time. (See, in general, Reisch, *Gr. Weihgeschenken*, 117 ff., and Rouse, *Greek Votive Offerings*, 1902, 157-9.)

5 f. **subscriptions for the treasury**] ἐπιδόσεων,—'benevolences' contributed by the citizens in emergencies of the State; usually to defray the expense of military operations which had suddenly become necessary. In such cases the presidents (πρυτάνεις) of the Ecclesia made the appeal at a sitting of the house. Citizens who intended to subscribe then came forward severally and gave in their names. Meidias is accused by Demosthenes of having been backward on an occasion of this kind, and of having at last subscribed only in hope of escaping personal military service (*in Meid.* § 162). The double meaning of ἐπιδίδωμι—to 'contribute' in this way, and to 'make progress'—furnishes the point of a story about Phocion's dissolute son. 'Once, when subscriptions to the treasury were being made, he, too, came forward in the Ecclesia, and said "I also advance—" "*in profligacy!*" roared the House with one accord' (Athenaeus IV p. 168).

8. **celebrating his daughter's marriage**] Aristotle numbers among the fit occasions for magnificence 'those domestic events which occur only once—as a marriage, or the like' (*Eth. N.* IV 2). The two chief ceremonies of a Greek wedding are alluded to in the text: (1) *The sacrifice* called προτέλεια γάμων, celebrated by the father of the bride and the male relatives and friends. In Ach. Tatius II 12 this sacrifice is held on the morning of the wedding. (2) *The wedding-feast*, given usually at the bridegroom's house, but *by* the father of the bride, after she had been conducted thither. See Eur. *Iph. in Aul.* 718: '*Clytaem.* Have you yet offered the nuptial sacrifice to the goddess (Hera

126 ΑΝΕΛΕΥΘΕΡΙΑC ΚΕ'

αὐτοῦ θυγατέρα τοῦ μὲν ἱερείου πλὴν τῶν ἱερωσύνων τὰ κρέα
ἀποδόσθαι, τοὺς δὲ διακονοῦντας ἐν τοῖς γάμοις οἰκοσίτους
μισθώσασθαι· καὶ τριηραρχῶν τὰ τοῦ κυβερνήτου στρώματα αὑτῷ ἐπὶ τοῦ καταστρώματος ὑποστορέννυσθαι, τὰ
10 δὲ αὑτοῦ ἀποτιθέναι. καὶ τὰ παιδία δὲ δεινὸς μὴ πέμψαι εἰς
διδασκάλου, ὅταν ᾖ Μουσεῖα, ἀλλὰ φῆσαι κακῶς ἔχειν, ἵνα
μὴ συμβάλωνται· καὶ ἐξ ἀγορᾶς δὲ ὀψωνήσας τὰ κρέα
αὐτὸς φέρειν καὶ τὰ λάχανα ἐν τῷ προκολπίῳ· καὶ ἔνδον
μένειν, ὅταν ἐκδῷ θοἰμάτιον ἐκπλῦναι· καὶ φίλου ἔρανον
15 συλλέγοντος καὶ διειλεγμένου αὐτῷ προσιόντα προϊδόμενος,
ἀποκάμψας ἐκ τῆς ὁδοῦ, τὴν κύκλῳ οἴκαδε πορευθῆναι· καὶ

Teleia) for your daughter? *Agam.* I purpose it.... *Clyt.* And will you then give the wedding-feast which should follow?' According to Demosth. *in Onet.* I p. 869 one reason for giving a large wedding-banquet was the importance of securing witnesses to the fact of the marriage.

8 f. **he will sell the flesh**] instead of entertaining his friends with it: see note on c. XV, 5. Compare Alexis in Athen. XV p. 671: 'The very Triballians have no such customs, where they say that the sacrificer allows his guests to feast their eyes on the repast, and next day sells to the starving wretches what he set out for them only to look at.'

9. **the parts due to the priest**] Ameipsias in Athen. IX p. 368 E: 'The parts usually given to the priest are the ham, the rib, the left side of the face' (δίδοται μάλισθ' ἱερώσυνα | κωλῆ, τὸ πλευρὸν, ἡμίκραιρ' ἀριστερά).

11. **on condition that they find their own board**] οἰκοσίτους. When servants were hired to assist the slaves of the household on a special occasion, it was probably usual to give them, besides their wages, their meals. But the Mean man engages the assistants on the express understanding that they are to find their own food. In the comedy of the 'Breakfast-party' Crates makes an economical person boast of having extended this regulation to his guests, and 'celebrated the wedding on a basis of self-refreshment' (οἰκοσίτους τοὺς γάμους πεποιηκέναι Athen. XV p 671). In the *Casina* of Plautus a man places his servants at the disposal of a friend; who replies, 'be sure that they all bring their own food' (III 1, 7).

11. **when he is trierarch**] The duty of the trierarchy was not at this time burdensome. It consisted in maintaining the efficiency, for one year, of a trireme found, rigged and manned by the State (Dem. *in Meid* § 156). The average cost of this was about £240 (*ib.*). A law, passed probably in 340 B.C., had distributed the burden of the trierarchy according to an assessment of property, at the rate of one trireme for every ten talents (about £2400) of taxable capital. The taxable capital was ⅕th of the aggregate capital. No man, therefore, was liable to maintain a trireme at his *sole* charge unless he possessed at least £12,000. If he had less, he paid his proportionate share to a Company (συντέλεια) who maintained a trireme among them. This system had superseded that of working the trierarchy by permanent boards (συμμορίαι), which had been found in practice unfair to the poor; just as the still older plan of the simple or dual trierarchy had been oppres-

THE MEAN MAN. XXV (XXII)

the flesh of the animal sacrificed, except the parts due to the priest; and will hire the attendants at the marriage festival on condition that they find their own board. When he is trierarch, he will spread the steersman's rugs under him on the deck, and put his own away. He is apt, also, not to send his children to school when there is a festival of the Muses, but to say that they are unwell, in order that they may not contribute. Again, when he has bought provisions, he will himself carry the meat and the vegetables from the market-place in the bosom of his cloak. When he has sent his cloak to be scoured, he will keep the house. If a friend is raising a subscription, and has spoken to him about it, he will turn out of the street when he descries him approaching, and will go home by a roundabout way. Then,

---

sive to the moderately rich. (See Boeckh *Publ. Econ* bk IV c. 11.) Comp. note on c. XXIX, 26.

12. **on the deck**] Vessels of the larger size were usually, at this time, completely decked. Thucydides says that the ships which fought at Salamis 'had not *as yet* decks throughout' (I 14). In a trireme there would be little cabin room below, and officers as well as men would live almost entirely on deck. But some vessels had cabins, for we hear of an open boat (ἀστέγαστον) being exchanged for a decked one (ἐστεγασμένον) *on account of the wet weather* (Antipho de c. Herod § 26). Casaubon quotes a notice from Pollux (I 89) of the deck-cabin which the trierarch usually fitted up for himself, and supposes that the Mean man has avoided this expense, providing himself merely with rugs. Compare Alciphr. I 12: 'He lay down on some foreign carpets and wrappers, pretending that he could not lie *like other people* on the deck; these planks, he said, are harder than stones.'

14. **a festival of the Muses**] Aeschines says that some of the old laws contained regulations 'for the festivals of the Muses at schools and of Hermes in the palaestras' (*in Timarch.* § 10). The celebration of the Hermaea in a palaestra was the occasion on which Socrates was introduced to the young Lysis (*Lys.* p. 606 D).

On that occasion the young men and boys had held a sacrifice (*ib.* E). At the 'Musea' in schools there would be a similar sacrifice, and for this the pupils would be expected to contribute.

16. **when he has bought provisions**] See note on c. XVII, 16.

18. **sent his cloak to be scoured**] ἐκπλῦναι—properly said of washing linen, but here applied to the scouring of the woollen cloak by the fuller (γναφεύς). The process consisting in scouring—rubbing in a sort of white earth ('Cimolian clay') like the Roman *creta*—and carding to raise the nap. The Mean man, through not having a second cloak, probably condemns himself to an imprisonment of some length; for the fullers were not famous for punctuality. 'If they would only give people their cloaks when they want them, just after the summer solstice,' says a speaker in Aristophanes, 'we should never have pleurisy' (*Eccl.* 415). In Athen. XIII p. 582 a person is described imploring a faithless fuller to restore his cloak. (Aelian, *Varia Historia*, V 5, asserts that Epameinondas had only one cloak, and that a dirty one; and that, if he ever sent it to the fuller's shop, he stayed at home for lack of another)

19. **a subscription**] See note on c. V, 14.

128   ΑΙΣΧΡΟΚΕΡΔΕΙΑΣ ΚϚ'

τῇ γυναικὶ δὲ τῇ ἑαυτοῦ προῖκα εἰσενεγκαμένῃ μὴ πρίασθαι
θεράπαιναν, ἀλλὰ μισθοῦσθαι εἰς τὰς ἐξόδους ἐκ τῆς
γυναικείας παιδίον τὸ συνακολούθησον· καὶ τὰ ὑποδήματα
20 παλιμπήξει κεκαττυμένα φορεῖν καὶ λέγειν, ὅτι κέρατος οὐδὲν
διαφέρει· καὶ ἀναστὰς τὴν οἰκίαν ἐκκορῆσαι καὶ τὰς κλίνας
καλλῦναι· καὶ καθεζόμενος παραστρέψαι τὸν τρίβωνα, ὃν
αὐτὸς φορεῖ.

αἰσχροκερδείας κϚ'.

ἡ δὲ αἰσχροκέρδειά ἐστι περιουσία κέρδους αἰσχροῦ·
ἔστι δὲ τοιοῦτος ὁ αἰσχροκερδὴς οἷος ἑστιῶν ἄρτους ἱκανοὺς
μὴ παραθεῖναι· καὶ δανείσασθαι παρὰ ξένου παρ' αὐτῷ
καταλύοντος· καὶ διανέμων μερίδας φῆσαι δίκαιον εἶναι
5 διμοιρίαν τῷ διανέμοντι δίδοσθαι καὶ εὐθὺς αὐτῷ νεῖμαι·
καὶ οἰνοπωλῶν κεκραμένον τὸν οἶνον τῷ φίλῳ ἀποδόσθαι·
καὶ ἐπὶ θέαν τηνικαῦτα πορεύεσθαι ἄγων τοὺς υἱεῖς, ἡνίκα

23. **the women's market**] See note on c. 1, 28.

23 f. **the girl who is to attend her**] It seems to have been thought at this time a mark of severe simplicity that a citizen's wife of the richer class should appear in public with only *one* attendant. Plutarch tells a story of a tragic actor, who was playing a queen's part, refusing to go on the stage unless the choregus gave him several well-dressed handmaids. The house was kept waiting, until the choregus, who was at the side-scenes, pushed him on, exclaiming, loud enough for the audience to hear,—'Don't you see Phocion's wife always going out with one maid? Why must you demoralise the drawing-rooms (διαφθείρεις τὴν γυναικωνῖτιν) with your swagger?' (Plut. *Phoc.* 19).

24. **when she goes out**] 'Hard it is,' says Calonice in the *Lysistrata*, 'for women to go out' (v. 16). Solon 'regulated *the appearance of women in public*, their mourning, and their festivals, by a law prohibitive of everything disorderly or immodest (Plut. *Sol.* 21), and special officers to enforce these rules were appointed at Athens, as in other Greek cities. How early the Athenian γυναικονόμοι were instituted is uncertain: Boeckh thinks, in the time of Demetrius Phalereus, i.e. about 318 B.C. The institution, as Aristotle remarks, is essentially aristocratic: 'for how are you to prevent poor men's wives from going out?' (*Polit.* IV 15).

26. **as strong as horn**] He wears mended shoes and declares—in a vigorous metaphor—that they are as good as new.

26. **when he gets up**] On rising in the morning, he addresses himself to tasks which a needlessly meagre establishment imposes upon him.

27. **twist aside**] Had not much been written on παραστρέψαι, it would have

THE AVARICIOUS MAN. XXVI (XXX)

he will not buy a maid for his wife, though she brought him a dower; but will hire from the women's market the girl who is to attend her on the occasions when she goes out. He will wear his shoes patched with cobbler's work, and say that it is as strong as horn. He will sweep out his house when he gets up, and polish the sofas; and, in sitting down, he will twist aside the coarse cloak which he wears himself.

XXVI (XXX). THE AVARICIOUS MAN.

Avarice is excessive desire of base gain.

The Avaricious man is one who, when he entertains, will not set enough bread upon the table. He will borrow from a guest staying in his house. When he makes a distribution, he will say that the distributor is entitled to a double share, and thereupon will help himself. When he sells wine, he will sell it watered to his own friend. He will seize the opportunity of taking his boys

---

seemed impertinent to remark that he 'twists aside' the already well-worn cloak simply in order to save it from further attrition.

28. **the coarse cloak which he wears himself**] 'Himself' is added to emphasise the fact that his meanness is not shown merely in the administration of an office or a household, but affects the details of his personal habits. The τρίβων was a short mantle of coarse stuff. See Demosth. *in Conon.* § 34: 'men who are of a gloomy countenance *and affect the Spartan*, and wear coarse cloaks (τρίβωνας) and single-soled sandals.' The Acharnian rustics wear the 'tribon' (*Ach.* 184), and it seems to have been the ordinary dress of poor men. Bdelucleon in the *Wasps* (v. 1131) associates it with the democratic dicast. Socrates sometimes alludes to his 'poor cloak' (τρίβων ὀβρολί, *Protag* p 335 D). Being the ordinary dress of philosophers, it afterwards came to be regarded, like the cowl, as a badge of austere life.

1. **Avarice**] See note on c. XXIV, 1.

4. **when he makes a distribution**] μερίδας διανέμων. The statement is general no particular allusion need be sought. The word μερίς, however, seems to have meant especially the *portion of food* assigned to an individual at a public distribution or at a picnic: see Plut. *Symp.* II 10: 'most of the banquets in old times were distributions (δαῖτες), a portion (μερίδος) being assigned to each man at the sacrifices'. and in Athen. VIII, p 365 E, the money-contribution (συμβολή) made to a picnic by the guest is opposed to the portion, μερίς, allotted to him out of the common store.

6. **will sell it watered**] Compare Lucian's *Hermotimus*, c 59: 'I do not exactly see how you make out the resemblance between philosophy and wine —unless, indeed, it is in this particular, that philosophers sell their wares as tavern-keepers do,—a little watered, as a rule, and adulterated, and of short measure.'

J. T. 9

προῖκα ἐφιᾶσιν οἱ θεατρῶναι· καὶ ἀποδημῶν δημοσίᾳ τὸ
μὲν ἐκ τῆς πόλεως ἐφόδιον οἴκοι καταλιπεῖν, παρὰ δὲ τῶν
10 συμπρεσβευόντων δανείσασθαι· καὶ τῷ ἀκολούθῳ μεῖζον
φορτίον ἐπιθεῖναι ἢ δύναται φέρειν καὶ ἐλάχιστα ἐπιτήδεια
τῶν ἄλλων παρέχειν· καὶ ξενίων δὲ μέρος τὸ αὑτοῦ ἀπαιτή-
σας ἀποδόσθαι· καὶ ἀλειφόμενος ἐν τῷ βαλανείῳ εἰπών,
σαπρόν γε τὸ ἔλαιον ἐπρίω, τῷ παιδαρίῳ, τῷ ἀλλοτρίῳ
15 ἀλείφεσθαι. καὶ τῶν εὑρισκομένων χαλκῶν ὑπὸ τῶν οἰκετῶν
ἐν ταῖς ὁδοῖς δεινὸς ἀπαιτῆσαι τὸ μέρος, κοινὸν εἶναι φήσας
τὸν Ἑρμῆν· καὶ ἱμάτιον ἐκδοῦναι πλῦναι καὶ χρησάμενος
παρὰ γνωρίμου ἐφελκύσαι πλείους ἡμέρας, ἕως ἂν ἀπαιτηθῇ·
καὶ τὰ τοιαῦτα· Φειδωνίῳ μέτρῳ τὸν πύνδακα ἐγκεκρουμένῳ

8. **the lessees of the theatre.** The theatre of Dionysus was rented from the Government by a lessee, or company of lessees, who undertook to keep it in repair, and received the entrance-money. As lessees they were called θεατρῶναι: as receivers of the entrance-money, θεατροπῶλαι. (Pollux, VII 199.) The earlier name for the lessee was 'the architect' (ἀρχιτέκτων)—i.e. the superintendent of repairs, etc., in connexion with the theatre. Demosthenes speaks of asking the 'architect' to keep places for distinguished visitors (*de Cor.* § 28). The free days referred to here were probably at some of the minor festivals

10. **the money allowed to him by the State**] A small allowance for travelling expenses was made by the State to its ambassadors. The Athenian envoys to Persia in the *Acharnians* receive each two drachmas—about 1s. 8d.—a day, and this was the pay of a θεωρός, or member of a sacred mission, at the same period. *Wasps* 1189. The members of the second embassy to Philip in 347 B.C. were absent three months, and received 1000 drachmas among them (Dem. *de F. Legat.* § 158). If, as seems probable, they were ten in number, this would not be much more than one drachma apiece daily.

11. **load his servant**] who attends him on the embassy. Slaves groaning under heavy packs were among the stock personages of comedy: thus in the opening of the *Frogs* Dionysus is moved by the complaints of Xanthias, who is toiling after him with the baggage, to give up the ass to him (1—29). In Xen. *Memorabilia*, III 13, 16, a person who complains of fatigue after a journey on foot is asked what the slave who trudged behind had to carry. 'My bed-furniture (στρώματα) and the rest of my baggage' is the answer. Demosthenes is described as attended on one of his embassies to Macedonia by 'two men carrying packs' (στρωματόδεσμα: Aeschin *de F. Legat.* § 99).

14. **the presents**] ξενίων—meaning especially the *provisions* furnished to ambassadors by the Government of the city in which they were staying. For this sense of the word see Herod. VI 35, where a man sitting at his door calls out to foreigners whom he sees passing, and offers them 'lodging and *entertainment*' (καταγωγήν καὶ ξείνια). Plutarch uses ξένια to translate the Roman *lauta*,—the present of provisions made in old times to foreign ambassadors by the Quaestors (Plut *Quaestiones Rom* 47)

14. anointing himself at the bath] Compare notes on c. XIV, 28, and c XII, 6.

18 **to cry 'Shares in the luck!'**]

THE AVARICIOUS MAN. XXVI (XXX)

to the play, when the lessees of the theatre grant free admission. If he travels on the public service, he will leave at home the money allowed to him by the State, and will borrow of his colleagues in the embassy; he will load his servant with more baggage than he can carry, and give him shorter rations than any other master does, he will demand, too, his strict share of the presents,—and sell it. When he is anointing himself at the bath, he will say to the slave-boy, 'Why, this oil that you have bought is rancid'—and will use someone else's. He is apt to claim his part of the halfpence found by his servants in the streets, and to cry 'Shares in the luck!' Having sent his cloak to be scoured he will borrow another from an acquaintance, and delay to restore it for several days, until it is demanded back.

These, again, are traits of his. He will weigh out their rations to his household with his own hands, using 'the measure

---

lit. 'to say that the Hermes is for both of us,' κοινὸν εἶναι τὸν Ἑρμῆν. Hermes was the gain-giver, whether he gave it by commerce, in his quality of ἐμπολαῖος (Ar. *Plutus* 1155); or smiled, as δόλιος, on some fraud which won it; or, as ἡγεμόνιος, guided men to where it glittered in their path or struck their spade. Compare Lucian, *The Boat* c. 12 · *Adeimantus* (who says that he has been dreaming golden dreams). 'You have come upon me at the very height of my opulence and luxury.' *Lucinus*. 'Shares in your luck! (κοινὸς Ἑρμῆς)—that phrase which comes so readily. Out with your treasures for all to see!' When a Roman dug up a pot of coins in his garden, it was Hercules, not Mercury whom he thanked (Pers II 10, Hor. *S.* II 6, 13). But there was a Latin phrase answering to κοινὸς Ἑρμῆς: Sen. *Epp.* 119, 1, 'When I have made a lucky find, I do not wait for you to cry 'Shares!' ('*in commune!*'), but myself say it for you.'

18 f. **sent his cloak to be scoured**] See note on c. XXV, 18.

22 f **the measure of the frugal king**] Φειδωνίῳ μέτρῳ—alluding to Pheidon, king of Argos about 750 B.C., by whom was introduced the standard of weights and measures sometimes known as the 'Pheidonian' (Strabo VIII 3, 33), more usually as the 'Aeginetan,' which were generally used in Greece before the time of Solon. (In Aristotle's *Constitution of Athens*, c. 10, we are told for the first time that the Pheidonian measures of capacity were smaller than the Solonian, ἐπ' ἐκείνου (Solon) γὰρ ἐγένετο καὶ τὰ μέτρα μείζω τῶν Φειδωνείων) The joke on the name 'Pheidon' seems to have been popular. The miserly stage-father was sometimes so called: see Athen VI p 223 (quoting from a poet of the Middle Comedy): 'When some *Pheidon* or *Chremes* is hissed off the stage' Alciphr III 34: 'Most of the newly-rich at Athens are shabbier than *Pheidon* or *Griphon*' ('Niggard'—probably another personage or Comedy). Strepsiades in the *Clouds* wished to call his son Pheidonides (v 65). (Pheidon, whose date is quite uncertain, is said by Herodotus, VI 127, to have 'made the *measures* for the Peloponnesians'; and, in later times, *measures* bearing his name were apparently in use for various purposes in different parts of Greece, including Athens. It has generally been supposed that they were larger than the Solonian; the text, however,

ΑΙΣΧΡΟΚΕΡΔΕΙΑΣ ΚΣ΄

20 μετρεῖν αὐτὸς τοῖς ἔνδον, σφόδρα ἀποψῶν, τὰ ἐπιτήδεια· καὶ
ὑποπρίασθαι φίλου δοκοῦντος πρὸς τρόπου πωλεῖν, καὶ
ἐπιβαλὼν ἀποδόσθαι· ἀμέλει δὲ καὶ χρέος ἀποδιδοὺς τριάκοντα μνῶν ἔλαττον τέτταρσι δραχμαῖς ἀποδοῦναι· καὶ τῶν
υἱῶν δὲ μὴ πορευομένων εἰς τὸ διδασκαλεῖον τὸν μῆνα ὅλον
25 διὰ τὴν ἀρρωστίαν ἀφαιρεῖν τοῦ μισθοῦ κατὰ λόγον· καὶ
τὸν Ἀνθεστηριῶνα μῆνα μὴ πέμπειν αὐτοὺς εἰς τὰ μαθήματα
διὰ τὸ θέας εἶναι πολλάς, ἵνα μὴ τὸν μισθὸν ἐκτίνῃ· καὶ
παρὰ παιδὸς κομιζόμενος ἀποφορὰν τοῦ χαλκοῦ τὴν ἐπι-
καταλλαγὴν προσαπαιτεῖν· καὶ λογισμὸν δὲ λαμβάνων παρὰ
30 τοῦ χειρίζοντος ✱ ✱ ✱. καὶ φράτορας ἑστιῶν αἰτεῖν τοῖς ἑαυ-

appears to imply the opposite. Whatever may have been true of the Pheidonian *measures of capacity*, the Pheidonian *weights* were certainly heavier than the Attic (195 135) in the 5th and 4th centuries (see Prof. Percy Gardner in Smith's *Dict. of Antiquities*, ed. 3, II 448). On Pheidon in general, cp. Busolt's *Griechische Geschichte*, I, ed. 2, p. 611 f., and Macan on Herodotus, l. c.; also Wilamowitz, *Aristoteles und Athen*, I 43, and Mr G. F. Hill's *Handbook of Greek and Roman Coins*, p 6 n)

(23. **with the bottom dinted inward**] πύνδαξ means the same as πυθμήν. Pollux, X 79, quotes from the *Triptolemus* of Sophocles, ἀπυνδάκωτος κύλιξ, as synonymous with ἀπύθμενος. He also quotes from Aristophanes the phrase, ἐσκρουσαμένους τοὺς πύνδακας, and, from Pherekrates, λαβοῦσα μὲν τῆς χοινικος τὸν πύνδακ' εἰσέκρουσεν)

(23 f **carefully brushing the rim**] In Pollux, IV 170, dry measures that are over full are described as τὰ οὐκ ἀπεψημένα· τὸ δὲ ἀποψῶν ἐργαλεῖον ('the implement used for levelling them') is called ἀπομάκτρα ἢ σκυτάλη ἢ περιστροφίς. Cf. Juvenal, XIV 126, 'servorum ventres modio castigat iniquo ')

27 **to withhold four drachmas**] i e about 3s out of £120 Compare Earle's character of *A Sordid Rich Man*: 'Hee loues to pay short a shilling or two in a great sum, and is glad to gaine that, when he can no more.' (*Microcosmographie* p. 100 ed. Arber.)

28. **throughout the month**] It seems to be implied here that school-accounts were usually settled, as interest on loans was paid, at the end of the month — Compare Demosth. *in Aphob.* 1 p. 828: 'To such a pitch of avarice (αἰσχρο-κερδείας) did he go, that he actually robbed my teachers of their fees.'—The saving thus effected must have been small, unless the Athenian schoolmaster were better paid than the Roman, to whom Juvenal says, after enumerating his toils (VII 949)—

This do, and take, upon the year's account,
What jockeys get for one successful mount.

31. **because there are so many festivals**] Especially (1) the *Anthesteria* on the 11th, 12th, and 13th, 1 e. in about the first week of March. On the 12th, or 'Pitcher-day,' 'it was the Athenian custom that presents, as well as their regular fees, should be sent to the Sophists, who used themselves to invite their acquaintances to an entertainment' (Athen. X p. 437) Hence Eubulides in the *Comastae*· 'You affect the Professor (σοφιστιᾶς), wretch, and long for the Pitcher-feast, with its pay and presents' (*ib*). (2) The *Lesser Mysteries* of Demeter, held on the banks of the Ilissus: Plut *Demetr.* 26. (3) The *Diasia*,—'the greatest festival of

THE AVARICIOUS MAN. XXVI (XXX)

of the frugal king,' with the bottom dinted inward, and carefully brushing the rim. He will buy a thing privately, when a friend seems ready to sell it on reasonable terms, and will dispose of it at a raised price. It is just like him, too, when he is paying a debt of thirty minas, to withhold four drachmas. Then, if his sons, through ill-health, do not attend the school throughout the month, he will make a proportionate deduction from the payment; and all through Anthesterion he will not send them to their lessons because there are so many festivals, and he does not wish to pay the fees. When he is receiving rent from a slave, he will demand in addition the discount charged on the copper money; also, in going through the accounts of his manager, <he will challenge small items>. Entertaining his

---

Gracious Zeus (Μειλίχιος), held without the walls, at which a great multitude offer public sacrifice, not of victims, but of the fragrant fruits of the soil' (Thuc. 1 896). —Not only would the scholars have all these holidays: they would also be expected to make presents to their master.

32. rent from a slave] Aeschines mentions among the items of a legacy 'some nine or ten slaves, skilled workmen in the shoe-making trade, each of whom paid their master a daily rent (ἀποφοράν) of two obols; the foreman (ἡγεμών) of the workshop paying three' (*in Timarch.* § 97). Nicias possessed 'a thousand slaves employed in the silver mines, whom he hired out to Sosias a Thracian, on the condition of his paying one obol daily, clear of taxes, for each of them' (Xen. *Vect.* IV 14). The Greek slave was regarded as capital; the Roman slave, mainly as a luxury. 'Romans,' says Athenaeus, 'have great multitudes of slaves, but do not make them sources of revenue...Most Romans employ the greater part of their slaves in personal attendance' (συμπραΐοντας: Athen. VI p. 272).

33. the discount charged on the copper money] The Avaricious man is paid by his slave in copper obols. Silver obols being generally preferred, the copper coin had to be exchanged at a small discount. The master insists on the slave paying this difference.—Copper money seems to have first come into general use about the time of Alexander. Before that time the only copper coin was the χαλκοῦς, rather less than a farthing. even the obol (1½*d*) was of silver The copper issue at Athens in 406 B.C. (Ar. *Frogs* 720–6) was exceptional (see Boeckh *P. E.*).—Compare Athen. IV § 6 (describing the extortions of an Athenian fishmonger) —'Then when *you* pay *him* his money, he always exacts Aeginetan coin' (the Aeginetan talent being to the Attic as 5 3),—'and if *he* has to give *you* change, he moreover pays you in Attic (προσαπέδωκεν Ἀττικά), and so on both sides he clears the agio' (τὴν καταλλαγὴν ἔχει). (The silver drachma of Aegina, which was equivalent to 10 Attic obols, was larger than the Attic drachma of 6 obols, and was known in Athens as the παχεῖα δραχμή (Pollux, IX 76). The copper (or bronze) coinage introduced in 406 became illegal about 394 (*Eccl.* 815–22), but was reissued in large quantities from 350 to 322, the year in which Theophrastus succeeded Aristotle as the head of the Lyceum. In the same year Athens became subject to the Macedonian Antipater, and lost the right of coining money in her own name (Head's *Historia Numorum*, ed. 1887, pp. 314–6).)

ΔΕΙΛΙΑC ΚΖ'

τοῦ παισὶν ἐκ τοῦ κοινοῦ ὄψον, τὰ δὲ καταλειπόμενα ἀπὸ τῆς τραπέζης ῥαφανίδων ἡμίσεα ἀπογράφεσθαι, ἵνα οἱ διακονοῦντες παῖδες μὴ λάβωσι· καὶ συναποδημῶν δὲ μετὰ γνωρίμων χρήσασθαι τοῖς ἐκείνων παισὶ, τὸν δὲ ἑαυτοῦ ἔξω 35 μισθῶσαι καὶ μὴ ἀναφέρειν εἰς τὸ κοινὸν τὸν μισθόν. ἀμέλει δὲ καὶ συναγόντων παρ' αὐτῷ ἀποθεῖναι τῶν διδομένων ξύλων καὶ φακῶν καὶ ὄξους καὶ ἁλῶν καὶ ἐλαίου τοῦ εἰς τὸν λύχνον· καὶ γαμοῦντός τινος τῶν φίλων καὶ ἐκδιδομένου θυγατέρα πρὸ χρόνου τινὸς ἀποδημῆσαι, ἵνα 40 <μὴ> πέμψῃ προσφοράν· καὶ παρὰ τῶν γνωρίμων τοιαῦτα κίχρασθαι, ἃ μήτ' ἂν ἀπαιτῆσαι μήτ' ἂν ἀποδιδόντων ταχέως ἄν τις κομίσαιτο.

δειλίας κζ'.

ἀμέλει δὲ ἡ δειλία δόξειεν ἂν εἶναι ὑπειξίς τις ψυχῆς

36. **his clansmen**] See note on c. XXIV, 18. The banquet is in this case given at the Avaricious man's house, but at the joint expense.

37. **register the half-radishes**] In the *Frogs* 987 the penurious citizen asks, 'Where is the stick of garlic which was left yesterday?' Juvenal's miser is well known (XIV 129):

Who, in September, spreads a new repast
With mince, kept under padlocks, from the last,
Who hoards, to make the sultry morrow glad,
One bean, a shred of lobster, half a shad;
And counts, ere he imprisons for a week,
Each fine-split fibre of the stringy leek.

40. **will let his own slave out for hire**] When slaves were hired by one citizen from another, it was usually for the purposes of some business requiring a large number of hands. A mineowner, for instance, would rather hire men than encumber himself by purchase with a large and permanent staff, which might lie on his hands if the works were suddenly suspended or contracted. See Xen. *Vectig* IV 16 'But why speak of old instances (like that of Nicias, above, on l. 32)? To this day there are numbers of men in the silver mines leased out (ἐκδεδομένοι) in this way.'

42. **a club-dinner**] We have seen how the Penurious man and the Avaricious man behave as semi-official hosts: the one in entertaining his parishioners, the other his clansmen. The same spirit is carried by the Avaricious man into strictly private entertainments. A few friends have arranged a joint dinner-party which is to be given at his house, and have sent in the necessaries. this store he plunders. When the contributions to a club-dinner were in *kind*, as here, it was properly δεῖπνον ἀπὸ σπυρίδος,—when in *money*, δεῖπνον ἀπὸ συμβολῶν (which Lucian calls συμφορῶν, *Lexiph.* 6): Athen VII p 292. Athenaeus there uses the phrase δεῖπνον συνάγειν, to *get up* such a party. Compare Ter. *Eun.* III 4, 1. 'Yesterday a party of us met in the Peiraeus, to arrange a club-dinner for to-day (*in hunc diem ut de symbolis esse-*

THE COWARD. XXVII (XXV)

clansmen, he will beg a dish from the common table for his own servants; and will register the half-radishes left over from the repast, in order that the attendants may not get them. Again, when he travels with acquaintances, he will make use of their servants, but will let his own slave out for hire; nor will he place the proceeds to the common account. It is just like him, too, when a club-dinner is held at his house, to secrete some of the fire-wood, lentils, vinegar, salt, and lamp-oil placed at his disposal. If a friend, or a friend's daughter, is to be married, he will go abroad a little while before, in order to avoid giving a wedding present. And he will borrow from his acquaintances things of a kind that no one would ask back,—or readily take back, if it were proposed to restore them.

XXVII (XXV). THE COWARD.

Cowardice would seem to be, in fact, a shrinking of the soul through fear.

---

mus). We made Chaereas our steward; rings were given (as pledges),—place and time appointed.'

46. **a wedding present**] On the first day after the wedding—called ἐπαύλια or the House-warming, as being the bride's first day in her new home—'the relatives bring gifts to the bridegroom and the bride' (Hesychius). But the chief occasion for wedding-presents was the third day after marriage, when the bride for the first time appeared unveiled. The gifts then made were called ἀνακαλυπτήρια. See Diod v 2: 'Some of the poets feign that at the marriage of Persephone and Pluto the island (Sicily) was given by Zeus to the bride as a wedding present' (ἀνακάλυπτρα). (Cp. Pherekydes of Syros, in Grenfell and Hunt's *Greek Papyri*, II (1897) 23, and in Diels, *Vorsokratiker*, II² 1 508, 12 (of the φᾶρος made by Zeus on his marriage with Hera), ταῦτά φασιν ἀνακαλυπτήρια πρῶτον γενέσθαι)

1. **Cowardice**] When 'cowardice' is said to be 'a shrinking of the soul through fear,' this is an explanation, but not a definition, of the term; for, as Aristotle says, there are things fearful 'above human endurance,' which the courageous man will not only fear but shrink from (*Eth. N.* III 6). The Coward either fears too much things which are really fearful, or takes things to be fearful which are not so (*ib*).—Compare the so-called Platonic *Definitions* p. 416, 'Cowardice tends to check impulse (ἀντιληπτικὴ ὁρμῆς), being the first cause of yielding.'

The phase of cowardice described here is the fear of death or bodily hurt, and is seen in two cases—on a voyage and in war. Theophrastus perhaps shared the view of his master that ἀνδρεία is strictly 'physical' courage only, and ought not to be extended, as it is in Plato's *Laches* p. 191 D, to what we call 'moral' courage, at least, the view of δειλία given here answers to this limitation. On the subjects of the chapter generally,

ΔΕΙΛΙΑC ΚΖ′

ἔμφοβος, ὁ δὲ δειλὸς τοιοῦτός τις οἷος πλέων τὰς ἄκρας
φάσκειν ἡμιολίας εἶναι· καὶ κλύδωνος γενομένου ἐρωτᾶν εἴ
τις μὴ μεμύηται τῶν πλεόντων· καὶ τοῦ κυβερνήτου †ἀνα-
5 κύπτων μὲν† πυνθάνεσθαι, εἰ μεσοπορεῖ καὶ τί αὐτῷ δοκεῖ
τὰ τοῦ θεοῦ· καὶ πρὸς τὸν παρακαθήμενον λέγειν, ὅτι φο-
βεῖται ἀπὸ ἐνυπνίου τινός· καὶ ἐκδὺς διδόναι τῷ παιδὶ τὸν
χιτωνίσκον, καὶ δεῖσθαι πρὸς τὴν γῆν προσάγειν αὐτόν· καὶ
στρατευόμενος δὲ πεζῇ τοὺς ἐκβοηθοῦντάς τε προσκαλεῖν
10 κελεύων πρὸς αὐτὸν στάντας πρῶτον περιιδεῖν, καὶ λέγειν, ὡς
ἔργον διαγνῶναί ἐστι, πότεροί εἰσιν οἱ πολέμιοι· καὶ ἀκούων
κραυγῆς καὶ ὁρῶν πίπτοντας εἰπὼν πρὸς τοὺς παρεστηκότας,
ὅτι τὴν σπάθην λαβεῖν ὑπὸ τῆς σπουδῆς ἐπελάθετο, τρέχειν

compare Arist. *Eth. N.* III 6. 'Properly, then, he would be called Courageous who is fearless about the noble death and about such things as bring it on and are sudden; and such especially are the chances of war. Not but that the Courageous man is fearless also on a sick-bed, or on the sea ; but he will not be so much so as sailors. For landsmen at once give up all hope of safety, and are ill-content with such a death, while sailors are sanguine by reason of their experience Moreover, the cases in which men show courage are those in which there is scope for valour (*ἐν οἷς ἐστὶν ἀλκή*) and in which to die is glorious; but in death by drowning or disease neither condition is present.'

3 f. **protest that the promontories are privateers**] The Persians, in their retreat after Salamis, actually mistook some sharp points (*ἄκραι λεπταί*) of the rocky Attic coast for ships (Her. VIII 107). As *ἡμιόλιος* means 'containing one and a half,' *ἡμιολία* was a ship with one and a half bank of oars,—the lower complete, the upper broken by a half-deck. *ἡμιόλιαι* are sometimes mentioned in connexion with this period as used in enterprises where light, handy craft were needed ; e g in the attempt of Aristoni-cus of Methymna to seize the harbour of Chios by night (B.C. 332, Arrian *An.* III 2, 4), and in the nocturnal attempt of Agathocles to surprise Messene (Diod. XIX 65)

5. **who has not been initiated**] Diod IV 43 (in the account of the voyage of the Argonauts).—'A great storm came on, and the chiefs were despairing of safety, when Orpheus, it is said, who alone of the ship's company was initiated in the rite' (of the Cabeiri), 'made his prayer to the Samothracian gods. Immediately the wind abated. And therefore storm-tossed voyagers ever made their prayer to the gods of Samothrace ' Ar. *Peace* 276: 'This is a crisis. But, if any of you happens to have been initiated at Samothrace, now is the time to pray.' The Coward refers here to the *Samothracian* Mysteries (which are also mentioned in Diod. V 49, and in the Scholium on Apollonius Rhodius, I 916. It was in the age of Theophrastus that the worship of the Cabeiri of Samothrace attained its greatest vogue : see Preller's *Gr. Mythologie*, I 863 ed. 1894). For the belief that irreligious companions are dangerous on a voyage, see Antipho *de caede Herod* § 82: 'I think you know that many men erenow, having blood on their hands, or

THE COWARD. XXVII (XXV) 137

The Coward is one who, on a voyage, will protest that the promontories are privateers, and, if a high sea gets up, will ask if there is any one on board who has not been initiated. He will put up his head and ask the steersman if he is half-way, and what he thinks of the face of the heavens; remarking to the person sitting next him that a certain dream makes him feel uneasy; and he will take off his tunic and give it to his slave; or he will beg them to put him ashore.

On land also, when he is campaigning, he will call to him those who are going out to the rescue, and bid them come and stand by him and look about them first; saying that it is hard to make out which is the enemy. Hearing shouts and seeing men falling, he will remark to those who stand by him that he has forgotten in his haste to bring his sword, and will run to the

---

being otherwise impure, have, as companions of a voyage, drawn into their own destruction those whose relations with the gods were blameless...All with whom I have sailed have had excellent voyages.' Aesch. *Theb.* 598 and Hor. *Od.* III 2, 26 are well known.

(6. **if he is half-way**] Diod. XVIII 34. Lucian, *D. Mort.*, 11 § 2, uses the phrase κατὰ μέσον τὸν πόρον of a vessel wrecked on the voyage from Sikyon to Kirrha. In the text, εἰ μεσοπορεῖ is rendered by Ast, *num medium cursum teneat* (cp. Hesychius, μεσοπορῶν· μέσην ὁδεύων). It is also held to mean, 'if he is keeping to the open sea,' cp. Homer, *Od.* III 174, πέλαγος μέσον εἰς Εὔβοιαν | τέμνειν, and Aelian, *Hist. An.* II 15, τεμνούσας.. μέσον τὸν πόρον τὰς ναῦς. Phrynichus, *Ecloga*, No. 391, disapproves of the use of the word by Menander (the pupil of Theophrastus).)

7. **what he thinks of the face of the heavens**] The Coward, verbally pious in his alarm, asks the steersman what he thinks—not of the face of the sky (τὰ τοῦ οὐρανοῦ)—but of the face 'of the god' (τὰ τοῦ θεοῦ). It is impossible to render the fineness of this touch; but it is necessary to represent it The Greeks ordinarily said 'It [he] rains,' etc., but when special reverence or emphasis was meant, '*the god* rains,' etc. So c. XVIII, 10, ' If *Zeus* would (be gracious enough to) send more rain, the crops would be better': Ar. *Wasps* 261, 'It is absolutely necessary that *the god* should give us rain.' Xen. *Hellen.* IV 7, 4, '*the god* made an earthquake.' 'The god ' of course means Zeus, who, etymologically, *is* the sky, djaûs: see Curtius, *Etym. Griech.* § 269.

11. **when he is campaigning**] The main body of the army in which the Coward is serving has already engaged the enemy. Reserve troops have been left in camp, with whom the Coward has managed to remain. These, or a portion of them, are now going out to the support of the main body. The Coward calls to the men hurrying past, and pretends to be uncertain which of the dark masses in the distance is the enemy. By this means he gains a brief delay; and, when the others insist on advancing, returns on pretence of seeking his sword.

16 **in his haste**] in his burning eagerness to hurl himself into the thick of the fight.

16 **his sword**] σπάθην. The ξίφος was a short, straight sword, with a blade of not much more than two feet. Iphicrates (about 395 B.C.) 'made the

ΔΕΙϹΙΔΑΙΜΟΝΙΑϹ ΚΗ'

ἐπὶ τὴν σκηνήν· καὶ τὸν παῖδα ἐκπέμψας καὶ κελεύσας
15 προσκοπεῖσθαι, ποῦ εἰσιν οἱ πολέμιοι, ἀποκρύψαι αὐτὴν ὑπὸ
τὸ προσκεφάλαιον· εἶτα διατρίβειν πολὺν χρόνον ὡς ζητῶν
ἐν τῇ σκηνῇ· καὶ ὁρῶν τραυματίαν τινὰ προσφερόμενον τῶν
φίλων, προσδραμὼν καὶ θαρρεῖν κελεύσας, ὑπολαβὼν φέρειν·
καὶ τοῦτον θεραπεύειν καὶ περισπογγίζειν καὶ παρακαθή-
20 μενος ἀπὸ τοῦ ἕλκους τὰς μυίας σοβεῖν, καὶ πᾶν μᾶλλον
ἢ μάχεσθαι τοῖς πολεμίοις· καὶ τοῦ σαλπιστοῦ δὲ τὸ πολε-
μικὸν σημήναντος, καθήμενος ἐν τῇ σκηνῇ <εἰπεῖν> ἄπαγ' ἐς
κόρακας· οὐκ ἐάσει τὸν ἄνθρωπον ὕπνον λαβεῖν πυκνὰ
σημαίνων· καὶ αἵματος δὲ ἀνάπλεως ἀπὸ τοῦ ἀλλοτρίου
25 τραύματος ἐντυγχάνειν τοῖς ἐκ τῆς μάχης ἐπανιοῦσι καὶ
διηγεῖσθαι ὡς κινδυνεύσας ἕνα σέσωκα τῶν φίλων· καὶ
εἰσάγειν πρὸς τὸν κατακείμενον σκεψομένους τοὺς δημότας,
τοὺς φυλέτας, καὶ τούτων ἅμα ἑκάστῳ διηγεῖσθαι ὡς αὐτὸς
αὐτὸν ταῖς αὑτοῦ χερσὶν ἐπὶ σκηνὴν ἐκόμισεν.

δεισιδαιμονίας κη'.

ἀμέλει ἡ δεισιδαιμονία δόξειεν ἂν εἶναι δειλία πρὸς τὸ

swords nearly twice as long as they had been before,' Diod. xv 44. This longer sword was called σπάθη, a word which sometimes translated the Roman *gladius*. Vegetius II 15, 'longer swords (*gladios*) which they called *spathae*.' (The word is used in Menander's *Misoumenos*, Pollux, x 146, ἀφανεῖς γεγόνασιν αἱ σπάθαι; and in his *Epitrepontes*, p. 62 Robert, χλαμύδα καὶ σπάθην τινὰ | ἐνεγκέ μοι. From the Latin *spatha* are derived the Italian *spada* and the French *épée*.)

(23. **keep the flies off**] τὰς μυίας σοβεῖν has been compared with Menander, *Frag.* 503, Πέρσαι δ' ἔχοντες μυιοσόβας ἑστήκεσαν)

25. **sounded the signal for battle**] τὸ πολεμικόν, the signal to charge (Xen. *An.* IV 3, 29), is opposed to τὸ ἀνακλητικόν, the note of recall (Plut. *Apopth. Lac.*

68).—This is the third and most pressing emergency which the Coward has had to meet. When the main body went into action, he remained with the reserves. When the reserves went out, he returned to look for his sword. Now the trumpeter goes through the camp, to summon forth any laggards who may chance to have stayed behind. The Coward affects to be busied with the wounded man.

30. **the men of his parish and of his tribe**] See note on c XXIV, 18.

1. **Superstition**] Ast regarded the use of δεισιδαιμονία in a bad sense as a reason for questioning the authenticity of this chapter. While the good sense of the word is found in Xen *Ages.* 11, 8, and *Cyrop.* III 3, 58, the bad sense, he contends, was of later date, and occurs for the first time in Polybius (VI 56 § 7 ·

THE SUPERSTITIOUS MAN. XXVIII (XVI)

tent; where, having sent his slave out to reconnoitre the position of the enemy, he will hide the sword under his pillow, and then spend a long time in pretending to look for it. And seeing from the tent a wounded comrade being carried in, he will run towards him and cry 'Cheer up!'; he will take him into his arms and carry him, he will tend and sponge him; he will sit by him and keep the flies off his wound—in short, he will do anything rather than fight with the enemy. Again, when the trumpeter has sounded the signal for battle, he will cry, as he sits in the tent, 'Bother! you will not allow the man to get a wink of sleep with your perpetual bugling!' Then, covered with blood from the other's wound, he will meet those who are returning from the fight, and announce to them, 'I have run some risk to save one of our fellows'; and he will bring in the men of his parish and of his tribe to see his patient, at the same time explaining to each of them that he carried him with his own hands to the tent.

XXVIII (XVI). THE SUPERSTITIOUS MAN.

Superstition would seem to be simply cowardice in regard to the supernatural.

---

circ. 160 B.C.). This criticism appears unsound. A word signifying 'fear of supernatural beings' may evidently have various shades of meaning according to the view of those beings entertained by the person who uses it. To say that δεισιδαιμονία never meant 'superstition' before the age of Polybius is in fact to say that doubts respecting the popular religion were never felt before his time. A term so general must always have had potentially a bad as well as a good sense. But the proof does not rest merely on *a priori* grounds. It is known that Menander—said to have been a pupil of Theophrastus (Diog. V 36 § 7)—wrote a comedy called Δεισιδαίμων, *The Superstitious Man*. And, when Aristotle says that an absolute ruler will be more powerful 'if his subjects believe that he fears the gods' (ἐὰν δεισιδαίμονα νομίζωσιν εἶναι), he adds—'but he must show himself such *without fatuity*' (ἄνευ ἀβελτερίας),—showing that the word δεισιδαίμων did not, to Aristotle's mind, exclude fatuity, as εὐσεβής would have done, *Polit.* V 11

See Plutarch, *de Superst.* c. 1: 'Ignorance or uneducated opinion about the gods divides at its source into two channels. On the one part it soon engenders in refractory characters (ἀντιτύποις ἤθεσι), as in a hard soil, Atheism. On the other part it engenders, as in a moist soil, Superstition' (Ultimately δεισιδαιμονία becomes, in Christian times, synonymous with 'impiety', *Etym. Magn.* παρὰ μὲν τοῖς Ἕλλησιν ἐπὶ καλοῦ, παρὰ δὲ ἡμῖν ἐπὶ τῆς ἀσεβείας. Chrysostom, in his Homily on *Ephesians* IV, says:—"The soul of

δαιμόνιον, ὁ δὲ δεισιδαίμων τοιοῦτός τις οἷος ἐπὶ κρήνῃ
ἀπονιψάμενος τὰς χεῖρας καὶ περιρρανάμενος ἀπὸ ἱεροῦ,
δάφνην εἰς τὸ στόμα λαβών, οὕτω τὴν ἡμέραν περιπατεῖν·
5 καὶ τὴν ὁδὸν ἐὰν ὑπερδράμῃ γαλῆ, μὴ πρότερον πορευθῆναι
ἕως διεξέλθῃ τις, ἢ λίθους τρεῖς ὑπὲρ τῆς ὁδοῦ διαβάλῃ·
καὶ ἐὰν ἴδῃ ὄφιν ἐν τῇ οἰκίᾳ, ἐὰν μὲν παρείαν, Σαβάζιον
καλεῖν, ἐὰν δὲ ἱερόν, ἐνταῦθα †ἱερὸν† εὐθὺς ἱδρύσασθαι·
καὶ τῶν λιπαρῶν λίθων τῶν ἐν ταῖς τριόδοις παριὼν ἐκ τῆς
10 ληκύθου ἔλαιον καταχεῖν καὶ ἐπὶ γόνατα πεσὼν καὶ προσ-

the Greeks is full of many fears, as 'When I left my house, the first to meet me was so and so; ten thousand evils are bound to befall me'; 'As I was going out, there was a throbbing below my right eye; this is a sure sign of tears.' If an ass bray, or if a cock crow, or if anyone sneezes, or, indeed, if anything happens, they are bound as it were by a thousand fetters, and there is nothing that they do not fear.")

4. from a temple-font] Vessels of water for sprinkling (περιρραντήρια) stood at the doors of temples. Among the treasures of Delphi Herodotus mentions two such vessels or fonts, one of silver, the other of gold, dedicated by Croesus (I 51). The ceremony of sprinkling was usually intended to purge a special defilement. Thus the messenger sent to Delphi for the sacred fire after the slaughter at Salamis 'purified his body and *sprinkled himself*' (Plut. *Arist.* 20); and the people of Miletus showed the fountain at which their fathers had *sprinkled* Achilles after he had slain the king of the Lelegae (Athen. II p. 43). What is for others an extraordinary purification the Superstitious man performs daily.

4. a bit of laurel-leaf] By carrying a laurel-leaf in his mouth, he places himself under the protection of Apollo the Averter. The same idea finds an ironical application in the proverb quoted by Erasmus (*Adag.* I i 79)—'I carry a laurel walking-stick'—i.e. a rod of virtue to chastise my enemies. In Lucian's *Twice Accused* c. 1, Zeus complains that Apollo is always flitting 'whither the priestess summons him, when she has drunk some holy water and *chewed some laurel*' 'To have bitten the laurel' is Juvenal's phrase for poetical inspiration (VII 19). (The prophylactic efficacy of the 'laurel,' or bay, is noticed in the *Geoponica* XI 2, 5, ἔνθα ἂν ᾖ δάφνη, ἐκποδὼν δαίμονες.)

5 f. if a weasel run across the path] Xen. *Apol. Socr.* 13: 'Others believe that it is by birds, by sounds, *by the objects that meet us* (συμβόλους) ..that the future is foretold.' Prometheus taught men to read 'the signs that met them on journeys' (ἐνοδίους συμβόλους· Aesch. *P. V.* 495). It was a warning sign, when the path was crossed by an unclean animal. Horace mentions some of these (*Od.* III 27, 1—7). Compare Ar *Eccl.* 792 'If a weasel were to rush across the road, they would stop levying war.'

6 f. until someone else has traversed the road] It was the old belief that the evil portended by omens was not aimed at any particular person; and that, therefore, it could be turned off from oneself to another by precaution, or (so to say) by a vigorous protest. See the story in Dio Chrysost. *Or.* XXXIV: 'A Phrygian was riding on a mule. Seeing a raven, and drawing a bad omen from it (οἰωνισάμενος), he threw a stone, and chanced to hit the bird. Delighted at this, and believing that *the mischief had been turned off upon the raven*, he remounted, and pursued his ride. The raven, however,

THE SUPERSTITIOUS MAN. XXVIII (XVI)

The Superstitious man is one who will wash his hands at a fountain, sprinkle himself from a temple-font, put a bit of laurel-leaf into his mouth, and so go about for the day. If a weasel run across his path, he will not pursue his walk until someone else has traversed the road, or until he has thrown three stones across it. When he sees a serpent in his house, if it be the red snake, he will invoke Sabazius,—if the sacred snake, he will straightway place a shrine on the spot. He will pour oil from his flask on the smooth stones at the cross-roads, as he goes by,

after a little while got up again; the mule, startled, threw her rider; and he broke his leg.' Ar. *Peace* 1063: '*Priest.* O mortals wretched and silly— *Trygaeus.* On *your* head the omen!'

7. **three stones**] These are thrown after the weasel, to symbolise, as in Dio's story, detestation of the evil power. Perhaps the same notion is to be traced in Columella's advice that three stones should be buried at the roots of orange-trees in order to prevent the fruit bursting on the branch (*de arb.* 23).

8 f. **when he sees a serpent in his house**] Ter. *Phormio* IV 4, 24: 'How many things happened afterwards to warn me! A strange black dog came into the house. A snake dropped from the roof into the impluvium. A hen crew.' So it is one of the omens which proclaim the divine origin of Hercules that 'two crested snakes sprang down the impluvium' (Plaut. *Amph.* V 1, 58).

8 f. **the red snake**] The παρείας was 'of a reddish colour, with a large, bright eye, a broad mouth, not biting dangerously, but gentle' (Ael. *Hist. An.* VIII 12). It was sacred to Asclepius (l. c.), and was also found in the temples of Dionysus (schol. Ar. *Plut.* 690). In Dem. *de Cor.* § 260 Aeschines is described 'leading those fine troops of bacchants through the streets,—squeezing the *red snakes*, and holding them on high above his head,—and crying *euoe, saboe!*'

9. **Sabazius**] Diod. IV 4: 'Some feign that there was yet another Dionysus long prior in time to this one. They say that a Dionysus was born of Zeus and Persephone,—he who by some is called *Sabazius*, whose birth and sacrifices and rites they celebrate stealthily, by night and in secret. He, they say, was of surpassing sagacity, and first essayed to yoke oxen, and by their means to achieve the sowing of crops; whence it is that they introduce him crowned with horns.'

9. **the sacred snake**] described in Arist. *Hist. An.* VIII 29 as 'a small kind of serpent, of which the larger kinds are afraid, its own length is a foot and a half. It is covered with hair. Wherever it bites, the flesh immediately mortifies all round.'

10 **a shrine**] The text is uncertain: see *Crit. App.* The sense, however, is clear:—the spot on which the 'sacred' snake was seen is consecrated. Plato complains that like acts of superstition have choked up Athens with votive chapels and altars. It is the custom, he says, of timid persons in any sickness or danger 'to promise seats to the gods and divinities and children of the gods; or, when they wake in terror from dreams and visions—often, too, when they recall things seen in waking hours—to contrive altars and rites as remedies for these, *and thus to fill every house, every quarter of the city*, with their foundations (ἱδρυομένους),' *Laws* IX p 909 E.

11. **the smooth stones at the cross-roads**] Cairns, piled at points where three roads met, were regarded as rude altars of the triform goddess, Hecate Trioditis, *Trivia*; and on these, at the new moon, offerings were laid The Superstitious man never passes such a

κυνήσας ἀπαλλάττεσθαι· καὶ ἐὰν μῦς θύλακον ἀλφίτων διαφάγῃ, πρὸς τὸν ἐξηγητὴν ἐλθὼν ἐρωτᾶν τί χρὴ ποιεῖν· καὶ ἐὰν ἀποκρίνηται αὐτῷ, ἐκδοῦναι τῷ σκυτοδέψῃ ἐπιρράψαι, μὴ προσέχειν τούτοις, ἀλλ' ἀποτραπεὶς ἐκθύσασθαι.
15 καὶ πυκνὰ δὲ τὴν οἰκίαν καθᾶραι δεινός, Ἑκάτης φάσκων ἐπαγωγὴν γεγονέναι· κἂν γλαῦξ βαδίζοντος αὐτοῦ ταράττηται, εἴπας, Ἀθηνᾶ κρείττων, οὕτω παρελθεῖν· καὶ οὔτε ἐπιβῆναι μνήματι οὔτε ἐπὶ νεκρὸν οὔτ' ἐπὶ λεχὼ ἐλθεῖν

---

cairn without pouring on it a few drops of oil from the flask which he is taking to the baths. Compare Lucian's *Alexander* c. 30· 'He was quite distempered in feeling towards the gods, and had the wildest beliefs about them. If he only saw *an anointed or crowned stone* anywhere, he straightway fell on his knees, worshipped it, and stood by it for some time, praying, and begging blessings from it.' Clemens Alexandrinus speaks of those 'who, as the common saying is, worship every stock and *every smooth stone*,' *Strom.* VII p. 302. (The corresponding Latin term is *lapides unguine delibuti, lubricati*, Apuleius, *Florida*, init, and Arnobius, I.)

13. **if a mouse gnaws through a meal-bag**] Plin *Hist. Nat.* VIII 57: (mice) 'are animals of no mean significance in public prodigies. They gave warning of the Social War by gnawing some shields at Lanuvium They warned Carbo of destruction at Clusium by gnawing the thongs which he used for his boots' (alluding to the battle in which he was defeated by Sulla in 82 B.C.). Augustine tells a story of someone, whose boots had been gnawed by rats, asking Cato how the portent was to be expiated, and of Cato replying that it would have been more portentous if the rats had been gnawed by the boots (*de doctr. Chr.* II). (Cp. Comic Fragm. Adesp 341, Kock —
If a mouse delves through an altar made of clay,
Or, having nothing else, *gnaws through a meal-bag*,
If a cock, while feeding, crows at eventide,
Some folk call this a sign)

14. **the expounder of sacred law**] The Athenian family of the Eumolpidae —descendants of the first high-priests of Demeter—had in their keeping that body of unwritten tradition which made up the sacred law. Three members of this family (acc. to Suidas) formed a board or council to which all ceremonial questions were referred. They did not profess, like the inspired seers, μάντεις, to read the future; their province lay wholly in the interpretation of precedent. To them, in concert 'with the guardians of the civil law, the seers, and (so) with the god himself,' Plato would entrust, for instance, the expiation of crime (*Laws* VIII p. 871 C). They were often consulted in cases where some special circumstances connected with a death made desirable some modification of the funeral ritual: see, e g , Demosth *in Euerg.* p. 1160.

(15 **give it to a cobbler to stitch up**] Herondas, VII 89 (to a cobbler), ἀλλὰ θύλακον ῥάψαι)

17. **to purify his house frequently**] Houses, as well as persons, were purified after a polluting presence. Antipho *de Chor.* § 37 'On the day after the boy's burial, before we had purified the house.' In Eur. *Her. Fur.* 922 sacrifice is held 'to purge the house' (καθάρσι οἴκων) from the stain of murder. Even the open air and the soil required purification from a moral taint: see Eur. *Helen.* 866

18. **Hecate has been brought into it by spells**] Plato speaks of the wandering jugglers (ἀγύρται) and soothsayers who beset a rich man's doors, offering to injure

and will fall on his knees and worship them before he departs. If a mouse gnaws through a meal-bag, he will go to the expounder of sacred law and ask what is to be done; and, if the answer is, 'give it to a cobbler to stitch up,' he will disregard this counsel, and go his way, and expiate the omen by sacrifice. He is apt, also, to purify his house frequently, alleging that Hecate has been brought into it by spells; and, if an owl is startled by him in his walk, he will exclaim 'Glory be to Athene!' before he proceeds. He will not tread upon a tombstone, or come near a dead body or a woman defiled by

---

his enemies 'at a slight outlay' (μετὰ σμικρῶν δαπανῶν) by persuading the gods 'with certain alluring charms or binding spells' to help (ἐπαγωγαῖς τισὶ καὶ καταδέσμοις, *Rep.* p 364 C). In the *Laws* (XI p. 933 D) he proposes to punish anyone who 'for the use of *binding or drawing spells*, or of incantations, or any such witchcraft whatsoever, shall be adjudged virtually a doer of violence' (ὅμοιος] βλάπτοντι). Compare Plut *de Superst.* c. 3, where the prophet tells a client who has come to him in alarm, 'Hecate has been paying you one of her riotous visits' ('Εκάτης κῶμον ἐδέξω).

18 f. **if an owl is startled by him**] Antiphanes in Athen XIV p 655 —
Men say that in the City of the Sun
Are phoenixes, Athene has her owls;
Doves are most honoured by the Cyprian Queen;
Hera of Samos loves her gilden brood,
The bright birds conscious of admiring eyes

(Menander, Fragm. 534, 11 Kock :—
If anyone sees a dream, we are sore afraid;
If an owl has hooted, then we fear the worst.)

19 f. **Glory be to Athene!**] 'Ἀθηνᾶ κρείττων. Having startled her favourite bird, he seeks to propitiate the goddess by a compliment addressed to herself. 'Athene is the better goddess after all!'—preferable to and stronger than rival divinities. For the comparative, see Ovid *Met.* XIV 657, where Vertumnus greets Pomona with the words '*tanto potentior!*'—not unlike the Irish salutation, 'More power to you!'—He cannot mean 'Athene is stronger (than the evil power which sent this omen)', for, to an Athenian, the appearance of Athene's bird was a good omen Ar *Wasps* 1085 'However, we repulsed (the Persians) with the help of the gods towards evening; for an owl flitted through our host before the battle' Aelian says, indeed (*H. A.* x 37), 'When the owl attends a man hastening on some urgent errand, and *then suddenly stops* (ἐπιστᾶσα), it is not a good omen', i e. it is a friendly warning from the goddess to turn back.

20. **tread upon a tombstone**] μνήματι. Monuments to the dead were either upright slabs, στῆλαι: columns, κίονες: shrines, ἡρῷα: or flat tombstones, τράπεζαι (Plut. *vit dec. oratt.* IV 25; *mensae*, Cic. *de Legg.* VI 26). The inscription on a monument often contained imprecations on those who should in any way dishonour it: 'If any one shall strip this shrine of its ornaments, or open it, or in any other way disturb it, with his own hand or by another's, he shall be suffered neither to walk the earth nor to sail the sea, but shall be rooted out with all his race,' Boeckh *Corp. Insc.* 916. Compare Aul. Gell. X 15, 24 (the flamen dialis) 'never sets foot on ground where a corpse has been burned' (locum in quo bustum est).

21. **come near a dead body**] Eur *Alc.* 98, 'I see not before the doors the spring water for ablution, as is the usage at the doors of the dead.' The lustral water, χέρνιψ, was usually set there in

144 ΔΕΙΣΙΔΑΙΜΟΝΙΑΣ ΚΗ'

ἐθελῆσαι, ἀλλὰ τὸ μὴ μιαίνεσθαι συμφέρον αὐτῷ φῆσαι
20 εἶναι· καὶ ταῖς τετράσι δὲ καὶ ταῖς ἑβδομάσι προστάξας
οἶνον ἕψειν τοῖς ἔνδον, ἐξελθὼν ἀγοράσαι μυρσίνας, λιβανω-
τόν, μίλακα, καὶ εἰσελθὼν εἴσω στεφανοῦν τοὺς Ἑρμαφροδίτους ὅλην τὴν ἡμέραν· καὶ ὅταν ἐνύπνιον ἴδῃ, πορεύεσθαι
πρὸς τοὺς ὀνειροκρίτας, πρὸς τοὺς μάντεις, πρὸς τοὺς
25 ὀρνιθοσκόπους, ἐρωτήσων τίνι θεῷ ἢ θεᾷ εὔχεσθαι δεῖ· καὶ
τελεσθησόμενος πρὸς τοὺς Ὀρφεοτελεστὰς κατὰ μῆνα πο-

---

an earthen vessel (ὄστρακον, Ar. *Eccl.* 1025), in order that friends passing out from their visit to the house of death might wash off the defilement —The Superstitious man is not content with this remedy for the pollution. He refuses to incur it at all,—thus declining one of the duties of kinship and friendship—the visit to a corpse while it was laid out (c. note on XIII, line 10 f.).

21 f. **a woman defiled by childbirth**] Eur. *Iph. in Taur.* 381.—

I blame the niceties of Artemis,
Who, if a man has put his hand to blood,
Or touched a corpse, or her whom childbed stains,
Bans him her altars, counts him as defiled,
Herself delighting in the blood of men

23 **the fourth and seventh days of each month**] (1) The 4th of each month was sacred to Hermes. Ar. *Plut.* 1128, '*Hermes.* Nothing of any sort does any one offer to us gods any longer. *Karion* No, nor will. *Hermes* Woe is me for the cake baked on the fourth of the month' (2) The 7th of the month was sacred to Apollo: 'for on it Leto bare Apollo of the Golden sword' (Hes. *Opp* 768).

25. **myrtle-wreaths, frankincense**] Aristoph. *Wasps* 861: 'Bring out fire, some one, with all speed, and myrtle-wreaths and frankincense, that we may first offer prayer to the gods.'

25. **smilax**] Worn by bacchants. Eur. *Bacch.* 105. 'Thebes, nurse of Semele, crown thyself with ivy; bloom with the fair blossoms of the delicate smilax, and make thyself a bacchanal with branches of oak or pine' The description of the *smilax* in Theophrastus, *Hist. Plant.* III 18, 11, with its ivy-like leaf, its white and *fragant flower*, and its *red berries*, shows that, in the *Bacchae*, 108, 703, it must be identified with the *smilax aspera*, and not with the convolvulus. In the present passage the word μίλακα has no manuscript authority, but is a very plausible conjecture.)

26. **the Hermaphrodites**] Hermaphroditus, son of Hermes and Aphrodite, was probably one of the household deities (Petersen *de cultu Graec. domestico* p 65). See Alciphro III 37 : 'I had woven a harvest-wreath and was on my way to the temple of Hermaphroditus, to offer it to him of Alôpekê' (meaning τῷ μακαρίτῃ, her late husband) ('Dici videntur maiorum utriusque sexus effigies cubiculares sub specie Hermarum biformium consecratae,' Lobeck, *Aglaophamus*, 1006. The cult of the Cyprian Aphroditos had been introduced into Athens during the 5th century; but the present passage is the earliest example of the name Hermaphroditos. A Hermes-bust of this type (figured in the *Annali*, 1884, tav. d' agg L) is represented crowned with pine-leaves (cp Roscher, *Lex. Mythol.* s.v. p. 2320); and another (reproduced in S Reinach's *Répertoire des Vases Peints*, I 472) has a Satyr standing before it and a Maenad behind it, both of whom bear the Bacchic thyrsus)

27. **when he has seen a vision**] The belief in *some* dreams as foreshadowing good or evil was universal in the ancient

childbirth, saying that it is expedient for him not to be polluted. Also on the fourth and seventh days of each month he will order his servants to mull wine, and will go out and buy myrtle-wreaths, frankincense, and smilax; and, on coming in, will spend the day in crowning the Hermaphrodites. When he has seen a vision, he will go to the interpreters of dreams, the seers, the augurs, to ask them to what god or goddess he ought to pray. Every month he will repair to the priests of the Orphic

world, and by no means confined to the superstitious. It is the anxiety to ascertain the precise import of *any* trivial dream which is here the mark of the Superstitious man.—Aesch. *Pers.* 202:—

Such were the phantoms that appalled my sleep;
But, when I rose, in clear streams from the spring
I washed my hands and with sweet-smelling flame
Came near the altar, fain to dedicate
Gifts meet for gods who turn mischance aside

(In Soph. *Electra*, 636, 644 f, Clytaemnestra 'uplifts her prayers for deliverance from her present fears,' prompted by 'the vision which she saw last night in doubtful dreams.')

27 f the interpreters of dreams, the seers, the augurs] He has recourse to one of three classes of diviners: (1) The special *Interpreters of dreams*. In spite of the general belief in dreams, the professors of a special dream lore were laughed at as early as the time of Aristophanes: see the *Wasps* 53, 'Shall I not hire him for two obols, with all his cleverness in telling dreams?' Alciphro III 59: 'I mean to go to one of the people who sit with boards (πινάκια) before them by the temple of Iacchus, undertaking to tell dreams—pay my two drachmas—and relate the vision which appeared to me in my sleep' A work in five books on the Interpretation of Dreams (ὀνειροκριτικά) by Artemidorus (circ. 150 A D.) is still extant. (2) The *Seers*, μάντεις. In the large sense, anyone was so called who spoke by the direct inspiration of the gods; and the various τρόποι μαντικῆς are enumerated in Aesch. *P. V.* 492—507. But μαντική meant especially divination *by sacrifice*,

either from the appearance of the victim (ἱερομαντεία) or from that of the flame (πυρομαντεία). (3) *The Augurs*. Augural science never became so elaborate or so important in Greece as at Rome. The Greek instinct for 'spiritual freedom and clearness' rebelled against a system of minute technicalities: see Curtius *Hist. Gr.* bk II c. 4, trans. Ward.

29. priests of the Orphic Mysteries] The mythical personage Orpheus, regarded by the oldest legends as the servant of Apollo, was regarded by a later legend as the priest of an Infernal god, Dionysus Zagreus. As early as the 7th century B.C. were formed Orphic Brotherhoods, 'who, under the guidance of the ancient mystical poet Orpheus, dedicated themselves to the worship of Dionysus' (Müller *Hist. Gr. Lit.* I p. 231). This cult bore a strong affinity to Indian asceticism: (*a*) in regarding the body as a prison from which the enlightened man seeks to achieve the deliverance of the soul. Plato *Cratylus* p. 400 C: 'I think, however, that this term ('body,' σῶμα) was the especial invention of the Orphic sect (οἱ ἀμφὶ 'Ορφέα)—signifying that the soul is in a state of punishment, for whatsoever cause; and is girt about, for its safe keeping, with the image of a prison. This, then, is, as its very name imports, the soul's *safe lodging* (σώζεσθαι), until it has paid its debts.'—(*b*) In prescribing a life of ceremonial purity: e g as regards diet; Plat. *Laws* VI p. 782 C: 'Orphic lives, as they are called, were led by those of our race who lived then, adhering to the use of all inanimate things, but abstain-

ρεύεσθαι μετὰ τῆς γυναικός, ἐὰν δὲ μὴ σχολάζῃ ἡ γυνή,
μετὰ τῆς τίτθης καὶ τῶν παιδίων· καὶ τῶν περιρραινομένων
ἀπὸ θαλάττης ἐπιμελῶς δόξειεν ἂν εἶναι· κἂν ποτε ἐπίδῃ
30 σκορόδων ἐστιώμενον τῶν ἐπὶ ταῖς τριόδοις, ἀπελθὼν κατὰ
κεφαλῆς λούσασθαι, καὶ ἱερείας καλέσας σκίλλῃ ἢ σκύλακι
κελεῦσαι αὐτὸν περικαθᾶραι· μαινόμενόν τε ἰδὼν ἢ ἐπίληπ-
τον, φρίξας εἰς κόλπον πτύσαι.

ing from everything wherein is life': and as regards bodily purity,—the Orphics wearing linen only, like the Egyptian priests to whom Herodotus compares them, II 81.

Such, in its original character, was the Orphic worship; as such, no doubt, it long had pure and earnest votaries. But already in Plato's time the name of the 'Orphic Mysteries' was traded upon by begging priests. *Rep.* p. 364 D: 'Prophets and quacks (μάντεις—ἀγύρται), besetting rich men's doors, exhibit books by Musaeus and Orpheus, those descendants of Selene and the Muses; according to which they offer sacrifice, persuading not only individuals but states that (forsooth) deliverance and purification from deeds of wrong are obtained by sacrifices *and childish mummeries* (παιδιᾶς ἡδοναί). These things they call their 'rites,' which deliver us from the ills beyond the grave : but, if we do not offer them, dread things await us.' Plut. *Apophth. Lacon.* p. 224 E: "Philippus, the Orphic priest, was very poor, but said that those who were initiated in his rites were happy when life was over. 'Why, then, foolish man,' he was asked, 'do you not die at once, and have rest from bewailing your poverty and wretchedness?'"

30. **accompanied by his wife**] It appears from this passage that women and children were admitted to the Orphic Mysteries. This was the case also at the Mysteries of the Cabeiri Plut. *Alex.* 2: 'It is said that Philip fell in love with Olympias on the occasion of his being initiated in her company at Samothrace, he being then a boy, and she a girl.' Women were admitted also to the Mysteries of the Eleusinian Demeter: Demosth. *in Meid.* § 158. (Attic Comedy in the time of Theophrastus regarded women as τῆς δεισιδαιμονίας ἀρχηγούς, Strabo, p. 297.)

31. **if she is too busy**] Observe the irony. Greek wives were seldom busy

32f. **sprinkling themselves with sea-water**] In Plut. *de Superst.* c. 3 the dream-teller advises the person who consults him to 'dip himself in the sea.' Circe, in the *Argonautica*, washes herself with sea-water after an alarming dream (Apoll. Rh. IV 669). Purification on the seashore was the ceremony of the second day of the Great Eleusinia, when worshippers were summoned with the cry ἅλαδε, μύσται. In Theocr. XXIV 44 salt is added to fresh water to increase its purifying efficacy.

34. **the garlic at the cross-roads**] A 'supper' for Hecate was placed at each new moon on the piles of stones at the cross-roads (see note on l. 11). Ar *Plutus* 595. 'Hecate can tell us whether it is better to be poor or hungry. She says that well-to-do or rich people send her a supper every month · whereas poor people snatch it away when it has hardly been put down' (The plaintiff in Dem. *in Cononem*, p. 1269 § 39, describes the defendant and his friends as feasting on 'Hecate's supper,' but we are not expressly told that garlic was one of the ingredients.) Plutarch (*de Superst.* c. 10) quotes a mention of Hecate as 'fastening at the cross-roads on the guilty wretch who has

THE SUPERSTITIOUS MAN. XXVIII (XVI)

Mysteries, to partake in their rites, accompanied by his wife, or 30 (if she is too busy) by his children and their nurse. He would seem, too, to be of those who are scrupulous in sprinkling themselves with sea-water; and, if ever he observes anyone feasting on the garlic at the cross-roads, he will go away, pour water over his head, and, summoning the priestesses, bid them carry a squill 35 or a puppy round him for purification. And, if he sees a maniac or an epileptic man, he will shudder and spit into his bosom.

gone after her foul supper' (καθαρμάτεσσιν ἐπισπομένῳ). The Superstitious man holds that he has been defiled by the mere sight of such wickedness.

(34 f. **pour water over his head**] A Greek inscription of the imperial age, found near Sunium, requires the worshippers at a certain temple to keep themselves 'pure from garlic and from pork,' and 'to pour water over their heads,' λουσαμένους κατακέφαλα, before entering the shrine, Dittenberger, *Sylloge*, no. 379)

(35. **the priestesses**] The γρᾶες of Plutarch, *de Superst.* 168 D, and the ἀπομάκτριαι of Pollux, VII 188)

35 f. **carry a squill or a puppy round him**] The object of all those ceremonies in which the offerings were carried round the person or place to be purified was to trace a charmed circle, within which the powers of evil should not come. Polyb. IV 21: the Mantineans 'held a purification, and carried victims round the city and the whole territory.' In the Roman *ambarvalia* the victim was carried thrice round the cornfields. Plaut. *Amph.* II 2, 154: 'Why do you not order a procession round her, as a madwoman' (*pro cerrita circumferri*)? (Menander fr 530, 21 Kock.—'let the women run right round, to disenchant thee,' περιμαξάτωσάν σ' αἱ γυναῖκες ἐκ κύκλῳ | καὶ περιθεωσάτωσαν)

35. **a squill**] Lucian *Menippus* c. 7:

'At midnight he took me to the Tigris, and purified me, rubbing me clean, and moving solemnly round me with torches and squills and divers other things.'

36. **a puppy**] Plut. *Quaest Rom.* c. 68 · 'The Greeks used, and to this day use, the dog for purifications They carry forth puppies, with other expiatory offerings, to Hecate, and touch all round (περιμάττουσι) with a puppy those who need restoration to purity, calling that sort of purification περισκυλακισμός.'

37. **spit into his bosom**] A custom connected with the belief already referred to (l. 6 f) in this chapter—that threatened evil could be averted by acts or words expressive of violent repugnance to it. Plin. *Hist. Nat.* XXVIII 4, 7 : 'We guard ourselves against epilepsy by spitting,— that is, we hurl back the plague (*contagia regerimus*). In like manner we repel the evil eye, and the lame man who jostles us on the right-hand side. We also ask pardon from the gods for any overbold hope by spitting into the bosom.' Lucian *The Boat* c 15: 'Nay, Adeimantus, you wax insolent, and forget to spit into your bosom.' Polyphemus, in Theocr. VI 39, takes this precaution against a nemesis on his beauty. In such cases—where a nemesis was deprecated—the idea of self-abasement was perhaps present. (In a fragment of Callimachus, 235, 'the women spit thrice into their bosoms,' and similarly in Theocritus, VI 39)

ὀλιγαρχίας κθ'.

δόξειε δ' ἂν εἶναι ἡ ὀλιγαρχία φιλαρχία τις, ἰσχύος,
οὐ κέρδους γλιχομένη, ὁ δὲ ὀλίγαρχος τοιοῦτος οἷος, τοῦ
δήμου βουλευομένου, τίνας τῷ ἄρχοντι προσαιρήσονται τῆς
πομπῆς τοὺς συνεπιμελησομένους, παρελθὼν ἀποφήνασθαι,
5 ὡς δεῖ αὐτοκράτορας τούτους εἶναι· κἂν ἄλλοι προβάλλωνται
δέκα, λέγειν· ἱκανὸς εἷς ἐστιν· τοῦτον δὲ ὅτι δεῖ ἄνδρα

1. **The Oligarchical temper**] ὀλιγαρχία, which properly denotes a form of government, stands here for ὀλιγαρχικότης—that habit of mind to which oligarchy is congenial. Compare, as analogous, the use of δυσσέβεια in Soph *Ant* 922 to denote, not the quality itself, but the character in men's eyes of the person who has that quality: τὴν δυσσέβειαν εὐσεβοῦσ' ἐκτησάμην: 'by being pious I have gained *the name of* impious.'

This Character and the following—that of the φιλοπόνηρος or Patron of Rascals—are essentially companion sketches. They are a pair of political caricatures, resting upon the fundamental antithesis of Athenian politics—government by the Few as contrasted with government by the Many. The partisan of either side is described from the point of view of the other; the oligarch, as loathing the mass of his fellow-citizens and ever tending towards a despotism, the democrat, as naturally attracted to whatever is low and tricky. There are two places in Greek literature where the bolder features of this contrast, and the commonplaces of recrimination which it suggested, are set forth with especial clearness,—the dialogue in the *Wasps* between the Admirer and the Loather of Cleon (471—724); and the whole speech of Isocrates *On the Peace*.

It is interesting to remember that, at the period to which the Characters of Theophrastus belong, the changes of party-fortune were unusually rapid, and party-feeling was perhaps more than usually keen. After his victory at Crannon in 322 B.C. Antipater abolished the democracy at Athens, and established an oligarchy. His death in 318 was followed by the democratic reaction to which Phocion fell a victim. In 317 the oligarchy was reconstituted by Cassander. It lasted till the nominal restoration of the democracy by Demetrius Poliorcetes in 307 B.C., with which the contest of parties in the old sense may be said to have finally closed. Thenceforth the question was mainly as to the particular agent in whom the Macedonian government of Athens should be vested. (At the date of the composition of the *Characters*, 319 B.C., the oligarchs, led by Phocion, were still in power.)

2. **covetous, not of gain, but of power**] See *Crit. App.* The wealthy oligarch was usually accused of bribing in order to get power; the needy democrat, of seeking power in order to be bribed. Thus in the *Wasps* the oligarch is greeted as 'hater of the people, enamoured of monarchy' (v. 473). He retorts—'father, you choose *these* men to rule over us, and then they take fees from the cities at the rate of thirty talents a town' (v. 672).

4. **whom they shall associate with the archon**] The First Archon would of course take a prominent part in a great public procession, and, if he was also to arrange it, would require the assistance of special colleagues or fellow-stewards. Hipparchus was assassinated in the act of marshalling (διακοσμοῦντι)

XXIX (XXVI). THE OLIGARCH.

The Oligarchical temper would seem to consist in a love of authority, covetous, not of gain, but of power.

The Oligarchical man is one who, when the people are deliberating whom they shall associate with the archon as joint directors of the procession, will come forward and express his opinion that these directors ought to have plenary powers; and, if others propose ten, he will say that 'one is sufficient,' but that

---

the Panathenaic procession. Thuc. I 20. These assistants of the archon on a particular occasion must not be confused with his regular assessors, πάρεδροι Each of the three principal archons might have two such assessors to aid him throughout his year of office; since, having been elected by lot, he might chance to be no man of business (πραγμάτων ἄπειρος, Dem. *in Neaer.* § 72). The six Thesmothetae had in like manner their 'advisers,' σύμβουλοι: Dem. *in Theocr.* § 37. (In Aristotle's *Constitution of Athens*, c. 56, we are told that the Archon superintended the sacred procession in the Great Dionysia in conjunction with the ten stewards, ἐπιμεληταί, of that festival. These were at first elected by show of hands in the Assembly, but at the time when the treatise was written, 328—325 B C., they were appointed by lot. If the text refers to the Great Dionysia, it shows clearly that, by the date of the composition of the *Characters* of Theophrastus, 319 B.C., the old method of electing by show of hands had been restored. It was apparently still in force in 280 B.C.)

5. **the procession**] '*The* procession' at Athens was that of the Greater Panathenaea. This festival was held in the August of every fourth year, the third of each Olympiad. The procession (was marshalled in the outer Cerameicus. Entering Athens by the Dipylum, it passed along the main street of the inner Cerameicus; subsequently, it probably swept round the western slope of the Areopagus:) and finally, ascending to the Acropolis, offered to Athene Polias the saffron robe embroidered with her victories. The frieze of the Parthenon represented the procession of which that temple was the goal. (For the *loci classici* on the Panathenaic procession, see Michaelis, *Der Parthenon*, pp. 213, 327 f, and, for a recent discussion of its probable course, Judeich's *Topographie von Athen*, 1905, p. 171 f) There were two other great πομπαί, both annual,— at the Great Dionysia in March, and at the Great Mysteries in September.

6. **ought to have plenary powers**] αὐτοκράτορας εἶναι. At Athens this word meant especially 'empowered to act without reference to the Ecclesia.' Thus, in the panic upon the mutilation of the Hermae in 415 B C , the Senate of Five-Hundred was made αὐτοκράτωρ (Andoc. *de Myst.* § 15). In the revolution of 411 B C. Peisander convoked the Ecclesia, and then proposed the appointment of ten Commissioners who should be independent of it (αὐτοκράτορας: Thuc. VIII 67). The opposite to αὐτοκράτωρ is ὑπεύθυνος, responsible to the public assembly. An ambassador, of course, might in another sense have 'plenary power' (to negotiate) but would still be 'responsible.'

7. **if others propose ten**] The Oligarch's first demand is that the new stewards of the procession shall not be responsible to the Ecclesia. He now makes a further demand—that this irresponsible power shall not even be divided, but shall be vested in one man. This is

εἶναι· καὶ τῶν Ὁμήρου ἐπῶν τοῦτο ἓν μόνον κατέχειν, ὅτι
οὐκ ἀγαθὸν πολυκοιρανίη· εἷς κοίρανος ἔστω, τῶν δὲ
ἄλλων μηδὲν ἐπίστασθαι. ἀμέλει δὲ δεινὸς τοῖς τοιούτοις
10 τῶν λόγων χρήσασθαι, ὅτι δεῖ αὐτοὺς ἡμᾶς συνελθόντας
περὶ τούτων βουλεύσασθαι καὶ ἐκ τοῦ ὄχλου καὶ τῆς ἀγορᾶς
ἀπαλλαγῆναι, καὶ παύσασθαι ἀρχαῖς πλησιάζοντας καὶ ὑπὸ
τούτων ὑβριζομένους ἢ τιμωμένους· <καὶ> ὅτι ἢ τούτους δεῖ
ἢ ἡμᾶς οἰκεῖν τὴν πόλιν· κατὰ μέσον δὲ τῆς ἡμέρας ἐξιών,
15 τὸ ἱμάτιον ἀναβεβλημένος καὶ μέσην κουρὰν κεκαρμένος καὶ
ἀκριβῶς ἀπωνυχισμένος σοβεῖν, τοὺς τοιούτους λόγους
<λέγων, διὰ> τὴν τοῦ Ὠιδείου· διὰ τοὺς συκοφάντας οὐκ
οἰκητέον ἐστὶν ἐν τῇ πόλει· καὶ ὡς ἐν τοῖς δικαστηρίοις

---

a hint how he would act if he had the framing of a constitution. His oligarchy would soon pass into a monarchy. cf. note on l. 4.

10 **'No good comes of manifold rule'**] From *Iliad* II 204. Odysseus is urging the Greeks to hear their chiefs in council. To the powerful he is persuasive; 'but when, on the other hand, he saw a man of the people and found him making a noise, him he would strike with his staff and loudly upbraid. Friend, sit quiet, and listen to the speech of others who are thy betters Assuredly we cannot all be kings here, we Greeks. *No good comes of manifold rule; let there be one ruler,* to whom the son of shrewd-minded Cronos hath given the sceptre and laws, that he may be king over his people.' The Oligarch's appeal from democracy to the poetry of divine right is the best touch in this sketch.

11 **of the rest he is absolutely ignorant**] A knowledge of the Homeric poems was one of the essentials of a good education. Isocr. *Panegyr.* § 159: 'I fancy that Homer's poetry gained the greater renown because he nobly praised those who warred against barbarians; and that for this cause our ancestors did honour to his artistic skill both by musical contests and in the education of the young, that, by often hearing his verses, they might thoroughly learn *the hereditary hatred of barbarians* (τὴν ἔχθραν τὴν ὑπάρχουσαν πρὸς αὐτούς), and, through admiration of the valour of those who went against Troy, might become emulous of deeds like theirs.' Xen. *Symp.* III 5: 'My father, anxious that I should become a good man, made me learn all Homer's poetry; and now I could say off (ἀπὸ στόματος εἰπεῖν) the whole Iliad and Odyssey'

(12 f. **we must get clear of the rabble**] In 322 B.C, on the submission of Athens after the Lamian war, Antipater disfranchised 12,000 of the poorer citizens and settled some of them in Thrace. In 319, on the death of Antipater, the exiles were restored (Plutarch, *Phokion* 28; Diodorus XVIII 18 and 66). These are the democratic 'rabble' that the Oligarch wants to get rid of. Cp. Droysen's *Gesch. des Hellenismus* II i, 80 f, 211 f, 219.

14. **we must leave off courting office**] Some officials—e g. the Generals, and ambassadors—were appointed by election (αἱρετοί) in the Ecclesia. The Oligarch scorns to be at the mercy of the popular Assembly.

16. **about the middle of the day**]

THE OLIGARCH. XXIX (XXVI)   151

'he must be a *man*.' Of Homer's poetry he has mastered only this one line,—

No good comes of manifold rule; let the ruler be one:

of the rest he is absolutely ignorant. It is very much in his manner to use phrases of this kind: 'We must meet and discuss these matters by ourselves, and get clear of the rabble and the market-place'; 'we must leave off courting office, and being slighted or graced by these fellows'; 'either they or we must govern the city.' He will go out about the middle of the day with his cloak gracefully adjusted, his hair daintily trimmed, his nails delicately pared, and strut through the Odeum Street, making such remarks as these: 'There is no living in Athens for the informers'; 'we are shamefully treated in the courts by

---

He will not deign to mix with the crowd in the market-place during the working-hours of the morning. Towards noon, when tired men are going home to their siesta (note on c. XXIV, 28), he will appear fresh and trim, and take gentle exercise in a street (leading past the Odeum of Pericles).

17. **with his cloak gracefully adjusted**] τὸ ἱμάτιον ἀναβεβλημένος. This perfect participle is sometimes used, without a qualifying adverb, in what may be called its pregnant sense—to express that the cloak is *thoroughly* or *carefully* adjusted. See Demosth. *de Fals. Legat* § 251: 'He said that the sobriety of the popular speakers of that day is illustrated by the statue of Solon with his cloak *drawn round him* and his hand within the folds' (εἴσω τὴν χεῖρα ἔχοντα ἀναβεβλημένον). In c. VII, which has wrongly been compared, ἀναβαλόμενος has no such pregnant sense.—The cloak, ἱμάτιον, was a square piece of cloth: it was thrown over the left shoulder, brought under the right arm, and then thrown over the left shoulder again. This was ἐπὶ δεξιὰ ἀναβάλλεσθαι, 'to put on the cloak from left to right.' Ar. *Birds* 1597 (to a Triballian): 'Why do you dress in this left-handed way?' (τί ἐπ' ἀριστέρ' οὕτως ἀμπέχει;) Plut. *Theaet.* p. 175 E (a man may possess vulgar accomplishments, and yet not know how) 'to put on his cloak from left to right *like a freeman*' (ἐλευθέρως).

17. **his hair daintily trimmed**] The man of Petty Ambition is ridiculed for having his hair cut too frequently (c. VII): the philosophers (Ar. *Clouds* 834), for never having it cut at all. The μέση κουρά, not mentioned elsewhere, is perhaps simply the mean approved by Athenian fastidiousness. (It is the mean represented in the Lateran statue of Sophocles, and in the busts of Isocrates and Epicurus.) A like attention to καιρός was exacted in regard to the length of the cloak: see note on c. XXIV, 25.

18. **the Odeum Street**] See *Crit. App* and, on the Odeum, the note on c. XVIII, 13. (It is practically certain that the text refers to the Odeum of Pericles, East of the Theatre of Dionysus. The Street of the Tripods, identified by the Choragic Monument of Lysicrates and by the remains of less important monuments East of the Acropolis, may well have led to the Odeum, East of the Theatre.)

(19 **There is no living in Athens**, etc.] Pseudo-Demosth. *In Theocr* p. 1342 § 65, 'Against informers, like the defendant, where can we go to obtain safety?')

20. **the informers**] Isocrates con-

δεινὰ πάσχομεν ὑπὸ τῶν δικαζόντων· καὶ ὡς θαυμάζω τῶν
20 πρὸς τὰ κοινὰ προσιόντων, τί βούλονται· καὶ ὡς ἀχάριστόν
ἐστι τὸ πλῆθος καὶ ἀεὶ τοῦ νέμοντος καὶ διδόντος· καὶ ὡς
αἰσχύνεται ἐν τῇ ἐκκλησίᾳ ὅταν παρακάθηταί τις αὐτῷ
λεπτὸς καὶ αὐχμῶν· καὶ εἰπεῖν· πότε παυσόμεθα ὑπὸ τῶν
λειτουργιῶν καὶ τῶν τριηραρχιῶν ἀπολλύμενοι; καὶ ὡς
25 μισητὸν τὸ τῶν δημαγωγῶν γένος· καὶ τὸν Θησέα πρῶτον
φῆσαι τῶν κακῶν τῇ πόλει γεγονέναι αἴτιον· τοῦτον γὰρ
ἐκ δώδεκα πόλεων εἰς μίαν καταγαγόντα λῦσαι τὴν βα-
σιλείαν· καὶ δίκαια αὐτὸν παθεῖν· πρῶτον γὰρ αὐτὸν
ἀπολέσθαι ὑπ' αὐτῶν· καὶ τοιαῦτα ἕτερα πρὸς τοὺς ξένους
30 καὶ τῶν πολιτῶν τοὺς ὁμοτρόπους καὶ ταῦτα προαιρουμένους.

demns the tendency to associate the informers—those pests of Athenian life—with the democratic side in politics: 'One of the ways in which we may mend the affairs of the city...is by ceasing to regard the informers as representative men of the people (δημοτικούς), and to identify the better class (τοὺς καλοὺς κἀγαθούς) with oligarchy' (*de Pace* § 133). Still, as money was the object of the professional informer, the rich must have suffered most from him; and a rich Oligarch would naturally look upon him as one of the plagues of a democracy The 'sycophant' was a character peculiar to Athens (Ar *Ach.* 904). The best picture of him is drawn in the pseudo-Demosth. *First Speech against Aristogeiton*:—'He moves through the market-place like a viper or a scorpion with sting erect, darting this way or that, seeking whom he may afflict with misfortune or calumny or any evil, and so, by putting him in fear, extort money' (*in Arist.* 1 § 52). When Aristotle was asked 'what he thought of Athens,' he is said to have replied—'A glorious place; but there—

ὄχνη ἐπ' ὄχνῃ γηράσκει, σῦκον δ' ἐπὶ σύκῳ:
Pear after pear grows old, and fig on fig':

i.e. the material for the sycophant never fails.

20 in the courts] The jury-courts were in their constitution, their tone and their practice thoroughly democratic. No institution was so hateful to the true Oligarch. Nothing, on the other hand, was more delightful to the ordinary dicast than the temporary abasement of rank and wealth at his bar Philocleon in the *Wasps* undertakes to show that the dicast's position is 'inferior to no sovereign's' (v. 549) After describing the abject defendant, his flatteries, his prayers, his pleading wife and whining children, he triumphantly concludes—'Is not this a great empire? Is not this *a flouting of wealth?*' (v. 575).

26. public services and trierarchies] The representative of a property amounting to 3 talents (τριτάλαντος οἶκος, Isaeus *de Pyrrh. h.* § 80),—i e. about £720—or upwards, was liable to the 'liturgies.' These may be classed as (1) the annual: Dem. *adv. Lept.* § 21: 'those who perform the yearly, recurring (ἐγκυκλίους) liturgies,—viz. the choregi, the gymnasiarchs and the entertainers' (ἑστιάτορες, who gave banquets to the several tribes). (2) The periodic, at longer intervals: e.g. the sacred mission (θεωρία) to Delos, to Olympia and to the Pythian festival in every fourth year; and to the Isthmian and Nemean games in every second. (3) The extraordinary: e g. missions to the oracle at Delphi. The trierarchy in so far belongs to this third class that the

the juries'; 'I cannot conceive what people want with meddling in public affairs'; 'how ungrateful the people are—always the slaves of a largess or a bribe'; and 'how ashamed I am when a meagre, squalid fellow sits down by me in the Ecclesia!' 'When,' he will ask, 'will they have done ruining us with these public services and trierarchies? How detestable that set of demagogues is! Theseus' (he will say) 'was the beginning of the mischief to the State. It was he who reduced it from twelve cities to one, and undid the monarchy. And he was rightly served; for he was the people's first victim himself'

And so on to foreigners and to those citizens who resemble him in their disposition and their politics.

---

number of vessels required by the state of course varied at different times. As organised in (prob.) 340 B.C. the trierarchy was perhaps specially unpopular with rich men; since under the old system of permanent boards (συμμορίαι) they had often paid less than their share: see note on c. XXV, 11.

27. Theseus] Thuc. II 15: 'In the time of Cecrops, and in that of the early kings down to Theseus, the population of Attica was divided among several towns, each having its town-hall and its magistrates; and, except in a season of alarm, they did not assemble to take counsel with the king... But when Theseus came to the throne...he dissolved the local town-councils and magistracies, and made the present city, with one council and one town-hall, the metropolis of the whole people. From that time to the present day the Athenians celebrate to the goddess the public festival of the Union' (συνοικία). This festival was held early in the October (Boedr. 17) of each year. It has been remarked that in the *Eumenides*—which, according to one view, was a conservative protest against the reform of the Areopagus—Theseus, the hero of the commonwealth, is made prominent, as if to conciliate the popular party (vv. 356, 380). His centralising policy finds no favour with the Oligarch, who would prefer that of which oligarchical Sparta was so fond—the διοι-κισμός, or breaking up of a town into several villages (Polyb IV 27, 6).

(**29 undid the monarchy**] Aristotle's *Constitution of Athens*, c. 41, describes the constitution of Theseus as 'a slight deviation from absolute monarchy.' In Plutarch's *Theseus*, 32, Menestheus, the prototype of the demagogue, describes Theseus as having deprived the Eupatridae of their royal rule in the country-districts of Attica and substituted a single foreign king for the many excellent kings of indigenous race)

30. he was the people's first victim himself] Plutarch tells the story thus. In the absence of Theseus and Peirithous on an attempt to carry off Coré, daughter of Aïdoneus king of the Molossians, a sedition was excited at Athens by one Menestheus, 'first of mankind, as they say, to attempt demagogy.' Theseus on his return tried to restore his old power, but was 'borne down by demagogues and faction' (κατεδημαγωγεῖτο καὶ κατεστασιάζετο). Having abdicated, and pronounced a curse upon the Athenians at Gargettos ('where is now the Araterium'), he withdrew to Scyros. In that island he was killed by a fall from the cliffs; Plut. *Thes.* 32—35. (Theophrastus himself, in a lost political work, πολιτικὰ τὰ πρὸς τοὺς καιρούς, stated that Theseus 'was the first to be ostracised at Athens,' Suidas *s.v* ἀρχὴ Σκυρία, in Wimmer's Fragm. of Theophrastus, 131.)

φιλοπονηρίας λ΄.

ἔστι δὲ ἡ φιλοπονηρία ἐπιθυμία κακίας· ὁ δὲ φιλοπόνηρός ἐστι τοιόσδε τις οἷος ἐντυγχάνειν τοῖς ἡττημένοις καὶ δημοσίους ἀγῶνας ὠφληκόσι καὶ ὑπολαμβάνειν, ἐὰν τούτοις χρῆται, ἐμπειρότερος γενήσεσθαι καὶ φοβερώτερος·
5 καὶ ἐπὶ τοῖς χρηστοῖς εἰπεῖν, ὡς γίνεται· καὶ φῆσαι, ὡς οὐδείς ἐστι χρηστός, καὶ ὁμοίους πάντας εἶναι· καὶ ἐπισκῶψαι δέ, ὡς χρηστός ἐστι· καὶ τὸν πονηρὸν δὲ εἰπεῖν ἐλεύθερον, ἐὰν βούληταί τις εὖ σκοπεῖν· καὶ τὰ μὲν ἄλλα ὁμολογεῖν ἀληθῆ ὑπὲρ αὐτοῦ λέγεσθαι ὑπὸ τῶν ἀνθρώπων,
10 ἔνια δὲ ἀγνοεῖν φῆσαι· εἶναι γὰρ αὐτὸν εὐφυῆ καὶ φιλέταιρον καὶ ἐπιδέξιον· καὶ διατείνεσθαι δὲ ὑπὲρ αὐτοῦ ὡς οὐκ ἐντετύχηκεν ἀνθρώπῳ ἱκανωτέρῳ· καὶ εὔνους δὲ εἶναι <αὐ>τῷ ἐν ἐκκλησίᾳ λέγοντι ἢ ἐπὶ δικαστηρίου κρινομένῳ· καὶ πρὸς τοὺς καθημένους δὲ εἰπεῖν δεινὸς ὡς οὐ δεῖ τὸν ἄνδρα ἀλλὰ τὸ

---

1. **The Patronising of Rascals**] The last sketch described the Oligarch as shrinking from contact with the people,—marvelling why they should wish to meddle in affairs,—striving to keep all power in the hands of a coterie. In this chapter he is given his revenge. At Athens the word πονηρός had what may be considered its political sense. It described a particular rank growth of character which sprang, amidst much that was good, out of the soil of Athenian democracy. In the representative democratic institutions—the Ecclesia and the law-courts—there was one great vice, arising from the very smoothness of the machinery and from the want of checks upon its swift, sweeping action. This was the insecurity of the individual. No man's character, property, even life was safe for a day from accusations which could be cheaply made, and which, when made in malice, were heard under the influence of rhetoric. Hence the terrible importance of the professional informer. Now the ideal πονηρός is to the συκοφάντης as genus to species. He is the man who avails himself without scruple of all those opportunities for extorting money, grasping power, or gratifying spite which a masterly knowledge of the available weapons can suggest. He is the skilled bully of the public assembly and of the law-courts,—the finished knave which Strepsiades aspired to become under the lessons of the sophist, and which the Aristophanic Cleon already is. He is such a man as is described in the First Speech against Aristogeiton, where the meaning of πονηρία (§ 39) is thus drawn out (§ 41):—'He storms in the Ecclesia, falling furiously on all of you; and, for every advantage which he gains over you collectively in the Assembly, for this, when he has left the platform, he prosecutes you individually—calumniating, begging, extorting.'

3. **those who have lost lawsuits**]

XXX (XXIX). THE PATRON OF RASCALS.

The Patronising of Rascals is a form of the appetite for vice. The Patron of Rascals is one who will throw himself into the company of those who have lost lawsuits and have been found guilty in criminal causes; conceiving that, if he associates with such persons, he will become more a man of the world, and will inspire the greater awe. Speaking of honest men, he will add 'so-so,' and will remark that no one is honest,—all men are alike; indeed, one of his sarcasms is, 'What an honest fellow!' Again, he will say that the rascal is 'a frank man, if one will look fairly at the matter.' 'Most of the things that people say of him,' he admits, 'are true; but some things' (he adds) 'they do not know; namely that he is a clever fellow, and fond of his friends, and a man of tact'; and he will contend in his behalf that he has 'never met with an abler man.' He will show him favour, also, when he speaks in the Ecclesia or is at the bar of a court; he is fond, too, of remarking to the bench, 'The question is of

---

Persons who made a practice of bringing vexatious lawsuits in the hope of occasionally getting a verdict would soon be competent masters in effrontery. 'Great is he, too, in lawsuits,' is said of the Reckless man (c. XVI). Strepsiades, in his exhaustive list of the qualities which make up the perfect πονηρός, hopes that he may one day be 'an old hand at lawsuits' (περίτριμμα δικῶν: *Clouds* 547).

3 f. **and have been found guilty in criminal causes**] The habit of getting up lawsuits (δίκαι) implies hardened impudence; the man who has been repeatedly convicted in public causes (γραφαί) is presumably a hardened criminal. The φιλοπόνηρος takes lessons in both the lighter and the graver branches of his subject.

16. **to the bench**] He undertakes to advocate the cause of the man who is on his trial, and addresses the judges in his favour. Both in public and in private causes the defendant was allowed to apportion as he pleased the fixed time given to him for speaking. He might, if he liked, surrender part of it to an advocate, though he was always expected to say at least a few words himself. The advocate was usually either a private friend or a person directly interested in the issue,—the taking of fees being forbidden under penalty of an indictment for bribery (Dem. *adv Steph* II § 26). Thus Demosthenes spoke for Ctesiphon against Aeschines, and for Phanus against Aphobus.

16 f. **the question is of the cause, etc.**] He exhorts the jury to show that they are no respecters of persons,—not to be biassed against the defendant because he is poor,—to decide solely on the merits of the case. Appeals of this kind are, in fact, very common in the orators: see, for example, the speech against Meidias. A speaker who knew how to use this topic skilfully could, in an Athenian court, exercise a good deal

156   ΦΙΛΟΠΟΝΗΡΙΑC Λ'

15 πρᾶγμα κρίνεσθαι· καὶ φῆσαι αὐτὸν κύνα εἶναι τοῦ δήμου,
φυλάττειν γὰρ αὐτὸν τοὺς ἀδικοῦντας· καὶ εἰπεῖν ὡς οὐχ
ἕξομεν τοὺς ὑπὲρ τῶν κοινῶν συναχθεσθησομένους, ἂν τοὺς
τοιούτους προώμεθα. δεινὸς δὲ καὶ προστατῆσαι φαύλων
καὶ συνεδρεῦσαι ἐν δικαστηρίοις ἐπὶ πονηροῖς πράγμασι,
20 καὶ κρίσιν κρίνων ἐκδέχεσθαι τὰ ὑπὸ τῶν ἀντιδίκων λεγό-
μενα ἐπὶ τὸ χεῖρον.

[καὶ τὸ ὅλον ἡ φιλοπονηρία ἀδελφή ἐστι τῆς πονηρίας,
καὶ ἀληθές ἐστι τὸ τῆς παροιμίας, τὸ ὅμοιον πρὸς τὸ ὅμοιον
πορεύεσθαι.]

---

of terrorism under the form of deprecation.

18. **the watch-dog of the people**] Compare the pseudo-Demosth. *in Aristog.* I § 40: 'What, then, is the defendant? Some, I suppose, will say—'a watch-dog of the people.' Of what breed? Of such a breed that he will not bite those whom he takes for wolves, but will himself devour the sheep that he pretends to guard' (and Xen. *Mem.* II 9, 2. In Cicero, *pro Sex. Roscio*, 56, accusers are compared to 'the dogs on the Capitol.' The phrase was taken up by Camille Desmoulins, in his *Discours de la lanterne*, and the word *aboyeur* became the technical term for an informer under the Reign of Terror, cp. Zielinski, *Cicero im Wandel der Jahrhunderte*, p 326, ed. 1908). The metaphor 'watch-dog' was less homely to Greek ears than it is to ours. It finds place in one of the stateliest passages of Greek tragedy, Aesch *Agam.* 591, where Clytaemnestra is speaking of herself as the faithful οἰκουρός during the absence of her lord:

and coming may he find,
Even as he left, the *Watcher* of the house,
To him leal-hearted, hostile to his foes.

It is somewhat curious that in the same language the dog should have been a proverb at once for shamelessness (κυνώπης, etc) and for noble fidelity. The dog Argos in the *Odyssey* bears witness to a Greek feeling for his species very different from that usual in the East.

21. **to form conspiracies in the law-courts**] συνεδρεῦσαι ἐν δικαστηρίοις. He has already been described as assisting his friends in the character of advocate (n. on l. 16). He now intrigues for them in the character of judge. When the panel of 500 or more jurors has been appointed to try a cause, the favourer of the worthless defendant forms a clique (συνεδρεύει) in his interest He conspires with a few of his numerous colleagues to give the man every chance. Conspiracies of another kind are often mentioned in the orators,—where 'a gang of confederates' combined to bring on or defeat an action (τὸ ἐργαστήριον τῶν συνεστώτων, Dem.

THE PATRON OF RASCALS. XXX (XXIX)

the cause, not of the person.' 'The defendant,' he will say, 'is the watch-dog of the people,—he keeps an eye on evil-doers. We shall have nobody to take the public wrongs to heart, if we allow ourselves to lose such men.' Then he is apt to become the champion of worthless persons, and to form conspiracies in the law-courts in bad causes, and, when he is hearing a case, to take up the statements of the litigants in the worst sense.

[In short, sympathy with rascality is sister to rascality itself; and true is the proverb that 'Like moves towards like.']

---

adv Pantaen. § 39: ἐργαστήρια μοχθηρῶν ἀνθρώπων συνεστηκότων, adv. Zenoth. § 10). But here the word συνεδρεύειν seems to show that the conspirator is on the bench.

22. and, when he is hearing a case, etc.] The last sentence described him as arranging with his brother-jurors, before the trial comes on, that the person in whom he is interested shall receive favour. The present sentence describes his ordinary conduct when a case is actually in progress before him, whether his sympathies are particularly engaged or not.

23. in the worst sense] A certain shallow cynicism—as shown in his remarks on honesty—is characteristic of the φιλοπόνηρος. It reappears in this trait. Neither of the parties to *this* cause being so eminently knavish as to enjoy his exclusive favour, he comforts himself with the conclusion that both are knaves. The usage of the Athenian law-courts permitted strong and abundant personalities. The believer in general depravity takes these conventional asperities ἐπὶ τὸ χεῖρον,—i.e. in the fullest and worst sense which a literal acceptation can fix upon them.

25 Like moves towards like] *Od.* XVII 218, 'The god ever draws like to like.' Arist. *Eth. N.* VIII 1, 6, "There are no slight controversies about (friendship). Some make it a certain likeness, and friends, those who resemble us; whence the sayings 'like to like,' 'jackdaw to jackdaw,' and so forth. Some on the contrary say that all such persons are potters to each other" (Hes. *Opp.* 25, 'Potter spites potter, bard hath grudge to bard'). An examination of the proverb 'like to like'—ending in nothing more definite than the conclusion that pure contrariety is incompatible with friendship—will be found in Plato's *Lysis*, pp. 214 ff. (Arist. *Rhet.* I 11, 25, "All things akin to one, and like one, are pleasant to one, as a rule,—as man to man, horse to horse, youth to youth; whence the proverbs, 'mate delights mate,' 'like to like,' 'a beast knows his fellow,' 'jackdaw to jackdaw,' and so forth ")

CRITICAL APPENDIX

CRITICAL APPENDIX

A list (1) of the MSS of the Characters, (2) of the principal Editions and Commentaries, is given by Foss (Teubner, 1858). In his Preface he has some remarks on the different classes and ages of the MSS and on some of the editions. The relation of the MSS to each other is fully discussed by Petersen in his Introduction.

From a comparison of these authorities, with occasional help from other sources, the following account has been drawn up. It is given here because it may be convenient to those who intend to make a critical study of the Characters to have in a compact form the principal facts about the MSS and some notice of the best editions

The editions of Ast, Foss, Sheppard, Petersen and Ussing are the only ones which the writer of these notes on the text has had before him. The varietas scripturae appended to the edition of Foss, and the apparatus criticus given at the foot of each page by Petersen, supply the necessary materials for forming a judgment on disputed passages. Ast, Foss and Ussing give in their commentaries the best conjectures of previous editors.

(Since the publication of the first edition, in 1870, further information on the text of the MSS and on the conjectures of recent critics has been recorded in the edition prepared by the *Philologische Gesellschaft* at Leipzig and published by Teubner in 1897. This has been followed by the annotated editions of Romizi, Florence, 1899, Fraenkel and Groenboom, Leyden, 1901, and Edmonds and Austen, London, 1904, and, finally, by the critical text edited by Diels, Oxford, 1909. With a view to this last edition, each of the three leading MSS, A, B, and V, has been reproduced by photography, and special care has been bestowed on the accurate record of their readings.)

I. MANUSCRIPTS.

The extant MSS of the Characters (50 of which are identified, and 10 others enumerated in the Leipzig edition) exhibit three different recensions or editions, viz

1. The Vulgate, or that recension which appears in 48 of the 50 MSS. Of these, 35 contain the first 15 Characters, as they stand in the traditional order (see p. 34); 6 the first 23, and 7 the first 28. The two oldest and best are usually called 'Paris A, B,' being nos. 3264 (now 2977) and 2751 (now 1983) in the National Library in Paris. These contain the first 15 Characters only. A is probably of the 9th century, B of the 10th Dubner thinks that both belong to the early part of the 10th. (Both are assigned to the 11th by Abraham in Studemund's *Jahrb.* 1885, 759 f; and B, which is placed early in the century, is more carefully transcribed than A. Both have been photographed for Diels.)

2. A recension found in one MS, no. CX in the Vatican Library. This contains the last 15 Characters only, and is the only MS which has the 29th and 30th. Also, in cc. 15—28, it gives additions which are found in no other MS. It is sometimes called (as by Foss) 'Palatinus,' sometimes (as by Ussing) 'Vaticanus.' Petersen designated it as the Palatino-Vatican (PVat. of Jebb's ed of 1870. It is now distinguished from the four Vatican MSS which were formerly in the Palatine Library. In the Leipzig edition of 1897, and in the present edition, as in that of Diels, it is denoted by V). Foss thinks that it was written in the 13th century. (In the Leipzig edition it is assigned to the 13th or 14th. It was collated by Badham and Cobet, it was carefully examined by G. Lowe on behalf of Ribbeck, and it has been completely photographed for Diels.)

3. A recension found in one MS, now in the Library at Munich (no. 505). This contains the first 21 Characters, and gives them in a shorter form than any other MS. It is usually called the Munich Epitome. At the beginning it has an index to all the thirty Characters. It belongs to the 14th or 15th century. (It was first printed by Wurm in 1822, more accurate copies have since been published by Petersen, 1859, Christ, 1860, by Diels, in his *Theophrastea*, 1883, and in the Leipzig edition of 1897.)

Characters 29 and 30 (nos. 30 and 26 in our Translation, see p. 35) were first published from V in 1786 at Parma by J. C Amaduzzi. The additions made to cc 15—28 by V were first published in 1798 by J. A. Goez, in the Anecdota Graeca of Siebenkees, which he edited after his friend's death (and in the complete text published in the same year). For many years afterwards the students of the Characters were divided into two schools; those who denied, and those who allowed, the authenticity of the extra matter in V.

The principal impugners of V were Coray, in his edition published at Paris in 1799; Ast, in his edition, Leipzig, 1816; and Hottinger, in his German Translation, Munich, 1821. Ast does not even admit into his text the additions found in V, but prints them in small type at the foot of the page; c. 29 [30] he regards as wholly spurious, c. 30 [26] as patched together from fragments of cc. 9 [15], 10 [24], 22 [25]. But he is not consistent; for, in a passage of c. 22 [25], καὶ τῇ γυναικὶ δέ. .μὴ πρίασθαι, and in another of c 24 [4], καὶ βαδίζων ἐν ταῖς ὁδοῖς τὰς διαίτας κρίνειν, he admits part of the supplement in V and rejects the rest. The earliest champions of that MS were J. G. Schneider,—whose first edition appeared at Jena in 1799, the second at Leipzig in 1818,—and S. N. J Bloch, in his edition published at Leipzig in 1814. But the turning point in the opinion of scholars on the question was the appearance of three dissertations published successively at Halle in 1834—6 by H E. Foss. In these he defended very forcibly and elaborately the genuineness of the supplements in V and of its two extra chapters. Among his earliest converts were E. Meier and F Dubner, the latter of whom published his edition at Paris in 1840. Since that time V has been generally acknowledged to be the best as well as the fullest authority for cc. 15—28, and the authenticity of cc. 29, 30 has been considered as established.

The arguments in favour of V are stated by Dr E. Petersen, in an essay which gained a University prize at Bonn in 1857, and which he published, slightly altered, in 1859. He agrees with Foss in the main, but differs from him in a few particulars. A full analysis of his essay would be out of place here, but an outline of his argument may be useful to those who wish to read it. (1) In respect to the supplements in V, it is argued that there are (a) cases in which they can be proved to be genuine by their intimate and necessary coherence with the text of the Vulgate: pp. 4—17; (b) cases, in which, though they cannot be proved genuine, there are no sufficient grounds for condemning them: pp. 17—19. (2) The opinion that the Munich Epitome represents the true text, and that the other two recensions are paraphrases of it, is examined and refuted. It is shown that, of all possible hypotheses as to the relations of the three recensions to each other, the only probable one is that V came from the same archetype from which were derived, but less immediately, the Vulgate on the one hand and the Epitome on the other pp. 19—24. (3) The several families of the MSS which have the Vulgate text are then examined: pp. 24—55. (4) Lastly, the probable relation between V and the archetype of the Vulgate and Epitome is more exactly defined. From the same book which was the source of V was made another copy; in which the last leaf, containing on its inner page a part of c. 30 [c. 26 ll. 6—33 in our text] had by accident been shifted to a place next c. 11 [17]. The leaf originally last but one, and which contained c. 29 [30], was thus left last; and, being exposed to ill-usage, became illegible, and was left out by transcribers. From this copy was taken (with sundry omissions) the archetype of the Vulgate. Hence in the Vulgate cc. 29, 30 do not appear, but a part of c. 30 is found in c. 11 (see *Crit. App.* xvii, 14). And from this copy came also the Munich Epitome.—The archetype of V, —which would thus have been the common ancestor of all our MSS,— was probably not much older than the 10th century (pp. 55, 6 compare p 23).

(The following is the *Stemma* of the MSS proposed by Otto Immisch on p. xliii of the Leipzig edition :

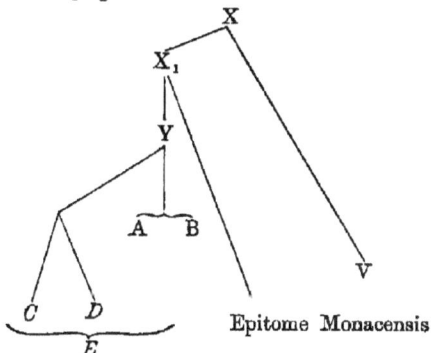

Here X is the archetype of all our existing MSS, and X_1 a copy of the same, in which part of c. 30 was placed next to c. 11 [17] V is the Vatican MS; A and B the principal Paris MSS; C and D represent the two groups of MSS with part of c 30 [26] placed next to c. 11 [17], C containing cc. 1—28, and D, cc. 1—23, while E represents the later MSS corresponding in contents to A and B, i.e. having only cc. 1—15 and placing part of c 30 [26] next to c. 11 [17]. Y is an intermediate epitome, which is the source of all the MSS except V.)

II. Principal Editions and Commentaries.

(1) *Editions with 15 Characters.*

1527. Pirckheymer publishes at Nuremberg an edition of the first 15 Characters—the first after the revival of letters. (This edition was founded on a MS presented in 1515 to Pirckheymer by Giovanni

Francesco Pico della Mirandola; the Latin translation was executed by Pirckheymer, who dedicated the work to Albrecht Durer.)

(1531. Andrea Cratander publishes at Basel an anonymous translation of the first 15 Characters, founded on a MS differing from that of Pico. This translation is ascribed to Politian by Conrad Gesner, and by F. Morell in his Paris ed. of 1853.)

(2) *Editions with 23 Characters*

1552. G. Battista Camozzi, in an edition of Aristotle, published in Venice, includes 23 of the Characters, along with other writings of Theophrastus. (This is the source of the edition of H. Stephanus, Paris, 1557, and of other editions published in 1561—84.)

(3) *Editions with 28 Characters.*

1599. Isaac Casaubon, in the second and third of his three editions (1592, 1599, 1612), prints 28 Characters, the 5 new ones from 4 MSS in the Palatine Library at Heidelberg. It was even then known that the number of the Characters was not complete; for indices to 30 had been found in some MSS But nearly two centuries more elapsed before the missing chapters were found

1712 Peter Needham published at Cambridge an edition in which the novelty was the weight given to the two Paris MSS A, B, in the first 15 chapters, but he did not follow them consistently (His edition includes the notes and emendations of Casaubon, with prelections, on the first 13 Characters, identified by Bentley as part of the professorial lectures delivered by Duport in Cambridge during the Civil War.)

1737. J. C de Pauw publishes at Utrecht an edition with some good conjectures, for which he is often quoted.

1739. J. C. Schwartz, in an edition published at Coburg, follows Needham chiefly, but alters and conjectures audaciously

1757. J. J. Reiske, in his *Animadversiones in Auctores Graecos* (I pp. 96—106), has some good notes on the Characters.

(1761. C A. Klotz publishes at Jena and Leipzig his *Animadversiones in Theophrasti characteres ethicos*.)

1763. J F. Fischer, like the other editors, founds his edition on the majority of inferior MSS, forsaking the two Paris MSS of which Needham had recognised the importance (Fischer gives a full account of all the earlier editions, and of the emendations proposed in them.)

1786. J. C Amaduzzi publishes at Parma the two long-missing Characters 29 and 30, from a MS in the Vatican library (no. CX). Prospero Petroni, librarian of the *bibliotheca Alexandrina* in Rome, had (in 1743) announced his intention to produce an ampler edition of the Characters with the aid of the Vatican MS

1788. J. P. Siebenkees copies cc. 15—30 from the Vatican MS, for insertion in his Anecdota Graeca, collected in Italian libraries. He dies before publishing the book, and it is edited by J. A Goez, who also produces a separate edition of the Characters (*infra*, 1798).

(4) *Editions containing 30 Characters.*

1798. J. A. Goez publishes at Nuremberg an edition including Siebenkees' transcript of the Vatican text of cc. 15—30. (The numerous errors in this transcript are pointed out by Cobet, in *Mnemosyne* VIII (1859) 310—338.)

1799. Coray's edition appears at Paris. He maintains strongly that the supplements discovered in the Vatican MS are spurious. His notes and (in some cases) his conjectures are good.

1799. J G. Schneider, in his first edition published at Jena, adopts and defends the Vatican supplements His edition is one of the most important, and is constantly referred to by later editors. (His *editio minor* appeared in 1800. His text of the Characters was afterwards included in his edition of the whole of Theophrastus, published at Leipzig in 1818—21.)

(1802. Schweighauser publishes in Paris his *Annotationes* to a new edition of the French translation by La Bruyère.)

1814. S. N. J. Bloch (a Danish scholar) publishes at (Altona and) Leipzig an edition in which he follows Schneider in maintaining the authenticity of the Vatican supplements.

1816 F. Ast publishes at Leipzig an edition in which he reasserts the view of Coray that the extra matter in V, including c. 29, is spurious . c 30 he regards as a patchwork from other chapters.

(1818—25. Kuchler publishes his *Observationes*, I at Leipzig, 1818, and II at Naumburg, 1825.)

(1820. Boissonade's *Theophrasti characteres tentati* is published in Wolf's *Lit. Analekten*, II 88—90, Berlin.)

1821 J. J. Hottinger publishes at Munich a German Translation, in which he takes nearly the same view as Ast.

1822. Chr. Wurm publishes in the Munich Journal of Philology (*Acta Phil Mon* III 363 ff) the first 21 Characters, in a shorter form than that of the Vulgate, as he had found them in a MS at Munich (the

Epitome). F Thiersch (in his epilogue to this article) maintains the view that this epitome gives the proem, and at least the first five chapters, in their genuine form, the Vulgate having been amplified by interpolation.

1830—50. E. Meier brings out at intervals five critical essays on the Characters. While writing these, he adopted the view of Foss respecting the Vatican MS (Meier's essays are reprinted in his *Opuscula*, II, 1863, 190—262.)

(1831. Dobree's *Notae in Theophrastum* are published in his *Adversaria*, I 161, ed. Scholefield, I 139, ed Wagner, 1875.)

(1834. Orelli publishes at Zürich his *Lectiones Theophrasteae*)

1834—6. H E. Foss, in three dissertations published in three successive years at Halle, maintains (1) that the Munich text is not complete, but a mere epitome; (2) that all the Vatican supplements are genuine.

1840. F. Dubner, in his edition published at Paris, takes the same view.

(1849. G A. Hirschig publishes at Utrecht his *Annotationes in Theophrastum*)

(1850—63 Nauck suggests some emendations in 1850, *Philologus* v 383 f., and in 1863, *Mélanges Gr Rom.* II 477—9.)

1852 J. G Sheppard publishes in London an edition in which he recurs to the theory that the Vatican additions are spurious He adopts, but modifies, the text of Ast. This Commentary is interesting for its illustrations from modern literature.

1857. J. A. Hartung's edition appears at Leipzig He adopts the Vatican supplements.

1858. H. E Foss publishes in Teubner's series an edition of the text of the Characters, with the 'Varietas Scripturae' appended. In this he used a collation of V made in 1843 by Charles Badham. (At Altenburg, in 1861, Foss published his Commentatio quarta.)

(1858—74. Cobet proposes emendations in *Novae Lectiones* (1858), *passim*; corrects the errors of Siebenkees in *Mnemosyne*, VIII (1859), 310—338; and proposes further emendations in *N. S.* II (1874), 34—72, and *Variae Lectiones*, ed. 2 (1873), reprinted in Bursian's *Jahresbericht*, II 1294 f. Cobet holds that we must rely entirely on the two Paris MSS, A and B, for the text of cc. 1—15, and on the Vatican MS for that of cc. 16—30.)

(1858—61. F. Hanow publishes at Leipzig his dissertation *De Theophrasti characterum libello*, produced at Bonn in 1858; and the two parts of his *Symbolae Criticae*, produced at Züllichau in 1860—1.)

(1859. Meineke proposes emendations in *Philologus*, XIV (1859), 403 ff.)

1859 E Petersen's essay on the MSS of the Characters and on the history of the book appears at Leipzig. He gives also the text of the Characters, with a collation of several MSS at the foot of each page; and also prints (on pp. 158—164) the Munich epitome of the first 21 chapters. (This text has since been revised by Christ in the *Sitzungsberichte* of the Munich Academy, 1860, 635 ff, it has also been printed in Diels' *Theophrastea*, 1883, and in the Leipzig edition, 1897.) Petersen's essay is altogether a most valuable book.

(1860. Kayser proposes emendations in the *Heidelberg Jahrbucher*, 611—624; and Moritz Schmidt in *Philologus*, XV 541 f.)

1868 J. L. Ussing publishes a volume containing the Characters of Theophrastus, the 10th book of Philodemus περὶ κακιῶν, and (in an appendix) two short extracts from Rutilius Lupus and from the Rhetorica ad Herennium. The chief value of the book consists in the excellent though somewhat scanty commentary (which is limited to 86 small pages). In dealing with the text he is usually cautious, but now and then makes emendations which show more ingenuity than instinct for the language.

(The following editions, and contributions to the criticism or explanation of the Characters, have appeared since 1868

1869—73. Haupt proposes emendations in (1) *Hermes*, III (1869) 336 f, (2) *ib.* V (1871) 29 f; (3) *ib.* VII (1873) 295 f; reprinted in *Opusc.* III 2 (1876) 434 f, 498 f, 592 f (on cc. 1, 14, 16, 20, 21)

1870. R. C. Jebb. The Characters of Theophrastus, an English Translation from a Revised Text, with Introduction and Notes; pp XII + 328, small 8vo. London and Cambridge.

1870—83. Ribbeck discusses the Characters in *Rhein. Mus.* XXV (1870) 129 ff; *On* εἴρων, *ib.* XXXI (1876) 381—400, *Alazon*, pp. 193 (Leipzig, 1882); *Kolax*, pp. 113, in *Abh.* of Saxon *Gesellschaft* (Leipzig, 1883). See below (1889).

1870—3. Usener comments on cc. 1, 5, 6, 8, 9, 16, 20, 21 in *Rhein. Mus.* XXV (1870) 605 ff, and XXVIII (1873) 434 f.

1871. H van Herwerden publishes *Bijdrage tot de verklaring en kritiek van de Charakteres van Theophrastus*, in Proceedings of Amsterdam Academy, II i (1871) 241—311.

1871. Madvig proposes emendations in *Adversaria Critica*, I 478 f.

1873. L. Schmidt, in a Marburg program, comments on the meaning of εἴρων in Ariston and Theophrastus. Cp. Bursian's *Jahresbericht*, 1 207 f.

1874 Buecheler publishes *Conjectanea* in Fleckeisen's *Jahrbücher*, CIX 691. Cp. Eberhard in Bursian, *l.c.*, II 1298.

1882. E. L. Hicks, in the *Journal of Hellenic Studies*, III 128—143, quotes Athenian inscriptions to illustrate cc. 13 [10] and 21 [7].

1883—98. (1) Diels publishes his *Theophrastea* in 1883, in a program of the Königstadtisches Gymnasium, Berlin. He supports Cobet's opinion that our text must be founded, for the first 15 chapters, on the Paris MSS A and B, and, for the second 15, on the Vatican MS, which contains these only. By a new collation of A and B, he shows that B is superior to A; and he suggests that a longer and a shorter excerpt were made from the Vatican MS, that a combination of B (for the first 15 chapters) with the longer excerpt (for the rest) is the source of the Munich epitome, and a combination of B with the shorter excerpt is the source of the later MSS, those containing 23 and also those containing 28 chapters. This view is criticised in the Leipzig edition, p. XLI f. (2) In the *Deutsche Litt.-Zeit.* of 1898, 750 ff, Diels reviews the Leipzig edition.

1884—9 G F. Unger suggests emendations in *Philologus*, XLIII (1884) 218, XLIV (1885) 740; XLV (1886) 218, 244, 277, 368, 438, 448, 552 f, 613, 641, XLVI (1888) 56, XLVII (1889) 374 f. See Bursian's *Jahresbericht*, XLII 267, L 19, LXXV 69

1885. H. Blumner suggests emendations in Fleckeisen's *Jahrbucher*, CXXXI 485 f. See Bursian, *l.c.*, XLII 267.

1887. W. Werle publishes at Coburg a program proposing a number of transpositions in the text. See Bursian, *l.c*, LXXV 68 f

1888—93. Zingerle proposes emendations in the *Zeitschrift f d osterreich. Gymnasien* (1888) 706 f; (1893) 1066 ff. See Bursian, *l c.*, LXXIX 279 f.

1889—98. Gomperz publishes in the *Sitzungsberichte* of the Vienna Academy, CXVII (1889) *Abh.* 10, a paper on the Characters, in which he opposes the view that they consist of excerpts from one or more writings of Theophrastus, and maintains that they are derived from the 'Ethical Characters' ascribed to that author He, nevertheless, disputes the genuineness of the *definitions* of the several Characters. In this paper he misunderstands Ribbeck's position. The sequel may be found in two papers in the *Rhein. Mus.* XLIV (1889), (1) by Ribbeck, on pp 305 f, and (2), by Gomperz and Ribbeck, on pp. 472 f. See Bursian, *l.c.*, LXXV 67 f. In the *Sitzungsberichte* CXXXIX (1898) 11—15,

Gomperz reasserts his opinion on the spuriousness of the *definitions*, and discusses some points in the text of c 21 [7].

1890. Weil discusses two historical allusions in c. 7 [19] in the *Revue de Philologie*, XIV 106 f See Bursian, *l c.*, LXXV 69.

1891. C. J. Babick publishes at Leipzig a dissertation *De deisidaimonia veterum*, including emendations on c. 28 [16]. Cp. Bursian, *l.c.*, LXXIX 128 f.

1891. Blaydes proposes, in *Hermathena*, VIII 1—13, a number of corrections of the Teubner text of 1858.

1892 Naber proposes emendations in *Mnemosyne*, N. S , XX 319 —337. Cp. Bursian, *l.c*, LXXIX 127 f.

1893 Van der Mey proposes emendations in the *Contos-Sylloge*, Leyden, 71 ff.

1894. P. Sakolowski, in the *Gr. Studien H. Lipsius dargebracht*, Leipzig, 157 f, follows in the lines of Ribbeck, *Rhein. Mus.* XXV 139, in the reconstruction of chapter 11 [17] Cp Bursian, *l c.*, LXXXVIII 46.

1895—6. Munsterberg proposes emendations in the *Wiener Studien*, XVI (1895) 161 ff , and XVII (1896) 217 ff.

1897. Otto Immisch gives a detailed account of 50 MSS, discusses the recension of the text, and adds a conspectus of the literature of the subject, on pp. VIII—LVI of an edition prepared by the Leipzig *Philologische Gesellschaft*. Here, and elsewhere, he points out that the Characters have survived solely as part of a collection of rhetorical writings, the nucleus of which is formed by Aphthonius and Hermogenes. They may therefore be regarded as supplementary to Hermogenes, περὶ ἰδεῶν, II 2—9. Among the other contributors to this edition (which includes critical and explanatory notes and a German translation) are M. Bechert, A. Gieseke, R. Holland, J. Ilberg, R. Meister, and W. Ruge. A few valuable notes have been added by Curt Wachsmuth, and by F. Studniczka, who has superintended the selection of the illustrations from works of ancient art. In this edition the most important emendations are recorded in the critical notes at the foot of the page, while other proposals are incidentally mentioned in the course of the commentary. In the sequel, the letter *L* is used to denote this edition and its editors.

1898 P. Wendland points out, in *Philologus*, LVII 104, that the work was once included in the celebrated Paris MS, no. 1741, probably in an edition containing only 15 Characters.

1898 Otto Immisch, in *Philologus*, LVII 193, argues that the work was originally a *parergon* to the rhetorical writings of Theophrastus.

1899. Domenico Bassi, in the *Rivista di Filologia*, XXVII 280—2,

BIBLIOGRAPHY

draws attention to a MS of cc. 1—15 (dated 1426) in the Ambrosian library, C 82 *sup*.

1899. Romizi publishes at Florence a critical edition of the text with an Italian translation, and with Latin notes on the text and Italian notes on the translation. The Introduction reviews the work of Italian scholars in connexion with the Characters of Theophrastus, pp. ix + 198.

1901. J. M. Fraenkel and P. Groeneboom, of Utrecht, publish an edition of the text at Leyden, with critical notes in Latin, and explanatory notes in Dutch, pp. 65; reviewed by P. Wendland in the Berlin *Philologischer Wochenschrift*, 1902, p. 323 f.

1902. Von Wilamowitz-Moellendorff includes c. 2 [1] κολακεία, 14 [13] ἀναισθησία, 21 [7] μικροφιλοτιμία, 25 [27] δειλία, and 30 [26] αἰσχροκέρδεια, in his *Griechisches Lesebuch*, Berlin, 1902 etc

1904. J. M. Edmonds and G E. V. Austen produce a school-edition. In the Introduction they deal with the Life and Times of Theophrastus, discuss the date, origin, authorship and titles of the Characters, and mention the principal MSS, but they erroneously follow editions previous to that of 1897 in supposing that the principal Vatican MS (V) is identical with one of the four Palatine MSS (no 149) in the Vatican, whereas the Palatine MS (no 149) is now known to be different from V, being in fact the same as the *Palatinus Neveleti* In the notes special attention is paid to the Greek of Theophrastus. There are 24 illustrations from works of ancient art. Mr Edmonds has since published suggestions on the text in the *Classical Quarterly* see below, 1908.

1904 Grenfell and Hunt publish in the *Oxyrhynchus Papyri*, IV 155, no. 699, a fragment of a compendium of the Characters including the end of c. 25 [27] and the beginning of c. 26 [29], ascribed to the early part of the third century A.D. c. 26 begins thus. [η ολι]γ[αρχ]ια εστ[ιν φιλαρχια] τις ισχυος ι[........ γ]λιχομενη, where the letter next to ισχύος may be ι, γ, η, π, or κ (cp. *Classical Quarterly*, 1908, 164)

1905. W Roberts, in the *Athenaeum*, no. 4045, 6 May, p. 562, draws attention to the discovery of ten leaves of an edition of the Characters printed at the Oxford press of Joseph Barnes in 1604

1905. P. Grindor discusses a few passages in the *Revue de l'instruction publique en Belgique*, XLVII 163—8.

1908 J. M. Edmonds publishes in the *Classical Quarterly*, pp. 119 f, 161 f, 'Contributions to a New Text of the Characters' Most of his suggestions are quoted in the present *Appendix*.

1909. Diels publishes at Oxford a text of the Characters, with brief critical notes, including a careful record of the readings of the three principal MSS, A, B, and V, and a selection from the more important emendations.)

ΘΕΟΦΡΑΣΤΟΥ ΧΑΡΑΚΤΗΡΕΣ] The MSS call the book simply χαρακτῆρες. Diogenes v 47 cites it as ἠθικοὶ χαρακτῆρες, and from him some modern editors have adopted the adjective

προοίμιον] Needham, Pauw and Coray give the heading as προοίμιον: Goez, Schneider and others as Θεόφραστος Πολυκλεῖ. Most MSS, acc. to Ast, have no heading at all. (The heading is omitted in *L*, the Leipzig ed. of 1897.)

(2 τί γὰρ δήποτε] τί ἄρα δήποτε Madvig)

19. ποιήσομαι τὸν λόγον ἀπὸ τῶν τὴν εἰρ. ἐζηλωκότων] The two Paris MSS, and another of less authority, omit the words τὸν λόγον ἀπό Hence Foss reads on his own conjecture ποιήσομαι μνείαν. (For εἰρωνείαν Buecheler proposes χείρονα αἵρεσιν or τὰ χείρονα.)

(25. καθιστάναι] Vulg. καταστῆσαι. Paris A and B, καθεστάναι. Some of the ordinary MSS apparently have καθιστάναι, the reading preferred by Foss and adopted by Petersen and Ussing.)

I (II)

(3 πορευόμενον ἅμα] ἅμα πορευόμενον A, B, Cobet and *L*)

(4 πρὸς σὲ] *L* : πρός σε ed 1870 εἰς σὲ, proposed by Cobet, is found in some MSS)

(6. καθημένων] συγκαθημένων is preferred by Cobet, *Mnemos.* 1874, p. 35.)

(7. ἀπ' αὐτοῦ] ἀφ' αὐτοῦ Ribbeck and Cobet.)

(11 δυοῖν] The variant δυεῖν is preferred by Wilamowitz. It becomes common in inscriptions of the Macedonian age, cp. Kuhner-Blass, *Gr Gr.* 1 1 633.)

(12 f. καίπερ ἔχεις] The normal construction καίπερ ἔχων is preferred by Herwerden, and is printed in Wilamowitz' *Lesebuch.* Blaydes proposes καίτοι.)

14 f καὶ ἐπαινέσαι δὲ ἀκούοντος] Foss transposes this clause, placing it after ὁρῶντος αὐτοῦ below (l 20) But it is in keeping with the character of the Flatterer that, though he has desired the others to be silent, he himself praises the speaker in loud whispers. Ussing brackets the words as spurious. (ἀκούοντος A and B, the former really having ἀκοῢ, wrongly read as ἀκοντος or ἄκοντος; hence ᾄδοντος was proposed by Reiske and Cobet, and αὐλοῦντος by Eberhard.)

CHARACTER I

15. εἰ παύεται] Vulg. εἰ παύσεται (retained in *L*). But εἰ with the fut. indic. is out of place here: it would mean 'if, as is the case, he is destined to stop.' Foss's ἐπὰν παύσηται, which Ussing adopts (and Edmonds prefers), is too far from the MSS. Ast (followed by Dubner) reads εἰ παύεται, and suggests ἢν παύσηται. The former seems best. *When* his patron—who perhaps is not a fluent speaker—pauses and is at loss for a word, the Flatterer encourages him. ἐπὰν παύσηται, which supposes him to say 'ὀρθῶς' once for all at the end of the speech, is not only a rash conjecture, but appears to give a less pointed meaning. (εἰ παύσαιτο, proposed by Reiske, is adopted by Wilamowitz.)

21. καὶ συνωνούμενος δὲ κρηπῖδας] Vulg. καὶ συνωνούμενος ἐπὶ κρηπῖδας, i.e. 'going with him to the slipper-market to buy'; but to supply the idea of motion from συνωνούμενος is very harsh. Petersen alters ἐπί to ἔτι, and transposes it to a place between εἶναι and εὐρυθμότερον—greatly to the enfeebling of the latter word. Fischer's correction (1763) of ἐπί to δέ appears the best at present. (ἐπικρηπῖδας, *Oberschuhe*, Wachsmuth, followed by *L* and by Wilamowitz, Ἰφικρατῖδας Schmidt; ἐπὶ κρηπίδων, 'in the shoe-market,' Diels.)

(23. πρὸς σέ] *L* πρός σε, ed. 1870.)

26. παρακείμενος] So Ast, Foss (and Wilamowitz), some MSS having παρακειμένων. The others (including A and B) mostly have παραμένων (retained in *L*), but this is evidently a corruption, perhaps from παρα-(κει)μένων (once supposed to be the reading of A and B). Ussing, with Gronovius, τῷ παρακειμένῳ.

27. ὡς μαλακῶς ἐσθίεις] Ast, οὐ μαλακῶς ἐσθίεις, 'you are uncomfortably placed at table.' Casaubon conj ὡς μαλακῶς ἑστιᾷς Foss ὡς μαλακῶς <ἔχων> ἐσθίεις. But the context shows that the Flatterer is praising the fare. His words imply that the host is accustomed to delicate living. With Casaubon's ingenious ἑστιᾷς an adverb such as λαμπρῶς would have been more appropriate than μαλακῶς

29. καὶ ἔτι ταῦτα λέγων περιστεῖλαι αὐτόν] The words ταῦτα λέγων had got out of their place, a copyist having written them after καὶ μήν. Reiske, followed by Ast, Foss, and Ussing, has restored them to their right place. Petersen leaves them in the wrong one, after καὶ μήν, and alters περιστεῖλαι to περιστείλαι, understanding apparently: 'he asks *whether* he *shall* wrap him up': in which sense εἰ περιστεῖλαι is not Greek. (καὶ εἴ τι περιστείλῃ αὐτόν καὶ μὴν ταῦτα λέγων *L*. καὶ μεταξὺ ταῦτα λέγων is suggested by Edmonds. καὶ μὴ ταῦτα λέγων A, B. καὶ ἅμα ταῦτα λέγων, Diels.)

(30 προσκύπτων] is proposed by Valckenaer for προσπίπτων, which is retained by *L*.)

36. πάντα—οἷς] Vulg. πάντα—ᾧ. corrected by Ast. There can be little doubt that ᾧ was a slip of the pen. If it were to be kept, I should like to read πᾶν τι for πάντα. Ussing reads on his own conj. εἰ. (Cobet, in 1874, proposed πᾶν...ᾧ· Diels prefers πάντῃ...ᾧ.)

II (V)

4. ἀμφοτέραις ταῖς χερσὶ μὴ ἀφιέναι] Schneider thought that λαβών or ἐπιλαβόμενος had dropped out after χερσί, and Foss inserts λαβόμενος in brackets This seems unnecessary μὴ-ἀφιέναι = ἔχων διατελεῖν.

6 ἔτι ἐπαινῶν] So most MSS. Foss and Petersen ἔτι αἰνῶν, with Par. A, B, and others. Orelli's conjecture ἔτι ἐπινεύων has been adopted by Dubner, Hartung, and Ussing: rashly, I think. (ἔτι was omitted by Needham, followed in L.)

(8 κοινὸς] κοινὸς εἷς A, B , hence κοινός τις Cobet and Unger)

12 f. καθίστασθαι] So Foss, Petersen, Ussing, with Par. A, B, etc. Vulg. καθίσαι, and so Ast; which I should prefer, did not the word καθίστασθαι appear to be used with something of an ironical tone: 'he manages to establish them beside him.' The middle voice helps the irony. (καθίσασθαι is proposed by Cobet.)

(14. θλιβόμενος] The passage which follows in the MSS (καὶ πλειστάκις —ἡ παλαίστρα), retained in this place by Coray and Ussing and L, is transferred to VII 6—24, as suggested by Ansaldo Cebà in his Italian translation, Genoa, 1620 Casaubon had already noticed that it was out of place in the present chapter.)

III (XV)

6. οὐκ ἂν γένοιτο διδομένων] Vulg. οὐκ ἂν γένοιτο διδόμενα · so L, with Foss and Ussing,—the latter thinking it corrupt. Meier attempted to render the vulgate:—'They are not likely to prove presents'· i.e. 'I shall be expected to pay for them by a return-present' a very strained version, which would, besides, require δεδομένα. Reiske, whom Schneider follows, conjectured οὐκ ἂν γένοιτο δεδομένων but I prefer Ast's οὐκ ἂν γένοιτο διδομένων, because διδόμενα, things *offered*, is more appropriate here than δεδομένα, things *given*. Petersen conj. οὐκ ἂν δέχοιτο διδόμενα not, as Ussing reports him, δεδομένα. (The text was proposed by Bernard, and accepted by Dubner etc.; οὐκ ἂν γεύσαιτο τῶν διδομένων was subsequently suggested by Cobet, and οὐκ ἂν δέχοιτο διδόμενα by F. W. Schmidt. Diels conjectures οὐκ ἂν γένοιτο <ἀντι>διδόμενα.)

7 f. οὔτε τῷ χρώσαντι αὐτόν...οὔτε τῷ ὤσαντι οὔτε τῷ ἐμβάντι] MSS οὔτε τῷ ἀπώσαντι αὐτόν. οὔτε τῷ ὤσαντι οὔτε τῷ ἐμβάντι. Schneider and Petersen correct ἀπώσαντι to ὤσαντι, and put the second ὤσαντι in

brackets; believing that, when ἀπώσαντι had been written by mistake, ὥσαντι was written in the margin as a correction, and thence found an independent place in the text. Ussing adopts this view. To me it seems more probable that ἀπώσαντι is a corruption of something else than merely ὥσαντι. A list of *several* petty annoyances which the Surly man cannot pardon seems almost necessary to the spirit of the passage. Petersen's ῥυπώσαντι (found in some MSS, and accepted in *L*) is a little too strong, and though ῥυπάω (intr.) is common, the transitive ῥυπόω is a very rare word. Ast's χρώσαντι seems precisely what is wanted. (οὔτε τῷ ἀπώσαντι αὐτὸν ἀκουσίως [οὔτε τῷ ὥσαντι] Diels, who follows Schneider in striking out, as a *varia lectio*, the words in brackets, and points out that ἀπώσαντι is here properly applied to 'pushing another person off the pavement')

13 ἐθελῆσαι] Petersen (followed in *L*) proposes ἐθελήσειεν.

IV (XXIV)

4. μεμνῆσθαι φάσκειν· καὶ βαδίζων ἐν ταῖς ὁδοῖς τὰς διαίτας κρίνειν τοῖς ἐπιτρέψασι] Vulg. μεμνῆσθαι φάσκειν ἐν ταῖς ὁδοῖς καὶ βιάζειν τὰς διαίτας κρίνειν ἐν τοῖς ἐπιτρέψασι. V places the words καὶ βιάζειν before ἐν ταῖς ὁδοῖς. For βιάζειν Schweighauser (and Sheppard independently) conj. βαδίζων: which, as the best available correction, I have taken, omitting ἐν before τοῖς ἐπιτρέψασι with Schneider, Foss and Ussing. (βιάζειν and ἐν are retained in *L*.) Foss καὶ φράζειν (for βιάζειν) ἐν ταῖς ὁδοῖς, τὰς διαίτας κρινεῖν (for κρίνειν) τοῖς ἐπιτρέψασι. Ussing on his own conj. καὶ ὑπτιάζειν τὰς διαίτας κρίνειν τοῖς ἐπιτρέψασι, 'haughtily declines (*superbe abnuere*) to decide cases' etc., omitting the words ἐν ταῖς ὁδοῖς as corrupt: Petersen suspects them also. Ast μεμνῆσθαι φράζειν (for φάσκειν)· καὶ τὰς διαίτας κρίνειν ἐν ταῖς ὁδοῖς· rejecting ἐν τοῖς ἐπιτρέψασι altogether. (Diels accepts βαδίζων, and proposes in the sequel κρίνειν ἐν <τάχει> τοῖς ἐπιτρέψασι.)

8. μισθουμένους] So (Stroth), Foss, Ast, Herwerden and Cobet, for the manuscript reading μεμισθωμένους, retained by Hottinger, Sheppard, Ussing, Petersen (and *L*). Ast's objection to μεμισθωμένους, that it could only mean *mercede conductos*, whom therefore the hirer has a right to summon at an early hour, is not convincing, since it is conceivable that μεμίσθωμαι, like γέγραμμαι, etc., may have been used as a Perfect Middle, and that οἱ μεμισθωμένοι τι may have meant *qui aliquid conduxerunt*. But the present μισθουμένους is better as denoting that the bargain is still in progress.

9. μὴ λαλεῖν τοῖς ἐντυγχάνουσι, κάτω κεκυφώς, ὅταν δὲ αὐτῷ δόξῃ, ἄνω πάλιν] So Foss and Ussing (and *L*). Vulg. ὅταν δὲ αὐτῷ δόξῃ ἐστιᾶν

(and so Shepp.). V ὅταν δὲ αὐτῷ δόξῃ, ἄνω πάλιν· καὶ ἑστιῶν κ.τ.λ. There can be no doubt that the words ἄνω πάλιν in V, if not sound, at least represent something which stood between δόξῃ and καὶ ἑστιῶν, and contrasted the conduct of the ὑπερήφανος in not speaking to those he met with some other feature of his conduct. I once conjectured for ἄνω πάλιν, ἀνακαλεῖν: 'When he walks in the streets he will not speak to those he meets, keeping his head bent down; or, when so it pleases him, *will call them back.*'

16. διωθεῖν] So the MSS, followed by Ast, Sheppard and Ussing. Ast, however, conjectures διαθεῖν, and Sheppard διαθεῖναι. Foss and L (and Fraenkel and Groeneboom) accept διαθεῖναι, without naming Sheppard. (διαθεῖναι was also proposed by Naber; διελθεῖν by Buecheler.)

17. αὐτῷ] αὐτῷ is proposed by Edmonds.

19. πρός σε] πρὸς σὲ L. ληψομένους] So Foss and Ussing. Sheppard (Buecheler and L) ληψόμενος with the MSS, Ast ληψόμενον.

V (I)

Almost every editor has taken a different view of the order in which the clauses between λαλεῖν οὐ μισεῖν and ἀκούσας τι μὴ προσποιεῖσθαι (l. 3—l. 14) should be arranged. Foss has been the boldest in transposing, Ussing has adhered most nearly to the MSS. I have observed absolutely the order of the sentences in the MSS. In writings of this kind, where every sentence has an independent point and is not necessarily in direct connexion either with what precedes or with what follows, that order of the clauses which is found in the manuscripts ought not, surely, to be disturbed without strong reason. In the present case the arrangement which has authority seems at least as good as any which has been effected by conjectural changes. (The order of the MSS is also retained in L.)

3 f. λαλεῖν, οὐ μισεῖν] (retained in L) Ast, with one MS, φιλεῖν, οὐ μισεῖν. But λαλεῖν is both more probable and more graphic. Ussing encloses οὐ μισεῖν in brackets. Hartung (and others) propose ὡς οὐ μισῶν (accepted by Fraenkel and Groeneboom). (Pierson, quoted by Naber, writes ὁμιλεῖν for λαλεῖν, οὐ μισεῖν.)

7. πρὸς τοὺς ἀδικουμένους] Ussing ingeniously (but unnecessarily) conjectures πρὸς τοὺς ἀδικ<α ἡγ>ουμένους, 'to those who think that the things said against him are unjust.' Foss, who transposes the clause to a place after συλλυπεῖσθαι ἡττωμένοις, reads πρὸς αὐτοὺς ἀδικουμένους— i.e. οἷς ἐπέθετο λάθρα.

(10. βουλεύεσθαι] βουλεύσεσθαι A, preferred by Blaydes, who compares the emended text in l. 16, σκέψεσθαι.)

CHARACTER V

(11. ὀψὲ γενέσθαι αὐτόν] So Ussing; all the MSS have αὐτὸν (L) αὐτῷ is preferred by Foss; αὐτοῦ is suggested by Edmonds, 'he arrived late *on the scene*,' '*on the actual spot*.')

(12 f. <ὡς ἀργύριον οὐκ ἔχει· καὶ πωλῶν λέγειν>] The lacuna was first noticed by Salmasius. Ribbeck proposes: <δοὺς πολὺ φῆσαι ὡς οὐ πλουτεῖ· καὶ πωλῶν φῆσαι>.)

(13. φῆσαι] Schneider: φήσει MSS. 14 φῆσαι] *v.l.* φήσει.)

(16. σκέψεσθαι] Casaubon (quoting Menander:—οἱ τὰς ὀφρῦς αἴροντες...καὶ σκέψομαι λέγοντες). σκέψασθαι MSS (followed by *L*); *v.l.* ἐσκέφθαι.)

19. καὶ λέγειν ἑαυτὸν ἕτερον ἀκηκοέναι] Petersen's conjecture, adopted by Ussing with the change of λέγειν into λέγει γάρ. It is the best correction which has been made of a hopeless passage. The MSS give λέγει ἑαυτὸν ἕτερον γεγονέναι, which Casaubon vainly tried to explain. 'He says that he has become another person,' i.e. has been mistaken for another, whose words or actions have been imputed to him. 'Vous me prenez pour un autre.' Clearly this will not do. but Foss and *L* adopt it, with λέγεις αὐτὸν for λέγει ἑαυτόν. Ast καὶ λέγειν, αὐτὸν ἕτερον γεγονέναι: 'he will say 'To think that he (the person from whom his friend has heard the story) should have changed so completely!',—*i.e.* 'to think that the man who told *you* this story should have told *me* a story so different' This is worse than the vulgate itself I once conjectured καὶ λέγεις αὐτὸ (for ἑαυτὸν) ἕτερον γεγονέναι, 'You describe the occurrence as having been of a different sort', which agrees well with what immediately follows,—'This, however, was not the story that he told me.' But, for this sense, we should have expected ἑτέρᾳ rather than ἕτερον: and I now prefer Petersen's emendation. (Immisch proposes λέγεις ἑαυτοῦ ἕτερον γεγονέναι, and Edmonds λέγεις, <αὐτὸν> ἑαυτοῦ κ τ λ)

(20 παράδοξόν μοι τὸ πρᾶγμα ἄλλῳ τινὶ λέγε] placed after ἐκπλήττομαι by Foss (who was followed by Jebb in the *text* of his edition of 1870, but not in his *translation*).)

23 f. εὑρεῖν ἔστι τοῦ εἴρωνος] The two best MSS (Paris A, B) have εὑρεῖν ἔστιν οὐ χεῖρον ὄν. Vulg., οὗ χεῖρον ἔστιν εὑρεῖν οὐδέν—probably a conjecture adapted to the old barbarous interpretation which made the accusatives πλοκὰς καὶ παλιλλογίας (really governed by εὑρεῖν) depend on πιστεύεις. Foss εὑρεῖν ἔστιν, οὗ χεῖρον οὐδέν. This would do, if it were possible that εὑρεῖν ἔστι could stand alone for εὑρεῖν ἔστιν ἐν τῷ εἴρωνι. There is great probability in Ussing's conjecture that ΕΣΤΙΝΟΥΧΕΙΡΟΝΟΝ is an old corruption of ΕΣΤΙΤΟΥΕΙΡΩΝΟΣ. (Diels prefers τῶν εἰρώνων.)

J. T.

VI (XXIII)

1. **δόξειεν ἄν**] has some manuscript support, and is (on general grounds) preferred by Coray and Ast: δόξει is found in most MSS (L). **προσποίησις**] So Foss and Ussing,—Foss assigning the emendation to Auber (ed. 1582) and Reiske, Ast, to Schneider. Ast himself keeps the vulg. προσδοκία, but believes that the text originally had προσποίησις ἀγαθῶν οὐκ ὄντων πρὸς δόξαν ('with a view to reputation'), and that προσδοκία arose from these words having been omitted and then written in the margin. I doubt if a Greek writer could have said πρὸς δόξαν in this sense; he would have said rather ἕνεκα δόξης or ἐπὶ δόξῃ. (Edmonds defends the exceptional use of προσδοκία, in the sense of 'acceptance, taking to oneself, assumption,' by comparing Hesychius, προσδέχεται· προσποιεῖται.)

2 f. **ἐν τῷ δείγματι**] Vulg. ἐν τῷ διαζεύγματι: explained by Coray as the isthmus joining the Peiraeus to the mainland, by Ussing, as a mole dividing the two parts of its great basin (the Kantharus and the Emporium). Casaubon conj. δείγματι, which Ast adopts. The topography of the Peiraeus is well known from ancient writers, but nowhere is τὸ διάζευγμα mentioned, whereas τὸ δεῖγμα exactly suits the context. This, however, would not in itself be a sufficient reason for adopting the emendation, were it not intrinsically probable. (Cobet accepts δείγματι, while L, Wilamowitz, and others, retain διαζεύγματι.)

(3. **αὐτῷ**] αὐτῷ is preferred by Edmonds here and in lines 14, 17, 30.)

(7 f. ἀπολαύσας. λέγειν] ἀπολαῦσαι. λέγων MSS (L).)

8 **Ἀλεξάνδρου**] The MSS have Εὐάνδρου, corrected by Auber to Ἀλεξάνδρου. He has been followed by Casaubon and by all subsequent editors except Goez and Sheppard. The latter thinks, with Coray, that Evander may have been some general of Alexander of whom we know nothing. But the fact that we know nothing of him is in itself the best argument against the reading. The names of Alexander's generals, the names of all who were prominent during his period, are known from the detailed narratives of Plutarch, Arrian and Quintus Curtius. Nowhere is an Evander named to whom this allusion could refer. It is difficult to suppose that there can have been a military leader so universally known that a braggart, incapable of selection and attracted only by the largest names, should boast to a chance companion of acquaintance with him; and of whom not a word is said in the full histories of the time which have come down to us. That the age of Alexander is referred to is shown, of course, by the allusion to Antipater.

9. ὡς αὐτῷ εἶχε] Schneider thought that some such adverb as φιλικῶς was wanted, and Ussing that αὐτῷ ought to be πρὸς αὐτόν. But cf. Xen. *Cyr.* VII 5, 58, ἐννοῶν ὅτι.. παρασκευάζοιτο οἰκεῖν ἐν πόλει τῇ μεγίστῃ τῶν φανερῶν, αὕτη δὲ οὕτως ἔχοι αὐτῷ ὡς πολεμιωτάτη ἂν γένοιτο, 'was so disposed to him that it was likely to become most hostile' (οἰκείως αὐτῷ εἶχε Cobet, <ὅπ>ως αὐτῷ εἶχε *L*)

(11. δὴ φῆσαι] Coray · ψηφῆσαι V : φῆσαι *L*.)

13. τριττὰ δή] V, Foss, Ussing, *L*.—In the collation of V by Siebenkees τριττὰ δή was wrongly reported as τρίτον ἤδη, whence Ast's conjecture τὸ τρίτον ἤδη, adopted in his own text and in Sheppard's. (τρίτον δή is found in some MSS)

(15. συκοφαντηθῇ] <καὶ ὅτι> is added by Foss (*L*))

16. περαιτέρω ὡς φίλος ὢν πλεῖν ἢ προσήκει Μακεδόσι] Vulg. (retained by *L* and Wilamowitz) περαιτέρω φιλοσοφεῖν προσῆκε Μακεδόσι, which it has been attempted to explain 'the Macedonians ought *to have been more thoughtful*' (i.e. 'than to offer me a privilege which would make me unpopular at Athens') Schneider was for changing Μακεδόσι to Μακεδόνων, 'ultra quam Macedones sapere decebat.' The sense thus extracted (or rather extorted) from φιλοσοφεῖν is, I think, impossible. Ussing's correction of φιλοσοφεῖν to φίλος ὢν πλεῖν appears to me not only very brilliant but almost certain. The ὡς which is then wanted before φίλος might easily have dropped out after the final ω of περαιτέρω The omission of ἢ before προσήκει would have been a natural result of the corruption of φίλος ὢν πλεῖν to φιλοσοφεῖν προσήκει for προσῆκε is Ussing's (and is also proposed by Cobet. Madvig proposes φίλος εἶναι ἢ προσήκει.)

(17. πλείω] πλείους V, *L* ; πλεῖον Eberhard)

20. ἑξακοσίας] The variant ἑξακοσίους was the mistake of a copyist, who was puzzled by the ordinary omission of δραχμάς, and referred the numeral to τοῖς ἀπόροις τῶν πολιτῶν. (Diels regards the passage as corrupt)

(22. καὶ δέκα] κδ' Cichorius (Wilamowitz, *L*) ; δέκα Casaubon and Hartung ; ὡς δέκα Naber, ἑκκαίδεκα Petersen.   φῆσαι] conjectured by Lycius for φήσας (retained in *L*).)

(24. λειτουργίας λελειτούργηκε] The forms in ληιτ- are found in inscriptions of the 4th century)

24 f. προσελθὼν δὲ τοὺς ἵππους τοὺς ἀγαθοὺς τοῖς πωλοῦσι] Vulg. προσελθὼν δ' εἰς τοὺς ἵππους τοὺς ἀγαθοὺς πωλοῦσι. V inserts τοῖς before πωλοῦσι. (εἰς τοὺς ἵππους—τοῖς πωλοῦσι *L*.) I cannot persuade myself that προσελθὼν εἰς τοὺς ἵππους is Greek ; and have little doubt that the preposition was inserted by a scribe who did not see that προσελθών was to be taken with the dat. τοῖς πωλοῦσι which governs

τοὺς ἵππους τοὺς ἀγαθούς. So c. IV (vulg. XXIV) προσελθεῖν οὐδενί, c XVII (vulg. XI), ἡττημένῳ προσελθεῖν, etc. This is Sheppard's view, who, however, puts τοῖς before τοὺς ἵππους. It seems unnecessary to move it from its place in V

30. καὶ ὅτι] καὶ διότι L.

VII (XXI)

1. **δόξειεν ἄν**] δόξει V (L).

4. **ἀγαγών**] V; v.l. ἀπαγαγών; ἀγαγεῖν Foss (L)

(5. **αὐτῷ**] αὐτῷ is preferred by Edmonds.)

(6 **ποιῆσαι**] omitted by Haupt and Petersen, altered into σπεῦσαι by Cobet, ζητῆσαι by Eberhard.)

6 f. **καὶ πλειστάκις δὲ ἀποκείρασθαι**] The passage which follows here, down to the words τούτου ἐστὶν ἡ παλαίστρα (l 24), stands in the MSS at the end of c. II (vulg. c V) περὶ ἀρεσκείας That it is foreign to the character of the ἄρεσκος has been allowed by almost all commentators since Casaubon, except Coray and Ussing. (Petersen, in printing it with the chapter περὶ ἀρεσκ., is merely performing his editorial duty to the MSS, and does not enter upon the further question) It must suffice here to point out the broad distinction between the ἄρεσκος and the μικροφιλότιμος, on which depends the unsuitableness of this passage to the former Both are vain, but the ἄρεσκος desires to be popular for his qualities, the μικροφιλότιμος, to be admired for his advantages. Among those who agree in rejecting the passage from the chapter περὶ ἀρεσκείας two views prevail Casaubon, followed by Schneider and others, supposes it to be a fragment of a chapter περὶ βαναυσίας or ἀπειροκαλίας, 'Of Vulgarity.' Ast, Foss and others assign it to this chapter, περὶ μικροφιλοτιμίας,—Ast adding it at the end after εὐημερεῖ,—Foss introducing it after Αἰθίοψ ἔσται. I agree with Foss, except that I do not separate the clause καὶ ἀποδιδοὺς μνᾶν ἀργυρίου, κ.τ λ., from that in which the Aethiopian slave is mentioned, and with which it is, I think, closely connected in sense

13. **ξένοις δὲ ἐπιστάλματα εἰς Βυζάντιον ἁλμάδας**] Vulg. ξένοις δὲ εἰς Βυζάντιον ἐπιστάλματα (retained in L). As Ast perceived, a word has fallen out here, denoting that special thing which was sent to Byzantium, as the dogs to Cyzicus and the honey to Rhodes. He himself guessed πέμματα, 'sweetmeats.' Another conjecture made by Foss appears so good that I have adopted it in the absence of anything certain. ἁλμάδες, pickled olives, were among the regular Athenian exports, and ἁλμάδας might easily have fallen out if ἐπιστάλματα had been written by mistake *after* Βυζάντιον. Foss himself discards ἐπιστάλματα, reading εἰς Βυζάν-

τιον ἀποστέλλειν ἀλμάδας. But ἐπίσταλμα is a perfectly good word in the sense of ἐπεσταλμένον τι, i.e. *a commission* given by the person abroad to his friend at Athens, and is supported by the contrast with ἀγοράζειν αὐτῷ μὲν μηδέν. He buys, not for himself, but on commission for others. ἐπιστέλλειν would mean 'sends as presents'; and the contrast would then be less clear. Ussing, on his own conjecture, ξένοις δὲ εἰς Βυζάντιον ἐπισκάλματα (a word which does not occur), 'leathers for rowlocks.'

(14. εἰς Κύζικον] πέμπειν omitted in both the Paris MSS, but found in others, is added by *L*.)

18. τῶν σκολιῶν <τῶν> ἐκ Λακεδαίμονος is suggested by Edmonds.)

20. παλαιστριαῖον] So Foss, Petersen, Ussing (and *L*), with the best MSS. Others παλαιστρικόν: Ast παλαιστρικήν

(21 χρῆσαι] The Paris MSS have χρὴ νῦν ἀεί, others χρᾶν ἀεί or χρᾶνυ ἀεί or simply ἀεί. χρῆσαι ἀεί, proposed by Petersen, is accepted by Ussing. χρωννύναι, or κιχράναι, is proposed by Needham; χρηννύναι by Foss, followed by *L*. κιχράναι is preferred by Cobet, who in l. 22 proposes ἐν ἐπιδείκνυσθαι.)

23. ἐπεισιέναι ἐπὶ <τῷ εἰπεῖν τὸν ἕτερον> τῶν θεωμένων πρὸς τὸν ἕτερον] In the MSS there is a lacuna. Vulg εἰπεῖν ἐπὶ τῶν θεωμένων πρὸς ἕτερον, the two best MSS (Paris A, B) having ἔπεισιν for εἰπεῖν, and πρὸς τὸν ἕτερον for πρὸς ἕτερον. Both ἔπεισιν (i.e. ἐπεισιέναι) and εἰπεῖν are prob. right. The first τὸν ἕτερον was omitted by a copyist who saw that the words were coming after τῶν θεωμένων, and did not see that they were wanted twice. Foss's restoration ἐπεισιέναι ἐπὶ <τῷ εἰπεῖν τὸν ἕτερον> seems almost certain. Ussing gives ὕστερον ἔπεισιν ἐπὶ τῷ εἰπεῖν τινα (for τὸν ἕτερον) τῶν θεωμένων· but ἔπεισιν is against the uniform structure of all these Characters, which are strings of infinitives, and τινὰ πρὸς τὸν ἕτερον is awkward. (ἐπεῖναι, ἐπιέναι, ἐλθεῖν and ἐπεισελθεῖν have also been suggested. *L* has ἔπεισιν ἐπὶ <τῷ εἰπεῖν τὸν ἕτερον> τῶν θεωμένων πρὸς τὸν ἕτερον.)

(30—32. καὶ κολοιῷ δὲ—πηδήσεται] inserted before l 25 (καὶ βοῦν θύσας) in V.)

34. κλάδος Μελιταῖος] So Sheppard and Foss (and *L*), with the MSS Toup's conjecture καλὸς Μελιταῖος has been adopted by Ast (writing ὁ καλός), Petersen and Ussing. If the μικροφιλότιμος had inscribed upon his dog's grave 'The Beautiful Melitean,' he would have been caricaturing the well-known formula of disconsolate lovers · e.g. Luc. *Amor.* 16, where the beloved object is Aphrodite herself, 'Every wall was scored, every tree with soft bark proclaimed 'Aphrodite the Beautiful.'' This would have been a joke quite foreign to the spirit of the pompous μικροφιλότιμος. The two instances of καλός in epitaphs

quoted from Iamblichus (in Photius pp. 246—7) only show that this use of it was rare. (Gomperz compares with κλάδος the poetic use of ὄζος, θάλος, ἔρνος in dedicatory or sepulcral inscriptions.)

(34. δακτύλιον] Naber, followed by *L*, Wilamowitz, and others, proposes δάκτυλον, a model of a finger presented as a votive offering to Aesculapius.

Evidence as to dedicated *rings* has been collected by Mr F. H. Marshall, in his *Catalogue of the Greek and Roman Finger-Rings in the British Museum*, pp xxix, xxxiv. In a letter to Dr Sandys, Mr Marshall suggests that the manuscript reading δακτύλιον is 'much the more probable'; ...' the bronze ring must have been one of the cheapest votive offerings which it was possible to make, and the whole point of the passage is that extravagant care was bestowed upon so paltry an object';.. 'the nearest approach to a votive *finger* in the British Museum is to be found in the votive bronze hands wearing rings, mentioned in the *Catalogue of Rings*, p. xxiii')

35. ἐν τῷ Ἀσκληπιοῦ] The MSS ἐν τῷ Ἀσκληπιῷ or Ἀσκληπιείῳ (V). Ast τῷ Ἀσκληπιῷ. Foss, Ussing, Sheppard (and *L*), ἐν τῷ Ἀσκληπιείῳ.

35 f. στιλπνῶν καὶ ἀλείφων] Vulg. στεφανοῦντα ἀλείφεσθαι. V στεφανοῦντα ἀλείφειν (*L* conjectures στεφανοῦν ἀλείφειν). The corruption of the passage probably lies beyond any remedy which can now be applied to it. Ast reads στεφανῶν καὶ ἀλείφων, referring τοῦτον to Asclepius: but clearly it refers to δακτύλιος. Foss's στιλπνῶν ('burnishing') for στεφανῶν is the best attempt at emendation which has been made. στιλπνός, 'glistering,' is common enough, and the verb has the authority of Epictetus in the 1st century. Ussing suggests τοῦτον ἐκτρίβειν σμήγματι (unguent) καὶ ἀλείφειν (The correction ἀλείφων was made by Coray, and by Cobet.)

(36 συνδιοικήσασθαι παρὰ τῶν πρυτάνεων] Herwerden's excellent suggestion, διοικήσασθαι παρὰ τῶν συμπρυτάνεων, is independently proposed by Gomperz and is accepted by Fraenkel and Groeneboom, and by Wilamowitz.)

39 f. ἐθύομεν οἱ πρυτάνεις τῇ μητρὶ τῶν θεῶν τὰ ἱερὰ ἄξια καὶ καλά] Vulg. ἐθ. οἱ πρυτ. τὰ ἱερὰ τῇ μ. τῶν θ. ἄξια καὶ καλά. V, ἐθ. οἱ πρυτ τὰ ἱερὰ τῇ μ. τῶν θεῶν τὰ γὰρ ἄξια καὶ τὰ ἱερὰ καλά. Ussing gives, I think, the true account of the confusion in V. First τὰ γάρ was written for τὰ ἱερά· then τὰ ἱερά was added in the margin, and thence crept in wrongly before τῇ μητρί and again before καλά. Foss, emending V, reads ἐθ. οἱ πρυτ. τῇ μ. τῶν θεῶν· καὶ ὑμεῖς δέχεσθε τὰ ἀγαθά· τὰ γὰρ σφάγια (for ἄξια) καὶ τὰ ἱερὰ καλά. (*L*, following Petersen, has —ἐθύομεν οἱ πρυτάνεις τὰ ἱερὰ τῇ Μητρὶ τῶν θεῶν, τὰ ἱερὰ ἄξια καὶ τὰ ἱερὰ καλά:

CHARACTERS VII, VIII

Wilamowitz proposes ἐθύομεν τῇ μητρὶ τῶν θεῶν τὰ Γαλάξια, καὶ τὰ ἱερὰ καλά, the Γαλάξια being a festival of the 'Mother of the Gods,' at which frumenty (γαλαξία) was offered to the Goddess, *Eph. Arch* 1860, no 4097; Bekker's *Anecdota*, p. 229 αἴσια (for ἄξια) had been proposed by Cobet and others.)

(42. εὐημερεῖ] The MSS have εὐημερεῖν with a variant εὐημερεῖ. Needham suggested εὐημέρει. *L* prints εὐημερῶν, disapproved by Gomperz.)

VIII (XXVII)

5. ἡρῷα] Schneider's correction for ἥρωα, V. Ἑρμαῖα is conjectured by Meier and adopted by Foss

7. αἱρεῖν] Vulg. αἱρεῖσθαι. which Ast renders 'bovem *capessere*, bovi *manum inicere*': and in this sense the commentators generally seem to acquiesce But, though in the *Iliad* (XVI 140) we have ἔγχος εἵλετο, 'he took (his own) spear,' etc., it is improbable that in Attic prose αἱρεῖσθαι could mean 'to seize' The word, and perhaps the passage, is corrupt. In the mean time, to make, at least, sense, I write αἱρεῖν. (For αἱρεῖσθαι V, αἵρεσθαι is proposed by Bergk, Blaydes, Meier and Ad. Wilhelm, and accepted by *L* and by Edmonds, and Fraenkel and Groeneboom, the phrase τὸν βοῦν αἵρεσθαι being found in Ephebic inscriptions, e g in *C I.A.* II 467, ἤραντο δὲ καὶ τοῖς μυστηρίοις τοὺς βοῦς ἐν Ἐλευσῖνι)

13 ἐν δεκάταις συνάγειν τοὺς μεθ' αὑτοῦ συναυλήσοντας] V, which alone has this clause, gives καὶ ἕνδεκα λιταῖς συνάγειν τοὺς μετ' αὐτοῦ συναύξοντας, which is nonsense. Ast conjectures καὶ ἐν δεκάταις συνάγειν τοὺς μετ' αὐτοῦ ᾄσοντας Foss καὶ ἐν δεκάταις σὺν αὐλὴταῖς συνάγειν τοὺς μετ' αὐτοῦ συνάξοντας I have taken Ast's ἐν δεκάταις, and for συναύξοντας written συναυλήσοντας. The υ in συναύξοντας preserves a trace of this If λ had been left out by accident, H would speedily have been corrupted to Ξ. (For ΔΕΚΑΛΙΤΑΙΣ Ad Wilhelm proposes ΔΕΚΑΔΙΣΤΑΙΣ, δεκαδισταί being the name of a club, which met on the 10th day of the month, cp. *Bull de corr Hell.* XII 303. This is adopted in *L*, which has ἐν δεκαδισταῖς συνάγειν τοὺς μετ' αὐτοῦ συναύξοντας, accepted by Fraenkel and Groeneboom Cobet proposed συνάξοντας)

14. παίζειν] MSS πέζειν· Schneider παίζειν, and so most editors. Ast proposes καὶ μακρὸν ἀνδριάντα παίειν (so Pauw), καὶ πρὸς τὸν ἑαυτοῦ ἀκόλουθον διατοξεύεσθαι, κ τ λ : Coray πιέζειν: see Notes

(16. παρ' αὐτοῦ] παρ' ἄλλου, with no verb following, is proposed by Unger.)

17. <κελεύειν>] The insertion of this word, which is not in the

MSS, but which (or something like it) the sense demands, was proposed by Reiske. Schneider introduced it in his 1st ed., only to eject it in his 2nd. It is now adopted by Foss, Petersen and Ussing. (παραινεῖν, proposed by Hanow, is adopted in *L*)

19. ὦσι πλησίον] πλησίον is wanting in V, which has, however, a lacuna after ὦσι. Foss, followed by Ussing, inserts it on conjecture. Ast proposed ἴωσι for ὦσι, Schneider παρῶσι, Foss formerly ἴδωσι. (*L* has ὦσι<ν> <ἐγγὺς> γυναῖκες, where ἐγγὺς is due to Meister. The double lacuna in V, ὦσι...γυναικ , is filled by Diels by proposing:— ὦσι <χοροὶ> γυναικ<ῶν>.)

IX (XII)

(1. ἐπίτευξις] Ruge and Holland, quoting [Plat.] Def. 413 c, εὐκαιρία, χρόνου ἐπίτευξις, add χρόνου, adopted by *L* and others. Dobree and Cobet proposed ἔντευξις.)

4 f. δίκην ὠφληκότι ἐγγύης προσελθὼν κελεῦσαι αὐτὸν ἀναδέξασθαι] αὐτὸν Vulg αὐτὸν Foss, Petersen, Ussing (and *L*) But the usual phrase was ἀναδέχομαί τινι: Polyb. v 16, 8 seems to be the only example of ἀναδέχομαί τινα in this sense. and I have no doubt that αὐτόν (referring to ὁ τὴν δίκην ὠφληκώς) is right. Then, however, we must alter the manuscript reading ὠφληκότα into ὠφληκότι, for προσελθὼν could not in prose be followed by an acc of the person · it has the dat. in cc. IV (vulg. XXIV), XVII (XI), and (prob.) VI (XXIII). The same correction was proposed by Pauw in his ed of 1737. Ast cuts the knot by omitting αὐτόν altogether.

(11 πρόθυμος] προθύμως Blaydes.)

13. τόκαν] Vulg. τόμον: but one of the best MSS has τόκον, and, since Ast, this has been universally adopted. To request 'a slice' at a season of feasting might be ἀναίσχυντον, but would not be ἄκαιρον.

(16. ὀρχησόμενος] 'minded to dance'; Casaubon's correction of ὀρχησάμενον, accidentally retained in the text of the former ed)

16. ἑτέρου] Vulg. ἑταίρου Foss ἑτέρου, with several MSS, including Paris A, B, and so Petersen and Ussing (and *L*, and others).

X (XIII)

(1. περιεργία] <ἡ> περιεργία is proposed by Buecheler and adopted by *L* and others)

(1. δόξειεν ἄν] The Paris MSS, amongst others, have δόξει (*L*).)

4 ἐνστάς] A, B ἔν τινι στάς. Ast (followed by Fraenkel and Groeneboom) supposes this to be a corruption of ἀναστάς, which he omits after ἐπαγγέλλεσθαι, and puts here. He thinks that an annotator

CHARACTERS IX—XI

wrote in the margin, as a note upon ἀναστάς,—ἔν τινι στάς 'in one manuscript there is στάς': but this is more ingenious than probable. When anything beside the variant itself was added, it was usually γρ. (γράφεται) no copyist could have written ἔν τινι in that sense. Foss reads, on his own bold conjecture, συνδικήσας Reiske's ἐνστάς is the best correction that has been suggested. (ἔν τινι στὰς is retained in L and understood as a reference to the form of rhetorical argument called ἔνστασις ἀντείπας is proposed by Naber, and ἀντανωστὰς by Diels.)

(5. πλεῖον] v.l. πλείω (L) and πλέον.)

6. καὶ οὕς] Ast arbitrarily omits καί. (Ussing and Cobet also omit τοὺς before μαχομένους.)

(7. ἀτραποῦ ἡγήσασθαι] τὴν ὁδὸν καταλιπών is added in L from the Munich Epitome.)

(10. παραγγέλλει] The variant παραγγελεῖ is preferred by Cobet, Hirschig, Blaydes, and L.)

(11 μαλακιζομένῳ] After this word a lacuna is indicated in L; δοῦναι is inserted by Coray.)

12 εὖ ποτίσαι] MSS εὐτρεπίσαι, 'to arrange': which Ast explains 'in lecto iacentem attollit et *ita componit* (hoc est enim εὐτρεπίσαι, i. q. μετεωρίζειν ap. Hippocratem), ut commode bibere possit.' But this is to make the word mean too much. No one could see that a breach of the doctor's order against giving the patient wine was hidden in εὐτρεπίσαι. Foss's emendation, εὖ ποτίσαι, is very brilliant, and, I think, almost certain. Ussing hesitates to take it, and suggests ἀναρριπίσαι, 'febris ardorem in aegroto excitare', which few will prefer. (L, and Fraenkel and Groeneboom, retain εὐτρεπίσαι.)

XI (XX)

(5 περιπατήσῃ] βηματίσῃ, the reading of the Munich Epitome, is discussed by Edmonds. With μασώμενος σιτίζειν, cp. Ar *Eq.* 716 f.)

7. πανούργιον] V (which alone has this clause) καὶ πανουργιῶν τοῦ πάππου καλεῖν Various corrections of πανουργιῶν have been tried: Foss's πανούργιον ('little rascal') is the least unsatisfactory and improbable. Schneider πανουργότερον Petersen clumsily πανουργιῶν πλεότερον Ast suggested πᾶν ἔργον τοῦ πάππου, 'das ganze Wesen des Grosspapas.' He and Ussing take πάππου to be the genitive of πάππος But surely it is the gen of πάππας. (πανούργημα was proposed by Usener and Cobet In L, πανουργιῶν is obelised as corrupt; Fraenkel and Groeneboom have <τῶν> πανουργιῶν.)

(8. οἰκείων] οἰκετῶν Cobet and Unger.)

(8. εἰπέ] In V εἶπον corrected into εἴπερ has led Ribbeck to suggest εἶπον, accepted by L and by Fraenkel and Groeneboom)

9. ποία τις ἡμέρα;] Vulg. εἰπὲ μάμμη, ὡς ποίᾳ ἡμέρᾳ με ἔτικτες, V εἰπὲ μάμμη, ὅτ' ὠδίνες καὶ ἔτικτές με, τίς ἡμέρα; From a combination of these Foss reads ποία τις ἡμέρα; and so Petersen (but adding ἦν unnecessarily). (τίς ἡμέρα is retained instead of ποία τις ἡμέρα in L.)— [Here there follows in V a hopelessly corrupt clause, about which only one thing is clear, that the ἀηδία consists in the coarseness; and which I have not translated.—καὶ ὑπὲρ αὐτῆς δὲ λέγειν ὡς ἡδύ ἐστι, καὶ ἀμφότερα δὲ οὐκ ἔχοντα οὐ ῥᾴδιον ἄνθρωπον λαβεῖν· *et pro matre respondere dulcem esse rem* (sc τὸ παιδοποιεῖν), *neque veio facile hominem invenire qui alterum* (τὸ ἡδὺ) *sine altero* (τὸ λυπρόν) *habeat*,' i.e ἡ παιδοποιοῦσα ἥδεται, ταύτην ἀνάγκη καὶ τίκτουσαν ὠδίνειν. Ast, Foss, Petersen, Ussing have all exercised their ingenuity on the sentence But none of them has got out a more intelligible sense than that which the reading of the MS itself gives (Diels conj. καὶ ὑπὲρ αὐτοῦ δὲ λέγειν ὡς ἡδύς ἐστι καὶ ἀμφοτέρωθεν εὖ γεγονότα, *nobilem a patre et a matre,* οὐ ῥᾴδιον ἄνθρωπον λαβεῖν.)]

9. καὶ <λέγειν> ὅτι ψυχρὸν ὕδωρ, κ.τ.λ.] (λέγειν is not added in L) The passage from here to the end is very corrupt. Ast transfers it to the end of c. VI (XXIII) περὶ ἀλαζονείας. But there is no reason to doubt that it belongs to the ἀηδής. The ἀλαζών boasts of great things; the ἀηδής, boasting of his cool cistern and his kitchen-garden, does not rise to the magnificence of the ἀλαζών. This is mentioned merely as one of the particular traits in which is seen his general characteristic —Illbreeding.

(10. αὐτῷ] αὐτῷ is preferred by Edmonds.)

ib λάχανα πολλὰ ἔχων καὶ ἁπαλά] Here V (alone) adds ὥστε εἶναι ψυχρόν: whence Foss conjectures ὥστε <ἀεὶ τὸν οἶνον> εἶναι ψυχρόν. Ussing leaves a lacuna, but thinks that we should read κῆπος λαχ. ἐχ π. καὶ ἁ. κρείττων ἐστὶν ἢ μάγειρος, κ.τ.λ To me there seems no doubt that the words ὥστε εἶναι ψυχρόν were a gloss upon λακκαῖον. (In Bloch's edition, they are placed in brackets after λακκαῖον.)

12. μεστὴ γὰρ ἀεί] MSS μεστὴ γάρ ἐστι (retained in L). Foss, Dubner and Hartung μεστὴν γὰρ ἀεί. The sense seems to require ἀεί: but there is no reason for changing μεστή to μεστήν. (μεστὴ γὰρ ἀεί is accepted by Fraenkel and Groeneboom)

14. καὶ ξενίζων δὲ δεῖξαι] Foss needlessly transposes the words ξενίζων δέ to a place before ὅτι ἡ οἰκία αὐτοῦ, and inserts φῆσαι after them (αὐτοῦ] αὐτοῦ L.)

15 f. καὶ παρακαλῶν δὲ ἐπὶ τοῦ ποτηρίου, εἰπεῖν ὅτι τὸ τέρψον τοὺς πα-

ρόντας παρεσκεύασται, κ.τ.λ.] Vulg καὶ παρακαλεῖν δὲ ἐπὶ τοῦ ποτηρίου ὅτι τέρψον τοὺς παρόντας: omitting all that follows, which is only found in V. Ast understood this· 'He will exhort (the parasite) with the words 'Amuse the company.'' But the ὅτι before the *imperative* is questionable in classical Greek, and τὸ τέρψον, the reading of the best MS, is no doubt right. (ὅτι is omitted by Casaubon, followed by Fraenkel and Groeneboom.)

XII (XIX)

3. μεγάλους] *v.l.* μεγάλας: μέλανας Herwerden (*L*, and Fraenkel and Groeneboom).

(4. αὐτῷ] αὑτῷ is preferred by Edmonds.)

4. αὐτὰ] Vulg. ἔχειν γὰρ καὶ τὸν πατέρα καὶ τὸν πάππον: V, ἔχειν γὰρ αὐτὸν καὶ τὸν πατέρα καὶ τὸν πάππον Dubner altered αὐτόν to αὐτοῦ (preferred by Edmonds): Meier, whom Foss follows, to αὐτά. Petersen, keeping αὐτόν, makes the strange mistake of translating it as if it were αὐτός (αὐτὸν is retained in *L*.)

5. αὐτοῦ] V, which alone has this clause, αὐτὸν τὸ γένος. Foss, Petersen and Ussing follow Siebenkees in inserting εἰς before τὸ γένος · Foss alters αὐτόν to αὑτῷ, Ussing to ἑαυτὸν (reading εἴς τε γένος) · I prefer αὑτοῦ.

7. χρώμενος χρίεσθαι] For these two words the vulgate has simply χρῆσθαι. V, χρώμενος σφύζεσθαι ('to throb'). A great many corrections of σφύζεσθαι have been proposed, but none is probable. Ast φλύζεσθαι ('to boil over'), Petersen ὄζεσθαι, Coray σπογγίζεσθαι, Schweighauser (after Visconti) σφίγγεσθαι, ('vestimento se constringere,') Foss σφαιρίζειν. One of the good MSS has χρίεσθαι (which was another conjecture of Coray's). This makes good sense, and may have been corrupted through its likeness to χρώμενος. (σφύζεσθαι is simply marked as corrupt in *L*. Diels conjectures συρίζεσθαι.)

(8. λεπτὸν] ἄπλυτον Naber.)

(8. ἀναβαλόμενος] The present tense (which is less natural) is found in V.)

(9. ἐξελθεῖν] The passage that follows in the MSS, καὶ εἰς ὀρνιθοσκόπου—τῷ οἰνοχόῳ, is transferred by Ast and Foss to the end of c. XVII (XI), βδελυρία.)

XIII (XIV)

1. ἔστι δὲ ἡ ἀναισθησία] Vulg. codices· ἔστι δὲ καὶ ἡ ἀναισθησία A. ἔστι καὶ ἡ ἀν. B. Ast follows Needham in omitting καί on the authority of several MSS. (καὶ is found in A and B; omitted by *L*.)

7. λαβών <τι>] τι, which is wanting in the MSS, was first supplied by Gesner, whom Foss, Ussing and most other recent editors follow. Petersen supplies ἀργύριον.—(The Munich Epitome has ἀποθείς τι.)

12 f. καὶ τὰ παιδία ἑαυτοῦ—ἐμβάλλειν] (τὰ παιδία τὰ ἑαυτοῦ is preferred by Edmonds.) Foss (who has τὰ παιδία ἑαυτῷ—ἐμβάλλειν) transfers the whole clause to the Character of the ὀψιμαθής, c. VIII (XXVII). But it is appropriate to the ἀναίσθητος, as a mark of stupid inadvertence· see Notes (The MSS are divided between κόπους ἐμβάλλειν (A etc.) and κόπον ἐμβαλεῖν (B etc.); the latter is adopted in L.)

15 f ἡδύ γε τῶν ἄστρων ὄζει, ὅτε δὴ οἱ ἄλλοι λέγουσι τῆς γῆς] The corruption in this passage is utterly desperate. Vulg ἡδύ γε τῶν ἄστρων νομίζει ὅτι δὴ καὶ οἱ ἄλλοι λέγουσι πίσσης (retained in L, where it is described, in Casaubon's language, as a *conclamatus locus*). I have followed Ast in taking Coray's ὄζει for νομίζει, and Schneider's τῆς γῆς for πίσσης Ast thinks that the words ὅτι δὴ καὶ οἱ ἄλλοι λέγουσι τῆς γῆς were added by a commentator who wished to explain the point of the ἀναισθησία he says 'How sweet is the smell from the stars' (*because, of course, other people say, 'from the earth'*). But it is more probable that ὅτι should be ὅτε Foss fills out the sentences thus:—ἡδύ γε τῶν ἄστρων <τὸ φῶς φαινομένων δὲ τῶν ἄστρων>, ὅ τι δὴ καὶ οἱ ἄλλοι λέγουσι, πίσσης <μελάντερον εἶναι τὸ σκότος > This is to rewrite Theophrastus; nor could ὅ τι δὴ καὶ οἱ ἄ λέγουσι mean 'whatever other people may say.'—Every interpretation which has been proposed requires the omission of καί before οἱ ἄλλοι. (Schneider, in his text of 1818, retains τῆς πίσσης, but, in his note in vol IV 839, proposes τῆς γῆς. This proposal, as Schneider was aware, had already been made in 1805 by the younger Schweighäuser, who was led to it by a passage of Cratinus, τῆς γῆς ὡς γλυκὺ | ὄζει See Schweighauser's Athenaeus, *Notae*, 1805, vol. VII 682.)

17. κατὰ τὰς ἱερὰς πύλας] All the modern editors, except Ussing, have adopted the emendation of Meursius, Ἡρίας for ἱεράς, 'the Gate of Tombs' (ἠρία). This is, I think, rash. For (1) the MSS agree on ἱεράς and we know that there was a gate at Athens called the Sacred· Plut. *Sulla* c. 14. (2) Ἡρίαι (or Ἡριαῖαι, proposed by Sylburg and approved by Curt Wachsmuth, Fraenkel and Groeneboom, and Wilamowitz) is a strange adjective. The Etym. Magn. has, indeed,—Ἡριά, 'A gate at Athens, so called because the dead were carried out at it to the tombs (ἠρία)' But this looks like guesswork; nor is there any mention elsewhere of an Erian Gate. Dr Smith, in his excellent article *Athenae* in the Dict of Geogr, places it conjecturally on the north of the city, 'since the burial-place of Athens was in the outer Cerameicus.' But

CHARACTERS XIII, XIV

this was a cemetery for those only who received *public* burial (Ar. *Aves* 395), and besides would be approached more conveniently from the N w., where stood the Dipylum, and probably the Sacred Gate Becker states (possibly on the authority of Pollux IX 15) that the space outside the walls between the Peiraic Gate on the s.w. of Athens and the Itonian Gate to the E. of it was a public burial-ground for the poor, for metoeci and for foreigners; and in this space places the Erian Gate, —where Dr Smith, on better grounds, places the Melitean But Becker, *Charicles* exc. to sc. IX, gives no proofs. (Judeich, *Topographie von Athen*, 1905, p. 129 f, places the 'Gate of Tombs,' or 'Erian Gate,' immediately to the South-West of the Dipylum, the position usually assigned to the 'Sacred Gate,' which Judeich places further South, at a point 240 metres beyond the Peiraic Gate No mention of the 'Erian Gate' has been discovered, either in literature or in inscriptions.)

XIV (IV)

14 f. καὶ ἀριστῶν δὲ ἅμα τοῖς ὑποζυγίοις ἐμβαλεῖν· καὶ κόψαντος τὴν θύραν ὑπακοῦσαι αὐτός] The two Paris MSS and one other omit the words καὶ κόψαντος, and have no point after ἐμβαλεῖν. The other MSS have ἐμβαλεῖν τὴν θύραν· καὶ κόψαντος τὴν θύραν ὑπακοῦσαι αὐτός Ast follows Casaubon in altering the first τὴν θύραν into τὸν χόρτον. I agree with Foss, Petersen and Ussing in thinking that it can be understood. The confusion in the MSS probably arose thus. First the words καὶ κόψαντος dropped out Then, as ἐμβάλλειν τὴν θύραν was a common phrase, it was assumed that τὴν θύραν belonged to ἐμβαλεῖν. When καὶ κόψαντος were replaced, they were accordingly inserted after, instead of before, τὴν θύραν, and the latter words were repeated by a transcriber who saw that κόψαντος required them, but did not see that they had merely to be transposed from the preceding clause (καὶ κόψαντος is omitted by *L.*)

(15. καὶ <ἑστιῶν> τὸν κύνα, κ.τ.λ.] is suggested by Edmonds, the *Epit. Mon.* having ἐσθίοντα.)

(17 f. λαμβάνων] λαβὼν, the reading of the two Paris MSS, is adopted by *L.*)

18. λίαν λέγων λευρὸν εἶναι] Vulg. λίαν μὲν λυπρὸν (three MSS λυπηρόν). There is some doubt about the μέν, which, Dubner says, looks in Paris A more like μενόν. (μεν῀ is the reading of A, and μ̄῀ that of B, both meaning nothing but μέν) Foss and Ussing adopt Casaubon's conjecture, and alter it to λέγων. I doubt whether this is right, but it is the best remedy that has been proposed. Of course 'λίαν μὲν λυπρὸν εἶναι' might be treated as a quotation between inverted commas; but

the omission of λέγων would be harsh, and for μέν we should then expect γάρ. Various emendations of λυπρόν—which Ussing vainly defends as meaning 'sorry,' 'poor,'—have been attempted; e.g. λεπτόν, ῥυπαρόν, and Petersen's bolder διὰ τὸ μὴ λαμπρὸν εἶναι. I suspect that the true word is λευρόν. The Rustic likes new, bright money. he complains that the coin offered to him is too old and worn. (λίαν μὲν λυπρὸν is printed in L, while the highest probability is there assigned to Duport's λεπρόν, cp. Herodas vi 36, χιλίων εὔντων | ἕνα οὐκ ἂν ὅστις λεπρός ἐστι προσδώσω, where there is a variant σαπρός. For μὲν λυπρὸν Diels conjectures μολυβρὸν.)

(19 ἅμα ἀλλάττεσθαι] ἀνταλλάττεσθαι Eberhard, Cobet, and Naber.)

19 ἐὰν τὸ ἄροτρον χρήσῃ] εἰ τὸ ἄροτρον ἔχρησεν A (followed by L).

20 <ἀπαιτεῖν>] In the MSS the verb after τῆς νυκτός, which the sense demands, has been lost. Ast supplies αἰτεῖν, Foss ἐξαιτεῖν, Casaubon ἀπαιτεῖν, and so Ussing. (The Munich epitome has ζητεῖν.)

23 εἰ σήμερον ὁ ἄρχων νουμηνίαν ἄγει] Vulg εἰ σήμερον ὁ ἀγὼν νουμηνίαν ἄγει Ast tried to make sense by omitting ὁ ἀγών, so that the subject to ἄγει should be ὁ ἀπαντῶν. I have adopted the emendation ὁ ἄρχων, proposed (by Darbens and Bloch, and accepted) by Ussing: see Notes (ὁ ἀγὼν is marked as corrupt in L Diels proposes εἰ σήμερον ὁ ἀγών, <καὶ εἰ> νουμηνίαν ἄγει)

(24. εὐθὺς ὅτι βούλεται καταβὰς] ὅτι βούλεται εὐθὺς καταβὰς Cobet, followed by Fraenkel and Groeneboom.)

24 f. καὶ τῆς αὐτῆς ὁδοῦ] This clause stands in the MSS after ἐγκροῦσαι Foss and Petersen (and L) follow Schneider in placing it, as seems necessary, after ἀποκείρασθαι.

(25 παριὼν] omitted by Casaubon and Cobet, followed by Fraenkel and Groeneboom.)

25. τοῦ ταρίχους] Ast is right, I think, in reading with Sylburg τοῦ ταρίχους (partitive gen) for τοὺς ταρίχους (retained in L) The form ὁ τάριχος is used by Herodotus, but in Attic (e g. Ar. *Eq.* 1246, *Ach.* 967) τὸ τάριχος, already used in this chapter, was far more common.

(25 f. καὶ ἐν βαλανείῳ—ἐγκροῦσαι] bracketed by Diels)

XV (IX)

4. εἶτα θύσας] Petersen shifts εἶτα to a place before πρὸς τοῦτον ἀπελθών in the preceding clause, and inserts καί before θύσας. But πρῶτον μέν in the first clause appears to confirm εἶτα in the second. (In L a lacuna is marked between these words)

(6 ἄρτον καὶ κρέας ἄρας] So A, ἄρας κρέας καὶ ἄρτον L, quoting the variant ἄρας κρέας τε καὶ ἄρτον)

CHARACTERS XIV, XV

7. τιμιώτατε] A etc.: τίμιε B etc. The conjecture of Salmasius, Τίβιε, a common slave's name, has been adopted by Foss, Petersen and Ussing. But τιμιώτατε, besides having authority, has more point. By it, as Ast says, 'impudentia hominis mirifice augetur.' (The evidence in favour of Τίβιε is strengthened by the fact that it is the reading of the Munich epitome which also has in the margin the *scholium*:—Τίβιε: δουλικὸν ὄνομα ὡς καὶ Δρόμων καὶ Γέτας καὶ τὰ τοιαῦτα, cp. Lucian, *Timon* 21, *De mercede conductis* 25; Galen x 4, Strabo, p 304, and Schol. Aristoph. Ach. 243, quoted by Diels, *Theophrastea*, 19 Τίβιε has been accepted in all the recent editions. Τίβειε is the form supported by Menander)

10. ζωμόν] All the MSS, except four of the best, have ζυγόν. but, as Ast says, this was probably an attempt to explain ἐμβάλλειν. The balance is τάλαντον, the beam, ζυγόν, the scales, πλάστιγγες. ζυγόν could not be used for πλάστιγξ

(13. θεωρεῖν] συνθεωρεῖν Cobet.)

(13. τοὺς υἱεῖς] τοὺς υἱοὺς is proposed by Edmonds. This would explain the reading of B, in which the similarity between τοὺς and υἱοὺς may have led to the omission of the latter To explain the corruption, Diels points out that the readings of the Paris MSS, τοὺς εἰς B, τοὺς ὡς εἰς A, τὴν ὑστεραίαν, show that either εἰς was dropped *after* υεις, or the termination εις *before* εἰς. The remaining letter u was then left out (as unintelligible) by B, while it was interpreted as ∾, i e ὡς, by A.)

(15 τὴν ἀλλοτρίαν οἰκίαν] τὴν is omitted by Cobet, who inserts τοὺς before χρήσαντας in l. 17.)

(16. ἄχυρον] ἄχυρα AB (Diels).)

(17. χρήσαντας] τοὺς χρήσαντας Munich Epitome, Cobet and *L*.)

20 καὶ εἰπεῖν ὅτι λέλουται, κᾆτα ἀπιών, οὐδεμία σοι χάρις] Vulg καὶ εἰπεῖν ὅτι λέλουται ἀπιὼν κἀκεῖ οὐδεμία σοι χάρις. Pauw conjectured καὶ εἰπεῖν, ὅτε λέλουται, ἀπιών Κάλει, οὐδεμία σοι χάρις 'he will say, when he has bathed and is going away. Summon me—I owe you no thanks' i.e. 'if you want to get your fee, you must bring an action, for I do not consider that I owe you anything, having acted as my own bath-servant' But the boast, ὅτι λέλουται, appears characteristic, and therefore I would not change ὅτι to ὅτε: and the advice to bring an action seems a rather cumbrous joke. Ast adopts κάλει, but retains ὅτι. Foss alters εἰπεῖν to εἰπών, and for κἀκεῖ boldly substitutes κραγεῖν. My remedy is simple. By merely changing κἀκεῖ to κᾆτα, and placing it *before* ἀπιών, perfectly good sense is obtained from the manuscript text. Ussing alters κἀκεῖ to δὲ καί (κακεί is marked as corrupt in *L* Edmonds, who in his text adopts Ribbeck's proposal, καὶ ἀπιὼν καλεῖν, has since suggested καὶ εἰπεῖν ὅτι Λέλουμαι, ἀπιών, κἀκείνου οὐδεμία σοι χάρις Fraenkel

and Groeneboom print καὶ εἰπεῖν ἀπιών, ὅτι Λέλουμαι καλῶς· καί· Οὐδεμία σοι χάρις. Holland, in L, suggests ἀπιὼν δέ, Κὰρ εἶ, 'a mere Karian,' a term of abuse)

XVI (VI)

2 f. **κακῶς ἀκοῦσαι καὶ λοιδορηθῆναι δυνάμενος**] καί, which is wanting in the best MSS, has been restored by most modern editors (though not by L), and is undoubtedly right Foss (followed by Petersen) reads κακῶς ἀκοῦσαι, λοιδορηθῆναι δυναμένοις. He calls δυναμένοις 'certissima coniectura': what it means, he does not explain, and I do not understand. But there can be little doubt that he and Ussing are right in taking λοιδορηθῆναι as a deponent aorist, having an active sense. Demosthenes so uses it in two places: (1) *in Meid.* p. 558 § 132 οἷα ἐδημηγόρησε παρ' ὑμῖν .., κατηγορῶν καὶ φάσκων ὄνειδος ἐξελθεῖν τὴν στρατιὰν ταύτην τῇ πόλει· καὶ τὴν λοιδορίαν ἣν ἐλοιδορήθη Κρατίνῳ περὶ τούτων. (2) *in Conon.* p. 1257 § 5 λοιδορηθέντος δ' αὐτοῖς ἐκείνου καὶ κακίσαντος αὐτούς. (Herwerden proposes ἑκὼν κακῶς ἀκοῦσαι, accepted by Fraenkel and Groeneboom.)

5. **προσωπεῖον μὴ ἔχων**] μή has been restored from two MSS by Meier, who however changes ἔχων to ἔχειν; and so Foss. Ussing rightly keeps ἔχων. Casaubon had conjecturally inserted οὐκ, and was followed by Ast. (οὐκ ἔχων is accepted by Fraenkel and Groeneboom. The negative is not adopted by L Edmonds suggests ἀγοραῖός τις καὶ παντοποιός ἀμέλει δυνατὸς καὶ ὀρχεῖσθαι νήφων τὸν κόρδακα, καὶ προσωπεῖον ἔχων ἐν κωμικῷ χορῷ ἀνασεσυρμένος περιάγειν.)

(7. **μάχεσθαι τοῖς τὸ σύμβολον φέρουσι**] The reading in AB, τούτοις τοῖς, suggests to Diels the conjecture τούτοις οἳ δὶς τὸ σύμβολον φέρουσι)

(11. **τὸ δεσμωτήριον**] The Munich Epitome has κέραμον In the Leipzig ed., Meister, who quotes Π v 387 χαλκέῳ δ' ἐν κεράμῳ δέδετο, and Hesychius, κέραμος· δεσμωτήριον, suggests that the original text was κέραμον (τὸν κέραμον πλείω χρόνον οἰκεῖν κ.τ.λ.), which has been ousted by the glossarial note, δεσμωτήριον. The *Et. Magn.* says that κέραμος was the Cyprian name for 'prison')

12 **καὶ τούτων δ'**] Vulg. καὶ τοῦτο δ'· Ast καὶ τούτων δ': whom Ussing and L follow, but (with Needham) omit δ', which is also omitted in the variant καὶ τοῦτ'.

12 f. **τῶν περιισταμένων τοὺς ὄχλους**] περιίστανται usu. means 'they place themselves (stand) around', but here, 'they place around themselves'. 'hominum turbam circum se colligunt' Ussing. Compare παρίστασθαι, 'to draw over to one's own side'

(16 **ἀκοῦσαι**] διακοῦσαι Unger.)

21 f. **καὶ οὐκ ἀποδοκιμάζειν δέ**] Vulg. οὐκ ἀποδοκιμάζων δέ Meier

corrected the part. to the infin., and inserted καί before οὐκ: so Foss. (L omits καί.) Ussing retains the vulgate; but the infin. appears absolutely necessary. Observe that in negative clauses depending on οἷος, δεινός we have in the Characters usually μή, but sometimes οὐ e.g. c. III (vulg XV) τοιοῦτος οἷος οὐκ ἔχειν συγγνώμην: c. IV (XXIV) τοιόσδε οἷος... προσελθεῖν πρότερος οὐδενὶ θελῆσαι.

22 οὐδὲ καπήλων ἀγοραίων στρατηγεῖν] Vulg. οὐδ' ἅμα πολλῶν ἀγοραίων στρατηγεῖν (retained in L) Nothing can be made of the ἅμα. It is absurd to say that he does not disdain to be captain *even of many* ἀγοραῖοι *at once*, as if a more modest person would have been στρατηγός of one at a time One German editor proposed to eject it altogether. Ast was for changing ἅμα πολλῶν to παμπόλλων. But the context itself supplies, I think, the true remedy. The ἀγοραῖοι of whom this man is prince or patron are, it appears, the keepers of the small provision-shops in the market-place, of which he makes the round for the purpose of levying the interest on his loans. In ΟΥΔΑΜΑΠΟΛΛΩΝ is concealed, I am persuaded, nothing but ΟΥΔΕΚΑΠΗΛΩΝ, the corruption of the first ε into α having been followed by that of κ into μ The idea of a *host* involved in στρατηγεῖν would lend countenance to the false πολλῶν. (Some MSS have οὐδ' ἀλλ' ἅμα πολλῶν, a combination of two texts Diels acutely conjectures οὐδ' ἀλλαντοπωλῶν.)

27. ἐργώδεις δέ εἰσι, τὸ στόμα εὔλυτον ἔχοντες] Vulg. ἐργώδεις δέ εἰσιν οἱ στόμα εὔλυτον ἔχοντες. I follow Ast in reading τό for οἱ With οἱ the sentiment is general; with τό, the subject to εἰσί is οἱ ἀπονενοημένοι understood, and the sentence is what it was meant to be—a commentary on the chapter.

XVII (XI)

(3. <ἀσχημονεῖν> is simply a substitution for the grosser phrase in the original.)

6. τὰ μύρτα] The reading of the two Paris MSS, adopted by Foss, Petersen and Ussing. The rest (except one which has τὰ μύρα) give τὰ μῆλα, which Ast prefers on the ground that ἀκρόδρυα is a generic term, including both shell-fruits and soft fruits, and that κάρυα—μῆλα represent these two species But the disjunctive ἢ is against this view (The Paris MS A has καί.) (Immisch, in L, regards ἢ τὰ ἀκρόδρυα as a glossarial note on κάρυα. Theophrastus himself, *De Odor.* 5, uses ἀκρόδρυα of 'nuts,' as contrasted with 'apples' and 'pears,' while Athenaeus, 52 A, observes that κάρυα was used for ἀκρόδρυα by Attic and other writers.)

9. περιμεῖναι κελεῦσαι] These words are preserved only in some of

the inferior MSS, but there seems to be little doubt of their genuineness.

10. ἡττημένῳ] The MSS give ἡττωμένῳ. Schneider's conjecture ἡττημένῳ has been accepted by Ast, Foss, Petersen and Ussing. (ἡττωμένῳ is retained by *L*, comparing c. V (1) 5, συλλυπεῖσθαι ἡττωμένοις, and regarding the present ἡττᾶσθαι as used in a perfect sense.)

11 f. καὶ ὀψωνεῖν—μισθοῦσθαι] Foss has unnecessarily transferred this clause to c. I (II), inserting it after the words διακονῆσαι δυνατὸς ἀπνευστί. The MSS (including A and B) have ἑαυτόν: Casaubon's ἑαυτῷ has been adopted by most editors; Furlan's αὐτός by Ast. (αὐτὸς ἑαυτῷ is proposed by Herwerden and Cobet.)

14 f μεθύσκεσθαι μέλλει] A long passage, now assigned by universal consent to c. XXVI (XXX), καὶ οἰνοπωλῶν—παῖδες λάβωσι, used to follow here.

15. καὶ εἰς ὀρνιθοσκόπου] The passage from here to the end stands in the MSS in c. XII (XIX), following the words εἰς ἀγορὰν ἐξελθεῖν (l. 9). Ast, followed by Foss and most recent editors, has transferred it hither. Petersen (Introd. p. 46) thinks that it belongs to c. XI (XX). My own impression is that part of it, viz. as far as the words ὥσπερ ἀστεῖόν τι πεποιηκώς, belongs, as Ast thinks, to this chapter: the remainder, καὶ αὐλούμενος δέ, κ.τ.λ., to c. XI (XX). But there is no warrant for dissecting it in this manner. I have therefore dealt with the entire passage in the way approved by Ast and Foss.

17. ὥσπερ ἀστεῖόν τι πεποιηκώς] ὥσπερ ἀστεῖόν τι is Bernard's excellent emendation (adopted by Petersen) of the MSS, ὡς τεράστιόν τι (retained in *L*), which is usually explained 'something portentous': the βδελυρός *laughing* as if he had done 'something of evil omen.' But it is more natural that he should laugh 'as if he had done something clever.' Ast's remark '*ὡς* non est *quasi*, sed *quia, quod*,' will not bear close inspection. ὡς, in places such as this, expresses the view—correct or false—taken by the doer of the action.

19. τί οὐ ταχὺ παύσαιτο] This, the reading of V, is now generally adopted; as by Foss, Petersen and Ussing. The βδελυρός asks τί οὐ ταχὺ ἐπαύσω, which becomes in oratio obliqua τί οὐ ταχὺ παύσαιτο. The sense is the same, but in a more lively form, as that given by the other MSS, μὴ ταχὺ παυσαμένη. Coray and Ast altered this to τῇ ταχὺ παυσαμένῃ, supposing that the βδελυρός reproves the player for ceasing to play before he has ceased to sing. (Eberhard and Ribbeck's suggestion, τί οὕτω ταχὺ ἐπαύσατο, is accepted in *L*. οὕτω was also proposed by Unger.)

XVIII (III)

10. πλόϊμον] So Foss, Petersen and Ussing, after Dubner, who found this form in all the MSS which he collated, including three of the best: vulg. πλώϊμον (found in some MSS, and retained by Wilamowitz and L, with a reference to Lobeck, *ad Phryn*. 615).

10. εἰ ποιήσειεν ὁ Ζεὺς ὕδωρ] πλεῖον is added after ὕδωρ by the two Paris MSS, followed by Needham, Dubner and L. Fischer suggested that it was probably introduced to balance βελτίω. He is followed by Ast in rejecting it. (In ed. 1 the editor was under the impression that πλεῖον was *omitted* by the Paris MSS. The reverse is the case.)

(15 f Πυανεψιῶνος..Ποσειδεῶνος] Πυανοψ. and Ποσιδ. are the forms attested by inscriptions and adopted in L. τὰ Ἀπατούρια is proposed by Naber, the Paris MSS A and B have Ἀπατούρια.)

16 f. κἂν ὑπομένῃ...μὴ ἀφίστασθαι] In the MSS this clause stands after σήμερον. Schneider was the first editor who transferred it to the place which it now occupies in nearly all editions. Ussing leaves it in its old position, and considers that the spurious addition begins at καὶ ὡς Βοηδρομιῶνος, κ.τ.λ.

18. τοὺς τοιούτους τῶν ἀνθρώπων] Casaubon's conjecture that φεύγειν ought to be inserted here has been adopted by Foss It seems unnecessary.

XIX (VII)

4. (αὐτοῦ] αὑτοῦ is suggested by Edmonds.)

5 f. ὑποβάλλειν, εἶπας σύ; μὴ ἐπιλάθῃ] This, the reading of the vulgate, is retained by Ussing and Petersen (the latter, however, giving ἐπιβάλλειν); and seems decidedly preferable to that proposed by Casaubon, which several modern editors (including L) have adopted, ὑποβάλλειν εἶπας· σὺ μὴ ἐπιλάθῃ. I cannot agree with Foss that the vulgate requires the insertion of καί before μὴ ἐπιλάθῃ. The words εἶπας σύ, μὴ ἐπιλάθῃ ὃ μέλλεις λέγειν, are closely connected in sense, and do not represent two distinct remarks The two Paris MSS, A and B, have ἐπιβάλλειν, one ἐπιβαλεῖν: the rest ὑποβάλλει (or ὑποβάλλειν). Needham restored ὑποβάλλειν, which is now generally accepted.

11. ἀπογυιώσῃ] The best MSS have ἀπογυμνώσῃ, which Petersen endeavours to defend in the sense, 'when he has *despoiled*' (as the victor strips and despoils a slain foe)—a figure for 'vanquished', but this will hardly do. Pauw conjectured ἀπογυιώσῃ· see *Il.* VI 264, μή μοι οἶνον ἄειρε μελίφρονα μή μ᾽ ἀπογυιώσῃς, μένεος δ᾽ ἀλκῆς τε λάθωμαι I think that this is probably right, and that the use of an epic word was meant to heighten the humour. The inferior MSS have ἀποκναίσῃ, which Foss

reads; but it has the air of a gloss by some one who despaired of ἀπογυμνώσῃ. (The latter is defended by Petersen, p. 171, and retained by L.)

14 f. **προμανθάνειν, τοσαῦτα προσλαλῶν**] Vulg. προμανθάνειν τοσαῦτα, καὶ προσλαλεῖν. The alteration of προσλαλεῖν to προσλαλῶν has been generally adopted, but the modes of dealing with the καί have been various. The obvious expedient of putting it before τοσαῦτα and keeping προσλαλεῖν weakens the passage intolerably. Before προσλαλῶν it could only mean 'actually,' and such emphasis is not wanted, while the omission of the article before διδασκάλοις makes it unlikely that καί stood before τοῖς παιδοτρίβαις. Petersen suggests τοσαῦτα δή (for καί): Foss, τοσαῦτα καὶ <τοιαῦτα>. I agree with Needham that it is to be omitted altogether. When προσλαλῶν became προσλαλεῖν, καί was inserted by some one who thought that τοσαῦτα belonged to προμανθάνειν (L has προμανθάνειν τοσαῦτα προσλαλεῖν κ.τ.λ.)

17. **πυθόμενος τὰ τῆς ἐκκλησίας**] Vulg. πυθόμενος τὰς ἐκκλησίας. It has been attempted to explain τὰς ἐκκλησίας as 'the days appointed for the meetings of the Ecclesia,' or 'the transactions in the Ecclesia'; but neither sense is tolerable. Ussing (followed by L) thinks that some words, connected with τὰς ἐκκλησίας by εἰς or πρός, have dropped out. I have adopted Petersen's conjecture of τὰ τῆς for τάς. Foss writes, on his own conj., πυθομένοις τὰς ἐκκλησίας. (Fraenkel and Groeneboom print τὰκ τῆς ἐκκλησίας.)

18 f. **τὴν ἐπ' Ἀριστοφῶντός ποτε γενομένην τοῦ ῥήτορος μάχην**] It is now the general opinion that τοῦ ῥήτορος was added by some one who confused the archon of 330 B.C. with one or other of his two more distinguished namesakes, Aristophon of Azenia and Aristophon of Collytus: see Notes. Casaubon proposed τῶν ῥητόρων (i.e. Demosthenes and Aeschines) but such a change would be very rash. (τοῦ ῥήτορος is retained in L, as a reference to Demosthenes; but τοῖς ῥήτορσι is suggested.)

19 f. **καὶ τὴν Λακεδαιμονίων ἐπὶ Λυσάνδρου**] The best MSS have ὑπό, and so Ussing (in his notes though by a misprint his text has ἐπί), and Peterson (and L). But, as Ussing himself says, ὑπό is suspicious, 'quoniam non significatur (proelium) a *Lysandro factum*, Λυσάνδρῳ scribendum videtur.' I doubt whether a Greek would have said ὑπὸ Λυσάνδρῳ when he meant 'under (the leadership of) Lysander.' He would rather have said, στρατηγοῦντος Λυσάνδρου. The reading ἐπί in some of the inferior MSS is probably the true one. Ast and Hottinger questioned the genuineness of this clause; and, if I felt sure that they were right in referring μάχη to the oratorical duel between Demosthenes

and Aeschines in 330 B.C, I should be inclined to agree with them. See Notes (Naber supposes that the text refers to some recent incident, and that the name of Kasandros is concealed under that of Lysandros, and the Macedonians under the Lacedaemonians.)

(27. εἰ—δόξειεν ἂν εἶναι] ἄν, omitted in B, is rejected by Cobet and Blaydes.)

29. βουλόμενα] The variant βουλόμενον, adopted by Foss, seems to spoil the sense

29 f λέγοντα, πάππα, λάλει τι ἡμῖν] Vulg. λέγοντα ταῦτα, λαλεῖν τι ἡμῖν. Sylburg's emendation of ταῦτα to πάππα, adopted by Hartung and Ussing, seems nearly certain. Petersen prefers the Homeric ἄττα (proposed by Casaubon). Needham suggested τέττα and Ribbeck τατᾶ. Foss λέγοντα βαυκαλᾶν· λαλεῖν τι ἡμῖν. βαυκαλᾶν is a late word meaning 'to sing a lullaby.' Ussing defends the imper. for infin in prose by Plat. *Crat.* 426 B · *Rep.* V 473 A But it is an essentially poetical construction, and would be out of place in this short, plain sentence. I have therefore adopted the easy correction λάλει, which has often been proposed before.

XX (VIII)

(2. ὧν βούλεται] Cichorius, in *L*, suggests a lacuna between these words. ὧν <πιστεύεσθαι> βούλεται is proposed by Diels.)

3. καταβαλὼν τὸ ἦθος] Casaubon conjectured μεταβαλὼν τὸ ἦθος. Ast renders the vulgate '*voltu demisso—blando et ita comparato ut alterum captet.*' If the text is right, this is probably the general sense, but ἦθος, though it sometimes denotes nearly what we mean by a man's 'air' or 'mien,' has nowhere the definite sense of 'countenance' I understand—'giving a demure, subdued air to his whole bearing'

4—6. πόθεν σύ, καὶ λέγεις τί; τί ἔχεις περὶ τοῦδε εἰπεῖν καινόν; καὶ ἐπιβαλὼν ἐρωτᾶν, μὴ λέγεταί τι καινότερον; καὶ μὴν ἀγαθά γέ ἐστι τὰ λεγόμενα] This is the reading of the vulgate, except that for τί ἔχεις it has καὶ ἔχειν Three good MSS have καὶ πῶς ἔχεις (followed by *L*), but πῶς ἔχεις εἰπεῖν καινόν is not Greek. Ussing therefore reads πῶς ἔχεις περὶ τοῦδε, and puts the words εἰπεῖν καινόν in brackets. To me it seems more likely that πῶς was inserted to mark a question after the second τί had been corrupted to καί Before ἐπιβαλών four MSS have ὡς, which is without meaning, for ἐπιβαλών is simply 'following up,' 'repeating' his question. Foss rewrites the whole passage conjecturally; among other changes he gives ὡς ὑποβαλών.

(13. Πολυπέρχων] Πολυσπέρχων (A) was the form adopted by earlier editors and in the first ed. of this work. But Πολυπέρχων, found in B, and in the Munich epitome, is the correct form, as attested by con-

temporary inscriptions, e.g. *C. I. A.* II 723. It has accordingly been adopted in *L*, which also (here and in l 23) prefers the form Κάσανδρος.)

(15. φήσει, τὸ πρᾶγμα βοᾶσθαι γὰρ ἐν τῇ πόλει] Probably with a view to securing an earlier position for γάρ, Cobet proposes <φανερὸν> φήσει <εἶναι> τὸ πρᾶγμα, βοᾶσθαι γὰρ ἐν τῇ πόλει. φήσει is here generally translated 'he will say,' in which case γάρ is used in an exclamatory sense 'Why!'; but it seems better to make φήσει emphatic, as in XXIII 8, ἂν ἐκείνη φῇ:—'he will say *yes*, for' (he will add) 'the town rings with it.' It is also so understood by Romizi (1899). *risponderà di sì, perche* etc.)

(18. αὐτῷ] ἑαυτῷ is suggested by Edmonds.)

(22. οἶδε] εἶδε Nauck)

(22 f. ταῦτα πάντα διεξιὼν, πῶς οἴεσθε; πιθανῶς σχετλιάζει] *L* prints πάντα (B) διεξιὼν † πῶς οἴεσθαι (AB) πιθανῶς σχετλιάζειν (AB). Fraenkel and Groeneboom follow the inferior MSS in printing: ταῦθ' ἅμα διεξιών, πῶς οἴεσθε πιθανῶς σχετλιάζει.) Diels proposes καὶ ταῦτα διεξιών πως, οἴεσθαι πιθανῶς σχετλιάζειν λέγων, *haec dum aliquo modo enarrat, apte se ad persuadendum lamentari opinatur cum dicit*, etc.)

24. ἀλλ' οὖν ἰσχυρός γε γενόμενος] Ast follows Casaubon in inserting γε, which seems almost necessary, and which might easily have been lost before γενόμενος. (Except with the imperative, ἀλλ' οὖν, as noticed by Edmonds, is almost invariably followed by γε.) Foss fills up the lacuna after γενόμενος with the words νῦν ὡς ἀσθενής ἐστι I should have preferred simply ἀπόλωλεν or some equivalent word, but I rather suspect that the lacuna was intentionally left by the author. These broken utterances, dying away in an unfinished sentence, constitute the very art of the λογοποιός. (Holland and Ilberg[1] suggest ἀλλ<ως> οὖν ἰσχυρὸς γενόμενος· accepted in *L*, where the lacuna is transferred to the next sentence:—καὶ ** δεῖ δ' αὐτόν γε μόνον εἰδέναι, where, for αὐτόν γε, there is a variant αὐτὸν σὲ Wilamowitz, in his *Lesebuch*, prints ἀλλ' οὖν ἰσχυρῶς γ' ἀμυνάμενος)   [1] *L*. anticipated by Auber and Herwerden.

34 f. ποίᾳ γὰρ ἐν στοᾷ, ποίῳ δὲ ἐργαστηρίῳ...οὐ διημερεύουσιν;] Vulg. ποίᾳ γὰρ οὐ στοᾷ . οὐ διημερεύουσιν. Schneider, feeling the want of ἐν, gave in his first edition οὐκ ἐνδιημερεύουσιν, and has been followed by Dubner, Hartung and Ussing It seems better, with Ast, to change the first οὐ, which is awkward, into ἐν. On the strength of ποία στοά, ποῖον ἐργαστήριον in some of the good MSS, Foss reads —ποία γὰρ οὐ στοά, ποῖον δὲ ἐργαστήριον, ποῖον δὲ μέρος τῆς ἀγορᾶς οὐ διημερεύουσιν; But τίς τόπος οὐκ ἔστιν, οὗ διημερεύω, could not stand for τίς τόπος ἔστιν οὗ οὐ διημερεύω; and ποίῳ μέρει is in all the MSS. (For variants in this paragraph, see *L*, p 64.)

CHARACTERS XX, XXI

XXI (XXVIII)

1. ἀγωγὴ τῆς ψυχῆς] So Ussing (and *L*) with Casaubon. The MSS have ἀγὼν τῆς ψυχῆς: but ἀγὼν εἰς τὸ χεῖρον cannot be right. (ἀγωγὴ ψυχῆς is preferred by Edmonds.)

3. εἰπεῖν] (V has οὐκοῦνδέ, with an indication that the word is corrupt. Immisch accordingly proposes οἰκονομεῖν, which he prints in *L*, and renders.—*verfahrt er nach einem formlichen Schema.* Diels, more satisfactorily, conjectures οὐκοῦν, φῆσαι.)

6. <Σωσίδημος>] This name is wanting in the MSS, and was first supplied by Meier's clever conjecture, which Foss and Ussing (and subsequent editors) have adopted. Ast, followed by Sheppard, spoils the passage by reading ἔπειτα (for ἐπειδὴ) δὲ εἰς τοὺς δημότας ἐνεγράφη.

7 f. καλεῖται γοῦν ἡ ψυχὴ <Κορινθιακῶς>] V (which alone has this clause) καλεῖται γοῦν ἡ ψυχὴ Κρινοκόρακα. Various attempts have been made to explain the corrupt word. The right clue is, I suspect, to be found in the fact that Κορινθία κόρη was a synonym for ἑταίρα (Plat. *Rep.* III p 404 D). cf. κορινθιάζεσθαι. The copyist first wrote Κρινθ— by mistake, leaving out the ο, then κορ in the margin, which came to be written in the text after Κρινθ, θ being then changed to ο. Κορινθ— thus became κρινοκορ—. What the rest of the word was, I do not pretend to say; but I believe that Κορινθιακῶς (from the adj. used by Xenophon etc.) represents the sense. (κρινοκόρακα is retained in *L*, where see p. 244 f.)

10. καὶ ἱκανὸς δέ] Foss's correction, adopted by Ussing, of the corrupt καὶ κακῶν δέ (Immisch, in his contribution to *L*, prints καὶ <ἀ>κάκων δὲ, '*und zu jemand Arglosem sagt er*')

11 f. ὑπὲρ ὧν οὐ πλανᾷ πρὸς ἐμὲ καὶ τούτους διεξιών] V (which alone has this clause) ὑπὲρ ὧν σὺ πλανᾷς πρὸς ἐμέ καὶ τούτοις διεξιών I follow Ussing in writing τούτους for τούτοις, and so connecting καὶ τούτους διεξιών with what precedes; Schneider and Foss, in writing πλανᾷ for πλανᾷς. The change of a single letter will now give good sense; for σύ read οὐ. The κακολόγος is always eager to *agree* with those who are depreciating the absent (Immisch, in *L*, has ὑπὲρ ὧν σὺ πλανᾷ πρὸς ἐμὲ· κἀπὶ (Casaubon) τούτοις διεξιών.)

14 κύνες] The word is wanting in the MSS, but is printed conjecturally in most editions since that of Ast. (αἱ κύνες *L*.)

15. συνέρχονται] (Schneider's and) Meier's conjecture, adopted by Foss (and others), for συνέχονται (retained in *L*).

15. ἀνδρολάλοι] Foss conj ἀνδρολάβοι (marked as corrupt in *L*; ἀνδροφάγοι is substituted by Ast, ἀνδροβόροι by Fraenkel and Groeneboom).

(16 αὐταὶ <ἐπὶ> θύραν τὴν αὔλειον ὑπακούουσι] <ἐπὶ> is due to Foss;

Schneider proposes <κατὰ>, and Kayser <παρὰ>, accepted by Diels. Petersen and Ussing, followed by L, retain the reading of the MS, αὑταὶ τὴν θύραν ὑπακούουσι. But ὑπακούειν θύραν is not Greek.)

17. εἰπών] V has εἶπου corrected from εἶπας (Cobet) or εἶπεν (Lowe and Diels), εἶπας L.

19 f. οὐδενὶ ὁμοία] οὐδὲν ὅμοιον L, the MSS varying between ὁμοία (V, followed by Cobet) and ὅμοιον.

(20 γυναικὶ τάλαντα] γυναικὶ ι' (=δέκα) τάλαντα, Cobet.)

20 f τάλαντα εἰσενεγκαμένῃ ἐξ, ἐξ ἧς παιδίον αὐτῷ γέγονε] V τάλαντα εἰσενέγκαμεν ἢ προῖκα ἐξ ἧς παιδίον αὐτῷ γεννᾷ (sic: in marg. γέγονε). Petersen emends thus: τάλαντα εἰσενεγκαμένῃ προῖκα ἐξ, ἥ τε παιδίον αὐτῷ γεννᾷ His restoration of ἐξ is certain; but he ought to have seen that the very fact of its having dropped out is the strongest argument for the ἐξ ἧς of the MS. ἐξ dropped out *because* it was followed by ἐξ. (δέκα τάλαντα is proposed by Hanow. Immisch, in L, reads προῖκα, ἐξ οὗ παιδίον αὐτῷ γεννᾷ (V, with γέγονε in margin); ἐξ ἧς γεννᾷ is defended by Edmonds γεννᾷ is bracketed by Diels.)

(22 f. τῇ τοῦ Ποσειδῶνος ἡμέρᾳ] Ast, omitting τῇ and ἡμέρᾳ, prefers Ποσειδεῶνος, making it a general reference to the winter month of December-January, rather than a special reference to a particular day in that month.)

(24. ἀναστάντος εἰπεῖν] ἐξαναστάντος <κακῶς> εἰπεῖν Cobet.)

25 τοὺς οἰκείους αὐτοῦ λοιδορῆσαι] So Foss (and L), with V (which originally had λοιδορεῖσθαι). Other MSS have λοιδορεῖσθαι If we read this (as Ussing and Petersen do), τοὺς οἰκείους ought probably to be altered to τοῖς οἰκείοις, since the Middle λοιδορεῖσθαι almost invariably takes a *dat.* of the object. (Ussing and Cobet insert τοῦ before τοὺς)

(26. κακὰ εἰπεῖν] *delet Hanow, quo glossemate inlato, αὐτοῦ intercidisse putat Diels.* (25) περὶ τῶν <αὐτοῦ> φίλων conieceret Herwerden (L).)

27 κακῶς λέγειν ἀποκαλῶν παρρησίαν] I follow Foss in placing the comma at τελευτηκότων, and not at λέγειν, for two reasons (1) an accus. in apposition with παρρησίαν, δημοκρατίαν, ἐλευθερίαν is required, this is supplied by (τὸ) κακῶς λέγειν. (2) We usually find κακῶς λέγειν τινά, but κακὰ λέγειν περί τινος. ⟨L has the same punctuation. Herwerden and Edmonds propose <τὸ> κακῶς λέγειν.⟩

28. ποιῶν] So V and Foss (and L). Petersen and Ussing, ποιεῖν.

29. ὁ τῆς δυσκολίας ἐρεθισμὸς] V ὁ τῆς διδασκαλίας ἐρεθισμός. For διδασκαλίας Ussing suggests διαβολίας (a merely poetical form); Coray κακολογίας, but this is utterly improbable Hottinger's δυσκολίας seems most likely. The copyist began δι—, then, seeing his mistake, started

afresh but, as he did not erase the former, διδασκαλίας arose out of [δι]δυσκολίας. If the whole comment is spurious, the want of necessary connexion between κακολογία and δυσκολία is no proof that the latter word did not stand here. (For διδασκαλίας Diels proposes ἰδίας κακίας. The comment is transferred by Hanow to the end of c. VIII (XXVII), ὀψιμαθίας.)

XXII (XVII)

1 f ἐπιτίμησις παρὰ τὸ προσῆκον τῶν δεδομένων] V has περὶ τῶν προσηκῶς δεδομένον, from which Foss gets περὶ τῶν προσηνῶς δεδομένων. But προσηκῶς is, as Ast points out, merely a corruption of προσηκόντως, and this of προσῆκον τῶν. (It is stated by Diels that V really has παρὰ τῶν προσήκ^τ, where the accent over η implies the reading προσήκοντα, and that over κτ the correction προσηκόντων. Following the latter clue, Diels independently proposes παρὰ τὸ προσῆκον τῶν δεδομένων.)

3 (ἐφθόνησάς μοι] Pauw's conjecture ἐφθόνησέ μοι is adopted by L and Wilamowitz.)

5 οὐ διότι οὐχ ὕει] οὐχ before ὕει is wanting in the MSS (and is omitted by L and Wilamowitz) It was first inserted by Needham, who is followed by Ast, Sheppard and Ussing.

8 εἴ τι ὑγιὲς] So Petersen and Ussing. The MSS have ὅτι, which Foss takes from ὅστις (ὅ τι is also preferred in L.)

11. ἄπεστιν] Two MSS have ἀπέστην, which Petersen prints, and which Coray thought might have arisen from ἀπέστη (ἀπέπτη Naber, ἀπέσβη F. W. Schmidt, ἀπόλωλεν Cobet, ἀπέθανεν Blaydes.)

15 ὅτε δεῖ τἀργύριον—ὀφείλειν] So (on Casaubon's conjecture) Ast, Sheppard, Ussing.—Foss keeps the MSS ὅτι, which Meier defended; but admits that ὅτε is a good emendation. (ὅτι is also retained in L)

XXIII (XVIII)

(1. ἀπιστία] <ἡ> ἀπιστία Buecheler, followed by L and others.)

4 f. καὶ φέρειν αὐτὸς τὸ ἀργύριον καὶ κατὰ στάδιον καθίζων ἀριθμεῖν] The MSS have φέρων, which Ussing keeps, omitting the καί before κατὰ στάδιον (L does the same.) It seems better, with Coray, Foss and Petersen, to read φέρειν

7 κυλικούχιον] Vulg. κοιλιούχιον. V κυλιούχιον, and so Petersen and Ussing (and L) Sylburg and Foss κυλικούχιον (Sylburg, approved by Naber, also proposed κλειδούχιον. Blumner suggests δακτυλιούχιον.)

11. ὕπνου τυγχάνειν] Ast inserts here, Foss after ἔξαρνοι γενέσθαι, the clause καὶ τοὺς ὅρους δέ. διαμένουσιν οἱ αὐτοί which usu stands in c. XXIV (X). As Meier shows, it need not be moved.

12 δύνωνται] I do not see how the δύναιντο of the vulgate, which

the editors pass by in silence, can stand. In those cases where ὅπως with opt. has reference to present time, the peculiarity is explained by attraction to a preceding optative: e.g. Aesch. *Eum.* 288, ἔλθοι—ὅπως γένοιτο τῶνδ' ἐμοὶ λυτήριος 'may Athene come that she may prove my deliverer from these things'—where γένηται might have been expected, but γένοιτο is allowed on account of ἔλθοι cf. Soph. *Ai.* 1222, *Phil.* 324. Here no such explanation is possible.

(13. **ἐκδοῦναι**] πλῦναι is added by Hirschig and Meineke (*L*). (Cp. XXV 14; XXVI 17.) ὅς for ὡς is due to Salmasius.)

(14. **γναφέως**] The manuscript reading is κναφέως in the present passage, and γναφεῖς in XXIV 26 with the variants κναφεῖς and κναφεῖς. κναφεὺς was the old Attic form, γναφεὺς the new; Schol. on Ar. *Plutus*, 166. In inscriptions, κναφεὺς (cent. VI) and Κνίφων (cent. V) are succeeded by γναφεῖον (cent. IV) and Γνίφων (cent. IV, III). In the former ed., as in *L*, κναφέως was printed here, and γναφεῖς in XXIV; in the present ed. the form used in the age of Theophrastus is adopted in both passages.)

16. **μόνον οὐ πυρώσας**] This is the reading of V (which alone gives the clause from ἂν δ' ἄρα το χρήσει, for χρῆσαι); and I see no good reason for disturbing it. πυροῦσθαι is used of gold standing the test of fire, Arist. *Hist. An.* III 5. If it was said that the ἄπιστος actually submitted his cups to this test, there would be reason to suspect the text. But it says μόνον οὐ πυρώσας. It is no more meant that he actually puts them through the fire than that he actually weighs them, or takes security. He only looks as if he would like to do all three things. It is merely a humorous hyperbole to express his extreme reluctance to grant the loan.—Elaborate attempts have been made to emend πυρώσας. Orelli and Foss independently conjectured, for μόνον οὐ πυρώσας, ὄνομ' ἐντυπώσας, 'having graven his name on the cups.' Foss and Petersen give in their texts μόνον ἐντυπώσας, understanding ὄνομα or something of the kind. Coray suggested ποσώσας. If a conjecture was to be made, a better one would, I think, have been μόνον οὐχ ὁρκώσας. but no conjecture is needed.

19. **αὐτὸν**] So Needham, Ast, Sheppard, Foss, Ussing. (αὐτῷ V: αὐτῷ Petersen.)

20 f. **πόσον; κατάθου**] MSS, πόσου κατάθου This probably corrupt passage is perhaps the most difficult in the Characters. The words μηδὲν πραγματεύου—συνακολουθήσω, found in the best MS, cannot on any sound principle of criticism be rejected as spurious, and it is clear that they represent the answer of the ἄπιστος to the buyer. κατάθου, then, is

said by the buyer; but in what sense? I follow Schneider, Foss and Petersen in rendering it *refer in tabulas*. Cf. pseudo-Demosth. p. 1401 · ταῦτα δὲ πάντα γέγραπται τὸν τρόπον ὅν τις ἂν εἰς βιβλίον καταθεῖτο. Schneider's view of the passage generally also seems to me, on the whole, the best. Three others should be noticed :—(1) Ast, following Casaubon and Coray, rejects μηδὲν πραγματεύου—συνακολουθήσω altogether. He reads ποσοῦ· κατάθου, οὐ γὰρ σχολάζω πέμπειν :—i.e. '*Buyer.* Reckon up the amount (and enter it in your books). *Seller.* Pay down; I have not time to send (to your house) for the money.' (2) Foss and Petersen differ from Schneider in reading πόσον (act imper. of ποσοῦν) καὶ κατάθον, '*Reckon up the amount* and put it down,' instead of πόσον, κατάθον. (3) Ussing understands the passage, not of buying, but of borrowing. For πόσον κατάθου he would read something like πόσον χρόνον ἔτι κατέχω, A person who has borrowed something from the ἄπιστος says 'How much longer may I keep it? for I have not time to send it just yet.' (*L* has πόσον, κατάθου. Madvig proposes. ποῦ σοι καταθῶ, οὐ γὰρ σχολάζω εἰπεῖν· μηδὲν πραγματεύου· ἐγὼ γὰρ ἕως ἂν σὺ σχολάσῃς, συνακολουθήσω)

21. <εἰπεῖν>] inserted conjecturally by Casaubon, Foss, Petersen and Ussing Schneider inserted λέγειν.

22. ἂν σὺ μὴ σχολάσῃς] The μή, first inserted by Schneider, is adopted by Foss and Petersen (but not by *L*) The sense seems to require it, as Ast saw, but he rejected the whole sentence.

XXIV (X)

(1. ἡ δὲ μικρολογία ἐστὶ] ἔστι δὲ ἡ μικρολογία *L*, with A and B)

(3. ἐλθὼν] omitted by *L*, with A and B ἀπαιτεῖν ἐπιτοκίαν, for ἐπὶ τὴν οἰκίαν, is proposed by Unger and accepted by Fraenkel and Groeneboom)

(3 συσσιτῶν] ὁ συσσιτῶν (AB) suggests ὁμοσιτῶν (Dietrich), accepted by *L*. ξένους ἑστιῶν Naber)

(4. τὰς κύλικας] τε κοίλικας (B) : τε κύλικας (A and *L*).)

6 πάντα φάσκειν εἶναι ἄγαν] So Ast, Foss and Ussing The best MSS have φάσκων, and omit ἄγαν From Ast's note, however, and from the fact that Foss prints it without comment, I infer that there is other authority for it. (No authority is given in *L*) Ussing prints it in smaller type, as a conjectural supplement. (*L* prints πάντα φάσκων εἶναι ** Unger proposes πάντα φάσκειν <ὤνια> εἶναι. Edmonds, πάντα φάσκειν <ἐν ἴσῳ> εἶναι. Diels, περιττὰ φάσκων εἶναι)

7. χύτραν ἢ λοπάδα] After χύτραν the two Paris MSS have εἶναι, out of which Petersen gets παλαιάν It seems more likely that it has merely

come in by mistake from the last clause. (Edmonds suggests χύτραν ἔνην, 'last year's pot or dish')

8. ἐκβαλούσης] So, with the best MSS, Foss, Petersen and Ussing (and L) Cf. c XVII (XI) ἐκβαλεῖν τὸ ποτήριον. There is in Greek no word which precisely renders our 'to *drop*' (accidentally). This must, in strictness, be expressed by a periphrasis with πίπτειν But ἐκβάλλειν seems to have been conventionally used *nearly* in that sense: see *Il.* XIV 419 etc Ast, with some inferior MSS, reads ἀποβαλούσης (proposed by Naber), which would have a more general meaning, 'having lost': and is less graphic than ἐκβαλούσης   (13. ἐλᾴαν] ἐλαίαν L.)

(13. φοίνικα] regarded as corrupt by Cobet, on the ground that 'there were no date-palms in Greece'; but Greek dates are expressly mentioned by Xenophon, *Anab.* II III 15, though they were inferior to the foreign varieties on which Theophrastus enlarges in *Hist Plant.* II VI 6—11, and failed to become ripe; cp. Xen. *Cyrop* VI 2, 22, Plut. *Mor.* 723 C D. Diels, *Theophrastea*, 10, suspects an Asiatic interpolator)

15 f ὑπερημερίαν πρᾶξαι καὶ τόκον τόκου ἀπαιτῆσαι] ἀπαιτῆσαι, added in some MSS, is omitted by L.

18. χρῆσαι] MSS χρωννύειν, but one χρωνύειν, and one ῥωννύειν. Ast and Schneider read χρᾶν· Casaubon conj. χρᾶν τινί. others χρᾶν οὐδενί, μηδενί, or ἑνί But χράω, in the sense of lending, occurs only in the fut. and aor. for the present Dem. p. 1250 uses κίχρημι and so κίχρασθαι c. XXVI (XXX) Foss, from a 'glossarium ἀνέκδοτον,' gives χρηννύειν, (followed by L), and in c. VII (XXI) a kindred form χρηννύναι[1]. Neither has much probability In the absence of any likely emendation, I have given χρῆσαι, in order at least to represent what was probably the sense. (κιχράναι Cobet.)

(19   οὐλὰς] ὀλὰς Munich Epitome, L)

20. θυλήματα] So Ast and Foss (and L) The word is known from Ar. *Pax* 1040. Petersen and Ussing keep the MSS θυηλήματα, which does not occur elsewhere; and θυηλή is a poetical form (But, as Diels points out, θυηλήματα has since been found in a Milesian inscription edited by Wilamowitz in the Berlin *Sitzungsberichte*, 1904, p 617 ; cp Stengel in *Hermes*, XXXIX 614.)

21—27. (καὶ τὸ ὅλον—ῥυπαίνηται ταχύ] regarded by Edmonds as a spurious addition)

22   καὶ κλεῖς] The variant τὰς κλεῖς suggests καὶ τὰς κλεῖς (L).

(23   ἰωμένας] perf part. from ἰόω, the present ἰουμένας is preferred by Blaydes)

---

[1] (Diels, *Theophrastea*, p 16 n , quotes χρηννύειν and ἐπιχρήννυται, or ἐπιχρείννυντο, from a passage ascribed to cent. X in a *lex Rhodia*.)

CHARACTERS XXIV, XXV

25. ὑπολυομένους] So Ast and Foss, with several MSS. As ὑπολυομένους in this context can be exactly illustrated from Aristophanes (see Note), it is astonishing that Petersen and Ussing (and L) keep ὑποδυομένους, which, it may be safely said, is nonsense. Ussing explains it 'medio die, quo tempore ceteri in publico versantur, *latebras quaerunt domique se condunt*, ne in vestimentorum elegantiam sumptus faciant' It means, then, 'slinking into concealment!' (ὑποδουμένους B: ὑποδομένους A. Similarly in Plutarch, *De audiendis poetis*, 24 D, καταδυσαμένους was wrongly written for καταλυσαμένους, cp. Nauck, Eur. Fragm. 994, ed. 1889.)

XXV (XXII)

1 f περιουσία τις ἀφιλοτιμίας ἐς δαπάνην ἔχουσα] MSS περιουσία τις ἀπὸ φιλοτιμίας δαπάνην ἔχουσα. I follow Casaubon, Ast and others in correcting ἀπὸ φιλοτιμίας to ἀφιλοτιμίας (a word used by Aristotle); and Ussing in inserting ἐς before δαπάνην. Schweighauser's ἀπουσία τις φιλοτιμίας has been tacitly adopted by Ussing. Foss reads περιουσία τις ἀποφιλοτιμίας δαπάνης ἔχουσα· but it is hard to believe in Fischer's ἀποφιλοτιμία, or that ἔχουσα could, in prose, stand with a genit. for ἀπέχουσα Ast proposes ἀπέχουσα. Casaubon's δαπάνην φεύγουσα is tempting, but, as Ast says, 'a vulgatae scripturae ductibus nimis recedit.' (Holland, one of the editors of L, suggests περιουσία τις <φιλοχρηματίας> ἀπὸ <ἀ>φιλοτιμίας δαπάνην ἐλλείπουσα. Diels proposes ἀπουσία τις [ἀπὸ] φιλοτιμίας δαπάνην ἐχούσης.)

3 τραγῳδοῖς] Foss and Petersen retain the manuscript reading τραγῳδούς: but Casaubon's correction, τραγῳδοῖς, is undoubtedly right. Compare the common phrase καινοῖς τραγῳδοῖς, '*at the representation of the new tragedies*' (also Lysias, *Or* XXIV § 10, κατασταθεὶς χορηγὸς τραγῳδοῖς, and *C. I. A.* IV, 2, 1280[b], ἑτέρα νίκη τραγῳιδοῖς). similarly, in Cic. *Epp.* X 31 *gladiatoribus = ludis gladiatoriis*

3. ἐπιγραψάμενος] I have little doubt that Schneider was right in thinking that this was the true correction of the ἐπιγράψας μέν of V (retained by L): 'having caused (midd.) his name to be inscribed upon it.' I do not think that μέν could stand as a sarcastic comment upon the fact that, shabby as was the offering, he yet took care to secure credit for it. Petersen tries to get this sense by writing μήν. Ussing more boldly μηδ᾽, but this seems plainly wrong. The ἀνελεύθερος is one who wants to get as much glory as possible for his money. He would not fail to record his victory, but he would record it cheaply. (Madvig proposes ἐπιγράψας μέλανι, approved by Gomperz.)

4 f. ἐκ τοῦ δήμου] The MSS agree on this, and I have left it, as it

can be taken with ἀναστάς. But I strongly suspect that we ought to read ἐν τῷ δήμῳ, referring to γινομένων. Ussing wanted τῷ δήμῳ, referring to ἐπιδόσεων. (The editors of *L* take ἐκ τοῦ δήμου with γινομένων)

5. σιωπῇ] Needham's correction of σιωπᾶν (retained by *L*).

6 πλὴν τῶν ἱερωσύνων] V has πλὴν τῶν ἱερέων: the other MSS πλὴν τῶν ἱερείων. Meier's conjecture ἱερωσύνων (cp. *C. I. A.* II 631), 'the parts reserved for the priest,' has been adopted by Dubner, Hartung and Foss See Ameipsias *ap.* Athen. IX, p. 368 E, δίδοται μάλισθ' ἱερώσυνα | κωλῆ, τὸ πλευρόν, ἡμίκραιρ' ἀριστερά, 'the ham, the ribs, and the left side of the face.' Bekker *Anecd.* p. 44: ἱερώσυνα· τὰ τοῖς θεοῖς ἐξαιρούμενα μέρη. Casaubon's ἱερῶν is adopted by Ussing Petersen reads on his own conj. μηρίων. (The editors of *L* retain ἱερέων in the text, but suggest γερῶν, 'gifts of honour,' in the notes.)

11. ὅταν ᾖ Μουσεῖα] After ὅταν ᾖ V (which alone has this clause) inserts τοῦ ἀποτιθέναι καὶ τὰ παιδία, which is now universally rejected as a confused repetition of what has preceded.

(13. καὶ τὰ λάχανα] καὶ (V) is omitted by *L*, with certain MSS.) Diels has ἐξ ἀγορᾶς δὲ ὀψωνήσας [τὰ κρέα] αὐτὸς φέρειν τὰ λάχανα.)

(15. διειλεγμένον] διηγγελμένου is suggested by Holland (in *L*).)

16 τὴν κύκλῳ] These words occur only in V: but Foss and Ussing seem right in regarding them as genuine. Cf. Plat. *Lysis* p. 203 A, πορεύεσθαι τὴν ἔξω τείχους. Petersen emends ἀποκάμψαι (for -ας) ἐκ τῆς ὁδοῦ καὶ (for τὴν) κύκλῳ οἴκαδε πορευθῆναι.

(17. προῖκα εἰσενεγκαμένη] as in XXI 20. Cobet proposes ἐπενεγκαμένη, as in Lysias XIX 14, Aeschin. *Ctes* 172, etc)

18 f ἐκ τῆς γυναικείας] So V, the sole authority here. Cobet, *Variae Lectiones*, p. 204, observes that ἀγορᾶς is to be supplied. Meier also defends it; and Petersen and Ussing receive it into their texts. Foss boldly writes εἰς τὰς ἐξόδους τὰς γυναικείας

20. παλιμπήξει] V πάλιν πήξει. Schneider was the first to write παλιμπήξει.

21 f. τὴν οἰκίαν ἐκκορῆσαι καὶ τὰς κλίνας καλλῦναι] The MSS have οἰκίαν καλλῦναι—κλίνας ἐκκορῆσαι and so Petersen and Ussing. Pauw's transposition of the verbs is adopted by Ast and Foss. (The order of the MSS is retained in *L*, where ἐκκορίσαι is adopted, as proposed by Casaubon and Coray.)

22 f. (ὃν αὐτὸς φορεῖ] Munsterberg, approved by Gomperz, proposes ὃν αὐτὸν φορεῖ, 'the only garb that he wears'; cp Aelian, *Var. Hist* VII 13, Ἀγησίλαος ἀνυπόδητος πολλάκις καὶ ἀχίτων προῄει, τὸν τρίβωνα περιβαλόμενος αὐτόν)

XXVI (XXX)

This chapter (usu. xxx) is found complete only in V · but the passage καὶ οἰνοπωλῶν—μὴ λάβωσι (6—33) stands, in those MSS which contain only the first 15 Characters, in the chapter on βδελυρία (usu. XI, in this ed. XVII). V places that passage here, inserting in it two additional clauses, viz. (1) καὶ ἱμάτιον ἐκδοῦναι—πλείους ἡμέρας (17 f). (2) καὶ τῶν υἱῶν δὲ μὴ πορευομένων—παρὰ τοῦ χειρίζοντος (23—30)

1. περιουσία κέρδους αἰσχροῦ] So the MS. Ast says that the peculiarity consists in περιουσία standing for *nimia cupiditas*. It consists rather, I think, in κέρδος standing for *cupiditas lucri*. Cf. Soph. *Ant.* 222, ἄνδρας τὸ κέρδος πολλάκις διώλεσεν, 'the *desire of* gain has often ruined men' Foss reads on his conj. περιποίησις, which means 'affectation of,' rather than 'effort to get.' Schneider inserted ἐπιθυμίας after περιουσία—clumsily. Hartung boldly, ἀπουσία φιλοτιμίας κέρδους ἕνεκα αἰσχροῦ. Probably αἰσχροῦ is a spurious addition. (For περιουσία, written ΠΟΥϹΙΔ, Cobet proposes ἐπιθυμία, written ΕΘΥΜΙΔ.)

(3. αὐτῷ] αὑτῷ is preferred by Edmonds.)

5. διμοιρίαν] So Petersen and Ussing: V διμοίρῳ (retained by *L*, and altered by Amaduzzi into δίμοιρον, which is accepted by Wilamowitz). The word διμοιρία is common. δίμοιρον, in this sense, is unknown.

(7. υἱεῖς] AB. υἱούς *L*.)

8. προῖκα ἐφιᾶσιν] Vulg. ἀφιᾶσιν (retained by *L*): but I think with Petersen and Ussing that ἐφιᾶσιν (sc. προῖκα θεᾶσθαι) is right.

8. οἱ θεατρῶναι] AB etc.: ἐπὶ θεάτρων V, ἐπιθέατρον Holland (*L*). (ἐπιθέατρον, 'a gallery,' is found in a Delian inscription of the 3rd century B.C., *Bull Corr. Hell.* XVIII 164.)

13. εἰπών] Ast, Foss and Ussing omit the καί of the vulg. before εἰπών, which Cobet alters into εἴπας, an alteration adopted by *L* and Wilamowitz.

(14. τῷ παιδαρίῳ] Cobet prefers εἴπας, σαπρόν γε τοὔλαιον, παιδάριον, and *L* prints παιδάριον.)

19 Φειδωνίῳ μέτρῳ] V φειδομένῳ (*L*, cp Alciphr. III 57, φειδωλῷ τῷ μέτρῳ): vulg. φειδωνίῳ, which is probably right, and which Ast and Ussing retain. (Φειδωνείῳ, Cobet and Wilamowitz.) See Notes.

19. τὸν πύνδακα ἐγκεκρουμένῳ] πύνδακα ἐκκεκρουμένῳ vulg.: ἐγκεκρουσμένῳ Casaubon (*L*). (πύνδακα εἰσκεκρουμένῳ is preferred by Edmonds.)

20. σφόδρα ἀποψῶν] (Cp. Pollux, IV 170.) In the vulgate these

words stand after τὰ ἐπιτήδεια. V has σφόδρα δὲ ὑποσπῶν before τὰ ἐπιτήδεια (*L*). With Ussing I follow the vulgate for the words, and V as regards their place.

20—22 καὶ ὑποπρίασθαι φίλου δοκοῦντος πρὸς τρόπου πωλεῖν, καὶ ἐπιβαλὼν ἀποδόσθαι] A passage too corrupt to be restored with much probability. The vulgate has simply ὑποπρίασθαι φίλου ἐπιλαβὼν ἀποδόσθαι: V, ὑποπρίασθαι φίλου δοκοῦντος πρὸς τρόπου πολεῖσθαι (*L*, marking the sentence as corrupt) I follow Ast and Foss in their general view of the sense, and in attempting to combine the vulgate and V. Ast proposes ὑποπριάσθαί τι, φίλου διδόντος πρὸς τρόπου, καὶ ἐπιβαλὼν ἀποδόσθαι 'he buys a thing privately, when a friend offers it on reasonable terms, and, having added to the price, sells it.' Foss, ὑποπρίασθαι φίλου δεδωκότος πρὸς τρόπου πωλεῖσθαι· εἶτα ἐπιλαβὼν ἀποδόσθαι i.e 'when a friend allows it *to be sold* reasonably.' In two points I would keep closer to the MSS (1) in retaining δοκοῦντος: (2) instead of inserting εἶτα, I should write πωλεῖν καί for πωλεῖσθαι. The awkward passive is thus got rid of, and the loss of καί explained. Coray's ἐπιβαλών for ἐπιλαβών may be supported from Arist *Polit* 1 11, 9, where ἐπιβάλλειν means to 'bid higher,' lit. 'to add to the price.' But the blot is πρὸς τρόπου. I much doubt whether πρὸς τρόπου πωλεῖν could mean 'to sell on reasonable terms,' though πρὸς τρόπου λέγειν (Plat. *Rep* p. 470 c) means 'to speak reasonably.' The corruption probably lies deep. (Other suggestions are quoted in *L*, p 266. Cobet, followed by Wilamowitz, proposes ὑποπρίασθαι φίλου δοκοῦντος πρὸς τρόπου τι ὠνεῖσθαι, εἶτα λαβὼν ἀποδόσθαι)

22. ἀμέλει δὲ καὶ χρέος] So the vulgate, which Ussing seems right in following. ἀμέλει, in these Characters, often adds spirit to the mention of an especially striking trait—here to the notice of a *very* shabby little artifice. '*It is just like him to* ..' Petersen without comment gives καὶ χρέη δέ (with V): Foss καὶ χρέος δέ.

24. τὸν μῆνα ὅλον] Ast leaves out these words, and reads below τὸν Ἀνθεστηριῶνα τὸν ὅλον.

29 f παρὰ τοῦ χειρίζοντος *** καὶ φράτορας] Ast, Foss and Ussing leave the lacuna in V after τοῦ χειρίζοντος without attempting to explain it. Ussing says : 'desiderari aliquid apparet ; nam necessario indicandum est quid administraverit ille quicum rationes putat.' (*L* follows V in omitting καί, in placing a lacuna after φράτορας, and also in omitting ἑστιῶν αἰτεῖν.)

36. συναγόντων παρ' αὐτῷ ἀποθεῖναι] The MS has παρ' ἑαυτῷ ὑποθεῖναι (*L*) Ast's correction is adopted by Foss and Ussing. The latter seems right in omitting παρ' ἑαυτοῦ before διδομένων (retained by *L* and

Wilamowitz): it was probably the mere error of a copyist whose eye had wandered back to παρ' ἑαυτῷ Foss seems right in altering ἑαυτῷ to αὐτῷ. (Unger proposes παρ' ἑκάστου διδομένων.)

40 <μὴ> πέμψῃ] So Ussing (and *L*): V has προπέμψῃ,—the προ probably from the line before, πρὸ χρόνου τινός. (προπέμψῃ is retained by Wilamowitz, and defended by Edmonds:—'so that he may *send a present beforehand*,' instead of taking it himself on the proper day; this would enable him to get off with a cheaper present.) Foss's προσπέμψῃ (apparently first proposed by Coray) is improbable.—μή, first added by Amaduzzi, the earliest editor of V, is obviously wanted by the sense.

XXVII (XXV)

(2 **ἔμφοβος**] Edmonds proposes ἐν φόβῳ or ἐν φόβοις, ἔμφοβος, in the sense of 'frightened,' being a late word.)

(3 f. εἴ τις μὴ μεμύηται τῶν πλεόντων] Blaydes omits μή, comparing Ar. *Pax* 276. Cobet prefers συμπλεόντων.)

4 f. καὶ τοῦ κυβερνήτου †ἀνακύπτων μὲν† πυνθάνεσθαι εἰ μεσοπορεῖ] ἀνακύπτων μέν is the reading of the best MS, V, and is printed by Foss, Petersen and Ussing. If it is right, it means, as Ussing says, that the δειλός had either covered his head or taken refuge below decks. 'et μέν importunum, ut ait Schneider, necessario delendum.' The inferior MSS have ἀνακύπτοντος αἰσθάνεσθαι. Ussing suggests that τοῦ κυβερνήτου ἀνακύπτοντος might mean, 'when the steersman raises his head,' in order to see over something which obstructs his view. (This is accepted by Wilamowitz, in the sense of 'gazing up into the sky to observe the stars.') The πυνθάνεσθαι of V must of course be retained. But besides the oddness of ἀνακύπτοντος in this sense, there is a further objection· εἰ μεσοπορεῖ must then mean 'whether he is steering the middle course'· 'diligentiam videas gubernatoris *in angusto freto* versantis' (Ussing). Now μεσοπορεῖν naturally means 'to be in middle course', in another sense—that of 'having come half way' So Diod. XVIII 34, μεσοπορούντων δ' αὐτῶν, 'in the middle of their voyage : and so Menander (4. 320) used it. Clearly the Coward asks 'whether they are half-way yet' (Wilamowitz understands μεσοπορεῖν as διὰ μέσης τῆς θαλάττης πορεύεσθαι, in contrast to the more cautious custom of hugging the shore.) The other MSS have ἀνακόπτοντος, which Casaubon understands to mean 'when the steersman *changes the ship's course*, the Coward asks whether he is keeping in mid-channel.' To this there are two objections. (1) that just stated—the sense given to μεσοπορεῖ (2) the sense of ἀνακόπτοντος ἀνακόπτειν ναῦν might, perhaps, have the

meaning of ἀνακρούεσθαι, 'to *back* the ship': compare the pass., said of a hesitating speaker, Luc. *Nigr* 35, ἐξέπιπτόν τε καὶ ἀνεκοπτόμην, 'I began to blunder and retract': and Arat. *Phaenom*. 346, quoted by Ast, ἀνακόπτει νῆα, 'quod Germanicus vertit, *inhibet iam navita remos*.' But I do not see how it could mean 'to change the ship's course' in any other way than by backing, nor how it could be said of the steersman. It would properly be applied, as by Aratus, to the rowers.

8. αὐτόν] So Ast and Ussing.—Foss and Petersen (and *L*) αὑτόν· Foss placing only a comma at χιτωνίσκον, to which he makes αὑτόν refer But surely the δειλός is more anxious for his life than for his clothes.

8—10. καὶ στρατευόμενος δὲ πεζῇ τοὺς ἐκβοηθοῦντάς τε προσκαλεῖν κελεύων πρὸς αὐτὸν στάντας πρῶτον περιιδεῖν] Vulgate, καὶ στρατευόμενος δὲ προσκαλεῖν πάντας πρὸς αὐτὸν καὶ στάντας πρῶτον περιιδεῖν V, καὶ στρατευόμενος δὲ πεζοῦ (ῇ superscr.) ἐκβοηθοῦντός τε προσκαλεῖν κελεύων πρὸς αὐτὸν στάντας πρῶτον περιιδεῖν (retained in *L*, with a lacuna after ἐκβοηθοῦντος). Ussing adopts the correction πεζῇ for πεζοῦ in V, and for ἐκβοηθοῦντος writes τοὺς ἐκβοηθοῦντας: in this I follow him, but not in putting πρὸς αὐτόν (MS αὑτόν) before κελεύων it can go with στάντας as well as with προσκαλεῖν Foss differs from Ussing only in omitting τοὺς (which, however, seems necessary) and in leaving πρὸς αὐτόν, as I do, in its place. Petersen proposes merely to write ἐκβοηθοῦντος τοῦ πεζοῦ for πεζοῦ ἐκβοηθοῦντός τε. One objection to this is that part of τὸ πεζόν is already fighting; it is to a small support-party that the Coward addresses himself Ast takes the vulgate, simply omitting στάντας, and, as usual, despising V. But πάντας is plainly wrong.

(11. πότεροι] The variant πότερόν is preferred by *L*.)

12. εἰπών] εἴπας Ilberg (*L*)· some MSS have εἰπεῖν.

14 καὶ τὸν παῖδα ἐκπέμψας] The καί is inserted conjecturally by Foss and Ussing.

(16 f. ὡς ζητῶν ἐν τῇ σκήνῃ· καὶ ὁρῶν] ὡς ζητῶν· καὶ ἐν τῇ σκήνῃ ὁρῶν *L*.)

22. <εἰπεῖν>} is not in the MSS, but is supplied by all the editors.

26. διηγεῖσθαι ὡς κινδυνεύσας ἕνα σέσωκα τῶν φίλων] So V, Foss, Petersen, Ussing. Vulg. διηγεῖσθαι ὡς κινδυνεύσας, ὡς σέσωκε τῶν φίλων. Foss and Petersen take κινδυνεύσας with σέσωκα, Ussing (and *L*) with διηγεῖσθαι ὡς. (This is confirmed by a comma after κινδυνεύσας in V. Casaubon and Cobet preferred σέσωκε.)

CHARACTERS XXVII, XXVIII

XXVIII (XVI)

2. ἐπὶ κρήνῃ] V has ἐπιχρωνῆν (which L prints, but marks as corrupt. Edmonds proposes ἐπ' Ἐννεακρούνου). The other MSS contain nothing corresponding to it, but read simply οἷος ἀπονιψάμενος τὰς χεῖρας. Siebenkees corrected ἐπιχρωνῆν to ἐπὶ κρήνην, which Schneider adopted,—saying, however, that he would prefer either ἀπὸ κρήνης or ἐπὶ κρήνην <ἐλθὼν καὶ> ἀπονιψάμενος. In the absence of any probable emendation, I give the dative. cf Od. XIII 408, ἐπὶ κρήνῃ, 'at a fountain'—Petersen ingeniously proposes ἔτι πρὼ ἤδη: Foss boldly prints ἐπὶ χοῶν που <γενόμενος> ἀπονιψάμενος τὰς χεῖρας, κ.τ.λ.: 'when he has been anywhere at the offering of libations to the dead.'—I once thought of εἴ τι ἔχρανεν, 'when anything has defiled him' (ἐπὶ κρήνῃ was independently proposed by Madvig.)

6. ἕως διεξέλθῃ] So Petersen (and L), with all the MSS. Most of the other editors insert ἄν But the omission of ἄν in such cases, though commonest in poetry, is not confined to it Thuc. 1 137, μηδένα ἐκβῆναι ἐκ τῆς νεὼς μέχρι πλοῦς γένηται.

7—8. καὶ ἐὰν ἴδῃ ὄφιν ἐν τῇ οἰκίᾳ, ἐὰν μὲν παρείαν, Σαβάζιον καλεῖν, ἐὰν δὲ ἱερὸν, κ.τ.λ.] V alone has the words, ἐὰν (without μὲν) παρείαν, Σαβάδιον (sic) καλεῖν, ἐὰν δὲ ἱερόν, .. (and so L, but with Σαβάζιον) With Ussing I insert μέν before παρείαν. Foss compresses and alters the sentence thus:—καὶ ἐὰν παρείαν ἴδῃ ὄφιν ἐν τῇ οἰκίᾳ, Σαβάζιον καλεῖν, ἐὰν δ' ἐπ' ἠρίου ('on a grave'—for ἱερόν). (Cobet prefers καὶ ὅταν ἴδῃ κ.τ λ.)

8. ἐνταῦθα ἱερὸν εὐθὺς ἱδρύσασθαι] Vulg. ἱερὸν ἐνταῦθα ἱδρύσασθαι, V ἐνταῦθα ἱερῶν [sic, ι in *rasura*] εὐθὺς ἱδρύσασθαι. Ussing adopts ἱερῶν in the sense of *aediculam*: but surely it is a vox nihili Petersen (followed by L) has taken Dubner's conjecture ἡρῷον. but I do not see how that mends matters. With Foss, I leave ἱερόν It is probably corrupt, but, as being a word of general sense, it might possibly mean a small shrine or altar, and nothing better has been proposed.

11. ἀλφίτων] ἀλφίτην V: ἀλφιτηρὸν Cobet (L). (ἀλφίτων is defended by Xen. *Hellen.* I vii 11, Aristot. *Hist. An.* vi 36, Babrius 108, 16 f)

(12. διαφάγῃ] διατράγῃ Hirschig and Cobet)

(14. ἐκθύσασθαι] Bernard's correction for ἐκλύσασθαι. The latter is defended by Edmonds, who compares Pollux I 33, μύσος λύσασθαι, ἐκλύσασθαι.)

16 f. κἂν γλαὺξ βαδίζοντος αὐτοῦ ταράττηται, εἴπας, κ.τ.λ.] V (the sole authority for the sentence) has κἂν γλαύ'κ βαδίζοντος αὐτοῦ ταράττεται καὶ εἴπας, κ.τ.λ. Badham corrects γλαύ'κ to γλαῦξ, the indic. to subj.,

and omits καί; and, with Ussing, I have followed him. Petersen does so too, except that he keeps καί, and inserts δειδίττεται before it, since the Munich Epitome has ὁμοίως γλαῦκας δειδίττονται: but this seems very improbable Foss (and L), κἂν γλαῦκες βαδίζοντος αὐτοῦ <ἀνακράγωσι>, ταράττεσθαι, καὶ εἶπας (cp Menander, fr. 534, 11 K., ἂν γλαῦξ ἀνακράγῃ, δεδοίκαμεν. This is approved by Babick and Blaydes). Ast conjectured that ταράττεται should be changed to παρίπτηται, 'fly past.' (Edmonds suggests κἂν γλαῦκες βαδίζοντος αὐτοῦ <αὐτῶσι>. Diels states that V really has γλαυκ̈, i.e γλαῦκες.)

(17. **Ἀθηνᾶ κρείττων**] Ἀθηνᾶ κρείττω, in the sense of *di meliora*, is proposed by Meineke and Jahn, and approved by Eberhard, Babick, and Blaydes.)

(17. **οὕτω παρελθεῖν**] παρελθεῖν οὕτω L.)

(20 **ἑβδομάσι**] ἑβδόμαις <φθίνοντος> Immisch (L). ἑβδόμ<αις ἐπὶ ταῖς εἰκ>άσι Unger.)

21. **λιβανωτὸν, μίλακα**] V, which alone has this, λιβανωτῶν πίνακα. so Coray and Schneider, but with λιβανωτοῦ —Meier, λιβανωτὸν, στύρακα (*storax*, for incense). Foss, λιβανωτὸν, πόπανα, 'cakes' (cp. Athen. 146 E, ὁ λιβανωτὸς εὐσεβὲς | καὶ τὸ πόπανον). Petersen's μίλακα, which Ussing has adopted, seems best. see Notes. (σμίλακα is the form found in Theophrastus, *Hist. Plant.* III XVIII 11.)

22. **εἰσελθὼν εἴσω στεφανοῦν**] εἰσελθὼν εἴσω * στεφανῶν Hartung (L). (εἰσελθὼν εἴσω <θῦσαι> στεφανῶν is proposed by Edmonds, who compares Menander, *Geneva Fragm*, καταλαμβάνω τοὺς θεοὺς, στεφανουμένους, τὸν πατέρα θύοντ' ἔνδον)

26 **πορεύεσθαι**] πορευόμενος Immisch (L).

(28 f. **καὶ τῶν περιρραινομένων ἀπὸ θαλάττης ἐπιμελῶς δόξειεν ἂν εἶναι**] placed in L before the previous sentence:—κατὰ μῆνα πορευόμενος μετὰ τῆς γυναικὸς—ἐὰν δὲ μὴ σχολάζῃ ἡ γυνή, μετὰ τῆς τίτθης—καὶ τῶν παιδίων· —the punctuation proposed by Usener.)

29. **ἀπὸ θαλάττης**] Schneider's ἀπό for the ἐπί of V has been received by Foss, Ussing and most editors. Cf. supra, περιρρανάμενος ἀπὸ ἱεροῦ.

29—31. **κἄν ποτε ἐπίδῃ σκορόδων ἐστιώμενον τῶν ἐπὶ ταῖς τριόδοις, ἀπελθὼν κατὰ κεφαλῆς λούσασθαι**] V has κἄν ποτε ἐπίδῃ σκορόδῳ [sic] ἐστεμμένων τῶν ἐπὶ ταῖς τριόδοις ἐπελθόντων [corrected into ἀπ. by the same hand] κατὰ κ. λούσασθαι (followed by L, with σκορόδῳ and ἀπελθών). Vulg. καὶ ἐπὶ ταῖς τριόδοις ἀπελθὼν κατὰ κεφαλῆς λούσασθαι. Ast corrected σκορόδῳ to σκορόδων, and ἐπελθόντων to ἀπελθών. These corrections confirm each other; for, when the ν of σκορόδων was lost, ἀπελθών was changed to ἀπελθόντων for the sake of τῶν, and ἀπ. to ἐπ for the sake of τριόδοις Ast also changed ἐστεμμένων to ἐφημμένον, 'one who has fastened upon,' 'laid hands upon', and in this, too, is followed by Ussing. But ἐφημμένον seems improbable. Here I have ventured to adopt an emendation of my own, because it is so near at once to the MS and to the sense required, as to appear highly probable. To *eat* the garlic (?) and other refuse placed for 'Hecate's supper' at the cross-roads is often mentioned as an impiety to which hunger drove the poor : see Ar. *Plut.* 595, Plut. *de Superst.* 10, (Dem. *in Conon.* 39, τὰ Ἑκαταῖα κατεσθίειν) For ἐστεμμένων read ἐστιώμενον, 'feasting upon.' With σκορόδων ἐστιᾶσθαι, compare Ar. *Vesp* 1306, καχύων εὐωχημένον, and so Char. XX (VIII), εὐωχεῖν λόγων.—Foss gives σκορόδῳ ἐστεμμένον, and keeps ἐπελθόντων, altering ταῖς τριόδοις to τὰς τριόδους. Petersen takes a strange view of the passage He reads —κἄν ποτε ἐπίδῃ σκορόδῳ ἐστεμμένων τῶν ἐπὶ ταῖς τριόδοις Ἑκάτῃ θυόντων [for ἐπελθόντων], κατὰ κεφαλῆς λούσασθαι 'If [one of] those who are sacrificing to H. at the cross-roads, crowned with garlic, cast an [evil] eye on him,' etc. The words τριόδοις ἑκάτῃ θυόντων were first corrupted, he supposes, to τριοδοισεισαπελθοντων, and εἰς then omitted (Pet. *introd.* p 5.)

(31. ἱερείας] The masc ἱερέας is preferred by Auber, and ἱερέα by G A Hirschig, supported by Blaydes, who quotes Ar *Plutus*, 1182, ὁ δ' ἂν ἐκαλλιερεῖτό τις | κἀμέ γ' ἐκάλει τὸν ἱερέα.)

(31. σκίλλῃ ἢ σκύλακι—περικαθᾶραι] Cobet prefers σκίλλῃ καὶ δᾳδί—περικαθῆραι, and Blaydes quotes Diphilus, IV 416, Προιτίδας ἁγνίζων κούρας—δᾳδὶ μιᾷ σκίλλῃ τε μιᾷ and Lucian I 466, II 153)

(32. μαινόμενόν τε] μαινόμενον δὲ Blaydes (*L*).)

(33. εἰς κόλπον πτύσαι] Hirschig and Cobet would prefix τρίς.)

XXIX (XXVI)

(1 δόξειε δ' ἄν] δόξειεν δ' ἄν *L*, δ' is omitted in some MSS)

1 f. ἰσχύος, οὐ κέρδους γλιχομένη] Vulg. ἰσχυροῦ κέρδους γλιχομένους : V ἰσχυρῶς κέρδους γλιχομένη (*L*). The favourite mode of emending the passage has been by adopting Pauw's conjecture of κράτους for κέρδους. Thus Foss ἰσχυροῦ κράτους. Petersen and Ussing, ἰσχυρῶς κράτους This seems to me rash Casaubon saw that κέρδους was genuine, but that a *not* was required with it; the love of power for its own sake, as felt by the oligarch, being opposed to that love of power for the sake of money with which demagogues were so often—as in Ar. *Vesp.* 672—reproached. He conjectured ἰσχυρὰ, κέρδους οὐ γλιχομένη. But a simpler remedy is, I think, at hand. The ἰσχυροῦ of the vulgate merely conceals ἰσχύος, οὐ. For ἰσχύς in the sense of δύναμις, cf. Thuc. II 97, ἦλθεν ἡ βασιλεία ἐπὶ μέγα ἰσχύος. (ἰσχύος καὶ κέρδους is proposed by Edmonds, who

observes that the fragment in *Oxyrh. Pap.* IV, no. 699, has ἰσχύος followed by an obscure letter which may be κ. 'The rest of the line is torn away, but καὶ κέρδους would exactly fill the gap.')

(2. ἀλίγαρχος] Casaubon's conjecture, ὀλιγαρχικός, is preferred by Edmonds as filling the space left in the Oxyrh. papyrus.)

(3 τίνας] οὕστινας is preferred by Cobet, who in l. 4 would omit τοὺς before συνεπιμελησομένους.)

(12 f ἀρχαῖς πλησιάζοντας—τιμωμένους] Cobet proposes ἀρχαιρεσιάζοντας καὶ ὑπὸ τούτων <μᾶλλον> ὑβριζομένους ἢ τιμωμένους)

12—14. καὶ ὑπὸ τούτων ὑβριζομένους ἢ τιμωμένους· <καὶ> ὅτι ἢ τούτους δεῖ ἢ ἡμᾶς οἰκεῖν τὴν πόλιν] Vulg καὶ ὅτι ὑπὸ τινῶν ὑβριζόμενος εἰπεῖν, δεῖ αὐτοὺς κἀμὲ τὴν πόλιν οἰκεῖν: V καὶ ὑπὸ τούτων ὑβριζομένους ἢ τιμωμένους ὅτι ἢ τούτους δεῖ ἢ ὑμᾶς οἰκεῖν τὴν πόλιν. I have followed Ussing. Foss and Petersen read with Schneider ὑβριζομένους <καὶ> ἠτιμωμένους. There is no difficulty about the καί—for, if ἠτιμωμένους had been corrupted into ἢ τιμωμένους, it would naturally have been omitted; but the perfect tense is an objection. We should have expected ὑβριζομένους ἢ ἀτιμουμένους, esp. as a *series* of insults is referred to. I think with Ussing that ἢ τιμωμένους, which is the reading of V, gives better grammar and better sense. The oligarch is indignant that it should be in the power of the people to slight or to honour him at will, and scorns their favours as much as their affronts. αὐτούς, which is found only in V, probably came in from αὐτοὺς ἡμᾶς just before with Ussing I omit it.

14. κατὰ μέσον δὲ] So Ussing for καὶ τὸ μέσον δὲ: he also omits καὶ before τὸ ἱμάτιον (retained by *L*).

16 f σοβεῖν, τοὺς τοιούτους λόγους <λέγων, διὰ> τὴν τοῦ Ὠιδείου] Vulg σοβεῖν τοὺς τοιούτους λόγους· διὰ τοὺς συκοφ., κ.τ λ V σοβεῖν τοὺς τοιούτους λόγους τ(ὴν) τ(οῦ) ὠδίω. Preller's τὴν τοῦ Ὠιδείου is adopted by Foss and Petersen (Holland in *L* suggests <κατὰ> τὴν τοῦ Ὠιδείου)· Ussing despairs of the words, and does not print them. To govern λόγους, Ussing inserts λέγων, Foss ἀφιείς; Petersen suggests τοῖς τοι. λόγοις. How τὴν τοῦ Ὠδείου is to be governed, no one explains; for σοβεῖν certainly cannot govern it. I have inserted διά, which may have been lost through a confusion with the other διά immediately following. But I have not much faith in τὴν τοῦ Ὠιδείου itself, and suspect that the fault lies too deep to be got at now. (V has τὴν τοῦ ὠδίω, written τ̄ ο̄ ὠδιω. The excellent emendation, τραγῳδῶν, has, accordingly, been proposed by Herwerden and, independently, by Diels.)

(18 οἰκητέον] οἰκη, superscr τ΄ and ×ωρ, V, implying, as Diels suggests, an unwarrantable alternative, οἰκήτωρ: οἰκητὸν Cobet and *L*. Some MSS read οἰκητέον ἐστὶ τὴν πόλιν.)

CHARACTERS XXIX, XXX

(19. τῶν δικαζόντων] Schneider's correction of the Vulg δικαζομένων (which is retained by L) is accepted by Foss and Ussing. Meier proposes δεκαζομένων, accepted by Cobet, Usener and Wachsmuth.)

20 f. καὶ ὡς ἀχάριστόν ἐστι τὸ πλῆθος καὶ ἀεὶ τοῦ νέμοντος καὶ διδόντος] The words τὸ πλῆθος καὶ ἀεί, wanting in the MSS, were supplied by Ast's almost certain conjecture, which Foss and Ussing adopt. (Edmonds proposes ὡς ἀχάριστόν ἐστι <τὸ> τοῦ νέμοντος καὶ διδόντος, 'how thankless the task is of the man who has to pay.')

(22 αὑτῷ] αὐτῷ is preferred by Edmonds.)

23. λεπτός] So Petersen and Ussing with the MSS; but it means *macer*, 'meagre,' 'starved-looking', not *tenuis* (pauper), as Ussing renders it. Foss, with Meier, λεπρός; (Eberhard and Buecheler, λιτός; Meineke, ἄλουτος or ἄνιπτος. Blaydes also proposes ἄλουτος.)

(25 f. καὶ τὸν Θησέα πρῶτον φῆσαι] τὸν Θ. πρῶτον φήσας L.)

26—8. τοῦτον γὰρ ἐκ δώδεκα πόλεων εἰς μίαν καταγαγόντα λῦσαι τὴν βασιλείαν] V, which alone has this, gives τοῦτον γὰρ ἐκ δώδεκα πόλεων καταγαγόντα λυθεῖσας βασιλ´ with a contraction after the σ, which is written above the line. Foss thinks that the MS had λυθεῖσαν βασιλείαν. Bold measures have been taken to supply the supposed lacuna. Foss reads, after εἰς μίαν, καταγαγόντα <τὰ πλήθη ἀφεῖναι τὴν κατα>λυθεῖσαν βασιλείαν. Meier's remedy, which Foss justly calls 'portentous,' is to copy after καταγαγόντα the greater part of Thuc. II 15. Ussing reads καταγαγόντα <τὰ πλήθη> παῦσαι τὰς βασιλείας but this, though it adds less to the text, uses the text itself still worse. I greatly prefer Ast's simple proposal to read λῦσαι τὴν βασιλείαν. It does not seem unlikely that the σ written over λύθει was meant simply to correct θ, and that the doubtful contraction after it was merely the article, and not, as has been supposed, αν or αι. The object of καταγαγόντα is τὴν πόλιν, understood from τῇ πόλει just before. αὐτῶν refers to the population of the δώδεκα πόλεις. (After καταγαγόντα Schneider adds <τὸν δῆμον> or <τοὺς δήμους>; Ilberg (in L) accepts <τὰ πλήθη>, and adds λῦσαι τὰς βασιλείας.) Cobet proposes εἰς μίαν συναγαγόντα <τὸν δῆμον κατα>λῦσαι τὴν βασιλείαν καὶ δίκαια [αὐτὸν] παθεῖν. Diels, who reads the text of V as λυθείσας βασιλείας, restores the whole passage as follows: καταγαγόντα <τὸν δῆμον αὐξῆσαι ὥστε πάντων κρατῆσαι τοὺς πολλοὺς> λυθείσης <τῆς> βασιλείας.

XXX (XXIX)

This chapter is found only in V.

(2. ἡττημένοις καὶ] bracketed by Cobet, altered into ἠτιμωμένοις καὶ by Unger.)

(5. καὶ φῆσαι, ὡς] καί φησιν ὡς L.)

6 f. καὶ ἐπισκῶψαι δὲ, ὡς χρηστός ἐστι] The MS has καὶ ἐπισκῆψαι δὲ, ὡς χρηστός ἐστι (retained by L). Nast's excellent emendation ἐπισκῶψαι has been adopted by Ussing. Coray, followed by Ast and Foss, reads ἐπισκῆψαι δὲ, ὅς χρηστός ἐστι, which, besides being awkward grammatically, gives a very tame sense

7 f. καὶ τὸν πονηρὸν δὲ εἰπεῖν ἐλεύθερον, ἐὰν βούληταί τις εὖ σκοπεῖν] The MS has ἐὰν βούληταί τις εἰς π..... (a lacuna of 5 or 6 letters). This lacuna has usually been filled up with πονηρόν or πονηρίαν. Coray proposed ἐάν που λοιδορῆταί τις εἰς πονηρίαν, or ἐὰν διαβάλληταί τις εἰς πονηρίαν. Foss reads, on his own conj., <καὶ> ἐὰν βούληταί τις εἰς π<ονηρὸν ἀποτείνεσθαι> τὰ μὲν ἄλλα ὁμολογεῖν, κ.τ.λ., where εἰς π ἀποτείνεσθαι means, I suppose, to *descant upon* a bad man; a very odd phrase. Hartung has probably, I think, come nearer to the truth Out of εἰς π . he gets εὖ σκοπεῖν Now I feel sure that the words ἐὰν βούληταί τις, κ τ.λ. are part of what the φιλοπόνηρος says. The rascal, he contends, is merely 'a frank independent man, *if one will look fairly at the matter*.' (Naber suggests εἰς π<εῖραν ἐλθεῖν>, Immisch, in L, proposes εἰς π<εῖραν λαβεῖν>.)

(9 ὑπὲρ αὑτοῦ] περὶ αὑτοῦ Cobet.)

10. ἔνια δὲ ἀγνοεῖν φῆσαι· εἶναι γὰρ αὐτὸν] The MS has ἔνια δὲ ἀγνοεῖν· φῆσαι γὰρ αὐτόν (retained by L). Foss, rightly, I think, inserts εἶναι between φῆσαι and γάρ, and puts a point at φῆσαι. Ussing adopts the conjecture, but, by an oversight, ascribes it to Petersen (Cobet prefers φῆσαι γὰρ ἂν αὐτόν, and Unger φανῆναι γάρ αὐτόν.)

11 ἐπιδέξιον] Before Badham collated V, it was supposed, on the report of Amaduzzi, that it contained ἐπίδοξον, which Ast prints. It is creditable to Schneider's sagacity that he conjectured ἐπιδέξιον, which now proves to be actually the word in the MS.

12 f εὔνους δὲ εἶναι <αὑ>τῷ ἐν ἐκκλησίᾳ λέγοντι] The MS, τῷ ἐν ἐκκλησίᾳ λέγοντι. Meier's αὑτῷ seems nearly certain, it is adopted by Foss and Ussing (and L).

(13 ἐπὶ δικαστηρίου] Meier's correction for ἐπὶ δικαστηρίῳ, retained by L.)

13 f. καὶ πρὸς τοὺς καθημένους δὲ εἰπεῖν δεινὸς] The MS καὶ προσκαθήμενος δέ Here again, Meier seems to have hit the truth with πρὸς τοὺς καθημένους, and is followed by Ussing (and L). For οἱ καθήμενοι, said of the judges in a law-court, '*the bench*,' see Andoc. *de Myst*. § 139, ᾧ οὐδ' ἂν ὑμῶν τῶν καθημένων οὐδεὶς ἂν οὐδὲν ἐπιτρέψειεν

GREEK INDEX
TO TEXT

ἄβρωτον ποιῆσαι, φακῆν, XIII 15; Menander, *Dysc.* 3
ἀγαθῇ τύχῃ, XIII 10
ἀγορά· VII 9, 30, X II 9, XVIII 8; XXIX 11; γυναικείας ἀγορᾶς, I 25 (cp XXV 19); πληθούσης ἀγορᾶς, XVII 5
ἀγοράζειν, VII 12
ἀγοραῖός τις, τῷ ἤθει, XVI 3
ἀγροικία, XIV 1
ἄγροικος, XIV 2
ἀγρός· I 34; VIII 11; XIII 5, 14, XIV 7
ἀγρυπνίαν, κατά, XIV 20
ἀγωγὴ τῆς ψυχῆς, XXI 1
ἀδολέσχης, XVIII 2
ἀδολεσχία, XVIII 1
ἀηδής, XI 2
ἀηδία, XI 1
ἀθεραπευσία σώματος, XII 1
Ἀθηνᾶ κρείττων, XXVIII 17
Αἰθίοψ, VII 5
αἱρεῖν (conj. αἱρεῖσθαι), τὸν βοῦν, VIII 7
αἰσχροκέρδεια, XXVI 1
αἰσχροκερδής, XXVI 2
ἄκαιρία, IX 1
ἄκαιρος, IX 2
ἀκρασία...λόγου, XIX 2
ἀκρόδρυα, XVII 6
ἀλαζονεία, VI 1
ἀλαζών, VI 2
Ἀλεξάνδρου, ἐστρατεύσατο μετ', VI 8
ἅλες· XIII 14, XV 5; XXIV 18; XXVI 37
ἀλέσαι, XIV 12
ἀλλ' οὖν γε, XX 24
ἀλμάδες· VII 13
ἀλφίτων, θύλακος· XXVIII 11
ἀλφὸν (ἔχων), XII 3
ἅμα, c. part, II 14, XV 11, XVII 7
ἀμαθία ἀσχήμων, XIV 1
ἀμέλει, I 24; II 3; IV 15, VI 1, VII 15, 35; VIII 6; X 1, XVI 4; XXI 16; XXIII 1, XXVI 22, 36; XXVII 1, XXVIII 1; XXIX 9
ἄν, οὐκ, c inf III 13, IV 14; XXIV 11; double ἄν, XXVI 41 f

ἀναβαλόμενος, ἱμάτιον, VII 29, XII 8; ἀναβεβλημένος, XIV 8, XXIX 15
ἀνάγεσθαι, XI 3
ἀναδέξασθαι (ἐγγύην), IX 5
ἀναθεῖναι· VII 34; XXV 3
ἀναισθησία, XIII 1
ἀναίσθητος, XIII 2
ἀναισχυντία, XV 1
ἀναίσχυντος, XV 2
ἀνακοινοῦσθαι, IX 3; XIV 6
ἀνακόπτειν, *Crit App.* XXVII 4
ἀνακύπτων, XXVII 4
ἀνανεύειν, VI 18
ἀνάπλεως, αἵματος, XXVII 24
ἀνασεσυρμένος, XVI 4
ἀναστρέψας, intrans I 24
ἀναφοραὶ τῶν λόγων, XX 11
ἀνδριάντα, παίζειν μακρόν, VIII 14
ἀνδρολάλοι, XXI 15
ἀνελευθερία, XXV 1
ἀνελεύθερος, VII 1, XXV 2
ἀνήρ· ἄνδρα κράτιστον εἰπών, II 3
Ἀνθεστηριῶνα μῆνα, XXVI 26
ἀντίδικος· II 8; pl XXX 30
Ἀντίπατρος· VI 13
ἀντιπροσειπεῖν, III 3
ἀνυπόδητος, XXIII 9
ἄξιος 'cheap,' XVIII 8, XXII 7, 9· ἐγγυητής, XXIII 14; τὰ ἱερὰ ἄξια, VII 40
ἀπάγεσθαι κλοπῆς, XVI 11
ἀπαγορεύοντος, X 10, ἀπαγορεῦσαι, XXIV 18
ἀπαιτεῖν· XXIII 12; XXIV 3, 16
ἀπαλλάττεσθαι, II 6; ἀπαλλαγῆναι, XXIX 12
ἀπάρχεσθαι, XXIV 4
Ἀπατούρια, XVIII 15
ἀπειπάσθαι, IX 12; ἀπείρηται, VI 15
ἀπήνεια ὁμιλίας, III 1
ἄπιοι· I 19
ἀπιστία, XXIII 1; ἄπιστος, XXIII 2
ἀπνευστί, I 25
ἀποβλέπειν I 3; 31
ἀπογράφεσθαι, XXVI 32

ἀπογυιώσῃ, XIX 11
ἀπογυμνώσῃ, Crit. App. XIX 11
ἀποδεδημηκώς, οὐδαμοῦ, VI 12
ἀποδιδόναι· III 5; VII 6, XXI 5; XXVI 23; ἀποδόσθαι, XXIV 10; XXVI 6
ἀποδοκιμάζειν· XIV 18, XVI 9, 21
ἀποδράσῃ, XXIII 19
ἀποκαλῶν, XXI 27
ἀποκαταστῆσαι, XIX 16
ἀποκεῖραι, VII 4, ἀποκείρασθαι, VII 7; XIV 24
ἀπολαμβάνων ἀργύριον ὀφειλόμενον, XIII 10
ἀπολαύσας, VI 7
ἀπονενοημένος, ὁ, XVI 2
ἀπόνοια, XVI 1
ἀποστερεῖ, XV 3
ἀποτραπείς, XXVIII 14
ἀποφορά· XXVI 28
ἀπουψῶν· XXVI 20
ἀπροβουλεύτων, λόγων, XVIII 2
ἀπωνυχισμένος, ἀκριβῶς, XXIX 16
ἀργυροθήκη· XXIV 22
ἀρέσκεια, II 1
ἀρέσκος, II 2
'Ἀριστοφῶντος, ἐπ', XIX 18
ἀριστῶν, XIV 14
ἁρμονικοί· VII 22
ἄροτρον, XIV 19
ἀρρωστήματα, συγγενικά, XII 4
Ἄρτεμις XXIV 5
ἀρύταινα· XV 19
ἀρχὴν εἰληφώς, XXI 24, ἀρχὰς πορίσασθαι, XIX 9, ἀρχαῖς πλησιάζοντας, XXIX 12; ἐξόμνυσθαι τὰς ἀρχάς, IV 6
ἀρχιτεκτονεῖν· εὖ ἠρχιτεκτονῆσθαι, I 33
ἄρχων, ὁ, XIV 23; XXIX 3
ᾆσαι, III 13
Ἀσία VI 10
Ἀσκληπιοῦ, ἐν τῷ, VII 35
ἀσκός, II 13
ἀσπίδα, ἐπί, VIII 5
ἀσπίδιον χαλκοῦν, VII 31
Ἀστείου τοῦ αὐλητοῦ, XX 9
ἀστραγάλους, δορκαδείους, VII 17
ἄστυ, καταβαίνων εἰς, XIV 21
ἀτελοῦς, ἐξαγωγῆς ξύλων, VI 15
ἀτραποῦ ἡγήσασθαι, X 7
αὐθάδεια, III 1
αὐθάδης, III 2
αὐλαίαν ἔχουσαν Πέρσας ἐνυφασμένους, VII 19
αὔλειος θύρα· XXI 10, αὔλεια θ. XXIII 7
αὐλητής XX 9
αὐλητρίς· XVII 11, 19
αὐλίδιον, VII 20
αὐλούμενος κροτεῖν, XVII 18
αὐτοκράτορας εἶναι, XXIX 5
αὑτός, 'his honour,' I 18, XXV 23
ἀφιλοτιμία· XXV 1
ἀχάριστον. τὸ πλῆθος, XXIX 20
ἄχυρον· I 10; XV 16

βακτηρίας ἐκ Λακεδαίμονος, VII 18
βαλανείῳ, ἐν, XII 6; XIV 26, ἐν τῷ β. VIII 18; XV 19, XXVI 13; ἐν τοῖς β. [XX 30]
βαλλάντιον, XXII 6
βασιλείαν, λῦσαι τήν, XXIX 27
βασιλεύς, ὁ, XX 13
βδελυρία, XVII 1
βδελυρός, XVII 2
βλασφημῆσαι, XVII 16
βοᾶσθαι, τὸ πρᾶγμα, XX 15
Βοηδρομιῶνος, XVIII 15
βοῦν, αἱρεῖν (conj. αἱρεῖσθαι), VIII 7; βοῦν θύσας, VII 25; βοῦν ἑστηκὼς θεωρεῖν, XIV 10
βραδυτὴς ψυχῆς, XIII 1
Βυζάντιον, VII 13

γαλῆ, XXVIII 5
γάμοις, ἐν τοῖς, XXV 7; κεκλημένος εἰς γάμους, IX 7
γενεαλογοῦντες, XXI 3
γένος κατὰ γένος, [Pro 11, 25], γένη τρόπων, [Pro. 12]
γῆν (Κιμωλίαν), XXIV 27
γλαύξ .ταράττηται, κἄν, XXVIII 16
γλιχομένη, XXIX 2
γνάθος XVI 26
γναφέως, XXIII 14; γναφεῖς, XXIV 26
γόνατα, πεσὼν ἐπί, XXVIII 10
γραμματιδίων, ὁρμαθούς, XVI 21
γυμνάσια (τῶν ἐφήβων) VII 10
γυμνός, XXIII 9
γυναικείας ἀγορᾶς, I 25; ἐκ τῆς γυναικείας, XXV 19, γυναικείου γένους κατηγορεῖν, IX 7

δᾷδα, μεγίστην, XVIII 13
δαιμόνιον, τό, XXVIII 2
δακτύλιον (δάκτυλον?) χαλκοῦν, ἀναθείς, VII 34
δανείζειν XVI 23; δανείζεσθαι V 12; XV 3, 16; XXVI 3, 10
δανειστικῆς, ἐργασίας, VI 4
δάφνην εἰς τὸ στόμα λαβών, XXVIII 4
δεῖγμα, VI 3
δειλία, XXVII 1; δ. πρὸς τὸ δαιμόνιον, XXVIII 1
δειλός, XXVII 2
δεῖνα, ὁ, III 2; XXI 2
δεινός, c. inf, III 11, 14; IV 8; V 18; VI 8, VII 15, 30; IX 8; XI 7; XIII 10, XIV 12; XV 2, XVI 8; XIX 11, 16; XXI 23; XXIII 13, XXIV 15 XXV 10; XXVI 16; XXVIII 15, XXIX 9; XXX 14, 18
δεισιδαιμονία, XXVIII 1
δεισιδαίμων, XXVIII 2
δεκάταις, ἐν, VIII 13
Δελφοί VII 4
δεσμωτήριον οἰκεῖν, XVI 11
δημαγωγῶν γένος, μισητόν.., XXIX 25

INDEX TO THE TEXT

δημοκρατία· XXI 27
δῆμος VII 37; XIX 21; XXV 5, XXIX 3; XXX 15
δημοσίᾳ, ἀποδημῶν, XXVI 8
δημοσίους ἀγῶνας ὠφληκόσι, XXX 3
δημόται XXI 6; XXIV 16; XXVII 27
διάζευγμα, Crit. App. VI 3
δίαιτα· II 7; IV 5; IX 15
διακονοῦντας, τούς, XXV 7
διακοντίζεσθαι, VIII 15
διανέμων μερίδας, XXVI 4
διάπειραν λαμβάνειν, X 11
διατείνεσθαι· XXIV 26; XXX 11
διατοξεύεσθαι, VIII 15
διαφόρου, τοῦ, XXIV 1
διδασκαλεῖον· XIX 13; XXVI 24
διδάσκαλος XXV 11; pl XIX 15
διείργειν τοὺς μαχομένους, X 6
διεξέλθῃ τις, ἕως, XXVIII 6
δικαίων, πολλὰ τῶν, XXII 13
δικαστήριον XVII 10; XXIX 18; XXX 13, 19
δίκην φεύγων εἰσιέναι, XIII 4 f; ὠφληκότι, IX 4; δίκας φεύγειν, διώκειν, ἐξόμνυσθαι, XVI 19 f., ὠφλήκασιν [XX 32]
διμοιρίαν, XXVI 5
Διονυσίων, ἐκ, XVIII 9, Διονύσια, τὰ κατ' ἀγρούς, XVIII 16
Διόνυσος· XXV 3
διότι=ὅτι, Crit. App VI 30
διφᾶν τὰ καλύμματα, XXIV 10
διφθέραι, XIV 23
διωθεῖν, ψήφους, IV 16
δόξειεν ἂν εἶναι, V 1, VI 1, VII 1, VIII 1, XIV 1; XIX 27; εἶναι ἂν δόξειεν, XIX 1; XXVII 1; XXVIII 1, 29; XXIX 1
δορκαδείους ἀστραγάλους, VII 17
δόρυ, ἐπί, VIII 4
δρέπανον, XIV 20
δυνατός, c. inf., I 25; XVI 4
δυοῖν ἡμερῶν· I 11
δυσχέρεια, XII 1
δυσχερής, XII 2

ἑβδομάσι, ταῖς, XXVIII 20
ἐγγράφειν· εἰς τοὺς δημότας ἐνεγράφη, XXI 6
ἐγγύης, δίκην ὠφληκότι, IX 4
ἐγγυητής XXIII 14, 17
ἐγκεκρουμένῳ, τὸν πύνδακα, XXVI 29
ἐγκώμιον, XVIII 4
ἔδραν στρέφειν, VIII 18
εἰδεχθής, XXI 19
εἰκών τὴν εἰκόνα ὁμοίαν εἶναι, I 34
εἶπας, XIX 5
εἴρων, V 2
εἰρωνεία, V 1; [Pro. 20]
εἰσιών, VIII 8; XIX 14
εἰσφέρειν ἔρανον· III 9, VI 22; XXI 13
Ἑκάτη XXVIII 15
ἐκβαλεῖν, 'to drop,' XVII 16, XXIV 8

ἐκδιδόναι θυγατέρα· XXV 5, XXVI 39; ἱμάτιον, XXIII 13, XXV 4, XXVI 17
ἐκθύσασθαι, XXVIII 14
ἐκκλησία· XIV 8, XIX 17; XXVIII 20; XXIX 22; XXX 13
ἐκκαρῆσαι, XXV 21
ἐκπλήττεσθαι V 19, XIV 10
ἐκπλῦναι, XXV 14; cp. κλῦναι
ἐλάα· XXIV 13
ἔλαιον XII 6; XXVI 37
ἐλευθερία· XXI 28
ἐλλύχνιον, XXIV 19
ἐμπόλημα· ' profit,' XVI 25
ἐνστάς, X 4
ἔντευξις, II 1; XI 1
ἐντυγχάνειν I 12; IV 3, 9, v 8; IX 1; XIX 3, 10; XXVII 25; XXX 2
ἐνύπνιον· XVIII 5; XXVII 7; XXVIII 23
ἐνυφασμένους, Πέρσας, VII 19
ἐξαγωγῆς ξύλων ἀτελοῦς, VI 14
ἐξενεχθῆναι νεκρούς, XIII 17
ἐξηγητής· XXVIII 12
ἐξόμνυσθαι, IV 6, XVI 20
ἑορτή· III 6
ἐπαγωγή, Ἑκάτης, XXVIII 16
ἐπὰν πορεύηται, IV 12
ἐπεντείνειν, τὸν λόγον, XX 16
ἐπὶ δόρυ ἐπὶ ἀσπίδα ..ἐπ' οὐράν, VIII 4 f
ἐπιβαλών, XX 5, XXVI 22; ἐπιβάλλεσθαι, I 29
ἐπιγελάσαι· I 11, 16
ἐπιγράψαι, VII 34; X 13; ἐπιγραψάμενος, XXV 3
ἐπιδείκνυσθαι, VII 22
ἐπιδείξεσιν, VII 23
ἐπιδέξιος· XXX 11
ἐπιδόσεις XXV 4
ἐπιθέατρον, Crit. App XXVI 8
ἐπιθυμία κακίας, XXX 1
ἐπικαταλλαγή· XXVI 28
ἐπικρηπῖδας, Crit App I 21
ἐπιλαβέσθαι, XIV 16, XX 12
ἐπίληπτος· XXVIII 32
ἐπιστάλματα, VII 13
ἐπιστέλλων, IV 17
ἐπίτευξις, IX 1
ἐπιτίμησις, XXII 1
ἐπιτρέπειν διαίτας, IV 5
ἐρανίζοντας, V 12
ἔρανος· III 9; VI 23, XXII 13; XXV 14
ἐργολάβος, XX 9
ἔργον διαγνῶναι, XXVII 11
ἐρεθισμός, ὁ τῆς δυσκολίας, [XXI 29]
ἐρήμους δίκας ὠφλήκασιν, [XX 32]
Ἑρμαφροδίτους, στεφανοῦν, XXVIII 22
Ἑρμῆς, κοινός, XXVI 17
ἑστιᾶν II 11, IV 10, XXVI 2, 30, XXIV 16, ἑστιωμένων, I 26, ἑστιώμενον (?), XXVIII 30
εὐαγγελιζόμενον, XXII 9
εὐδοκίμησεν, XIX 20
εὐημερεῖ, VII 42

INDEX TO THE TEXT

εὑρίσκειν· τί εὑρίσκει, III 5
εὐρυθμότερος· I 22
Εὐρώπη· VI 11
εὐρωτιώσας, ἀργυροθήκας, XXIV 22
εὐφυής· XXX 10
εὐωχήσειν, XX 8
ἐφελκύσαι, XXVI 18
ἔφηβοι, VII 11
ἐφοδεύειν, XVI 24
ἐφόδιον, XXVI 9
ἔχειν, κακῶς· X 12; XXV 11; ὡς αὐτῷ εἶχε, VI 9
ἔχεις, 'vipers,' [V 25]
ἐχῖνος XVI 20
ἕψαν, οἶνον, XXVIII 21
ἕως διεξέλθῃ τις, XXVIII 6

Ζεύς, as god of rain, XIII 15; XVIII 10; XXII 5
ζωγρεῖν· XX 14
ζωμός· XV 10; XXII 4; 'hash,' XX 17
ζωρότερον πιεῖν, XIV 12

ἦθος, καταβαλὼν τό, XX 3
ἡλικίαν, ὑπὲρ τήν, VIII 2
ἡμιολίας, 'privateers,' XXVII 3
ἥμισυ τῆς οὐσίας, τό, XXII 10; τὰ . ῥαφανίδων ἡμισέα, XXVI 32
ἡμιωβόλιον· XVI 23; XXIV 2
Ἡρακλεῖον, VIII 7
ἡρίαι πύλαι, Crit App XIII 17
ἡρῷον (conj), XXVIII 8, pl. VIII 5
ἡττημένῳ (conj), XVII 10, ἡττημένοις, XXX 2; ἡττωμένοις, V 5

θαλάττῃ, πολλὰ χρήματα ἐν τῇ, VI 4
θαύματα, 'a conjurer's performance,' VIII 9; XVI 6
θέα, VII 11; XV 12, XXVI 7, 27
θέατρον· I 32, VII 11, XIII 6, XVII 4
θεατρῶναι, XXVI 8
θεοῦ (= οὐρανοῦ), τὰ τοῦ, XXVII 6, τῇ μητρὶ τῶν θεῶν, VII 39
θεωρεῖν· XIII 6; XVII 5
Θησεύς XXIX 25
Θουριακὰς ληκύθους, VII 17
Θρᾷττα, XXI 7
θύλακος· XIV 20, XXVIII 11
θρίξ· μέλαιναν τρίχα, I 13
θυηλήματα, Crit App. XXIV 20
θυλήματα, XXIV 20
θύμου, 'thyme,' XIV 3
θύραν αὔλειον, XXI 16, αὔλειαν, XXIII 7; κόψαντος τὴν θύραν, XIV 15

ἰατρός· X 10
ἱερά· VII 37, 40
ἱερεῖ, παρὰ τῷ, VIII 11
ἱερεῖον· XXV 6
ἱερωσύνων, πλὴν τῶν, XXV 6
ἱκανός, c. inf., XVI 19, XXI 10
ἱμάτιον· I 8, 16; VII 8, 29; VIII 7;
XII 8; XXIII 13; XXIV 26; XXV 14; XXVI 17; XXIX 15
ἱματισμὸν ζητῆσαι, VI 26
ἱππάζεσθαι, VIII 12
ἱππέων, πομπεύσας μετὰ τῶν, VII 28
ἵππου ἀλλοτρίου, VIII 11; ἵππους ἀγαθούς, VI 25
ἰσχύος, conj., XXIX 1
ἰχθυοπώλια, XVI 25
ἰωμένας, κλεῖς, XXIV 23

καθᾶραι, οἰκίαν, XXVIII 15
καί . δέ, I 14, 15, II 8, 9, V 5; VI 7, 12, 16, 19, 24; VII 8, 15, 30, VIII 17; IX 11; X 4, XI 7, 14, XIV 11, 14; XVI 12, 21; XVII 17; XIX 13; XXI 10; XXIII 13, XXV 10, XXVIII 15, XXX 6 f, 13
καὶ μήν, I 30; V 20; XX 6
καινόν, καινότερον, XX 5; καινῶν λόγων, XX 8, καινὸν (ἀργύριον), VII 6
καίπερ ἔχεις, I 12
κακολογία, XXI 1
κακολόγος, XXI 2
καλλιστεύειν VIII 11
καπήλων ἀγοραίων στρατηγεῖν, XVI 22
κάρνα, XVII 6
καρφολογῆσαι I 10
Κάσσανδρος, XX 13, 23
καταβαλὼν τὸ ἦθος, XX 3
κατάθου, XXIII 1
κατακείμενος, παρ᾽ αὐτὸν τὸν καλέσαντα, VII 3, πρὸς τὸν κατακείμενον, XXVII 28
κατάξαντος, XXIV 7, κατεαγέναι, VIII 13
κατάστρωμα XXV 9
καταφρόνησις, IV 1
κειρομένοις, ἐν χρῷ, XXIV 25
κεκαττυμένα, παλιμπήξει, XXV 20
κεράσαι (οἶνον), X 5, κεκραμένον οἶνον, XXVI 6
κεφάλαιον, 'total,' IV 16, XIII 3
κεφαλῆς, κατά, XXVIII 31
κῆπος· XI 10, XXIV 12
κηρύττειν, XVI 10
κιβωτός XXIII 6; pl. XXIV 9
κίονες, XVIII 13
κλεῖς, XXIV 22
κλιμάκιον, VII 31 f
κλίνας, ἐλθὼν ἐπὶ τάς, VI 26; κλίνας καλλῦναι, XXV 21
κναφεύς or γναφεύς, Crit App XXIII 14
κοινός· II 8; κοινὸν Ἑρμῆν, XXVI 16; πρὸς τὰ κοινὰ προσιόντων, XXIX 20
κολακεία· I 1
κολοιός· VII 30, 32
κόνιν, παλαιστριαῖον, VII 20
κόποις, ἐμβάλλειν εἰς, XIII 13
κόρακας, ἄπαγ᾽ ἐς, XXVII 23
κόρδαξ· XVI 5
<Κορινθιακῶς>, conj. XXI 8
κουρά, μέση· XXIX 15
κουρεῖον, XVII 14

INDEX TO THE TEXT

κόφινος· XIV 19
κρεωπώλης· XV 8
κρήνῃ, ἐπί, XXVIII 2
κρηπῖδας, συνωνούμενος, I 21
κριθαί· XV 16
Κρινοκόρακα, Crit App. XXI 8
κροκύδα, ἀπὸ τοῦ ἱματίου ἀφελεῖν, I 9
κροτεῖν, XVII 4, 18
κυβερνήτης· XXV 8, XXVII 4
κυβεύειν, XVI 10
Κύζικος· VII 14
κυκεών· XIV 2
κύκλῳ, τήν, XXV 16
κυλικούχιον, XXIII 7
κύμινον, XXIV 19
κυναρίου Μελιταίου, VII 32
κύπτειν· κάτω κεκυφώς, IV 10
κύων XIV 15; pl, VII 14; XXI 14; κύων τοῦ δήμου, XXX 5
κωμάζειν, IX 4

Λακεδαιμονίων, XIX 19
Λακεδαίμονος, βακτηρίας ..ἐκ, VII 18
λακκαῖον (ὕδωρ), XI 10
Λακωνικὰς κύνας, VII 13
λαλεῖν, I 31, V 3; XIV 5, XIX 7, 30; λαλῇ, XI 3
λαλιά, XIX 1
λαλίστερος, XIX 27
λάλος, XIX 2, 25
λαμπάδα τρέχειν, VIII 6
λάχανα, XI 10; XXV 13
λειτουργίαι· VI 24; XXIX 24
λέπραν ἔχων, XII 2
λεπτός (?), XXIX 23
λευρόν (ἀργύριον), conj. XIV 18
λεχώ XXVIII 18
ληκυθίων μικρῶν, XXIV 24
ληκύθους, Θουριακάς, VII 18
λῆρος, XXI 14
λῃτουργίαι· Crit App VI 24
λιβανωτός· XXVIII 21
λιθοκόλλητα ποτήρια, VI 9
λίθων, λιπαρῶν, XXVIII 9, λίθους τρεῖς, XXVIII 6
λιπαρῶν λίθων, XXVIII 9
λογίζεσθαι· IV 15, XIII 3
λογοποιΐα, XX 1
λογοποιός, XX 2
λογοποιῶν, ὁ, XX 2
λοιδορηθῆναι, XVI 3; λοιδορουμένων, XVI 14
λοπ 's XXIV 7
Λύκων ὁ ἐργολάβος, XX 9
Λυσάνδρου, ἐπί, XIX 20

μαγειρεῖα, XVI 24
μαγειρεύειν, XVI 10
μάγειρος, XI 11
Μακεδονία VI 14; XX 21; Μακεδόσι, VI 16
μαλακιζομένῳ, X 11, μαλακισθῆναι, V 11

μαλακῶς ἐσθίεις, I 27
μάμμη, XI 13
μάντεις, XXVIII 24
μάρτυρας παραλαβεῖν, XIII 11
μαρτυρήσων, IX 5
μαστιγίας, XXI 10
μαστιγουμένου οἰκέτου, IX 13
μασώμενος, XI 5
μάχῃ· XIX 19; XXVII 25
μειράκια VIII 6
μελετᾶν, VIII 12, 19
μέλι Ὑμήττιον, VII 14
Μελιταίου, κυναρίου, VII 33, κλάδος Μελιταῖος, VII 34
μεμύηται, XXVII 4
μεμψιμοιρία, XXII 1
μεμψίμοιρος, XXII 2
μέν· ἐπιγραψάς μέν, Crit App. XXV 3; λίαν μέν, ib. XIV 18, μὲν οὖν, v (1) 1
μερίς XXII 3, pl. XXVI 4
μέσην κουρὰν κεκαρμένος, XXIX 15, τὸ μέσον τῆς ἡμέρας, XXIV 25
μεσοπορεῖ, XXVII 5
μεταξύ, c. part., XIX 5, 12
μέτρῳ, Φειδωνίῳ, XXVI 19
μή ('if') ῥιγοῖ, I 28
μητέρα, μὴ τρέφειν, XVI 10, τῇ μητρὶ τῶν θεῶν, VII 39
μικρολογία, XXIV 1
μικρολόγος, XXIV 2; -ων, XXIV 21
μικροφιλοτιμία, VII 1
μικροφιλότιμος, VII 2
μίλακα (conj.), XXVIII 22
μνᾶν ἀργυρίου, ἀποδιδούς, VII 6; κατὰ μνᾶν, VI 21, μνῶν, XXVI 23
μνῆμα, X 13
μόνον οὔ, XXIII 16
Μουσεῖα, XXV 11
μοχλός, XXIII 7
μύρον, XIV 3
μυροπώλιον, XVII 14
μυρσίναι XXVIII 21
μύρτα, XVII 6
μῦς, XXVIII 11
μυστηρίοις, XVIII 12
μύωψι, ἐν τοῖς, VII 29

νέμοντος καὶ διδόντος, τοῦ, XXIX 21
νεόττια, χρηστοῦ πατρός, I 21
νέωτα, εἰς, XVIII 11
νουμηνίαν ἄγει, XIV 23
νυκτός, τῆς, 'during the following night,' XIV 20; 'last night,' XVIII 4

ξένια XXVI 12
ξενίζων, XI 14
ξένος XXVI 3, pl II 8; VI 3, VII 13, XV 12, XVIII 9, XXVI 3, XXIX 29
ξενοδοχία VI 31
ξύλα XXVI 37

ὁδός IX 8, pl IV 4, 9
ὀδούς· ὀδόντας λευκούς, VII 7

ὄζει, τῶν ἄστρων,.. τῆς γῆς, XIII 16
οἰκέτου, μαστιγουμένου, IX 13
οἰκία· μισθωτή, VI 28, πατρῷα, VI 29
οἰκοσίτους μισθώσασθαι, XXV 7
οἰνοπωλῶν, XXVI 6
οἶνος ἐπαινέσαι τὸν οἶνον, I 26; οἶνον κεκραμένον, XXVI 6
οἷος, c. inf., XXIV 8; also preceded by
  τοιόσδε τις, IV 2; XXI 2; XXII 2; XXX 1
  τοιοῦτός τις, II 3; III 2; V 3; VI—XVII 2; XIX—XX 2; XXIII—XXV 2, XXVII—XXVIII 2
  τοιοῦτός ἐστιν, XVIII 2
  ἔστι τοιοῦτος, XXVI 2
  τοιοῦτος, XXIX 2 (exc. τοιοῦτόν τινα ὥστε, I 2)
ὀλιγαρχία, XXIX 1
ὀλίγαρχος, XXIX 2
Ὁμήρου ἐπῶν, τῶν, XXIX 7
ὁμιλία· ὁμιλίαν αἰσχράν, I 1; ἀπήνεια ὁμιλίας, III 1
ὀμνύναι μέλλων, X 16; πολλάκις ὀμώμοκα, X 17
ὅμοιον πρὸς τὸ ὅμοιον, τό, [XXX 33]
ὀνειροκρίται XXVIII 24
ὀνομαστί, XVII 8
ὄνον, ἑστηκὼς θεωρεῖν, XIV 10
ὄνυχας μεγάλους (μέλανας?), XII 3
ὄξος XXVI 37
ὁπλομάχοι· VII 22
ὅπως, c aor subj., V 21, XIX 30; c pres subj XXIII 12, c fut ind, IV 19, X 10
ὅρα μή V 22
ὄρεξις τιμῆς ἀνελεύθερος, VII 1
ὀρίγανον, XXIV 19
ὁρίζεσθαι, XIX 1
ὁρμαθοὺς γραμματιδίων, XVI 21
ὀρνιθοσκόπος XVII 15; XXVIII 25
ὅρους ἐπισκοπεῖσθαι, XXIV 14
Ὀρφεοτελεσταί XXVIII 26
ὀρχεῖσθαι III 13, VIII 20; IX 16, XVI 5
ὅρῳ περιλαβεῖν, II 1
ὅτε, preceded by καὶ πῶς; XXII 15
οὗ πορεύεται, X 8
οὐλαί XXIV 19
οὐράν, ἐπ', VIII 5
ὄφις παρεία, ὄφις ἱερός· XXVIII 7
ὄχλος XXIX 11
ὀψιμαθής, VIII 2
ὀψιμαθία, VIII 1
ὄψον, XI 11, XXI 22; XXVI 31
ὀψωνεῖν XV 7, XVII 11, XXIII 2; XXIV 17, XXV 12

παιδαγωγός· VIII 16, XV 14
παιδάριον XXVI 14
παιδιὰ ἐπονείδιστος, XVII 2
παιδίον, 'child,' XI 5; XXI 21, παιδία, II 10, XIII 12; XXV 10; παιδίοις, I 19, XIX 29; XXVIII 28
  παιδίον, 'slave-girl,' XXV 19

παιδοτρίβης· XIX 15
παίζειν, μακρὸν ἀνδριάντα, VIII 14
παῖς, 'slave,' XX 9, παιδός, I 32; παιδί, VI 27; VII 28; XIII 12; XXVII 7, παῖδα, X 5; XXIII 3, XXVI 28; XXVII 14; παισί, XXVI 31, 34
  παίδων (=παιδίων) παιδαγωγῷ, VIII 16
παλαίστρα VII 24; VIII 8, XIX 13
παλαιστριαῖος κόνις· VII 20
παλιμπήξει κεκαττυμένα, ὑποδήματα, XXV 20
πανδοκεῖον, XI 12
πανδοκεῦσαι, XVI 8
πανήγυρις, XVI 18
πανοῦργον τοῦ πάππου, XI 7
πάντες χρηστοί, on tombstones, X 16
παντοποιός (=παντοδαπός), XVI 4
πάππα, XIX 30
παράσιτος XI 14
παρασκευαστική, ἔντευξις ἡδονῆς, II 2
παρεία (ὄφις)· XXVIII 7
παρερρωγυίᾳ, φωνῇ, XVI 14
παρρησία· XXI 27
πέλεκυς, II 14
περιεργία, X 1
περίεργος, X 2
περιισταμένων τοὺς ὄχλους, τῶν, XVI 13
περιλαβεῖν, ὅρῳ, II 1
περιουσία, XXV 1; XXVI 1
περιπατεῖν, IV 3, VII 30; XII 3
περιρραίνεσθαι XXVIII 3, 28
περισπογγίζειν, XXVII 19
περιστεραί, Σικελικαί VII 16
Πέρσας ἐνυφασμένους, VII 19
πίθηκον θρέψαι, VII 15
πίθον, τὸν τετρημένον, XI 13
πλεθρίζων, VI 6
πλεῖν ᾖ προσήκει, VI 16
πληγὰς λαβών, IX 14
πλῆθος, ἀχάριστον, XXIX 21; κατὰ τῶν πληθῶν, XIX 21
πλήν, XXV 6
πληρώματα, 'audiences,' VIII 9
πλησιάζοντας, ἀρχαῖς, XXIX 12
πλόιμον, XVIII 10
πλῦναι, XXVI 17; Crit. App XXIII 13
ποδαπή, X 15
πολεμικόν, τό, XXVII 21
πολιῶν πώγωνα μεστόν, I 12
Πολυπέρχων, XX 13
πομπεύσας, VII 27
πομπή· XXIX 4
ποππύζων, XI 6
Ποσειδεῶνος, XVIII 16
Ποσειδῶνος ἡμέρᾳ, XXI 23
πόσον, III 4; XXII 3, 20
ποσῶν, 'reckoning,' VI 20; πόσου Crit. App XXIII 20
ποτήριον XI 16; XVII 17; λιθοκόλλητα ποτήρια, VI 9
ποτίσαι, εὖ, X 12

πράγμασιν, τῶν ἐν τοῖς, XX 18
πράως διαλέγεσθαι, V 7
πρὸ χρόνου τινός, XXVI 39
προαιρουμένους, ταὐτά, XXIX 30
πρόθυμος, c inf, IX 11
προϊδόμενος, XXV 15
προῖκα εἰσενεγκαμένῃ, XXI 20; XXV 17
προῖκα θεωρεῖν, XVI 8
προκόλπιον· XVI 20; XXV 13
προμανθάνειν, XIX 14
προμετωπίδιον, (βοός), VII 25
προπέμψαι II 5, XIX 16
προσαγορεύσας, II 3; προσαγορευθείς, III 3
προσκεφάλαιον, XXVII 16
προσκυνήσας, XXVIII 10
προσκύπτων, I 30
προσποιεῖσθαι V 10, 14
προσποίησις, V 2; VI 1; X 1
προστατῆσαι, XXX 18
προσφορά XXVI 40
προσωπεῖον, XVI 5
πρυτάνεις· VII 37, 39
πτύσαι, εἰς κόλπον, XXVIII 33
Πυανεψιῶνος, XVIII 15
πυκνά, VIII 18, XXVIII 15
πύλαι, ἱεραί, XIII 17
πύνδακα ἐγκεκρουμένῳ, XXVI 19
πυροί, XVIII 8
πυρώσας, XXIII 16
πύγωνα μεστὸν πολιῶν, I 12
πῶς οἴεσθε; XX 22

ῥαφανίδες XXVI 32
ῥῆσιν εἰπεῖν, III 13; ῥήσεις μανθάνειν, VIII 2
ῥήτορος, τοῦ, [XIX 19]
'Ρόδος· VII 14

Σαβάζιος· VIII 10; XXVIII 7
σαλπιστής, XXVII 21
σήμερον· XIV 23
σημήναντος, XXVII 22; σεσήμανται, XXIII 6
Σικελικαὶ περιστεραί· VII 16
σίκυος· XIII 12
σιτοδεία· VI 17
σιτοποιός, ἡ· XIV 13
σκέλη ἡρκυῖα, τά, XXI 13
σκέψεσθαι, V 16, Crit. App.
σκίλλη XXVIII 31
σκολιῶν (βακτηρίων), VII 18
σκορόδων ἐστιώμενον, XXVIII 30
σκύλαξ· XXVIII 31
σκυτοδέψης XXVIII 13
σοβεῖν, XXVII 20, XXIX 16
σοφισταί VII 21
σπάθη· XXVII 13
στάδιον, XXIII 4
σταθμός· XV 9
στέμματα· VII 26; XXIV 20
στεφανοῦν, XXVIII 22; ἐστεφανωμένος, VII 38

στηλίδιον, VII 33
στιλπνῶν, VII 35
στοά· I 5; [XX 31, 35]
στρατηγός· X 10; pl VII 12
στρέφειν, ἕδραν, VIII 18
στρογγύλων ⟨ληκύθων⟩, VII 18
στρώματα, XXIII 9; XXV 8
συγγνώμην, ἔχειν, III 7, V 5
συγκρούειν, IX 15
συκοτραγῆσαι, XXIV 12
σύκου ὁμοιότερα, II 11
συκοφάνται· XXIX 17
συκοφαντηθῇ, VI 15
συλλαβή, 'an epitome,' XVI 17
συλλέγειν, ἔρανον· XXV 15
συμβάλλεσθαι, VIII 5
σύμβολον, 'ticket,' XVI 7
συναγόντων παρ' αὐτῷ, of a 'club-dinner,' XXVI 36
συναυλήσοντας (conj.), VIII 14
συνδικάζων, XIX 24
συνδιοικήσασθαι, VII 36
συνεδρεῦσαι, XXX 19
συνεπιμελησομένους, τῆς πομπῆς, XXIX 4
συνθεωρῶν, XIX 24
συνοδοιπόρου ἀπολαύσας, VI 7
συντάξαι, IV 12, 16
συντερετίζειν, XVII 19
συνωνούμενος, I 21
συρίττειν, XVII 4
σφαιριστήριον, VII 20
σχετλιάζει, XX 22
Σωσίας, Σωσίστρατος, Σωσίδημος, XXI 5 f

ταινίαν ξυλίνην ἀναθεῖναι, XXV 3
ταμιεῖον· XIV 12
ταράττηται, κἂν γλαῦξ, XXVIII 16
ταριχοπώλια, XVI 25
τάριχος XIV 23; 25
ταχίστην, τήν, IV 20
τελούμενος, VIII 10; τελεσθησόμενος, XXVIII 26
τελωνῆσαι, XVI 9
τερετίζων, VIII 20
τετράσι, ταῖς, XVIII 20
τεχνῖται· 'artists,' VI 10
Τίβιος, Crit App. XV 7
τιμώτατε (?), XV 7
τίτθη XI 5
τίτυρος· VII 16
τοιόσδε τις (or τοιοῦτός τις) οἷος, c. inf passim, see οἷος, τοιοῦτόν τινα ὥστε, I 2
τόκος· IX 13; XVI 23; τόκος τόκου· XXIV 16; τόκοι· XVI 25; XXIII 12
τραγηματίζεσθαι, XVII 7
τράγον, ἑστηκὼς θεωρεῖν, XIV 10
τραγῳδοῖς, νικήσας, XXV 3
τράπεζα· VI 6; pl VII 9
τραυματίας· XXVII 17
τραχηλίσῃ, (βοῦν), VIII 7

τρέχειν, λαμπάδα, VIII 6
τρίβων· XXV 22
τριηραρχίαι· VI 23; XXIX 24
τριηραρχῶν, XXV 8
τριόδοις, ἐν ταῖς, XXVIII 9, 30
τρίχαλκον, XXIV 8
τρίχωμα· I 9
τρόπου, πρός, XXVI 21
τροχάζειν, XIII 13
τύπῳ λαβεῖν, ὡς, V 1

ὑγρῷ, ἐν, XIX 26
ὕδωρ, 'rain,' XVIII 10, ὕδωρ, ψυχρόν, λακκαῖον, XI 9 f
ὕει (ὁ Ζεύς), XXII 5; ὕοντος τοῦ Διός, XIII 15, cp. Chantonides, Ποικίλα Φιλολογικά, 740—774
Ὑμήττιον, μέλι, VII 14
ὑπακούειν· XIV 15; XXI 16
ὕπειξις ψυχῆς ἐμφόβος, XXVII 1
ὑπέρ (=περί), XXX 9
ὑπερημερίαν πρᾶξαι, XXIV 15
ὑπερηφανία, IV 1
ὑπερήφανος, IV 2
ὑποβάλλειν, XIX 5, ὑποβάλλεσθαι, XII 6
ὑπόδημα· I 22; pl. XIV 4, 26, XXV 19
ὑποζυγίοις, ἐμβαλεῖν τοῖς, XIV 14
ὑποκορίζεσθαι, XI 6
ὑπόληψις, XXIII 1
ὑπολυομένους, XXIV 25
ὑπομεῖναι, III 12, XIX 28
ὑπομονή, XVI 1
ὑποπριᾶσθαι, XXVI 21
ὑποστορέννυσθαι, XXV 9, ὑποστρῶσαι, I 33
ὕστερον, 'too late,' XXII 5

φακῆν ἕψων, XIII 14; φακῶν, XXVI 37
Φειδωνίῳ μέτρῳ, XXVI 19
Φῇ, 'says yes,' XXIII 8; cp Crit. App. XX 15
φιλαρχία, XXIX 1
φιλέταιρος, XXX 10
φιλοπονηρία, XXX 1
φιλοπόνηρος, XXX 1

φιλοπανία, VIII 1
φιλόσοφοι· VII 21
φοῖνιξ, XXIV 13
φράτορας ἐστιῶν, XXVI 30
φυλέται XXVII 28

χαλκεῖα, XV 18
χαλκοῦς pl XVI 6, XXI 21, XXVI 15
χαρίζοιο ἄν μοι, IV 18
χάρις, XV 20
χεῖρον, ἐπί, V 2 etc.; εἰς τὸ χεῖρον, XXI 1
χειροτονούμενος, IV 5
χελιδόνων λαλίστερος, XIX 27
χιτωνίσκος· XII 7
χολίκιον, XV 11
χορῷ, ἐν κωμικῷ, XVI 6
χρέος ἀποδοῦναι, XXVI 22
χρηννύναι, Crit. App. VII 21; χρωννύναι, ib. XXIV 18
χρῆσαι· VII 21; XIV 19, XV 17; XXIII 17, XXIV 18; χρησάμενος, XXVI 17;
χρηστός· XXX 5—7; 'πάντες χρηστοί,' X 16
χρίεσθαι, XII 7
χρίσματι ἀλείφεσθαι, VII 8
χρῷ, ἐν, XXIV 25
χρώσαντι, III 7
χύτρα XIII 14; XXIV 7

ψήφους διωθεῖν, IV 16, θεῖναι, VI 20, λαβὼν πάσας τάς, XXII 12; ψήφοις λογισάμενος, XIII 3
ψυχή, ἡ, XXI 7
ψυχρῶς, σκώψαντι, I 16

Ὠιδεῖον· XVIII 13, XXIX 17
ὠνητής IX 9
ὠνητιᾶν, VI 26
ὡς αὐτῷ εἶχε, VI 9, ὡς, c part., I 17; VIII 17, XXVII 16; ὡς ἄν, c part, VIII 17, ὡς, c. inf, ὁρῷ εἰπεῖν, XIII 1, ὁρῷ περιλαβεῖν, II 1; τύπῳ λαβεῖν, V 1
ὠφληκότι ἐγγύης, δίκην, IX 4; δημοσίους ἀγῶνας ὠφληκόσι, XXX 3; ἐρήμους δίκας ὠφλήκασιν, [XX 32]

ENGLISH INDEX

TO THE INTRODUCTION, NOTES AND BIBLIOGRAPHY

actors, XVII 4
advocates, XXX 16
Aeginetan standard of measures, XXVI 22
Aegospotami, battle of, XIX 23
Aethiopian slaves, VII 6
Alciphro, p. 3 n. 3
Alexander the Great, p. 5, VI 10; XX 15
Amaduzzi, J C., pp. 162, 166
ambassadors, presents to, XXVI 14
— travelling allowances to, XXVI 10
ambition, petty, VII 1
Anthesterion, festivals in, XXVI 31
Antipater, VI 14; XX 15
Apaturia, the, XVIII 15
apes, VII 19
arbitration, II 8
archery, VIII 18
'architect,' or manager of the theatre, XXVI 8
archon, assessors of, XXIX 4
Aristophon, XIX 22
Aristotle's *Ethics*, pp. 13–16; I 1; II 1, III 1; IV 1, V 1; VI 1, XXVII 1
arrogance, IV 1
Artemis, festivals of, XXIV 5
Asclepius, temples of, VII 38
Ast, F, pp 7, 17, 161, 163, 166
Athene, invocation of, XXVIII 19
Athenian troops, XXI 6
Athens, Metröum, VII 45
— Odeum, XVIII 13; XXIX 18
— sacred gate, XIII 21
athletics, Greek moderation in, XIII 15
augury in Greece, XXVIII 27 f
Austen, G. E. V, pp. 161, 171
avarice, XXIV 1; XXVI 1

Babick, C J, p 170
baggage carried by a slave, XXVI 11
ball, games at, VII 22
banks in market-place, VII 11
barber's shop, a lounge, XVII 15
bath, anointing oneself at the, XXVI 14
— cold, XXI 24 f
— warm, XXI 24 f

bathman, his duties, XV 20
baths, behaviour in the public, XIV 28
battle, signal for, XXVII 25
bench, addresses to, XXX 16
'benevolences' at Athens, XXV 5
birds sacred to several deities, XXVIII 18
'blasphieme,' in the Greek sense, XVII 17
Blaydes, F. H M., p 170
Bloch, S N J., pp 163, 166
Blumner, H., p. 169
boastfulness, VI 1
Boissonade, J. F., p 166
boorishness, XIV 1
bottomry, VI 4
boundaries, XXIV 16
Brillon, p. 32
Bruyère, La, pp. 30–32
bucranium, VII 28
Buecheler, F, p. 169
Burney, Charles, pp. 3, 5

Cabeiri (Κάβιροι), mysteries of, XXVII 3
cakes for sacrifice, XXIV 22
Camozzi, J B, p. 165
Casaubon, I, p. 165
'cask,' 'the pierced,' XI 15
Cassander, XX 11, 15, 27
'cause (not the person),' 'the question is of the,' XXX 16 f
childbirth, XXVIII 21 f
clansmen's feast, XXVI 36
cloak, VII 32, 42
— coarse, XXV 28
— fashionable length of, XXIV 25
— mode of wearing, XXIX 17
— sent to be scoured, XXIII 12; XXV 18; XXVI 18 f
— the breast of, a pocket, XVI 23
clothing, winter and summer, XII 7
club-dinners, XXVI 42
cobbler, XXVIII 15
Cobet, C. G., p. 167
coins, XXIV 9 f.; XXVI 33
— carried in the mouth, XVI 28
commanding officer, X 9

J. T.

15

226 INDEX TO THE NOTES, ETC.

complaisance, II 1
conjurers, VIII 11; XVI 6
conspiracies in law-courts, XXX 21
contractors, XX 11
cooks, hired, XVI 11
cook-shops, XVI 27
copper money, XXVI 33
Coray, pp. 162, 166
Corinth, the language of, XXI 9
couches, coverings for, VI 30
counting-board, IV 19; XIII 3
cowardice, XXVII 1
Cratander, A., p. 165
crier, public, XVI 10
criminal causes, XXX 3 f
cross-road offerings to Hecate, XXVIII 34
cross-roads, stones at, XXVIII 11
cucumbers, XIII 15
cupboard, XXIII 6
cup, dropping the, XVII 18
cups inlaid with gems, VI 11
— loan of, XXIII 14
cushions taken to the theatre, I 36
Cyzicus, VII 16

Danaids, allusion to the, XI 15
dancing, IX 21
dates, *Crit. App.*, XXIV 13
dead body, pollution from touching a, XXVIII 21
dead, laying out of the, XIII 10
decked vessels, XXV 12
Delphi, VII 5
deme, enrolment in a, XXI 6 f
demesmen, dinners of, XXIV 18
Diasia, the, XXVI 31
dicasteries, tone of the, XXIX 20
dice of deerhorn, VII 19
dice-playing, XVI 11
Diels, Hermann, pp. 16 n, 161, 169, 171
dinner-party, places at, VII 4
— presents to guests at, XV 6
Dionysia, the, XVIII 9
discount on copper money, XXVI 33
distraining, right of, XXIV 17
distrustfulness, XXIII 1
Dobree, P. P., p 167
dogs, Greek feeling towards, XXX 18
— in the halls of Greek houses, XIV 17
— Laconian, VII 10
— of Melita, VII 36, 37
doves, Sicilian, VII 19
dreams, belief in, XXVIII 27
— interpretation of, XXVIII 27
drill-serjeants, VII 24
dropping a cup, etc., a bad omen, XVII 18
Dubner, F., p. 167

Earle's *Microcosmographie* quoted, p. 17 n , pp 28–30; XIV 11; XXVI 27

Ecclesia, controlling power of, XXIX 6
editions, pp 164–172
Edmonds, J M , pp. 161, 171
education, Greek ideal of, VIII 22
elective offices, IV 6, XXIX 14
ephebeum in gymnasia, VII 12
epitaphs on pet-dogs, VII 36
— on women, X 14
Eumolpidae, XXVIII 14
evil-speaking, XXI 1
exports, duty on, VI 16

fairs, XVI 20
famine, VI 19
festival, tenth-day, VIII 16
festivals, XXVI 31
— presents sent to friends at, III 5
finger, votive, VII 38 n. and *Crit. App* VII 34
Fischer, J. F , p 165
fish-market, XVII 12
fish, salted, XIV 28
flattery, I 1
flies, XXVII 23
flute-playing, VIII 17; XX 11
food, distribution of, XXVI 4
Foss, pp 161, 163, 167
fourth day of month, sacred to Hermes, XXVIII 23
Fraenkel, J. M , pp 161, 171
frankincense, XXVIII 25
fuller, the, XXIII 13; XXV 18
'full market,' time meant by, XVII 5

gambling-houses, XVI 11
games, II 16
garlic at the cross-roads, XXVIII 34
garrulousness, XVIII 1
gates, Athenian, *Crit. App* XIII 21
genealogy, Greek love of, XXI 4
Generals, the Ten, VII 13
Goez, pp. 162, 166
Gomperz, Theodor, V 1 ; pp. 16 n., 171
Grindor, P., p. 171
Groeneboom, P., pp. 161, 171
grossness, XVII 1
grumbling, XXII 1
guests, presents to, XV 6
gymnasia, VII 12

hair, close-cut, a mark of mourning, XXIV 27
— daintily trimmed, XXIX 17
— worn long by youths, VII 5
hall-door, answering the, XXI 8
Hall's *Characterismes*, pp. 6, 24–26, 28–30
Hanau, F , p. 167
Hartung, J. A , p. 167
Haupt, M., p. 168
Hecate's agency invoked by spells, XXVIII 18

INDEX TO THE NOTES, ETC. 227

'Hecate's supper,' XXVIII 34
Heracles, temples of, VIII 8
herald's office, XVI 10
Hermaphrodites, XXVIII 26
Hermes, festivals of, XXV 14
— the giver of luck, XXVI 18
heroes, festivals of the, VIII 4
Herwerden, H van, p. 168
Hicks, E L, p. 170
hides worn by rustics, XIV 24
hired labour, XIV 8
Hirschig, G. A., p. 167
Homer, his place in Greek education, XXIX 11
— quoted, XXIX 10
hoops, children's, XIII 15
horses kept by rich men for the credit of the State, VI 29
Hottinger, pp. 163, 166
houses purified, XXVIII 17

ill-omened words, XIII 21; XVII 17
Immisch, Otto, pp. 164, 170
informers, public, VI 17; XXIX 20
initiation, rites of, VIII 20; XXVII 5
inn-keeping, XVI 9
insanity, XXI 33
interest, XVII 29
— compound, XXIV 17
— paid by the day, XVI 26
— paid by the month, XXIV 2; XXVI 28
irony, V 1

jackdaw, tame, VII 35
javelin-throwing, VIII 19
Jebb, R. C. (ed. 1870), p. 170
jug, the broken, XXIV 8
jury-courts, democratic tone of, XXIX 20

Kayser, K. L, p 168
Klotz, C. A., p. 165
knights, procession of, VII 30
Kuchler, p. 166

labourers, hired, XIV 8
Lacedaemonian victory, XIX 23
late-learning, VIII 1
laurel, a bit of, carried in the mouth as a charm, XXVIII 4
law-courts, XXII 13; XXIX 20; XXX 16
— conspiracies in the, XXX 21
law-suits, XIII 5; XVI 12, 22, XXX 3
leathern garments, XIV 24
Leipzig *Philologische Gesellschaft*, pp. 161 f, 164, 170
letters, IV 20
libations at dinner to deities, XXIV 5
'like to like,' XXX 25
'liturgies,' the Athenian, XXIX 26
loans between neighbours, XIV 21
loquacity, XIX 1

lustration, circular, XXIII 14; XXVIII 35
Lysander, XIX 23
Lysicrates, monument of, XXV 4

Madvig, J. N, p. 168
mantic art, XXVIII 27 f
manuscripts, pp. 161-4
marketing; usu. done by slaves, XVII 12
market-place, XVI 25, 27; XVII 5, 11 f
marriage-feast, XXV 8
mask, the comic actor's, XVI 5
meal-bag, the mouse and the, XXVIII 13
meals, servants', XXV 11
meanness, XXIV 1
measure, with the bottom dinted, XXVI 23
Megalopolis, battle of, XIX 22
Meier, E., p. 167
Meineke, A, p. 167
Melita, VII 36
Menander, p. 4; I 28; XIV 24; XXVII 6, 16, 23, XXVIII 1, 18, 35
mercenary troops, XXI 6
Metrôum, the, VII 45
Mey, van der, p. 170
mice, omens from, XXVIII 13
monarchy, Theseus and the, XXIX 27, 29, 30
money-lenders, VI 5
month, 4th and 7th days of the, XXVIII 23
Mother of the gods, VII 45
mourning in the house of death, XIII 10
Munsterberg, p 170
Muses, festival of, at schools, XXV 14
musical skill, Greek feeling for, VIII 17
musicians, professional, VII 24
myrtle-berries at dessert, XVII 6
myrtle-wreaths worn by sacrificers, XXVIII 25
mysteries of Eleusis, the greater, XVIII 12
— the lesser, XXVI 31
— the Orphic, XXVIII 29
— of Samothrace, XXVII 5
— torch at the, XVIII 12

Naber, S A, p 170
name, change of, XXI 5
Nauck, J. A, p 167
navigable season, the, XVIII 9
Needham, Peter, p. 165
'new-moon,' the fair day at Athens, XIV 25
news, XX 7
— from the Ecclesia, XIX 20
news-making, XX 1

oath of inability to accept public office, IV 6
Odeum, the, XVIII 13
Odeum-street, XXIX 18
offensiveness, XII 1
officials appointed by lot or by election, IV 22, 23

INDEX TO THE NOTES, ETC.

officiousness, X 1
oil used at the baths, XII 6
oligarchical temper, the, XXIX 1
omen, the evil threatened by, transferable, XXVIII 6
— words of evil, XVII 17
omens which cross the path, XXVIII 5
Orelli, J. Kaspar von, p. 167
Orphic societies, the, XXVIII 29
Overbury's *Characters*, pp. 27–29
owl, omen given by, XXVIII 18
ox, the more costly victim for sacrifice, VIII 9
Oxyrhynchus Papyri, p 171

palaestra and gymnasium, VIII 10; XIX 16
palaestra, private, VII 22
Panathenaea, the Great, XXIX 5
panegyris, XVI 20
parasites, XI 17
parents, neglect to maintain, punishable, XVI 11
parish-feast, XXIV 18
Pauw, J. C. de, p. 165
penuriousness, XXIV 1
perfumer's shop, a lounge, XVII 15
Petersen, E , pp. 10–16, 18 n 1, 19, 161, 164, 169
petty ambition, VII 1
'Pheidonian measures,' XXVI 22
philosophers, their conversazioni, VII 23
Phocion, XX 21
Pirckheymer, W., p. 164
places of honour at table, VII 4
plate lent between friends, XXIII 14
'plenary powers,' directors of a procession with, XXIX 6
Politian, p. 165
Polyperchon, XX 15
porches of Athens, I 6
Porson on the *Characters*, p. 7 n 3
'Poseidon's day,' XXI 25
possets, XIV 3
'potter spites potter,' XXX 25
presents to ambassadors, XXVI 14
— to friends at festivals, III 5
— to guests at dinner, XV 6
priestesses, XXVIII 35
priests, their perquisites, XXV 9
privacy little permitted by Greek manners, IV 17
procession, Dionysiac or Panathenaic, XXVIII 4, 5
— of the knights, VII 30
promontories mistaken for privateers, XXVII 3 f
public services at Athens, the, XXIX 26
puppies used in a rite of purification, XXVIII 36
purse usu carried by an attendant, XXIII 4
Pydna, XX 4

rascals, patronising of, XXX 1
rations, the slave's, XXIV 9
recitations, III 13
recklessness, XVI 1
'red' snake, the, XXVIII 8
Reiske, J. J , p. 165
Ribbeck, Otto, I 1, V 1, VI 1; p. 170
rings worn as amulets, VII 38, and *Crit. App* VII 34
'right wheel,' etc., VIII 5
Romizi, A , pp. 161, 171

Sabazius, VIII 13; XXVIII 9
'sacred' snake, the, XXVIII 9
sacrifice, dress worn at, VII 42
— followed by a banquet, XV 5
sacrifice, public, by the Senate, VII 41
— — form in reporting, VII 44
sacrificial parts reserved for priest, XXV 9
— victim, its neck bent back, VIII 9
Samothrace, mysteries of, XXVII 7
'satyri,' a species of ape, VII 19
Schmidt, L , p 169
Schneider, J G., pp. 9, 163, 167
schoolmasters' fees, XXVI 28
schools, law for privacy of, XIX 16
Schwartz, J C., p. 165
Schweighauser, J , p. 166
sea-water in purification, XXVIII 32
seals set on doors, XXIII 6
seers, XXVIII 27 f
Senate, presidents of the, VII 40
serenades, IX 4
serpent seen in a house, ominous, XXVIII 8
services, the public, XXIX 26
seventh day of month sacred to Apollo, XXVIII 23
shamelessness, XV 1
'shares in the luck!', XXVI 18
Sheppard, J G., pp 20, 161, 167
ships, large, completely decked, XXV 12
shoes, I 23
shops, VI 3
shrine, XXVIII 10
Siebenkees, pp 162, 166
siesta, at noon, XXIV 28
singing at dessert, III 13
slaves attend their masters in the streets, XXIII 18
— Greek and Roman treatment of, XXVI 32
— Greek familiarity with, XIV 6
— heavy-laden, XXVI 11
— let out for hire, XXVI 32, 40
— rations of, XXIV 9
slippers, I 33
smilax, XXVIII 25
snake, red, XXVIII 8 f
— sacred, XXVIII 9
Solonian standard of measures, XXVI 22
son, rejoicings for birth of, XXII 10

INDEX TO THE NOTES, ETC 229

soothsayer consulted in the smallest matters, XVII 17
'sophist' meaning specially 'rhetorician,' VII 23
Sosias, a Thracian name, XXI 5
Sosistratus, XXI 5
speech-writers, XXII 13
spells, malign, XXVIII 18
spitting into the bosom to avert evil, XXVIII 37
sprinkling, ceremony of, XXVIII 4
squill, XXVIII 35
stick, custom of carrying a, VII 20
stones, virtue of three, XXVIII 7
streets, demeanour in the, IV 11
stupidity, XIII 1
subscriptions for friends, V 14
— to the public treasury, XXV 5
superstition, XXVIII 1
sureties, IX 6
surliness, III 1
swallow, a proverb of loquacity, XIX 32
sword, long (*spatha*), XXVII 16

tableaux vivants, VIII 17
taverns in the market-place, XVI 25, 27
tax-farmers, XVI 9
temple-font, XXVIII 4
'tenth-day' festival, VIII 16
theatre, cost of places at, XV 13
— demonstrative audiences, XVII 4
— lessees of, XXVI 8
— seats of officials at, VII 13
theft, laws against, XVI 12
Theophrastus, his date, p. 7
— his death, p. 18; [Pro 6]
— his style, p 22
— his will, I 39
Theophrastus, his *Characters*, date of, pp 4—10; XXIX 1, 12 f
— — their probable origin, pp. 1–21
— — the excerpt-theory, pp. 9–16, 18; [Pro. 8]
— — the definitions, p. 19
— — their imitators, pp. 22–32
Theseus, his connexion with Heracles, VIII 8
— the hero of the commonwealth, XXIX 27
Thracian peltasts, XXI 6
— slaves, XXI 8
Thrasybulus, monument of, XXV 4
tickets, XVI 8
'tityri,' followers of Dionysus, VII 19
tombstones, various forms of, XXVIII 20
torch-race, VIII 7
torches at the Mysteries, XVIII 12
travel, foreign, Plato on, VI 13

trial, day appointed by archon, XIII 5
tribesmen, festivals, XXIV 18
'tribon,' a coarse cloak, XXV 28
trierarchy, the, XXV 11; XXIX 26
tripod, the prize of a choregus, XXV 4
trumpet, signals by, XXVII 8

Unger, G. F., p. 169
unguent instead of olive-oil, a luxury, VII 10
unpleasantness, XI 1
unseasonableness, IX 1
upholstery mart, VI 30
Usener, H. K., p. 168
Ussing, J. L, pp. 161, 168

vases, Thurian, VII 19
verdict, unanimous, XXII 13
vessels of water at temple-doors, XXVIII 43
vestibule of a Greek house, VII 28, XIV 17
votive chapels, etc, at Athens, XXVIII 10
voyage, danger of wicked companions in a, XXVII 5

walk after dinner, IV 3
walking in the streets, IV 11
walking-sticks, IV 11; VII 20
'watch-dog of the people,' XXX 18
water over the head, purification by pouring, XXVIII 34 f
weasel, ill-omened, XXVIII 5
wedding ceremonies, XXV 8
— feast, IX 8
— presents, XXVI 46
Weil, H, p. 170
Wendland, P, p. 170
Werle, W., p. 169
Wilamowitz-Moellendorff, U. von, p. 171
wine, frauds in selling, XXVI 6
— mixing of, X 6; XIV 13
witness, oath of inability to be a, XVI 22
witnesses to a claim for interest, XXIII 10
— to a payment, XIII 13
witchcraft, XXVIII 18
women admitted to the Orphic and other mysteries, XXVIII 30
— attended by slaves abroad, XXV 23
— privacy enjoined upon, XXI 18
— restrictions on freedom of, XXV 24
women's market, I 28; XXV 23
workshops, resorts for conversation, XVII 15 f
Wurm, Chr., p 166

Zeus, 'the heavens,' XXVII 7
Zingerle, A, p. 169

WORKS BY SIR R. C. JEBB

The Attic Orators from Antiphon to Isaeus. In two vols. 8vo. 25s.

Selections from the Attic Orators. Antiphon, Andocides, Lysias, Isocrates, Isaeus. Fcap. 8vo. 5s.
[*Classical Series.*

The Growth and Influence of Classical Greek Poetry. Crown 8vo 7s. net.

Modern Greece. Two Lectures. With Papers on 'The Progress of Greece' and 'Byron in Greece.' Globe 8vo. 4s. net. [*Eversley Series.*

Greek Literature. Pott 8vo 1s. [*Literature Primers.*

Humanism in Education. The Romanes Lecture, 1899. 8vo. Sewed. 2s. net.

Bentley. Crown 8vo. Library Edition. 2s. net. Popular Edition. 1s. 6d. Sewed. 1s. Pocket Edition. Fcap. 8vo. 1s net. [*English Men of Letters Series.*

LONDON: MACMILLAN & CO., LTD.

MACMILLAN'S
CLASSICAL LIBRARY
8vo.

ÆSCHYLUS.—THE SUPPLICES. A Revised Text, with Translation. By T G Tucker, Litt.D. 9s net.

—— THE CHOEPHORI. With Translation. By A. W. Verrall, Litt.D 10s net.

—— THE AGAMEMNON. With Translation. By A. W. Verrall, Litt.D. 10s net.

—— THE EUMENIDES. With Translation. By A. W. Verrall, Litt D. 10s. net.

ARISTOPHANES.—THE ACHARNIANS. With Translation. By W. J. M Starkie.

ARISTOTLE.—THE POLITICS. Books I.—V. By F. Susemihl and R. D. Hicks, M.A 18s. net.

—— ON THE CONSTITUTION OF ATHENS. By J. E. Sandys, Litt.D. 12s 6d. net

CICERO.—ACADEMICA. By J. S. Reid, Litt.D 12s 6d. net.

EURIPIDES.—IPHIGENEIA IN AULIS. By E. B. England, Litt.D. 6s. net.

HERODOTUS.—BOOKS I.—III. THE ANCIENT EMPIRES OF THE EAST. By Professor A H Sayce 13s net

—— BOOKS IV.—VI. By R W. Macan, D.Litt. Two vols. 20s. net.

—— BOOKS VII.—IX. By R W Macan, D.Litt Three vols. 30s. net.

HOMER.—THE ILIAD. By Walter Leaf, Litt.D. Vol. I. (Books I —XII) Vol II. (Books XIII.—XXIV) 15s net each.

—— THE HOMERIC HYMNS. By Thomas W. Allen, M A., and E E Sikes, M A 10s. 6d. net.

MARCUS AURELIUS ANTONINUS.—BOOK IV. OF THE MEDITATIONS. With Translation. By Hastings Crossley, M.A. 5s. net.

PAUSANIAS'S DESCRIPTION OF GREECE. Translated with Commentary by J. G Frazer, D C.L., LL D , Litt.D Six vols. 126s. net.

PINDAR.—THE NEMEAN ODES. By J. B Bury, Litt D. 10s. net.

—— THE ISTHMIAN ODES. By J B Bury, Litt.D. 9s. net.

PLATO.—PHÆDO. By R D. Archer-Hind, M.A. 8s. 6d. net.

—— TIMÆUS. With Translation. By R. D Archer-Hind, M.A. 13s. net.

—— THE MYTHS. Translated with Introduction, etc by J. A. Stewart, M A 14s net

PLINY.—CORRESPONDENCE WITH TRAJAN. By E. G. Hardy, M.A. 9s net

—— THE ELDER PLINY'S CHAPTERS ON THE HISTORY OF ART. Translated by K Jex-Blake. With Commentary and Introduction by E. Sellers, and Notes by Dr H. L. Urlichs. 12s. net.

TACITUS.—THE ANNALS. By G. O. Holbrooke, M.A. With Maps. 13s net

—— THE HISTORIES. By Rev. W. A. Spooner, M.A. 13s. net.

THEOPHRASTUS.—THE CHARACTERS. An English Translation, with Introduction and Notes by R. C. Jebb, M A. New Edition Edited by J. E. Sandys, Litt.D

THUCYDIDES.—BOOK VIII. By H. C. Goodhart, M.A. 7s. 6d. net.

LONDON: MACMILLAN AND CO., LTD.

www.ingramcontent.com/pod-product-compliance
Lightning Source LLC
LaVergne TN
LVHW010412271025
824340LV00030B/533